AF545231

S-PRES

52 Pages | 25 cents | Page A-1

Gunmen attack food convoy, kill Iran envoy

Gunfire foils efforts to reach starving Palestinians' camp

By Moha
Associ

Bl... ...nmen killed an Iranian e... ...hen they fired on t... ...hungry Pales...

...ives since ... 62,000

"Have you e... found any guerrillas in the world who say they're willing to surrender? ... What they want to discuss is not the end of the war, but power," the 62-year-old Christian Democrat president said.

Three efforts at peace talks have failed. The president said he would continue seeking a dialogue aimed at peace, but added, "Not one that only gives expectations without results."

Yugoslavia dissident sues in copyright case

BELGRADE, Yugoslavia (AP) — A prominent dissident has sued a former interior minister and two newspapers for alleged copyright infringement for disclosing parts of an unpublished manuscript he wrote on Yugoslavia's economic and social problems.

Vojislav Seselj, a sociologist, was convicted in July 1984 of counter-revolutionary activity ...the basis of the manuscript, ... was sentenced to eight ... in prison.

...Yugoslav Fede... ...d he had ...

World Roundup

north over the past 16 days, the military said.

In a statement Thursday, the South West African Territorial Force gave no details on the skirmishes. It said security forces suffered no losses.

South Africa administers South West Africa, also called Namibia, under a League of Nations mandate rescinded by the United Nations. It is fighting Angola-based guerrillas of the South West African Peoples Organization.

The statement said the latest fatalites brought to 235 the number of guerrillas killed this year. According to the Territorial Force's statistics, 645 insurgents were killed last year.

Iran official in Moscow for talks on relations

MOSCOW (A... Soviet Foreign Mini... ...A. Shevardn... Foreign Mi... ...ti be... ...t to ...eir

By ...
Asso...

BER... in East... cabare... end...

DEDICATION

To Oliver Gramling,
founder and longtime head of AP Broadcast.
Without him, this book and the standards it represents
might very well not exist.

The Associated Press
BROADCAST NEWS HANDBOOK

Incorporating the AP Libel Manual

Compiled and Edited by

JAMES R. HOOD and BRAD KALBFELD

Published by The Associated Press, 50 Rockefeller Plaza, New York, New York 10020.

Printing:
10 9 8 7 6 5 4 3 2 1

Library of Congress Cataloging in Publication Data:

Hood, James R., 1944–
The Associated Press broadcast news handbook.

Includes index.
1. Journalism—style manuals. 2. Broadcast journalism. 3. Libel and slander—United States. I. Kalbfeld, Brad, 1954–. II. Associated Press. III. Title.

PN4783.H57 070.4'15 81-12702 ISBN 0-917360-49-4 (pbk.) AACR2

Cover and Interior Design by Susan B. Trowbridge, Trowbridge Graphic Design

TABLE OF CONTENTS

PREFACE

Not long ago, if you asked for *The AP Broadcast News Stylebook,* you'd have been handed a skinny, 40-page booklet. There was nothing wrong with that booklet. There just wasn't much of it. We hope that this expanded *AP Broadcast News Handbook* will be valuable to broadcasters around the world, and that it will live through many future revisions.

For the beginner, this should serve as a handy primer, outlining the basics of good broadcast journalism. For the veteran, we hope that it will be a handy reference work which will be taken down from the shelf frequently.

The important thing is that it be used. We hope that future editions will be even more useful, and that you will let us know what should be added, revised, and deleted.

This opus was orchestrated largely by General Broadcast Editor Jim Hood and his deputy, Brad Kalbfeld, who somehow worked it into their other duties during the hectic events of 1980 and 1981.

We hope you enjoy it.

ROY STEINFORT
Vice President and Director
AP Broadcast Services

New York, 1981

ACKNOWLEDGMENTS

No book is created in a vacuum, but few grow as directly from another as this one.

The Associated Press Broadcast News Handbook is based to a large extent on *The Associated Press Stylebook and Libel Manual,* edited by Eileen Alt Powell and Howard Angione. It was their groundwork that made possible Section 2, "The Specifics of Broadcast Style," and Chapter 5, the "AP Libel Manual."

Roy Steinfort, AP Vice President and Director of Broadcast Services, is directly responsible for the creation of this book. It was he who insisted that the *Broadcast Handbook* be a full-length reference work instead of a mere pamphlet.

Louis Boccardi, AP Vice President and Executive Editor, and AP Managing Editor Wick Temple both lent their support to the project, reading the manuscript and giving us valuable insights.

Many others made valuable contributions as well, among them Bruce Hodgman, Night Supervisor of AP's Broadcast News Center. Designer Susan Trowbridge maintained her good humor despite frequent disasters. And finally, our thanks to Jane Kalbfeld, who helped keep the material organized and, in the process, found new meaning in the phrase "cut and paste."

JAMES R. HOOD
BRAD KALBFELD

INTRODUCTION

On the night of November second, 1920, a transmitter atop the Westinghouse Electric factory in Pittsburgh crackled to life. In the building below, people were busy on the telephone, taking down information from a newspaper office elsewhere in town. The information was run into the studio and read on the air—and radio station KDKA, reporting the results of the Presidential election, ushered in both commercial broadcasting and broadcast news.

There were no rules back then, no basic tenets of on-air reporting, no guidelines for newcomers to the business. In fact, there was no "business" to speak of; KDKA improvised as it went along.

Since then, broadcast technology has grown up, branching into new audio and video felds. The programming and commercial aspects of broadcasting have become complex. And broadcast journalists have developed their own set of ground rules: basic, simple standards of good practice.

They range from the trivial to the grandiose, from rules such as "use people, not person," to unbreakable laws such as "always attribute a story."

Many news organizations have, over the years, codified the basics. Among them is the Associated Press, which has the world's largest news-gathering operation and serves thousands of radio and television stations. AP Broadcast has established guidelines that work in newsrooms of three and newsrooms of 30. That's what this book is about.

Any stylebook serves two major functions: to give others the benefit of the organization's collective experience in the newsroom and to clear the air of basic stylistic questions, so more immediate and debatable matters can be tackled. After all, the main event in any newsroom isn't as much the style as the story.

SECTION ONE:

An Approach to Broadcast Style

1 THE ASSOCIATED PRESS

"We'll have dispatches from Hell before breakfast," General William Tecumseh Sherman said when he learned that three Civil War correspondents were missing.

That oblique tribute on the field of battle at Vicksburg more than 100 years ago is a good reminder that the news business hasn't changed all that much in recent history.

The tension between the press and those whose blunders and triumphs it traces has been around since the first epic poets took their tales of the gods to the crowds in the street.

Covering the Civil War was one of the first big tests for The Associated Press, and it was the first trial by fire of "objectivity"—an AP invention which was still regarded as an oddity in those days.

The AP had decided from its birth in 1848 that it would present the news fairly and impartially. In the days when each pamphleteer was pushing his own version of the truth, that was a pretty revolutionary notion.

But it paid off handsomely. In 1861, when the State Department prohibited telegraphic dispatches from wartime Washington, The Associated Press was the only agency exempted from the order because it devoted itself to straight reporting, without the luxury of opinion.

"My business is to communicate facts," said AP Washington Correspondent Lawrence Gobright a few years before war broke out. "My instructions do not allow me to make any comments upon the facts."

Not many years later, another bureau chief in the same job issued instructions to his staff, warning them against suppressing or publishing any story because of personal opinions. If anyone tried to violate the rule, the bureau chief said: "Throw him out of the window and report the case to the coroner."

Besides objectivity, the AP has for 133 years prided itself on accuracy, speed and innovation—not to mention lean, easy-to-read prose.

It came into being in 1848 and pioneered the notion of using the telegraph to distribute news to more than one point simultaneously.

It flourished from the start.

In 1849, Daniel Craig opened the first foreign bureau, in Halifax, Nova

Scotia. He gave up his carrier pigeon news service to join the new, modern AP. For years, he had been greeting New York-bound ships as they stopped off at Halifax, getting the latest news from Europe, and relaying it by pigeon. Now he sped the latest news to New York via telegraph—cutting days off the transmission time.

Just seven years later, the whole procedure was obsolete. The trans-Atlantic cable carried its first message in 1856 and the Halifax relay was no longer needed.

By then, Craig had moved to New York to become the head of the AP. He presided over the shut-down of the Halifax operation he had started just a few years before.

Now, more than 120 years later, the AP has taken to the skies again, abandoning land-based telephone lines for a new type of high-flying bird—the communications satellites which hover in stationary orbit 23,000 miles above the earth.

Presiding over that change is AP President and General Manager Keith Fuller, who in late 1979 announced a plan to convert all domestic news distribution—both print and audio—to satellites, and to install more than 900 earth stations in the United States alone.

"Once again, The Associated Press is providing a quantum leap in the dissemination of news and information to the American people," Fuller said.

"This system will break the economic bonds that have held back new and better services for the dissemination of vital information."

Fuller presides over a far greater enterprise than Craig would have imagined. The modern Associated Press has an operations budget approaching $150 million.

From an initial membership roster of six newspapers, it has grown to serve 1,400 newspapers and 5,600 broadcast stations in the United States alone.

It operates bureaus in 120 American cities and more than 130 foreign countries.

Each day it reaches more than a billion people, over one-third of the world's population.

As Fuller described it in a monograph prepared recently for a United Nations commission:

"The Associated Press is the single greatest source of accurate, timely information for the peoples of the world. The history of the AP has been, in a large sense, the history of impartial news coverage."

Or, as Mark Twain put it years earlier:

"There are only two forces that can carry light to all corners of the globe—the sun in the heavens, and The Associated Press down here."

In 1932, Mohandas Gandhi went Twain one better, when he told an AP reporter in Poona, India:

"I suppose that when I go to the Hereafter and stand at the Golden Gate, the first person I shall meet will be a correspondent of The Associated Press."

This book makes no claims to having a Heavenly Host bureau, despite the AP signals now carried to the fringes of space via satellite.

Nor is it its function to trace the fascinating history of an organization that is never stagnant, never satisfied.

It is instead intended to provide an overview of how The Associated Press serves its thousands of broadcast members. It is primarily a guide for AP staffers around the country, although it should also be useful for news personnel at member stations and for aspiring journalists in colleges and universities.

It is designed to further the AP goals mentioned earlier: accuracy, speed, innovation—and lean, easy-to-read prose.

AP BROADCAST SERVICES

Six young men reported for duty at AP headquarters on December 1, 1940.

Their job: Set up a special wire, written just for radio stations. One of them was Mitchell Curtis, who was to write later that the six saw their job as being rather simple: they were to find a way "to string words together in such a way that they listened well."

The AP then served few broadcasters. The few stations in membership received newspaper wires and had to rewrite all of the material for broadcast.

Curtis and his colleagues went to work and within a few weeks they were producing the first 24-hour AP Radio Wire. The first station to sign up was in New York City, but the service quickly spread across the country.

The next year, regional bureaus began adding state and regional news to the Radio Wire, and by the end of the decade, there were more than 1,000 stations taking the service.

The wire was just right for radio. It carried pre-scripted newscasts, sports shows, feature programming and background reports.

Then television came along and steadily expanded its news programming. TV stations began installing the Radio Wire in their newsrooms and soon the circuit was being called the AP Broadcast Wire.

By 1979, the wire went to more than 5,600 stations, far more than any other single AP service.

Instead of Curtis and his five co-workers, the Broadcast News Center in New York consisted of nearly 40 full-time news staffers. A separate audio network had been established in Washington, D.C., also with about 40 news people.

Then, something happened.

AP management conducted a detailed study of its services to broadcasters, and interviewed hundreds of station personnel to determine whether those services fit their day-to-day needs.

The conclusion?

The Broadcast Wire was carrying more information than most radio stations wanted. That's because it was trying to provide television with the detailed stories necessary for TV's longer newcasts. But it turned out that the larger TV stations wanted still more information; they said the Broadcast Wire was far too abbreviated for them.

The solution was obvious: It was time to re-invent the Radio Wire and to create a new wire tailored to the needs of television.

The AP Radio Wire, it was decided, should concentrate on fully-scripted news and information programming for stations which did not have large news staffs and could not devote much time to re-writing national and regional news.

In other words, the main job of the AP Radio Wire should be to "string words together in such a way that they listened well."

The APTV Wire would provide the reams of detailed source copy which TV stations need for their larger news operations.

A series of carefully-planned changes was instituted and by 1981, most of the program was complete.

The Radio Wire introduced a host of new scripts which could be integrated into modern radio formats; it de-emphasized lengthy, in-depth stories. The hourly news summaries were re-formatted to meet contemporary standards: stories became shorter and more conversational, and features of interest to modern-day radio audiences were added.

The TV Wire was designed to operate at highspeed—1,200 words per minute, 18 times faster than the Radio Wire. This made it possible to combine scripted news material from the Radio Wire with in-depth stories from AP newspaper circuits—thus giving TV newsrooms both the capsule versions which can be read directly on the air and the detailed source copy necessary for rewriting.

Like Daniel Craig and his pigeons, it's a story of how things often come full-circle. And it's a reminder that change is the only constant in journalism.

Change is not only constant; the rate of change, and the speed which existing services becomes obsolete, is increasing all the time. Broadcasting and communications in general are adapting constantly to new technology, changing demographics, new lifestyles and new rules of economic feasibility.

AP Broadcast is always looking for ways to improve service to existing members, and to provide new services for the new media which are being born in the 1980s.

• SERVICES

AP Broadcast Services is one of several major news divisions of The Associated Press.

It is headed by Roy Steinfort, Vice President and Director of Broadcast Services. He oversees the news, sales and administrative functions of the division. He is also repsonsible for the department which serves Cable Television systems and for Press Association, an AP subsidiary serving educational stations (which are not eligible for AP Membership) and private clients, including the government agencies and business firms that subscribe to the Radio Wire.

Here is a complete listing of the services AP offers to broadcasters and the cable TV industry.

AP Radio Wire: The basic service for most members, the Radio Wire contains ready-to-air newscasts, sportscasts and features of all kinds—including regular farm, business and entertainment scripts.

It is a combination of the national wire produced by the Broadcast News Center in New York and one or more state wires fed from state bureaus around the country.

AP Radio Network: AP's full-service radio network, established in 1974, now serves more than 1,000 stations. It is distributed by satellite, with an audio range of 8 kHz. APR, as it is commonly known, provides a complete range of network services, including five-minute hourly newscasts, regular sports shows, business and farm round-ups, and feature material.

It also offers the most comprehensive package of actuality and voice reports available anywhere. Each hour, a package of raw sound and voice reports is fed to affiliated stations for use in their locally-produced newscasts. The material to be fed is listed on the Radio Wire *before* it is fed on the network, so that stations can take only that material which appeals to them.

APR is produced from studios in Washington, D.C., and is discussed at length in chapter seven.

AP TV Wire: The first wire ever designed specifically for television, the TV Wire combines Radio Wire and newspaper-wire features with material prepared especially for television. It operates at 1,200 words-per-minute, providing far greater capacity than normal circuits. It is commonly known as APTV.

AP NewsCable: A special report for cable TV systems, NewsCable is produced by the Broadcast News Center in New York. It is an alpha-numeric feed which allows cable systems to operate a fully-automated news channel featuring national, state and regional news, weather, sports, business and farm news.

The information may be displayed on one channel or it may be split up and displayed on multiple channels, with one channel carrying national news, another carrying sports, etc.

AP LaserPhoto: The AP invented the WirePhoto process years ago, and at that time, it was the only system available for sending still pictures by wire.

Today, Laserphoto provides vastly improved quality and reliability. A laser beam traces the photographic image onto heat-sensitive paper, producing photos which rival glossy prints.

A worldwide network brings pictures from remote corners of the world directly into television newsrooms, often hours or days before live video can be obtained.

AP PhotoColor: A specially-produced color slide service for television stations. Stations receive two packages of PhotoColor slides each week, featuring color photos of people and places in the news as well as maps and graphics.

AP DataStream: The most complete news report available, DataStream is a 1,200 word-per-minute service recommended only for the largest stations.

It contains far more material than any other single circuit, and can be modified to suit individual needs.

• HOW IT WORKS

The AP Radio Wire represents the latest in technology, although it may not look like it to the casual observer.

Most AP Members are familiar with the teleprinter which delivers the news report directly to their station. It looks pretty simple and most people don't think much more about it.

But behind that printer is an electronic information-handling system second to none. Long before anyone had thought of calling them "Word Processors," AP was using video display terminals in conjunction with computers for speedy, accurate handling of news copy.

In fact, the AP was the principal developer of what is now called the "electronic newsroom," a system of information-handling which eliminates typewriters, telegraphers, and other obstacles to quick, accurate transmission of news and information.

Here's how it works.

There are AP computers scattered around the country, usually in major cities where larger regional bureaus are located.

Each of these computers serves several AP bureaus, which in turn are equipped with anywhere from one to 16 terminals, usually called CRTs—short for "cathode ray tube."

The CRT is the device you've seen in banks, airports, and other business places. It serves several functions: it's used in place of a typewriter by the writer who composes a story; it's used instead of a blue pencil by the editor who marks up the story; and it's used to execute the commands which cause the story to move on the wire, or to be stored in the memory for use later.

The CRTs are easy to use. They're faster than typewriters and it's much easier to make revisions in a story. The writer can go back and change words or whole phrases without affecting the rest of what has been written.

Better yet, the CRTs reduce the likelihood of typographical errors sneaking into copy.

Before the CRTs were developed, AP staffers used typewriters to write their stories. Then editors marked them up with pencils and handed them to a telegrapher—or "operator," as they were usually called.

The operator took the typewritten copy and used an old warhorse of a machine called a perforator to convert it to paper tape. In effect, the operator re-typed the copy while keeping a mental count of the number of spaces in each line. If he miscounted, the line was too long and the whole thing came out garbled.

Also, the operator had no hard copy of what he was typing. It was like using a typewriter with a cover over the paper; if he made a mistake, he couldn't see it until after it had moved on the wire.

Today, the CRT screen shows the newsman exactly how the copy will look, and it completely eliminates the re-typing step of the process.

There are other advantages to the computerized system. For one thing, it's not necessary to have a roomful of teleprinters to monitor several different circuits.

Instead, the computer can drive an "index"printer, which prints just the first few lines of each story coming into the system. The editors scan the index printer, watching for stories of interest to their area—and they can then call up on the CRT screens only the stories they need. If necessary, they can also run off a hard copy of the story on a monitor printer.

This not only saves paper, but also makes the newsroom a cleaner, quieter place to work by eliminating the large bank of printers that used to be a common sight in AP bureaus.

As this technology spreads to member newsrooms, stations will be able to enjoy the same benefits. And it will be easy for them to feed AP circuits into their newsroom computers, since a standardized format and program has already been worked out for such purposes.

The AP uses the "ASCII" (as'-kee) program, and ANPA standardized format and coding process.

These standardized codings have lots of advantages. For example, they will—if your computer is set up to handle it—feed state stories to the state news desk, national stories to the national desk, and so forth.

The computers can also search their memories for specific items, making it easy to find and retrieve a story which may not have been noticed by the editor on duty.

The computers "talk" not only to the CRTs in each bureau; they also talk to each other. Bureaus can exchange stories quickly and easily, and national copy can be automatically combined with regional copy.

Thus, national copy for the AP Radio Wire is fed from New York to the regional computers, where it is combined with state copy. The national wire carries about 40 minutes of copy each hour, with the state bureaus adding about 20 minutes of state and regional news.

The computers are programmed so that these percentages can be changed to reflect local conditions. So, in large states with heavy news commitments, some of the national copy can be deleted so that members receive expanded regional reports.

The computers use a sorting system which is based on a series of priority codes. These codes tell the computer how important each piece of copy is.

The codes are:

F — Flash
B — Bulletin
U — Urgent
R — Routine
LR — State Routine
LD — State Deferred
D — Deferred

Routine copy is filed with an "R" priority, so that it can be "bumped" by more pressing material. This allows the state bureaus to override national copy if there is an urgent story on the state level—and it also allows the national desks to override state copy during state sending periods if an urgent national or international story breaks.

3 TELLING THE STORY

Although the details may differ, most newsrooms hold to certain basic rules. Perhaps the most basic rule at the AP is that we are here to report the news impartially. We are reporters, not advocates.

Almost as important is this simple rule: Good writing is clear writing. The reporter's job is to tell the public what is happening and to explain—if possible—why it is happening. Above all, the story must be told in clear, simple language. The more complicated the story, the more important it is that it be told clearly.

In this Handbook, we will be looking at how stories can be put together effectively. Most of this advice should be as useful to reporters and editors at member stations as it is to AP staffers.

The AP Radio wire has developed its own style, especially suited for broad national audiences, but there is really very little that is different in writing news for a national audience and writing for a local audience. Whether you are serving thousands of newsrooms or thousands of listeners and viewers, you must be *quick, clear, accurate and fair.*

In actual practice, the story is first composed by the writer, then polished by the editor. Thus, this chapter deals with writing and the following one looks at editing.

• THE BASICS

Imagine this: You're walking to work and you see a terrific fire, eating away at a high-rise building. When you get to work, the first thing you're likely to say is: "This big building's on fire downtown."

Someone else arrives and says the fire department is closing the street. He'll probably say something like this: "They're closing Main Street down by Clinton. They're stringing hoses all over the place."

Later, you may hear that seven people died in the fire. That's probably the first thing you'd mention to the next person you talked to: "Seven people died in that fire this afternoon, the one in the Clinton Building on Main Street. They had the street closed for hours."

That's how you tell a story, in person or on the air. You lead with the newest and most important information, but you don't completely abandon the information that you relayed earlier.

That principle applies to written as well as spoken journalism. But broadcast news differs from print in several important ways, and they help determine how we tell a breaking story.

In the first place, broadcasters can tell the story as it is unfolding, on a minute-by-minute basis. This means that broadcast news can have an effect on the outcome of the event—which places a tremendous responsibility on all radio and TV reporters.

While it is our job to report the first story, it is also our responsibility to do so without causing panic, without unnecessarily drawing bystanders to the scene and without reporting unfounded rumors or speculation which may later turn out to be untrue.

Keep in mind, too, that our listeners and viewers can't go back and read the story again if we don't tell it clearly the first time. And finally, remember that broadcast news tends to be more personal than print. The vocal inflections, facial expressions and general attitude of the newscaster all influence the public's perception of the story. This means we must keep stories in perspective and make it clear that we may not have all of the answers at any given moment.

To return to the fire analogy, radio and television will be covering the story in much the same way as newspapers, with one important exception: the newspaper story will probably not be read until the fire is out. The broadcast stories will be heard while the flames are still raging, as well as after the fire is out.

We must therefore keep the public posted as the story unfolds, while also preparing the more complete wrap-ups to be aired later.

The local newspaper will be constantly updating its story as the event unfolds. You'll be doing the same, except that you'll be doing so publicly—on the air.

From the moment the first report comes in, it's a story for radio. Even though there's no way of knowing immediately whether it's just another routine fire call or whether it's a major story, radio still needs a brief story reporting that fire trucks are rushing to the scene. If nothing else, it's an advisory to motorists to watch for fire equipment and to steer clear of the congestion that's bound to develop.

Then the first word from the scene comes into the newsroom, either from the fire department or from a reporter who routinely went there. Flames are visible. They're shooting out of windows on the upper floors. And you learn that the building is being evacuated. A check of your reference file gives you the exact floor count, and you go with the story:

> *FIRE HAS BROKEN OUT IN THE CLINTON BUILDING DOWNTOWN. FIRE UNITS ARE ARRIVING NOW AND THE 30-STORY BUILDING IS BEING*

EVACUATED. THERE'S NO INDICATION YET JUST HOW SERIOUS THE FIRE IS, BUT WITNESSES SAY FLAMES ARE SHOOTING FROM WINDOWS ON THE UPPER FLOORS.

Note how closely this corresponds to the imaginary conversation recounted a few pages ago.

A few minutes later, you relay a police request to motorists to stay away from the area and you learn that a multiple alarm has been sounded:

MAIN STREET IS BEING CLOSED TO TRAFFIC FOR SEVERAL BLOCKS AROUND THE CLINTON BUILDING DOWNTOWN. FIRE BROKE OUT IN THE 30-STORY OFFICE TOWER A FEW MINUTES AGO AND FIRE UNITS FROM AROUND THE CITY ARE RESPONDING.

IF YOU'RE DRIVING, WATCH FOR THE FIRE TRUCKS AND AVOID THE MAIN AND CLINTON AREA. AMBULANCES ARE ALSO ON THE WAY, ALTHOUGH SO FAR THERE'S NO DEFINITE WORD OF ANY INJURIES IN THE FIRE AT THE CLINTON BUILDING DOWNTOWN.

The lead now is that the streets are being closed around the building. This is immediately important to anyone driving in the area—and keep in mind always that most people listen to the radio while driving. In the next sentence, we recount the fact that there's a fire in the Clinton Building for those who weren't listening to the first report.

Then we repeat—in different words—the advice that drivers should stay away from the area. And we note that ambulances are on the way, as is routine in such an event, even though there's no certainty yet that anyone has been hurt. This is important; never jump to conclusions about deaths and injuries. Remember that relatives and friends of the possible victims are listening to you, and you have a responsibility to them to be both accurate and prudent.

Finally, we repeat the basic information in the last sentence. This is always advisable in handling breaking stories, since most people don't really begin paying attention until you're well into the story. Remember the last time you heard an obituary on the radio but missed the identity of the deceased? It's pretty annoying.

Your next report on the fire includes some bad news: three people are dead, eight injured and several missing. That becomes the lead; the street closings and the details of the fire itself are secondary.

GRIM NEWS FROM FIRE OFFICIALS: AT LEAST THREE PEOPLE HAVE DIED IN THE FIRE THAT'S STILL BURNING OUT OF CONTROL IN THE CLINTON BUILDING. FIRE CHIEF EDWIN WILCOX SAYS FIREMEN HAVE CARRIED OUT THREE BODIES AND RESCUED EIGHT PEOPLE WHO WERE INJURED. WILCOX SAYS THERE ARE AT LEAST THREE MORE PEOPLE STILL INSIDE THE BURNING OFFICE TOWER.

WILCOX SAYS ALL OF THE DEAD AND INJURED SO FAR ARE CIVILIANS -- MEANING THEY'RE NOT POLICE OR FIREFIGHTERS.

FIVE FIRE COMPANIES ARE BATTLING THE BLAZE IN THE 30-STORY BUILDING AND TRAFFIC IN THE ENTIRE DOWNTOWN AREA IS BADLY CONGESTED. POLICE ARE PLEADING WITH DRIVERS TO STAY OUT OF THE AREA.

First, note that the listener is set up for the bad news. Note too that the report of deaths and injuries is clearly attributed, first to "fire officials," then to the chief himself. We also specify that "at least three" are dead, clearly signalling that there may be more, but not going out on a limb or unnecessarily dramatizing the situation.

In the second paragraph, we go along with the custom of police and fire departments to refer to everyone except themselves as "civilians." It is not strictly accurate, of course, which is why we explain it in the same sentence. It is important information, however, and it shouldn't be left out.

The last paragraph recaps what has been covered before and emphatically repeats the advice to drivers to stay away.

Notice that so far, none of these leads much resembles a print version of the story. All of them are written in the present tense and it is very clear that the story is changing every minute. It is when the fire is out and the final casualty count is in that the broadcast and print stories may begin to look alike. But first it is broadcast's job to spread the word that the fire is out.

THE FIRE IN THE CLINTON BUILDING IS OUT. THE ANNOUNCEMENT BY FIRE CHIEF EDWIN WILCOX COMES NEARLY FOUR HOURS AFTER THE FLAMES BROKE OUT -- KILLING THREE PEOPLE AND INJURING 16 MORE.

Once that is out of the way, we can deal with the story from a variety of angles for the next several hours or days. And now many of our broadcast stories will more closely resemble the print versions.

A FIRE THAT BURNED FOR NEARLY FOUR HOURS KILLED THREE PEOPLE AND INJURED 16 MORE IN A DOWNTOWN OFFICE BUILDING YESTERDAY. DAMAGE IS ESTIMATED IN THE (M) MILLIONS AT THE CLINTON BUILDING, A 30-STORY TOWER BUILT JUST THREE YEARS AGO.

THE FIRE INSPECTOR'S OFFICE IS TRYING TO FIND OUT WHAT CAUSED THE FIRE THAT SWEPT THROUGH THE UPPER FLOORS OF THE CLINTON BUILDING YESTERDAY.

ONE OF THE AREA'S LEADING BUSINESS EXECUTIVES PERISHED IN YESTERDAY'S FIRE IN THE CLINTON BUILDING. WAYNE SMITH WAS TRAPPED IN AN ELEVATOR ON THE BUILDING'S TOP FLOOR.

SMITH FOUNDED AN ELECTRONICS COMPANY AND WAS AN OFFICER OF THE FIRM WHICH BUILT THE CLINTON BUILDING JUST THREE YEARS AGO.

Writing for radio presents both a problem and an opportunity. The problem is that a top story must be told at least every hour, maybe more often, without becoming repetitive or boring. The opportunity is the flip side of the problem: radio, more than any other medium, has the aura of immediacy. It can tell every aspect of the story as it unfolds, and can explore various facets of the story after the fact.

This is possible because most radio stations have newscasts at least every hour, and often even more frequently. Most television stations and newspapers, on the other hand, have only one or two newscasts or editions each day and are thus limited to just a few approaches.

This situation is steadily changing, however, as television becomes increasingly able to televise live from almost anywhere with very little notice. Most major television stations now have helicopters, microwave equipment and small portable cameras which allow them to broadcast live from the scene of a major story. In practice, however, television tends to stay with its programming schedule and to present news only at regularly-scheduled times.

Broadcasting's emphasis on immediacy has given newspapers the opportunity to concentrate on analytical and investigative pieces, and to fill in the holes which broadcast news may have left.

What it all means is: Know your audience.

If you are writing an hourly radio newscast, you are updating your audience. While you must tell the bare bones of the entire story, the emphasis should be on the latest angle. This varies only slightly when you are writing "drive-time" newscasts, those aired during the hours when most people are traveling to and from work.

Most commuters want quick recaps of the top stories at that hour, and the chances are that they haven't been in touch with the news for the previous eight hours or so. This means you must be sure to cover the important angles of each major story, while still emphasizing the latest wrinkle in each.

In television newscasts, there is a stronger assumption that viewers want the story from the top. So you lead with the major development of the day, not the hour, and work your way along from there.

• PUTTING IT TOGETHER

Just as the nature of the story and newscast determine the lead, the lead itself sets the tone for the story, and helps determine what sentences will follow. Each sentence must flow logically from the previous. It is the only way the story will make sense to the listener.

With practice, logical story structure comes naturally to the writer;

experienced reporters begin to build the story even before reaching a typewriter or computer terminal.

Let's return to our fire story. The first-hour's lead went like this:

A FIRE HAS BROKEN OUT IN THE CLINTON BUILDING DOWNTOWN.

That lead naturally raises a question: how serious is it? The next sentence answers:

FIRE UNITS ARE ARRIVING NOW AND THE 30-STORY BUILDING IS BEING EVACUATED.

The facts are presented in a logical and orderly fashion that leaves no questions unanswered, that leaves the listener with the knowledge that he has heard all there is to tell at this point.

As the lead changes, the structure of the story changes, even though the same facts are being presented. You cannot simply plop a new lead atop an old story: it will raise new questions that have to be answered, which means a new second sentence, and, in turn, a new third sentence, and so on.

There was a time when broadcast writers, be they radio or television people, did little more than mark up newspaper copy. But those days are gone. Broadcast copy now demands a totally different structure, a different approach and writing style.

In fact, it is downright detrimental to simply rewrite the phrasing of newspaper copy. You must take it apart and weigh the facts, then put the whole thing back together again—in a new form. The best way to write a broadcast story is to tell it to *yourself,* polish it up a bit, then commit it to paper.

Here's a way to get into that habit.

Take the newspaper or wire copy from which you are writing and read it thoroughly. Try to gain a full understanding of the story: who's doing or saying what about whom?

Once you know the story well, turn the copy over and put it aside. Write your own story.

Do not refer to the source copy except to find a specific fact or quote. Concentrate on your lead, your second sentence—not the source copy's.

You'll soon find that you are building your own structure. Rather than relying on the source copy's approach, you'll have to come up with your own. That's the single most important step.

It takes a certain flair to do it correctly. And it takes a firm concept of your audience. Perhaps the best description of *that* was provided in the late '30s by Edward R. Murrow of CBS. The analogy may seem a bit dated, but the ideas behind it are as sound as ever:

Imagine yourself at a dinner table back in the United States with the local editor, a banker, and a professor, talking over the coffee. You try to tell what it was like, while the maid's boyfriend, a truck driver, listens from the kitchen. Talk to be understood by the truck driver while not insulting the professor's intelligence.*

It's not the kind of thing you can do by simply following a formula. But there are some guidelines that can help put you on the right path.

—Write simply, yet intelligently.
—Use the simple declarative sentence.
—Always keep the listener's ear in mind.
—Build your story logically.
—Always use appropriate attribution—and know the laws in your state.
—Be informal.
—Don't put stumbling blocks in your copy.
—Use contractions.
—Be grammatical.
—Avoid slang.
—Use words properly.

Write Simply, Yet Intelligently: News stories tend to be complicated, and the writer's task is to unravel them and present them in an understandable form. The stories should be simply structured, one fact leading into another. And there's no need to use a big word—or several—when one will do.

For example, why say "utilize" when you can say "use?"

Why say "exacerbated" when you mean "made worse?"

Why write "toxic material" when you mean "poison?"

Simple, direct words can be used in intelligent stories. In fact, they usually make them more understandable.

Use the Simple Declarative Sentence: The best way to say something is to simply come out with it. Direct statements, graceful but not flowery, are the basic building blocks of broadcast news writing.

Some examples:

THE RATIFICATION OF THE "SALT-TWO" TREATY IS UP TO THE SENATE. BUT VICE PRESIDENT MONDALE FIGURES IT CAN'T DO ANY HARM TO TAKE THE TREATY'S CASE TO THE PUBLIC.

THIS IS THE FINAL DAY OF THE OPEC OIL CARTEL MEETING IN CARACAS, VENEZUELA.

NO SHAH, NO FREEDOM FOR THE HOSTAGES. TEHRAN RADIO BROADCAST THAT STATEMENT TODAY.

Why waste words? If you can say it simply and directly, do it.

* Alexander Kendrick, *Prime Time* (Boston: Little, Brown & Company, 1969), p. 278.

Always Keep the Listener's Ear in Mind: Some words sound better together than others. Sentences, paragraphs and entire stories, much like music, have textures and rhythms. A series of short words may sound too staccato for the scene you are describing. On the other hand, you may want some rapid-fire wording to summarize the tense situation you are reporting.

Listen mentally to the words you are using. If they sound clumsy, or if it feels cluttered as you skip from one word to the next, rewrite the sentence. To make sense to the mind, a sentence must sound right to the ear. An example:

> *PRESIDENT CARTER FEARS THAT GRANTING CHINA MOST-FAVORED-NATION TRADE STATUS WILL BE BAD FOR OUR RELATIONS WITH RUSSIA.*

It is a long, clumsy sentence. It lacks grace; the words are falling all over each other, and the idea behind them seems to have been lost in the shuffle. It can be improved:

> *PRESIDENT CARTER'S AFRAID THAT RUSSIA WON'T LIKE IT IF WE GRANT BETTER TRADE TERMS TO CHINA.*

It's still a bit wordy. *Won't like it if* is a particularly difficult phrase to say. And if the newscaster has trouble saying it, the listener will know—and it will get in the way of comprehension.

The problem can be tackled by taking a different approach to the lead:

> *WHAT WILL RUSSIA THINK IF WE IMPROVE OUR TRADE RELATIONS WITH CHINA? PRESIDENT CARTER'S AFRAID THE SOVIETS WILL BE UPSET.*

Or, you could take a more oblique approach:

> *PRESIDENT CARTER'S LOOKING TOWARD MOSCOW AS HE CONSIDERS BETTER TRADE RELATIONS WITH PEKING. CARTER'S WORRIED ABOUT THE KREMLIN'S REACTION TO PROPOSALS TO IMPROVE CHINA'S STATUS AS AN AMERICAN TRADING PARTNER.*

Compare that to our first pass at this difficult set of ideas. Both versions contain the same facts. It is the approach and style that are different.

Build Your Story Logically: Once you've chosen a lead, think of the next obvious question it raises. Answer that question in the second sentence. Then consider what question *that* sentence raises—and answer it. The story must be a progression of facts that cover all major questions the listener could ask.

One of the more common mistakes in story structure is the failure to lay the groundwork for a fact you are introducing. You must set the listener up, so that every facet of the story fits into the whole. If the listener spends any time wondering what you are talking about, he will never get the point you're trying to make. For example, the following story leaves the listener reeling in confusion:

THE "WASHINGTON STAR" SAYS IT'S PEGGED THE MAN BELIEVED TO BE THE FIRST TO GO IN THE PRESIDENTIAL SHAKE-UP. HE'S A WHITE HOUSE COUNSEL -- ROBERT LIPSHUTZ. AND THE PAPER SAYS UNIDENTIFIED SOURCES HAVE SAID CARTER WILL ACCEPT HIS RESIGNATION FIRST.

The story might be better structured this way:

UNIDENTIFIED WASHINGTON SOURCES THINK THEY KNOW WHO'LL BE THE FIRST WHITE HOUSE STAFFER OUSTED IN THE ADMINISTRATION SHAKE-UP. ACCORDING TO A REPORT IN THE "WASHINGTON STAR," HE'S WHITE HOUSE COUNSEL ROBERT LIPSHUTZ.

The second story prepares the listener for the facts that are about to be presented. It establishes first that someone's going to be fired—and then says who it's likely to be. Another way to do the story would be to establish the fact of the shake-up first:

PRESIDENT CARTER IS WORKING ON AN ADMINISTRATION SHAKE-UP ... AND NOW COMES A REPORT ON WHO THE FIRST VICTIM MIGHT BE.

Once the potential for firings has been established it's only logical to go on to who the "victim" might be.

It's also possible to approach the story from the "victim" angle—and then establish what he's victim of:

A PUBLISHED REPORT SAYS ROBERT LIPSHUTZ WILL BE THE FIRST VICTIM OF THE CARTER ADMINISTRATION SHAKE-UP.

That lead logically suggests a second sentence providing attribution, which would prompt a third sentence saying who Lipshutz is and when he might go. In each of these examples, unlike the original, we start with one idea and progress—logically—from there.

Always Use Appropriate Attribution: A key aspect of that Washington Star story was the attribution: the newspaper quoted unidentified sources as saying that Lipshutz would be the first to go.

The writer had to clearly identify just who was reporting the statement—and what their source was.

The requirement for strong and clear attribution is a basic tenet of journalism: report the facts—only what you know to be true. Don't guess; don't draw conclusions.

So, for example, in the Lipshutz story, we didn't say he *will* be the first to go, or that he *apparently* is about to be fired, or even that he *might* be the first. We reported the fact that someone else has obtained information that he will be the first man to be fired. And we prominently attributed it all.

There are some cases where attriubtion is not needed. If the fire department says a building is on fire, it's a fairly safe bet that it is. If officials tell you the building is being evacuated, and your reporter on the scene tells you that there's a steady flow of people out of the building, you can go with the evacuation angle.

But if you have any reason to doubt the report, if it is not verifiable, or if it is an opinion instead of a fact, it must be attributed.

Of course, if you pick up the report from another source—a foreign news service, a newspaper or a radio station—you should attribute it in most cases.

And always err on the side of caution: when in doubt, pin it on someone. If you can't, hold off.

Attribution is especially important in public controversies and in criminal cases. If a politician accuses somebody of something, you must be careful to specifically and prominently say who's doing the accusing.

Similarly, if police report that a crime has been committed or an arrest has been made, and that report is the only source you have for the story, it is common practice to pin it all on the police. Of course, anything that is independently verifiable need not be attributed.

Which leads us to the question of what to do with "facts" reported by police, or in court, that are in legal doubt. You can't very well tack on the phrase, "according to police" every time one of these questionable matters comes up.

The answer is a modifier such as "alleged" or "accused." Such words *must* be used to make it clear that an unproved assertion is not being treated as fact.

What is at issue in most criminal cases is whether a crime was actually committed and/or whether the defendant is responsible for the crime.

It is important that you know just which one is at issue in a given case.

For example, if Mr. X is on trial for murder in the dismemberment slaying of Mr. Y, it is pretty clear that Mr. Y was the victim of a crime, not an accident or suicide. So, we don't need to constantly refer to an *alleged killing.*

However, whether Mr. X is the actual killer is in question. That is what the trial is all about. Therefore, Mr. X must be referred to as the *alleged killer, the accused slayer of Mr. Y, the defendant, the man charged with killing Mr. Y,* etc.

If Mr. Y is simply missing—disappeared without a trace—we have another situation entirely. We then have an alleged killing and a person charged with carrying out the alleged scheme. The prosecution will first have to establish that a crime has occured. Then it will try to pin it on Mr. X.

Keep in mind also that *accused* and *charged* are not necessarily the same thing.

Procedures vary widely from one state to another.

In some states, police may arrest someone and charge him with murder. In others, only the District Attorney or a similar authority may file such a charge.

Terminology varies widely. In some states, the proper phrase is that someone is *being held for investigation* of the crime.

Being arrested or detained is not the same thing as being formally charged. The charge must be filed in court, usually by the D.A. or by a Grand Jury. There is nearly always a hearing of some type in conjunction with the formal charge—sometimes a preliminary hearing, sometimes an arraignment.

It is very important to know the difference.

It is also important to handle police statements carefully.

"We got him. We got the killer," a county sheriff once said after his men arrested a suspect. The man had not been formally charged . . . and never was formally charged. He was released a few days later and could well have proceeded to sue the sheriff and any news outlet which had carried the assertion.

Don't *ever* say that John Doe *has been arrested and will be charged with murder.* You don't know that he will be—and if, in the end, he isn't, you're in trouble.

Know the Laws in Your State: When reading wire copy from another state, it is best not to make any changes in the wording of the section dealing with the status of criminal charges—since the person who wrote that section presumably knows the exact laws in his state. You don't, and the laws in your state may be different.

Be careful not to over-use the word *alleged.* It is one of those words that has a specific meaning and it is easy to fall into the habit of throwing it at any questionable situation. Remember that it has synonyms such as *accused, reputed, supposed,* and *purported.* And remember, too, that you can turn the sentence around and express the same thought in another way: "the purported spy" can become "the man who is accused of spying."

In any case, such modifiers protect both the writer and the accused. It is important that they be properly used. When dealing with stories where there is a legal or factual issue, make sure you know just what that issue is—and make sure your story reflects it.

As we saw in the Washington Star-Robert Lipshutz example before, attribution is central to stories in which the source does not want to be identified. It is crucial to the story that you establish—as firmly as possible—who the source is and what his qualifications are.

For example, suppose a Senator's administrative aide tells you that the Senator is about to resign, but asks that you not divulge his role in reporting the story. You might report:

A SOURCE SAYS SENATOR JOHN SMITH IS ABOUT TO RESIGN.

But that doesn't give the listener any indication of the reliability of the report: who is the source and why should he be believed?

You might firm it up by saying:

A SOURCE WHO OUGHT TO KNOW SAYS SENATOR JOHN SMITH IS ABOUT TO RESIGN.

But *ought to know* or *in a position to know* reflects a judgment on your part—and unfairly leaves the listener in the dark as to the facts of the case.

And it is to the facts that you must turn:

A SOURCE IN SENATOR JOHN SMITH'S OFFICE . . .
A SOURCE CLOSE TO SENATOR JOHN SMITH . . .
A SENATE SOURCE WHO ASKED NOT BE NAMED . . .

In each case, you come as close as possible to telling the listener just why the source is believable.

Another type of story that must be carefully attributed is public opinion polling. You must always credit the polling organization with the results. In addition, you must indicate that the results are based on a particular sampling—and reflect nothing more than a statistical projection of that sampling's responses.

For example:

THE LATEST GALLUP POLL GIVES PRESIDENT CARTER A LOWER POPULARITY RATING THAN EVER. THE POLL SUGGESTS THAT FEWER THAN ONE-THIRD OF THE COUNTRY LIKES THE JOB THE PRESIDENT IS DOING. GALLUP SAYS 29 PERCENT OF THOSE RESPONDING TO THIS WEEK'S POLL GAVE CARTER A POSITIVE JOB RATING. LAST MONTH, 35 PERCENT APPROVED OF HIS WORK.

Note that the story does not say that the President's popularity is down; it says that Gallup's *rating* of the President's popularity is down.

And the story does not say that the poll means that fewer people like the job Carter is doing; it says the poll *suggests* that fact. In each sentence, what we report is not where public opinion stands, but where the latest measure of public opinion stands.

Always be careful to prominently attribute poll results, to remind your audience that the numbers are based on a specific sampling (*29 percent of those responding to this week's poll*) and to say that the poll merely *suggests, predicts* or *estimates* the opinion of the nation as a whole.

There are several different styles of attribution. The one most often encountered in print is the *hanging attribution:*

SEVEN PEOPLE DIED AND 35 WERE INJURED IN A BUS CRASH ON A SLIPPERY HIGHWAY OUTSIDE NEW YORK CITY TODAY, POLICE SAID.

Of course, people don't talk that way and there is usually a more graceful way of using attribution in broadcast copy.

The most obvious is to put the attribution at the front of the sentence:

POLICE SAY SEVEN PEOPLE DIED AND 35 WERE INJURED IN A BUS CRASH ON A SLIPPERY HIGHWAY OUTSIDE NEW YORK CITY TODAY.

This is not much better than the "hanging" version, and it is a dangerous habit to fall into. For one thing, it is easy to lazily start every story with someone saying something:

POLICE SAY . . .
THE MAYOR SAYS . . .
THE PRESIDENT SAYS . . .

It is much better to use a little extra effort to work the attribution into the story in a natural and more graceful way:

A BUS CRASHED ON A SLIPPERY HIGHWAY OUTSIDE NEW YORK CITY TODAY, AND POLICE SAY SEVEN PASSENGERS WERE KILLED. THIRTY-FIVE OTHERS ARE REPORTED INJURED.

Or . . .

POLICE REPORT A MAJOR ACCIDENT INVOLVING A BUS THIS AFTERNOON. OFFICERS SAY THE BUS WENT INTO A SKID ON A SLIPPERY HIGHWAY NEAR NEW YORK CITY AND CRASHED INTO A GUARDRAIL. THE OFFICIAL CASUALTY COUNT AT THIS HOUR LISTS SEVEN DEAD AND 35 HURT.

There are as many ways to attribute a story as there are to tell the story. Don't fall into a rut.

Be Informal: There is a dialect in the English-speaking world known as *wire-ese.* It is the awful habit of falling into stodgy, stilted sentences that state the facts but put the listener to sleep. Wire-ese causes newscasters to drone on and on, prompts listeners to turn off their radios, and gives writers and wire services bad reputations.

You don't have to write that way.

After all, you don't think that way, and you don't speak that way.

Perhaps the principal cause of the persistent use of wire-ese is conventionality. Writers assume that, because they must tell the story, they must line up fact after fact, knocking them off like ducks in a row.

But that can be boring. And, again: people don't talk that way.

Instead, they use images, familiar phrases, sometimes colloquialisms, to get the point across.

As an example, take the Iranian hostage story, in which militants in Tehran held American diplomatic workers prisoner for months and months. It was, to the American public, a frustrating story as it was being played out, and one writer caught that in his lead:

> *IT'S HAPPENED AGAIN. NO SOONER HAD IRAN'S FOREIGN MINISTER MADE A CONCILIATORY STATEMENT ABOUT THE IRANIAN CRISIS THAN THE MILITANTS OCCUPYING THE U-S EMBASSY CONTRADICTED HIM.*

The lead catches the flavor of frustration, using a familiar phrase to do it.

In wire-ese, the story might have come out this way:

> *THE MILITANTS HOLDING THE AMERICAN EMBASSY IN TEHRAN SAY THE ONLY WAY THEY'LL RELEASE THEIR 50 HOSTAGES IS IF THE SHAH RETURNS TO IRAN. THAT CONTRADICTS FOREIGN MINISTER GHOTBZADEH, WHO EARLIER TOLD . . .*

Boring.

Economic stories are particularly prone to formula writing:

> *SEVERAL OF THE NATION'S LEADING BANKS HAVE RAISED THEIR PRIME LENDING RATE TO 15 AND THREE-QUARTERS PERCENT. THAT'S A RECORD, AND FOLLOWS LAST WEEK'S GOVERNMENT MOVE TO TIGHTEN CREDIT TO FIGHT INFLATION.*

There's nothing terribly wrong with that story. But compare it to this one:

> *MONEY IS GETTING HARDER TO COME BY. SEVERAL BANKS, LED BY CHASE MANHATTAN, TODAY BOOSTED BY ONE-HALF POINT THE RATE THEY CHARGE THEIR BEST CORPORATE CUSTOMERS TO BORROW MONEY. THAT PUTS THE SO-CALLED PRIME RATE BACK AT THE RECORD 15 AND THREE-QUARTERS PERCENT SET LAST FALL. AND IT FOLLOWS A MOVE LAST FRIDAY . . .*

Congressional stories—the House passed this, the Senate passed that—are also vulnerable:

> *A HOUSE-SENATE CONFERENCE COMMITTEE IS RESUMING WORK ON A COMPROMISE FEDERAL BUDGET. THE NEW FISCAL YEAR IS 17 DAYS OLD, BUT THE LAWMAKERS HAVE BEEN UNABLE TO COME UP WITH AN AGREEMENT ON A BUDGET BILL.*

Instead, one writer opted for more familiar words:

> *CONGRESS REMAINS A HOUSE DIVIDED. WITH THE NEW FISCAL YEAR 17 DAYS OLD, THERE'S STILL NO FEDERAL BUDGET. HOUSE AND SENATE CONFEREES ARE TO RESUME CONSIDERATION OF A PACKAGE TODAY.*

It's not that the wire-ese examples are badly written. They simply are not as good as the others. They lack the spark of imagination that makes copy move rather than plod.

Quite often, the flint for the spark is informality.

Take, as an example, this title:

ROBERT STRAUSS, THE HEAD OF PRESIDENT CARTER'S RE-ELECTION CAMPAIGN.

Why not:

CARTER CAMPAIGN CHIEF, or
CARTER RE-ELECTION CHAIRMAN.

Or, better yet, why not break up the title and put it in a sentence, so it comes out the way it would in conversation:

ROBERT STRAUSS, WHO HEADS THE CARTER CAMPAIGN . . .

The key to informal writing is to put yourself back at that mythical dinner table, telling friends and neighbors what's going on. Turn the story over in your mind a few times: what does it *really* mean—what's the point of the story? Or, who is this person I'm reporting about, what is his or her real significance?

After that kind of thinking, Strauss' title might come out like this:

ROBERT STRAUSS IS THE MAN HEADING THE EFFORT TO GIVE PRESIDENT CARTER FOUR MORE YEARS IN THE WHITE HOUSE, AND HE SAYS . . .

Remember the function of the writer: to tell the listener what's going on in terms that he can appreciate.

Another key to informality is to vary the lengths of your sentences. After a long one, write a short one. Keep the lengths mixed up, and keep the pacing appropriate to the story:

IT SEEMS GRIFFEN WAS, INDEED, A TECHNICIAN AT A HOSPITAL IN BALTIMORE NINE YEARS AGO, WHEN HE DECIDED TO TRY HIS HAND AT ROBBING BANKS. IT WAS A WHIM, HE SAYS, JUST ONE OF THOSE THINGS. HE PULLED IT OFF. THEN HE GAVE HIMSELF UP.

That was a feature story, and so the tone was a bit less formal than a news story, and the pace more leisurely. But the irony of trying to rob a bank on a whim, succeeding, and then giving up, was expressed in the pacing of the final two sentences.

Don't Put Stumbling Blocks in Your Copy: Just as the proper length and placement of a sentence or phrase can help a story move along, the improper placement or length can make the newscaster stumble.

As the story progresses, the copy, newcaster and listener all gain momentum. If a long and difficult phrase suddenly appears, that momentum will come to a crashing halt—and the story will lose direction and the listeners will lose interest.

(Of course, there are times when you want to stop the momentum. Often, if you want to shock or surprise a listener, you can let the momentum build up—and then throw in a very short sentence with the "zinger" in it. But that's done intentionally, what we're concerned with here are those unintentional zingers.)

Such stumbling blocks are, most often, caused by complicated attribution. The key in such cases is to break up the title and the name:

> *GENERAL ROBERT BARROW, THE NEW COMMANDANT OF THE MARINE CORPS, SAYS THE DRAFT MAY HAVE TO RESUME IN THE LATE 80'S.*

Try, instead:

> *THE MARINES' NEW COMMANDANT SAYS THE DRAFT MAY HAVE TO RESUME IN THE LATE 80'S. GENERAL ROBERT BARROW SAID THAT AS HE ...*

Some titles are even longer. They are impossible to get around, but at least their impact can be minimized:

> *THE HEAD OF THE NATIONAL OCEANIC AND ATMOSPHERIC ADMINISTRATION, JOHN SMITH, SAYS IT ISN'T TRUE.*

Try, instead,

> *JOHN SMITH HEADS THE NATIONAL OCEANIC AND ATMOSPHERIC ADMINISTRATION, AND HE SAYS IT ISN'T TRUE.*

Or, back into the title:

> *THE HEAD OF THE AGENCY INVOLVED DISAGREES. AND JOHN SMITH SAYS HIS NATIONAL OCEANIC AND ATMOSPHERIC ADMINISTRATION HAS THE FACTS TO BACK HIM UP.*

Use Contractions: People combine words all the time. Even college professors use *don't, won't,* and *can't,* and there is no reason why broadcasters shouldn't.

The number and types of contractions you use will depend on your personal style and the context of the story. But, as a rule of thumb, contractions help the story move along, help develop a familiar tone, and make it easier for the newscaster to read the story:

> *IT'S HAPPENED AGAIN ... PRESIDENT CARTER WON'T BE CAMPAIGNING ... SENATOR EDWARD KENNEDY'S CALLING ON ... THE GOVERNMENT ISN'T IN THE RED ...*

Be Grammatical: You obviously wouldn't use the contraction *ain't,* since it isn't grammatical. There are less obvious grammatical errors that make it to the air every day—and they shouldn't.

There's no denying that English is a complicated, seemingly irrational language. But there are certain rules that govern it, and they are best followed if the language is to be used as an effective tool of communication.

One of the best guides to good grammar is "The Elements of Style," by the late William Strunk, Jr., and E. B. White. This compact volume provides some basic, common-sense grammatical guidelines.

Avoid Slang: Conversational news writers are constantly walking that thin line between informality and slang. Don't step over it.

Colloquialisms, such as those cited in our discussion of informality, are often acceptable. But ungrammatical, utterly irreverent and downright incorrect words and phrases have no place in radio or television copy. When injected, they usually make the story sound silly, undermining the credibility of the writer, newsroom and newscaster.

The line between what's appropriate and what isn't is constantly shifting. Experience is the best tool in deciding whether to use a questionable phrase or word. But if in doubt, leave it out. And be prepared for the editor to be the final judge.

Use Words Properly: Proper use of the language is at the heart of effective communication. The person who can not choose the right word and use it correctly is in big trouble behind a typewriter or CRT.

There are, of course, the classic errors—mixing up *their* and *they're*, using the wrong form of *it's* and *its*. Fortunately, or maybe unfortunately, these words are *homonyms*. They sound the same on the air, whether they're correctly spelled or not. This saves many of us from sounding foolish, but it also lulls many broadcast writers into letting their writing become sloppier and sloppier, until finally it begins to show in their on-air presentation. It may also cause severe problems for a broadcast reporter who moves on to a different operation, one where clear and correct writing is demanded.

There are many pompous words currently in vogue in America, most of them nothing more than bloated, multi-syllabic versions of much simpler words.

Facility nowadays can be tacked onto anything. We have all seen signs for "auto storage facilities" (parking lots), "waste disposal facilities" (trash dumps) and "recreation facilities" (swimming pools). Many towns now have a "correctional facility" instead of a jail.

Many prison guards insist on being called "corrections officers."

Utilize threatens to replace *use,* and nearly no one has a job anymore; we all have *positions.*

A government agency not long ago issued a report on an airline accident, saying that the cause of the crash was "inadvertent impact with terrain." Simply put, the airplane flew into the ground.

Any living language is constantly changing—taking in words from foreign languages, assimilating terms from science and coining new words to describe new situations. At the same time, archaic and arcane words tend to die out. This is a natural process, and one which keeps the language useful. But if language is consistently misused, it will eventually lose its precision and those who speak that language will lose the ability to communicate precisely.

It is so obvious that it hardly needs to be stated that journalists have a tremendous impact on everyday usage. It is our job to know our language and to use it carefully and affectionately.*

It is, after all, all we have to work with.

* For an excellent treatment of this subject, see Edwin Newman, *Strictly Speaking* (Indianapolis: Bobbs-Merrill, 1974), and *A Civil Tongue* (Indianapolis: Bobbs-Merrill, 1976).

THE EDITOR'S EYE

Writers and reporters have difficult jobs. They must dig through reams of material, sit through hours of meetings or talk to scores of people trying to find a newsworthy story. Then they must seek substantiation, get quotes or film or tape to flesh out the story and put it all together in a form that will satisfy their editors.

The editors have even more difficult jobs. They must sift through all of the material their reporters and writers have given them that day, try to keep up with the flow of copy from their wire machines, listen to their networks and keep an eye on the clock.

The editor has several essential functions:

—To make sure there is enough copy to fill up the next newscast or edition or split period;
—To make sure there is not too much copy;
—To make sure the copy that is used is interesting, accurate and timely;
—To keep the writers and reporters reasonably happy;
—To keep the boss as happy as possible.

Please note that most of these functions conflict with the others. It is the editor's lot to juggle the conflicting needs and desires adroitly so that the news report is turned out each day in good order while the staff and management remain relatively content.

In short, it is the editor who must say yes or no. Thus, editors are usually not popular people.

In fact, the editor has become rather rare in broadcast journalism. Most radio stations combine the jobs of writer, editor and newscaster, so that one person must perform all of these functions on each shift. In many stations, there is no designated reporter, so that the writer-editor-anchorman must also serve that function, covering stories in person when he or she is not on duty at the station, or chasing stories on the phone when he or she is on duty.

If it is difficult for an editor to do one job well, it is even more difficult for a single person to perform all of the editor's functions while also acting as reporter, writer and newscaster.

Much of this chapter may seem irrelevant to such a person, but it may prove to be useful, since every reporter must also try to see his or her work from an editor's point of view. It's the only way to improve.

The writer/reporter uses research, legwork, the telephone and source copy from the wires or from newspapers to put together a newscast or story that explains the world as he or she sees it.

The editor, on the other hand, has access to a much greater amount of information. The editor reads many more incoming wires, receives copy from many reporters and stringers and scans all of the network material available at that hour. Usually, editors try to put themselves in the place of the listener. They constantly ask themselves if they would want to hear this story while driving down the freeway next to a cement truck. If not, they kill it, or at least shorten it.

A reporter who works enthusiastically and thoroughly usually becomes so engrossed in the story that it becomes hard to judge its value.

This obviously sets the stage for a confrontation, which is why the editor must also be a diplomat, one who can de-emphasize or delete a reporter's story without alienating the reporter.

Also, good writers are constantly searching for new ways to say things. Good editors are always watching the copy to be sure it is factually consistent with previous stories, and to be sure it is written in the proper style.

An editor must be careful to not inadvertently stifle creativity in the name of consistency. It is not the editor's job to re-write everything that crosses the desk just to fit some preconceived formula of what the story should say. But at the same time, the editor must ensure that the writer's words say what they are meant to say.

Fortunately, there are some guidelines to help editors deal with copy—and to help writers know what's likely to happen to their copy once the editors get hold of it.

Report the Facts: Our job is to report what happens. Any conclusions about whether what happens is good or bad are left to the public.

Reporters often form strong opinions about the stories they cover, and these opinions sometimes find their way into the copy. It is the editor's job to root them out.

Editors must also watch for instances in which the writer has inadvertently taken an assertion as fact.

Just because a White House official says that News Secretary James Brady is dead does not make it so, as so many news organizations learned—the hard way.

Don't Jump to Conclusions: This goes along with sticking to the facts. Frequently, a series of circumstances will seem to point to a certain conclusion, but be careful! It may not be so.

A few years ago, the Israelis sent fighter jets screeching over Beirut at rooftop level, breaking the sound barrier and terrifying the residents. A reporter filed a story about the incident, saying that unidentified jets had flown over Beirut at roof-top level, accompanied by deafening explosions and the sound of shattering windows.

A writer back in New York turned that story into a bombing. It seemed quite obvious to the writer that the story was describing a bombing raid.

The editor smelled something amiss, however, referred back to the original story, and caught the error. The story did not go out until it had been revised.

Check for Proper Attribution: It is the editor's job to be sure that every story is properly attributed and that redundant attribution is avoided.

Keep It Readable: Copy may be factually correct, but if it doesn't read well it is wasted effort. If the copy is turgid and stale, it must be brought back to life.

In too many cases, the editor will revise the copy himself. When at all possible, it should be thrown back to the writer with a clear explanation of what is wrong with it. This is the only way the writer will learn.

Keep It Short: Don't let the writer's pride keep you from pruning the copy. You're making the writer look better, after all. No one is too good to be edited, and any sentence can be tightened up, including this one.

Keep It Current: Frequently, a story will change between the time it is written and the time the editor gets to it. And sometimes, the writer will bury the lead, perhaps because he is not as up to date as the editor.

In such a case, the editor must put the latest angle at the top of the story.

For example, this story was turned in to the AP Broadcast desk one day in 1980:

> *THE "NEW YORK TIMES" AND THE "LOS ANGELES TIMES" REPORTED TODAY THAT LATE-NIGHT TELEVISION COMEDIAN JOHNNY CARSON WANTS TO LEAVE N-B-C'S "TONIGHT" SHOW. THE NEWSPAPERS BOTH SAY CARSON WILL LEAVE THE SHOW ON SEPTEMBER 30TH -- HIS 17TH ANNIVERSARY AS THE "TONIGHT" HOST.*

The editor found new information, however, indicating that Carson's attorney had confirmed that his client intended to quit. But the attorney refused to talk about a date.

So the copy was revised:

> *JOHNNY CARSON WANTS TO LEAVE N-B-C'S "TONIGHT" SHOW. AND SOME REPORTS HAVE IT THAT CARSON WILL LEAVE THE PROGRAM ON*

SEPTEMBER 30TH -- HIS 17TH ANNIVERSARY AS HOST OF THE SHOW. CARSON'S ATTORNEY . . .

Have the Proper References at Your Desk: The editor must always be mindful of spelling and punctuation—and correct pronunciations. As a back-up, it is good to have a dictionary, thesaurus and gazeteer on hand for easy reference. And an almanac wouldn't hurt. In addition to this book, the basic reference source for style and spelling is Webster's New World Dictionary.

The editor's job is to work with the writer to perfect the stories prepared for broadcast. By respecting the writer's work and intentions, and maintaining a close watch on the integrity of the copy, the editor can mold the staff into a good working unit that will produce readable, interesting and accurate copy.

5 AP LIBEL MANUAL

Associate Justice John Marshall Harlan once remarked that "the law of libel has changed substantially since the early days of the Republic."

And it has changed substantially since he made that observation more than a decade ago. The past 14 years have seen the Supreme Court of the United States decide several cases that made headlines and truly can be called landmarks.

But the working journalist remembers: the news stories which generate the most claims of injury to reputation—the basis of libel—are run-of-the-mill. Perhaps 95 of 100 libel suits are in that category and result from publication of charges of crime, immorality, incompetence or inefficiency.

A Harvard Nieman report makes the point: "The gee-whiz, slam-bang stories usually aren't the ones that generate libel, but the innocent-appearing, potentially treacherous minor yarns from police courts and traffic cases, from routine meetings and from business reports."

Most of these suits based on relatively minor stories result from factual error or inexact language—for example, getting the plea wrong or making it appear that all defendants in a case face identical charges.

Libel even lurks in such innocent-appearing stories as birth notices and engagements. The fact that some New York newspapers had to defend suits recently for such announcements illustrates the care and concern required in every editorial department.

Turner Catledge, retired managing editor of The New York Times, says in his book, "My Life and the Times," that he learned over the years that newspapers must be extremely careful in checking engagement announcements. He noted that "sometimes people will call in the engagement of two people who hate each other, as a practical joke."

In short, there is no substitute for accuracy. But, of course, this does not mean that accurately reporting libelous assertions automatically absolves the journalist of culpability.

Accurate reporting will not prevent libel if there is no privilege, either the constitutional privilege or the fair report privilege.

A fair and impartial report of judicial, legislative and other public and official proceedings is privileged—that is, not actionable for libel. But it is important to know, for instance, what constitutes judicial action. In many states there is no privilege to report the filing of the summons and complaint in a civil suit until there has been some judicial action.

Many libel suits occur in the handling of court and police news, especially criminal courts. Problems can arise in stories about crime and in identifying a suspect where there has been no arrest or where no formal charge has been made.

Don't be deluded into thinking a safe approach is to eliminate the subject's name. If the description—physical or otherwise—readily identifies him to those in his immediate area, the story has, in effect, named him.

When accusations are made against a person, it is always well to try for balancing comment. The reply must have some relation to the original charges. Irrelevant countercharges can lead to problems with the person who made the first accusation.

The chief causes of libel suits are carelessness, misunderstanding of the law of libel, limitations of the defense of privilege (including the First Amendment privilege) and the extent to which developments may be reported in arrests. These are discussed in detail in this manual, which is "must" reading for every Associated Press staff member. It should be reviewed periodically.

• LIBEL, DEFENSES AND PRIVILEGE

Libel is injury to reputation.

Words, pictures or cartoons that expose a person to public hatred, shame, disgrace or ridicule, or induce an ill opinion of a person are libelous.

Actions for civil libel result mainly from news stories that allege crime, fraud, dishonesty, immoral or dishonorable conduct, or stories that defame the subject professionally, causing financial loss either personally or to a business.

There is only one complete and unconditional defense to a civil action for libel: that the facts stated are *provably true.* (Note well that word, *provably.*) Quoting someone correctly is not enough. The important thing is to be able to satisfy a jury that the libelous statement is substantially correct.

A second important defense is *privilege.* Privilege is one of two kinds—absolute and qualified.

Absolute privilege means that certain persons in some circumstances can state, without fear of being sued for libel, material which may be false, malicious and damaging. These circumstances include judicial, legislative, public and official proceedings and the contents of most public records.

The doctrine of absolute privilege is founded on the fact that on certain occasions the public interest requires that some individuals be exempted from legal liability for what they say.

Remarks by a member of a legislative body in the discharge of official duties are not actionable. Similarly, libelous statements made in the course of legal proceedings by participants are also absolutely privileged, if they are relevant to the issue. Statements containing defamatory matter may be absolutely privileged if publication or broadcast are required by law.

The interests of society require that judicial, legislative and similar official proceedings be subject to public discussion. To that extent, the rights of the individual about whom damaging statements may be made are subordinated to what are deemed to be the interests of the community.

We have been talking about absolute privilege as it applies to participants in the types of proceedings described here.

As applied to the press, the courts generally have held that privilege is not absolute, but rather is qualified. That means that it can be lost or diluted by how the journalist handles the material.

Privilege can be lost if there are errors in the report of the hearing, or if the plaintiff can show malice on the part of the publication or broadcast outlet.

An exception: broadcasters have absolute privilege to carry the broadcast statements of political candidates.

The two key points are:

1. Does the material at issue come from a privileged circumstance or proceeding?
2. Is the report a fair and accurate summation?

Again, the absolute privilege legislators enjoy—they cannot be sued, for example, for anything said on the floor of the legislature—affords total protection.

The journalist's protection is not as tight. But it is important and substantial and enables the press to report freely on many items of public interest which otherwise would have to go unreported.

The press has a qualified privilege to report that John Doe has been arrested for bank robbery. If the report is fair and accurate, there is no problem.

Statements made outside the court by police or a prosecutor or an attorney may not be privileged unless the circumstances indicate it is an official proceeding.

However, some states do extend privilege to these statements if made by specified top officials.

Newspapers and broadcasters often carry accounts going beyond the narrow confines of what is stated in the official charges, taking the risk without malice because they feel the importance of the case and the public interest warrant doing so.

The source of such statements should be specified.

Sometimes there are traps.

In New York and some other states, court rules provide that the papers filed in matrimonial actions are sealed and thus not open to inspection by the general public.

But sometimes litigants or their lawyers may slip a copy of the papers to reporters. Publication of the material is dangerous because often the litigants come to terms outside of court and the case never goes to trial. So privilege may never attach to the accusations made in the court papers.

In one such case, the vice president of a company filed suit alleging that he was fired because the newspaper published his wife's charges of infidelity. The newspaper responded that its report was a true and fair account of court proceedings. The New York Court of Appeals rejected that argument on grounds that the law makes details of marital cases secret because spatting spouses frequently make unfounded charges. The newspaper appealed to the Supreme Court of the United States. But it lost.

Unless some other privilege applies, there is danger in carrying a report of court papers that are not available for public inspection by reason of a law, court rule or court order directing that such papers be sealed.

As stated earlier, a fair and accurate report of public and official proceedings is privileged.

There has never been an exact legal definition of what constitutes an official proceeding. Some cases are obvious—trials, legislative sessions and hearings, etc.

Strictly speaking, conventions of private organizations are not "public and official proceedings" even though they may be forums for discussions of public questions. Hence, statements made on the floor of convention sessions or from speakers' platforms may not be privileged.

Statements made by the president of the United States or a governor in the course of executive proceedings have absolute privilege for the speaker, even if false or defamatory. However, this absolute privilege may not apply to statements having no relation to executive proceedings.

President Kennedy once was asked at a news conference what he was going to do about "two well-known security risks" in the State Department. The reporter gave names when the president asked for them. This was not privileged and many newspapers and radio stations did not carry them. The Associated Press did because it seemed in the public interest to report the incident fully. No suits resulted.

After a civil rights march, George Wallace, then governor of Alabama, appeared on a television show and said some of the marchers were members of Communist and Communist-front organizations. He gave some names, which newspapers carried. Some libel suits resulted.

The courts have ruled that publishing that a person is a Communist is libelous on its face if he is not a Communist.

"The claimed charge that the plaintiff is a Nazi and a Communist is in the same category. . . . The current effect of these statements is the decisive test. Whatever doubt there may have been in the past as to the opprobrious effect on the ordinary mind of such a charge . . . recent events and legislation make it manifest that to label an attorney a Communist or a Nazi is to taint him with disrepute." (*Levy* v. *Gelber,* 175 Misc. 746)

The fact that news comes from official sources does not eliminate the concern. To say that *a high police official said* means that you are making the accusation. A statement that a crime has been committed and that the police are holding someone for questioning is reasonably safe, because it is probably true. However, there are times when the nature of the crime or the prominence of those involved requires broader treatment. Under those circumstances, the safest guide is whatever past experience has shown as to the responsibility of the source. The source must be trustworthy and certain to stand behind the information given.

Repetition of Libel: In reporting the filing of a libel suit, can we report the content of the charge? By so doing, do we compound the libel, even though we quote from the legal complaint?

Ordinarily, a fair and impartial report of the contents of legal papers in a libel action filed in the office of the clerk of the court is privileged. However, many states do not extend privilege to the filing of court actions; in such a case there is no privilege until the case comes to trial or until some other judicial action takes place.

But we have found that it is safe, generally speaking, to repeat the libel in a story based on the filing of a suit.

Fair Comment and Criticism: The publication of defamatory matter that consists of comment and opinion, as distinguished from fact, with reference to matters of public interest or importance, is covered by the defense of fair comment.

Of course, whatever facts are stated must be true.

The right of fair comment has been summarized as follows:

"Everyone has a right to comment on matters of public interest and concern, provided they do so fairly and with an honest purpose. Such comments or criticism are not libelous, however severe in their terms, unless they are written maliciously. Thus it has been held that books, prints, pictures and statuary publicly exhibited, and the architecture of public buildings, and actors and exhibitors are all the legitimate subjects of newspapers' criticism, and such criticism fairly and honestly made is not libelous, however strong the terms of censure may be." (*Hoeppner* v. *Dunkirk Pr. Co.,* 254 N.Y. 95)

Criminal Libel: The publication of a libel may result in what is considered a breach of the peace. For that reason, it may constitute a criminal offense.

It is unnecessary to review that phase of the law here because the fundamental elements of the crime do not differ substantially from those that give rise to a civil action for damages.

• PUBLIC OFFICIALS, PUBLIC FIGURES, PUBLIC ISSUES

In a series of decisions commencing in 1964, the Supreme Court established important First Amendment protections for the press in the libel area.

But in more recent decisions, the tide in libel has been running against the press, particularly in the unrelenting narrowing of the definition of a public figure. This was the single most active area of libel law in the decade of the '70s.

While the full impact of the later decisions is not yet clear, a review of the rulings since the mid-1960s shows the trend.

Three basic cases established important precedents. They did so in a logical progression. The cases were:

—*New York Times* v. *Sullivan* (1964)
—*Associated Press* v. *Walker* (1967)
—*Rosenbloom* v. *Metromedia* (1971)

In the *New York Times* case, the Supreme Court ruled in March 1964 that public officials cannot recover damages for a report related to official duties unless they prove actual malice.

To establish actual malice, the official was required to prove that at the time of publication, those responsible for the story knew it was false or published it with reckless disregard of whether it was true or false.

The decision reversed a $500,000 libel verdict returned in Alabama against The New York Times and four black ministers. The court said:

"The constitutional guarantees (the First and Fourteenth Amendments) require, we think, a federal rule that prohibits a public official from recovering damages for a defamatory falsehood relating to his official conduct unless he proves that the statement was made with 'actual malice'—that is, with knowledge that it was false or with reckless disregard of whether it was false or not."

This does not give newspapers absolute immunity against libel suits by officials who are criticized. But it does mean that when a newspaper publishes information about a public official and publishes it without actual malice, it should be spared a damage suit even though some of the information may be wrong.

The court said it considered the case "against the background of a profound national commitment to the principle that debate on public issues should be uninhibited, robust and wide-open, and that it may well include vehement, caustic and sometimes unpleasantly sharp attacks on government and public officials."

The ruling in the *New York Times* case with respect to public officials was extended by the Supreme Court in June 1967 to apply also to public figures.

In so holding, the court reversed a $500,000 libel judgment won by former Maj. Gen. Edwin A. Walker in a Texas state court against The Associated Press. The AP reported that Walker had "assumed command" of rioters at the University of Mississippi and "led a charge of students against federal marshals" when James H. Meredith was admitted to the university in September 1962. Walker alleged those statements to be false.

The court said: "Under any reasoning, Gen. Walker was a public man in whose public conduct society and the press had a legitimate and substantial interest."

The rulings in the *New York Times* and the *Associated Press* cases were constitutional landmark decisions for freedom of the press and speech. They offered safeguards not previously defined. But they did not confer license for defamatory statements or for reckless disregard of the truth.

The AP decision made an additional important distinction.

In the same opinion, the court upheld an award granted Wallace Butts, former athletic director of the University of Georgia, against Curtis Publishing Co. The suit was based on an article in the Saturday Evening Post accusing Butts of giving his football team's strategy secrets to an opposing coach prior to a game between the two schools.

The court found that Butts was a public figure, but said there was a substantial difference between the two cases. Justice Harlan said: "The evidence showed that the Butts story was in no sense 'hot news' and the editors of the magazine recognized the need for a thorough investigation of the serious charges. Elementary precautions were, nevertheless, ignored."

Chief Justice Warren, in a concurring opinion, referred to "slipshod and sketchy investigatory techniques employed to check the veracity of the source." He said the evidence disclosed "reckless disregard for the truth."

The differing rulings in the *Associated Press* and the *Saturday Evening Post* cases should be noted carefully. The AP-Walker case was "hot news"; the Post-Butts story was investigative reporting of which journalists are doing more and more.

Extension of the *Times* rule in one case was based on a column by Drew Pearson which characterized a candidate for the United States Senate as "a former small-time bootlegger." The jury held that the accusation related to the private sector of the candidate's life. Reversing this judgment, the Supreme Court said:

"We therefore hold as a matter of constitutional law that a charge of criminal conduct, no matter how remote in time or place, can never be irrelevant to an official's or a candidate's fitness for office for purposes of application of the 'knowing falsehood or reckless disregard' rule of *New York Times* v. *Sullivan*."

Another case was brought by a Chicago captain of detectives against Time magazine, which had quoted from a report of the U.S. Civil Rights Commission without making clear that the charges of police brutality were those of the complainant whose home was raided and not the independent findings of the commission. The court described the commission's documents as "bristling with ambiguities" and said Time did not engage in a "falsification" sufficient to sustain a finding of actual malice.

To this point, then, the important constitutional protections were extended to public officials and public figures.

Now for the third case in the important Supreme Court trilogy: *Rosenbloom* v. *Metromedia.*

This case concerned a suit brought against a Philadelphia radio station, WIP, by a former distributor of a nudist magazine in the area. The station had referred to material seized in a police raid as obscene and referred to an injunction suit against police as an attempt to force police to "lay off the smut literature racket."

The trial jury awarded a substantial verdict to the magazine distributor. But in 1971, the Supreme Court ruled in favor of the radio station, saying private individuals have no more protection than public officials and other public figures in matters that involve the public interest. The court said:

"The community has a vital interest in the proper enforcement of its criminal laws, particularly in an area such as obscenity where a number of highly important values are potentially in conflict: the public has an interest both in seeing that the criminal law is adequately enforced and in assuring that the law is not used unconstitutionally to suppress free expression."

The Supreme Court decisions starting with the *New York Times* case and continuing through the Philadelphia radio case offered new safeguards. But they did not confer license for making knowingly false defamatory statements or for reckless disregard of the truth. As the Supreme Court has stated: "There must be sufficient evidence to permit the conclusion that the defendant in fact entertained serious doubts as to the truth of his publication. Publishing with such doubts shows reckless disregard for truth or falsity and demonstrates actual malice."

The progression of the *New York Times, AP* and *Metromedia* cases was interrupted in June 1974 with the Supreme Court's decision in the case of *Gertz* v. *Robert Welch Inc.*

Gertz, a lawyer of prominence in Chicago, had been attacked in a John Birch Society publication as a Communist. There were additional accusations as well.

Gertz sued and the Supreme Court upheld him, ruling that he was neither a public official nor a public figure.

The decision opened the door to giving courts somewhat wider leeway in determining whether someone was a public person.

This also opened the way to giving state courts the right to assess what standard of liability should be used in testing whether a publication about a private individual is actionable.

For instance, some state courts have established a negligence standard (whether a reasonable person would have done the same thing as the publisher under the circumstances). The New York courts follow a gross negligence test. Others still observe the actual malice test in suits by private individuals against the press.

Bear in mind that the significance of the *Gertz* decision still is being developed, as new cases arise and are adjudicated. But at a minimum it opened the way to judgments the three earlier cases would seem to have barred.

More recently, in the case of *Time* v. *Firestone,* the Supreme Court again appears to have restricted the "public figure" and "public issue" standards.

The case stemmed from Time magazine's account of the divorce of Russell and Mary Alice Firestone. The magazine said she had been divorced on grounds of "extreme cruelty and adultery." The court made no finding of adultery. She sued.

She was a prominent social figure in Palm Beach, Florida, and held press conferences in the course of the divorce proceedings. Yet the Supreme Court said that she was not a public figure because "she did not assume any role of special prominence in the affairs of society, other than perhaps Palm Beach society, and she did not thrust herself to the forefront of any particular public controversy in order to influence resolution of the issues involved in it."

As in the *Gertz* case, the decision opened the way to findings within the states involving negligence, a standard less severe than the actual malice standard that was the base of three earlier landmark cases.

Supreme Court decisions, starting with *Gertz* and extending through *Firestone* and more recent cases, have consistently narrowed the class of persons to be treated as public figures under the *Times-Sullivan* and *AP-Walker* standards.

The *Times* rule has been left standing, but it is tougher and tougher to get in under it.

The court is rejecting the notion that a person can be a public figure simply because of the events that led to the story at issue. The courts are saying that public figure means people who seek the limelight, who inject themselves into public debate, etc. The courts are saying that involvement in a crime, even a newsworthy one, does not make one a public figure.

This means that the broad "public official" and "public figure" protections that came out of the *Times* and *AP* cases remain, but for shrinking numbers of people that are written about.

At the same time, the "reckless disregard of the truth" and "knowing falsity" standards of the *Times* decision also slip away, becoming applicable to fewer people as the public figure definition narrows.

And those standards are being replaced in state after state with simple negligence standards. In other words, the plaintiff, now adjudged to be a private citizen because of the recent rulings, must now prove only that the press was negligent, not reckless.

The difference is more than semantic. This development suggests that press lawyers will be relying more on some of the old standbys as defenses—plaintiff's inability to prove falsity, privilege, fair comment—and this puts the ball right back with editors and reporters.

Another recent Supreme Court decision which provoked wide press controversy came in the case of *Herbert* v. *Lando.*

The court ruled in 1979 that retired Army Lt. Col. Anthony Herbert, a Vietnam veteran, had the right to inquire into the editing process of a CBS "60 Minutes" segment, produced by Barry Lando, which provoked his suit. Herbert had claimed the right to do this so that he could establish actual malice.

The decision formalizes and calls attention to something that was at least implicit in the *Times* case: namely, that a plaintiff had the right to try to prove the press was reckless or even knew that what it was printing was a lie. How else could this be done except through inquiry about a reporter's or editor's state of mind?

So the ruling reminds plaintiffs' lawyers that they can do this and will, no doubt, be responsible for far more of this kind of inquiry than the press has had to face before.

A crucial test will be how far judges will let plaintiffs' lawyers range in their discovery efforts. Will they let the plaintiff widen the embrace of inquiry into stories other than the one at issue? Will they let the plaintiff rummage about the news room, probing unrelated news judgments, examining the handling of other unrelated stories, demanding to know why this investigative piece survived while that one died quietly on the kill hook?

That the questions are being prompted by the *Herbert-Lando* ruling is the best response to those who say that the decision didn't really mean very much.

The press should be certain that files include contemporaneous memoranda that will testify later to the care taken with the story and the conviction that it was true and fair.

It is too soon to tell whether the impact of the decision will be large or small. But editors and reporters must understand it and be prepared to cope.

• THE RIGHT OF PRIVACY

The right of privacy is a doctrine that has been developing in the past 60 years. It is recognized by statute in only a few states, including New York, but courts increasingly are taking cognizance of it. It is clearly an area to be watched.

The doctrine is based on the idea that a person has the right to be let alone, to live a private life free from publicity.

In 1890, two Boston lawyers wrote in the *Harvard Law Review:*

"The press is overstepping in every direction the obvious bounds of propriety and decency."

It is of interest that one of those lawyers, who later became Justice Brandeis, said years later in one of his dissents:

"The makers of our Constitution undertook to secure conditions favorable to the pursuit of happiness. They recognized the significance of man's spiritual nature, of his feelings and of his intellect. They knew that only a part of the pain, pleasure and satisfactions of life are to be found in material things. They sought to protect Americans in their beliefs, their thoughts, their emotions and their sensations. They conferred, as against the government, the right to be let alone—the most comprehensive of rights and the right most valued by civilized men." (*Olmstead* v. *United States,* 277 U.S. 438, 478)

When a person becomes involved in a news event, voluntarily or involuntarily, he forfeits the right to privacy. Similarly a person somehow involved in a matter of legitimate public interest, even if not a bona fide spot news event, normally can be written about with safety.

However, this is different from use of a story or picture that dredges up the sordid details of a person's past and has no current newsworthiness.

Paul P. Ashley, then president of the Washington State Bar Association, said in a talk on this subject at a meeting of The Associated Press Managing Editors Association:

"The essence of the wrong will be found in crudity, in ruthless exploitation of the woes or other personal affairs of private individuals who have done nothing noteworthy and have not by design or misadventure been involved in an event which tosses them into an arena subject to public gaze."

Here are details of a few cases brought in the name of right of privacy:

—A leading case centering on publication of details of a person's past concerned a man who as a child prodigy in 1910 had attracted national attention. In 1937, The New Yorker magazine published a biographical sketch of the plaintiff. He alleged invasion of privacy.

The court said "he had cloaked himself in obscurity but his subsequent history, containing as it did the answer to the question of whether or not he had fulfilled his early promise, was still a matter of public concern. The article . . . sketched the life of an unusual personality, and it possessed considerable popular news interest."

The court said further:

"We express no comment on whether or not the newsworthiness of the matter printed will always constitute a complete defense. Revelations may be so intimate and so unwarranted in view of the victim's position as to outrage the community's notions of decency. But when focused upon public characters, truthful comments upon dress, speech, habits, and the ordinary aspects of personality will usually not transgress this line. Regrettably or not, the misfortunes and frailties of neighbors and 'public figures' are subjects of considerable interest and discussion to the rest of the population. And when such are the mores of the community, it would be unwise for a court to bar their expression in the newspapers, books, and magazines of the day."

—The unsavory incidents of the past of a former prostitute, who had been tried for murder, acquitted, married and lived a respectable life, were featured in a motion picture. The court ruled that the use of her name in the picture and the statement in advertisements that the story was taken from true incidents in her life violated her right to pursue and obtain happiness.

Some courts have ruled that a person who is recognizable in a picture of a crowd in a public place is not entitled to the right of privacy. But if a camera singled him out for no news-connected reason, then his privacy is invaded, some courts have ruled.

—Another example of spot news interest: A child was injured in an auto accident in Alabama. A newspaper took a picture of the scene before the child was removed and ran it. That was spot news. Twenty months later a magazine used the picture to illustrate an article. The magazine was sued and lost the case, the court ruling that 20 months after the accident the child was no longer "in the news."

—In another case, a newspaper photographer in search of a picture to illustrate a hot weather story took a picture of a woman sitting on her front porch. She wore a housedress, her hair in curlers, her feet in thong sandals. The picture was taken from a car parked across the street from the woman's home. She sued, charging invasion of privacy. A court, denying the newspaper's motion for dismissal of the suit, said the scene photographed "was not a particularly newsworthy incident," and the limits of decency were exceeded by "surreptitious" taking and publishing of pictures "in an embarrassing pose."

—A woman took her two children to the county fair and went with them into the funhouse. A newspaper photographer took her picture just as a jet of air blew up her dress. She sued, and the Supreme Court of Alabama upheld the damages.

The Supreme Court of the United States ruled in January 1967 that the constitutional guarantees of freedom of the press are applicable to invasion-of-privacy cases involving reports of newsworthy matters.

The ruling arose out of a reversal by the Supreme Court of a decision of a New York court that an article with photos in Life magazine reviewing a play, "The Desperate Hours," violated the privacy of a couple who had been held hostage in a real-life incident. In illustrating the article, Life posed the actors in the house where the real family had been held captive.

The family alleged violation of privacy, saying the article gave readers the impression that the play was a true account of their experiences. Life said the article was "basically truthful."

The court said:

"The line between the informing and the entertaining is too elusive for the protection of (freedom of the press). Erroneous statement is no less inevitable in such case than in the case of comment upon public affairs, and in both, if innocent or merely negligent, it must be protected if the freedoms of expression are to have the 'breathing space' that they 'need to survive.'

"We create grave risk of serious impairment of the indispensable service of a free press in a free society if we saddle the press with the impossible burden of verifying to a certainty the facts associated in a news article with a person's name, picture or portrait, particularly as related to non-defamatory matter."

The court added, however, that these constitutional guarantees do not extend to "knowing or reckless falsehood." A newspaper still may be liable for invasion of privacy if the facts of a story are changed deliberately or recklessly, or "fictionalized." As with the *New York Times* and the *Associated Press* decisions in the field of libel, the *Life* case does not confer a license for defamatory statements or for reckless disregard of the truth.

• APPLYING THE RULES

We already have defined libel and explained the defenses available to the press. Let's now look at some applications.

In a society in which standards of right living are recognized by most persons, any accusation that a member of society has violated such standards must be injurious. Members of a community establish in the minds of others an estimate of what they are believed to be. Injury to that reputation may mean business, professional or social ruin.

One court decision put the matter this way:

"The law of defamation is concerned only with injuries to one's reputation. . . .

"Embarrassment and discomfort no doubt came to her from the publication; as they would to any decent woman under like circumstances. Her own reaction, however, has no bearing upon her reputation. That rests entirely upon the reactions of others. We are unable to find anything in this article which could appreciably injure plaintiff's reputation." (*Kimmerle* v. *New York Evening Journal Inc.,* 262 N.Y. 99)

In order to be libelous, it is not necessary that a publication impute criminal activity. The following was held to be libelous:

> **Pauper's Grave For Poor Child**
> "Unless financial aid is forthcoming immediately, the body of a 4-year-old boy who was run over Tuesday will be interred in Potter's Field, burying ground of the homeless, friendless and penniless, who die or are killed in New York City. The parents of this youngster are in dire financial straits, and at this writing have no alternative but to let their son go to this final rest in a pauper's grave.

The court said:

"It is reasonably clear, therefore that in some cases it may be a libel if the plaintiff has been written up as an object of pity. . . . The reason is that in libel the matter is defamatory not only if it brings a party into hatred, ridicule or contempt by asserting some moral discredit upon his part, but also if it tends to make him be shunned or avoided, although it imputes no moral turpitude to him." (*Katapodis* v. *Brooklyn Spectator Inc.,* 287 N.Y. 17)

A publication that does not discredit a person as an individual may nonetheless damage a person's professional status.

A story stated that after a man's body had been taken from the waters in which he had been swimming, he was pronounced dead by a doctor. Later the youth was revived. The doctor sued because of the implication that he had been unable to determine whether a person was living or dead.

Similarly, a publication may affect a business.

Companies are naturally sensitive to news stories that reflect on their business prospects and practices. There have been many such news stories in the field of environmental and consumer protection. The issues are complicated, and the legal aspects not always clear. Formal charges and allegations should be reported precisely and fairly.

Likewise, there is no alternative to precision in reporting any criminal charge.

Not only what is written, but the instruments used in transmitting it, must be considered in handling news. It is safer to say *acquitted* or *innocent,* rather than *not guilty* because of the danger that the negative may be dropped in transmission.

An essential element of an action for libel is that the complainant be identifiable to a third party. Nevertheless, the omission of names will not, in itself, provide a shield against a claim for libel. As was pointed out earlier, there may be enough details for the person to be recognizable.

A story may, by the use of a general description or name, make a libelous charge against an organized group. It is possible that any member of the group could bring an action on the story.

If the material is libelous and not privileged, then the question turns to proof.

Can the substance be established by documents, by testimony from trustworthy persons or by material from privileged sources? Hearsay evidence is not enough. It is not enough to show that somebody gave you the unprivileged information. The issue turns on proof.

Another libel pitfall is the mistaken identity case. There is no complete defense when a newspaper confuses a famous individual with a person bearing a similar name who gets into a scrape. Petty thieves running afoul of the law may give the names of famous persons—often old-time athletes—in the hope of getting leniency from a judge.

A few years ago a man chanrged with a minor crime appeared in Magistrate's Court in New York and gave as his name that of a once-great baseball pitcher. The magistrate gave the prisoner a suspended sentence. The real baseball player was a prosperous auto salesman, who threatened multiple suits when he read the story in the newspapers.

• POINTS TO REMEMBER

Obviously, the first question is whether it is libelous. That is, whether it is actionable on its face. If it is, can you prove it? Or is it privileged?

If the story is libelous or potentially libelous, if you can't prove it and if it is not privileged, don't move it. If it is already on the wire, *kill it at once.*

—Don't try to fix a possibly libelous story by elimination, correction, sub or new lead. If there is any unprivileged or unsafe material in the story, the dangerous portion *must be killed.* That is the only way in which material definitely can be removed from the report.

—Remember that privilege does not remove the need for careful reporting and the use of editorial judgment. In many cases, courts have held that it is up to the jury to decide whether a particular publication was a fair and true report or whether there was "actual malice."

—If it is decided that a name should be withheld from a crime story, be certain that no potentially troublesome descriptive phrases are given. *An elderly janitor of a nearby apartment house* could lead to a suit from every elderly janitor in the neighborhood.

—The fact that police are questioning someone about a crime does not necessarily justify the label *suspect*. In most cases, a detective's telling you that someone is a suspect is not privileged. Again, the basic questions: Could you prove it, if it came to that? Or is it privileged?

—Picture captions must be as accurate and objective as a news story. You can commit libel in a picture caption as damagingly as in a story.

—In writing about murder charges filed during a preliminary police investigation, it makes no difference legally whether you say John Doe is charged (a) with the murder of, (b) with murdering, or (c) with murder, in connection with the killing of Richard Roe.

AP counsel says:

"Each statement contains an accusation by The Associated Press that John Doe is guilty of murder. The accusation is made by implication in that the wording suggests that the charge was made by someone other than The Associated Press. That, however, does not relieve the AP of responsibility unless the publication is qualifiedly privileged.

"Thus a publication relating to a murder charge against John Doe in connection with the killing of Richard Roe must be either privileged, (based on official proceedings) or provably true."

6 KILLS AND CORRECTIVES

Prompt action must be taken when serious problems are found in a story which has already moved on the wire. If there is a possibility of legal action, the General Desk in New York must be consulted. There are no exceptions to this rule; even if a story has moved only on an AP Broadcast circuit, it is still the General Desk which will decide what needs to be done.

There are three ways to deal with problem stories: withholds, kills and eliminations.

A *withhold* is filed when the accuracy of a story has been seriously challenged and the AP cannot quickly confirm the story. A withhold should be followed as soon as possible by a kill or an elimination if further checking makes either necessary. If the story turns out to be correct after further checking, file an advisory releasing it and lifting the withhold.

A *kill* is needed for material that is libelous and unprivileged. The kill is mandatory. It may also be necessary to file a corrective story, as explained below.

An *elimination* is used when the story carries no threat of libel action but is objectionable for some other reason: error, poor taste, etc.

Remember: Consult immediately with the General Desk.

• KILLS

Material considered libelous and unprivileged requires a prompt kill. The kill is mandatory.

The only exception: If the last version of the story moved more than 24 hours before the problem was discovered, it will probably be too late for a kill, but a corrective will be needed.

In cases where the problem is discovered several hours after the story moved, the kill and any corrective should be sent as soon as the problem is found. Also, an advisory telling news directors of the kill and the full text of the corrective should be sent the next day at about the same time as the erroneous story. This is intended to ensure that the material finds its way to the members who used the original story.

The kill should say succinctly what was wrong with the original.

Example: *Smith not arrested.*

It should not say the original was libelous. Just state the factual problem. Always use a "b" priority for the kill and the following advisory. This form should be followed exactly:

B U L L E T I N K I L L
(NEW YORK) -- KILL THE ZYX COMPANY BANKRUPT STORY WHICH MOVED AT ——— EASTERN TIME. THE COMPANY IS N O T BANKRUPT.
THE AP

Follow the kill immediately with an advisory, stating whether a substitute story is planned:

K I L L ADVISORY
NEWS DIRECTORS:
THE NEW YORK STORY ABOUT THE ZYX COMPANY BEING BANKRUPT HAS BEEN KILLED. THE COMPANY IS N O T BANKRUPT.
A KILL IS MANDATORY.
MAKE CERTAIN THE STORY IS NOT AIRED.
A SUB WILL BE FILED SHORTLY. (Or: *NO SUB WILL BE FILED.)*
THE AP

Send an advisory the next day at roughly the same time as the original story:

K I L L ADVISORY
NEWS DIRECTORS:
A NEW YORK STORY FILED AT 12:10 P-M EASTERN TIME MONDAY UNDER THE SLUG ZYX-BANKRUPT HAS BEEN KILLED. THE ZYX COMPANY IS N O T BANKRUPT.
A KILL IS MANDATORY.
A SUB WAS FILED MONDAY AT 8:15 P-M, SLUGGED ZYX-PETITION.
THE AP

Circumstances will dictate whether a substitute story is required. (See *Correctives* below.)

Report Requirements: A copy of the story killed and the kill itself should be mailed promptly to the managing editor, together with a letter telling who made the error and how it was made. If necessary, AP counsel will contact you for further information.

The file sent by the bureau chief to New York should include four things:

1. Wire copy of the erroneous story, the kill and the kill notes.
2. Wire copy of the substitute story or corrective.
3. A copy of any source material used by the writer or editor in preparation of the story, including member clip, reporter's notes or whatever.
4. A factual explanation from the staff member(s) who handled the story as to exactly how the error was made—what they did, where the information came from, etc.

The covering letter should add relevant details not covered above. For example, how we became aware of the mistake, what contact we have had from oustiders on the matter, etc.

The bureau chief's letter and the staff member's memorandum should be factual reports of what happened. They are not the place for extraneous comments about individuals or bureau procedures.

Do not make any response to any letter or other communication in connection with any case where legal action seems possible without first consulting the managing editor or the General Desk.

• CORRECTIVES

A kill may necessitate a corrective story. As with a kill, a corrective must be approved by the General Desk before it is filed by a bureau.

It is preferable that a corrective be handled by mail. But if necessary it can be handled by telephone.

Do not feel you must be hasty in transmitting a corrective. When there is a factual error in the report, we want to correct it as quickly as possible. But remember that publication of a corrective does not safeguard us against legal action. You should be aware of any legal requirement in your state setting a time within which a corrective must appear.

The corrective story should identify the previous incorrect story by slug, dateline, and the date. As follows:

C O R R E C T I V E
NEWS DIRECTORS: MEMBERS WHO USED THE MARCH 15 STORY FROM NEW YORK SLUGGED "ZYX COMPANY BANKRUPT" ARE ASKED TO USE THE FOLLOWING STORY.

Remember that any story which has been on a broadcast circuit may well have been used before the kill has moved. Therefore, the corrective or subtitute story should acknowledge the previous error and set the record straight.

While each case must be considered individually, the proper form for the corrective or sub will often be a straight assertion at the start that a previous AP account was in error.

Example:

THE ASSOCIATED PRESS REPORTED ERRONEOUSLY ON MARCH 15TH THAT . . .

In no instance should the story use any apologetic phrase such as

THE ASSOCIATED PRESS REGRETS THE ERROR.

The corrective is to be simply a factual account.

Obviously, kills and correctives should be filed on all circuits where the original was transmitted. When a kill appears on any of the general news wires, the New York Broadcast Desk should check to determine whether the story was used on any of the broadcast circuits. If so, the kill and any subsequent correctives should be moved. If the story was not used on the broadcast wires, no further action is necessary—although the desk log should note that the matter has already been researched. This will save later shifts the trouble of checking through the files.

• WITHHOLDS

A withhold is filed when the accuracy of a story has been seriously questioned and The Associated Press cannot quickly confirm the story. A withhold should be followed as soon as possible by a kill or an elimination if further checking makes either necessary.

The form:

W I T H H O L D

(DENVER) -- WITHHOLD DENVER STORY SLUGGED "GOLD FIND," WHICH MOVED AT 10:30 A-M EASTERN TIME. AUTHORITIES SAY THE MINER'S STORY HAS BEEN QUESTIONED.

THE AP

If the information holds true after checking, file an advisory releasing the story.

• ELIMINATIONS

An elimination is used for matter that carries no threat of libel action but is objectionable for some other reason: poor taste, error, an old story inadvertently transmitted, etc.

The form:

B U L L E T I N   E L I M I N A T I O N

(DALLAS) -- ELIMINATE THE ASSASSINATION ANNIVERSARY STORY, WHICH MOVED AT 8:15 A-M EASTERN TIME. THE STORY IS OLD AND WAS TRANSMITTED INADVERTENTLY.

THE AP

AP RADIO NETWORK

The AP Radio Network relies not only on its staff of reporters to cover the news. It also relies on you—the general news staff of the AP and the thousands of members of AP worldwide.

Feeding material to APR is simple. All you need is a good tape recorder, microphone and a telephone. We'll tell you exactly how to feed your material a little later.

APR needs reports of all the major national and international stories each day, as well as the top stories from each region of the country. From domestic cities, call APR at (800) 424-8804; from overseas, call (202) 872-0548. You should be ready to tell the editor what your story is about and be ready to feed right away.

There are several types of feeds.

—*Voicers.* A verbal recounting of a news story, usually delivered by a reporter on the scene.

—*Actuality.* The "sound" of the news—a taped excerpt of a speech, a coach responding to a question in a locker-room interview or a fire chief describing the damage at the scene of the fire. An actuality, then, is the actual sound of the person about whom the story is being written.

—*Raw sound.* The sound of gunfire in Beirut, a marching band in the Inaugural Parade or the roar of the crowd at the Indianapolis 500 as the winner streaks across the line.

—*Wraparound.* A combination of a voicer with an actuality or raw sound, or both. The reporter tells the story, using actuality material to illustrate it. The most frequent example is the White House reporter recounting a statement by the president, and using a 15-second insert of the president himself making an announcement or responding to a question.

All of these are useful to APR.

Let's look at them in a little more detail.

Voicers: If you can write a good broadcast story, you can read it for the radio. Just tell the story, as though you were telling it to a friend; there's no need for a booming voice or a stilted delivery. Relax. Rehearse a few times, until you get a recording that sounds good to you.

Try to keep it to 40 seconds. Sign off with your name and the city.

A few pointers:

Remember that your listeners may be halfway around the world, so set the scene early.

Example:

FLOOD WATERS HERE IN KANSAS CITY ARE AT TREE-TOP LEVELS IN SOME AREAS . . .

Don't date your story. Avoid such phrases as *later this morning, late tonight,* etc. Emphasize color, background and elements that aren't likely to change. The latest details will be added by the newscaster, so you don't have to worry about that.

Actualities: These are the easiest for the novice to handle. If you're covering a news conference, get your mike as close to the main speaker as possible. Don't be shy. Microphones are common today and there's seldom an objection to them.

A small mike stand is an excellent investment. Anything that will get your mike off the table (where it will pick up extraneous thumps and scratches) and closer to the speaker will pay off in much cleaner audio.

It also is prudent to carry a roll of masking tape with you. Then you can tape your mike to the podium microphone or any other handy object.

And don't forget the public-address system. If you are close to a loudspeaker, just hold the mike in front of it. That works fine, especially where several people are speaking on the same platform, using different public address mikes. (Remember, there may be multiple p.a. mikes on the stage, but all the voices will come out of the loudspeaker together.)

Before you call APR, pick out the one or two best moments on tape, again trying to keep your cuts to 40 seconds at the absolute maximum. Keep track of where each cut is on your tape counter so you can find it quickly.

With some trial-and-error, you'll soon be recording news events with the best of them. You'll find that getting good audio is like taking a good photo: It's so easy that anyone can do it, but there are only a few who take the trouble to get it just right.

Raw Sound: If there is a 1980s corollary to the old adage that a journalist should always have pen and paper with him, it is this: carry your recorder with you as much as possible and at the slightest hint of action, turn it on and *leave it on.*

If you find yourself in the middle of a riot, or surrounded by a crowd wildly cheering the returning hostages, or standing next to a gun-wielding assassin, you will produce a priceless piece of tape.

One of the most dramatic pieces of tape in recent years was made March 30, 1981, when President Reagan was shot outside the Washington Hilton.

APR White House Correspondent Walter Rodgers had his recorder rolling and was shouting a question to the president when a man beside him opened fire. The sound of the gunshots, the screams and Rodgers' shocked comments were as chilling as the videotapes of the shooting.

If you have dramatic raw sound, you can feed it to APR, then feed your narration. The editors in Washington will mix the two together.

If you see something dramatic happen, describe it—and don't worry about sounding breathless or disorganized. Eyewitnesses to history always sound that way.

Wraparounds: These are simple and quite effective. First, find 10 or 12 seconds of actuality—the governor shouting down a heckler, for example. Then write the story around it.

Read the story, using a separate casette. Pause for just a few seconds in the space where the actuality should go.

Then feed the narration and the actuality to APR separately. Again, the editors will put them together in Washington.

Always sign off your wraparounds, don't let the piece end with actuality or raw sound. Just say your name and the city.

The same rules on datelines apply to APR as to the general news operation. You can't say you're in Kansas City unless you are really there.

Don't quibble about details, though. If the floods have forced you out of Kansas City and into Shawnee Mission, the Kansas City dateline still applies.

When assembling wraparounds, don't make the classic mistake of saying exactly the same thing the person on the actuality tape says.

Example:

> *THE PRESIDENT SAYS HE'S SHOCKED AND SICKENED BY THE DISASTER:* [Sound of President] *I AM SHOCKED AND SICKENED BY THIS DISASTER.*

Better:

> *THE PRESIDENT'S REACTION WAS EMOTIONAL:* [Sound of President] *I AM SHOCKED AND SICKENED BY THIS DISASTER.*

• THE RECORDER

Almost any casette recorder will work satisfactorily, but the *Superscope C202LP* is recommended for reliability and quality.

Set the recording level to "automatic" and you won't have to worry about adjusting the volume while recording. Don't worry about the tone control; it has no effect on recording.

When playing back, however, always set the tone control on full treble.

Set the volume control at maximum and then back off just a little. This will get the cleanest sound possible through the telephone lines.

It's easy to hook your recorder up to a telephone. All you need is a cord with a plug on one end and a pair of alligator clips on the other.

Plug the cord into the "earphone" or "monitor" plug on the recorder. Then, take the mouthpiece off the telephone and hook the alligator clips to the two prongs inside the handset.

Most pay telephones are built to resist vandalism and you won't be able to get the mouthpiece off. So always try to find a phone in an office or a nearby home that you can use.

That's all there is to it.

SECTION TWO:

The Specifics of Broadcast Style

• ABBREVIATIONS

Generally should be avoided, except when they help the listener understand the story and help you keep wordiness to a minimum.

Guidance on how a particular term should be handled is provided in the individual entries in this handbook.

Some general principles:

—Use only those abbreviations that are so familiar to both broadcaster and listener that they do not form a stumbling block to the flow of copy. For example, most everyone knows what the *AFL-CIO* is, so you need not spell it out. But the term *A-P-I* does not immediately bring to mind *American Petroleum Institute,* and so should not be used in any reference.

—The only titles that should be abbreviated are *Mr., Mrs., Ms.* and *Dr.*

—Do not abbreviate junior or senior, and do not set these words off with commas: *Martin Luther King Junior.* See **HYPHEN.**

• A-B-C

Acceptable in all references to the *American Broadcasting Companies* (the plural is part of the corporate name).

Headquarters is in New York. Divisions include A-B-C News, A-B-C Radio and A-B-C T-V.

• A-B-C'S

• ABLE-BODIED

• A-B-M, A-B-M'S

• ABOVE-BOARD

• ABSENT WITHOUT LEAVE

"AWOL" (ay'-wawl) is acceptable on second reference.

• ACADEMIC TITLES

Spell out such formal titles as *professor, dean, president, chancellor* and *chairman.*

• ACADEMY AWARDS

Presented annually by the Academy of Motion Picture Arts and Sciences. Also known as the *Oscars.*

• ACCEPT, EXCEPT

Accept means to receive.

Except means to exclude.

• ACCOMMODATE

• ACCUSED

A person is *accused of,* not *with,* a crime.

For guidelines on related words, see **ALLEGE; ARREST;** and **INDICT.**

• ACRONYMS

These are words that are formed from the first letters of a series of words. Use only those that are commonly known.

Acronyms should be put in quotes and should not be hyphenated: "NATO," "CORE," "SALT-Two."

See **ABBREVIATIONS.**

• ADDRESSES

Spell out all terms such as *road* or *drive.* Follow the rules for **NUMERALS.**

Street addresses should be put in copy only when they are specifically relevant to the story. They should not be put in parentheses.

If you want to make the use of the

address optional, put the address in an advisory to run with the story.

See **ZIP CODE.**

• ADJECTIVES

The abbreviation *adj.* is used in this book to identify the spelling of the adjectival forms of words that frequently are misspelled.

The **COMMA** entry provides guidance on punctuating a series of adjectives.

The **HYPHEN** entry provides guidance on handling compound modifiers used before a noun.

• AD-LIB (n., v., adj.)

• ADMINISTRATION

See the **GOVERNMENT, JUNTA, REGIME** entry for distinctions that apply in using these terms and *administration.*

• ADMINISTRATIVE LAW JUDGE

This is the federal title for the position formerly known as hearing examiner.

To avoid the long title, seek a construction that sets the title off by commas: *The administrative law judge, John Williams, disagreed.*

• ADMISSIBLE

• ADMIT, ADMITTED

These words may in some contexts give the erroneous connotation of wrongdoing.

A person who announces that he is a homosexual, for example, may be acknowledging it to the world, not admitting it. *Said* usually is sufficient.

• ADOPT, ADAPT

To *adopt* is to accept or approve: *The resolution was adopted. The child was adopted.*

To *adapt* is to change: *He had to adapt to the circumstances.*

• ADOPT, APPROVE, ENACT, PASS

Amendments, ordinances, resolutions and rules are *adopted* or *approved.*

Bills are *passed.*

Laws are *enacted.*

• ADVENTIST

See **SEVENTH-DAY ADVENTIST CHURCH.**

• ADVERBS

The abbreviation *adv.* is used in this book to identify the spelling of adverbial forms of words that frequently are misspelled.

See the **HYPHEN** entry for guidelines on when an adverb should be followed by a hyphen in constructing a compound modifier.

• ADVERSE, AVERSE

Adverse means unfavorable: *He predicted adverse weather.*

Averse means reluctant, opposed: *She is averse to change.*

• ADVISER

Not *advisor.*

• ADVISORY

An advisory is intended to pass on information which the AP has not put into story form. Advisories are not intended to be read on the air.

They give broadcasters information about how an event will be covered, or relay information which will be put into story form later. Sometimes they confirm that an event which had been expected to occur has in fact occurred.

A D V I S O R Y

THE POPE'S PLANE HAS LANDED IN BOSTON.

THE AP

ADVISORY

NEWS DIRECTORS:

PRESIDENT REAGAN IS EXPECTED TO ARRIVE AT ANDREWS AIR FORCE BASE IN 30 MINUTES. WE WILL TOP THE STORY AT THAT TIME AND MOVE A REVIEW OF HIS TRIP SHORTLY THEREAFTER.

THE AP

See **UPDATE.**

• AER LINGUS (AYR LIN'-GUHS)

The headquarters of the airline is in Dublin, Ireland.

• AEROFLOT (EHR'-OH-FLAWT)

The headquarters of this airline is in Moscow.

• AERO MEXICO

This airline formerly was known as Aeronaves de Mexico.

Headquarters is in Mexico City.

• AESTHETIC

• AFFECT, EFFECT

Affect, as a verb, means to influence. *The game will affect the standings.*

Affect, as a noun, is best avoided. It occasionally is used in psychology to describe an emotion, but there is no need for it in everyday language.

Effect, as a verb, means to cause: *He will effect many changes in the company.*

Effect, as a noun, means result: *The effect was overwhelming. He miscalculated the effect of his actions. It was a law of little effect.*

• AFL-CIO

Acceptable in all references for the *American Federation of Labor and Congress of Industrial Organizations.*

• AFRICAN

Of or pertaining to Africa, or any of its peoples or languages. Do not use the word as a synonym for *Negro.*

In some countries of Africa, *colored* is used to describe those of mixed white and black ancestry. In other societies *colored* is considered a derogatory word.

Because of the ambiguity, avoid the term in favor of a phrase such as *mixed racial ancestry.* If the word cannot be avoided, place it in quotation marks and provide its meaning.

See **COLORED.**

• AFTER

No hyphen after this prefix when it is used to form a noun:

AFTEREFFECT
AFTERTHOUGHT

Follow *after* with a hyphen when it is used to form a compound modifier:

AFTER-DINNER DRINK
AFTER-THEATER SNACK

See **HYPHEN.**

• AFTERWARD

Not *afterwards.*

• AGENCY FOR INTERNATIONAL DEVELOPMENT

The abbreviation *A-I-D* is acceptable on second reference.

• AGENDA

A list. It takes singular verbs and pronouns: *The agenda has run its course.*

The plural is *agendas.*

• AGES

Follow the rules for **NUMERALS** in expressing the ages of persons or objects.

Hyphenate the age when it is used

as a compound modifier: *the five-year-old agreement,* but *it was five years old.* Similarly, a youngster is *five years old* or *a five-year-old.*

Avoid redundancies in expressing ages. It is enough to say someone is a boy or girl without saying he or she is *young.*

See **BOY** and **GIRL.**

• AGNOSTIC, ATHEIST

An *agnostic* is a person who believes it is impossible to know whether there is a God.

An *atheist* is a person who believes there is no God.

• AID, AIDE

Aid is assistance.

An *aide* is a person who serves as an assistant.

• AIN'T

A dialectical or substandard contraction. Use it only in quoted matter or special contexts.

• AIR BASE

Two words. Follow the practice of the Air Force, which uses *Air Force Base* as part of the proper name for its bases in the United States, and *Air Base* for installations abroad: *Lackland Air Force Base, Texas,* but *Clark Air Base, The Philippines.*

On second reference: *the Air Force base, the air base, the base.*

• AIR CANADA

Headquarters is in Montreal.

• AIRCRAFT NAMES

Strive for readability. When the name includes numbers and letters, spell out the numbers and hyphenate: *D-C-Ten, L-Ten-Eleven, B-A-C One-Eleven, F-Four-C, MiG-21, C-Five-A, Phantom-Two.*

If the aircraft has only a model number, with no letters, it is not necessary to spell out the numbers: *707, 727, 737, 747, 757,* etc.

Wide-body jets—or *jumbo jets*—include the *D-C-Ten, L-Ten-Eleven,* and *747.*

Commercial aircraft are generally referred to as *airliners* or *jetliners.*

• AIRCRAFT TERMS

Use *engine,* not *motor: a twin-engine plane* (not *twin-engined*).

Use *jet plane* or *jetliner* only to describe those aircraft driven solely by jet engines. Use *turboprop* to describe an aircraft on which the jet engine drives a propeller. Turboprops are sometimes called *propjets.*

• AIR FORCE BASE

See **AIR BASE.**

• "AIR FORCE ONE"

The Air Force applies this name to any aircraft the President of the United States may be using.

But in ordinary usage, *"Air Force One"* is the name for the particular jet that is normally reserved for the president's use.

• AIR FRANCE

Headquarters is in Paris.

• AIR-INDIA

The hyphen is part of the formal name.

Headquarters is in Bombay, India.

• AIR JAMAICA

Headquarters is in Kingston, Jamaica.

• AIRLINE, AIRLINES

Major airlines are listed in this book separately by name.

Companies that use *airlines* in their

names include Alitalia, American, Continental, Eastern, Frontier, Hawaiian, Northwest Orient, Republic, Trans World, United and Western.

Companies that use *air lines* include Delta, Japan and Ozark.

Companies that use *airways* include Braniff, British, Pan American, World and Qantas (Kwan'-tuhs).

Companies that use none of these include Aer Lingus, Aeromexico, Air Canada, Air France, Air-India, Air Jamaica, Iberia, K-L-M, U-S-Air and Western Alaska.

On second reference, use just the proper name—as in *Delta*—or, if applicable, an abbreviation, such as *T-W-A* or *Pan Am.* Also acceptable is *the airline* or *the carrier.*

The generic term is *airline.*

• AIR MAIL

• AIRMAN

See **MILITARY TITLES.**

• AIRPORT

The first name of an individual and the word *international* may be deleted from the formal name of an airport in all references: *John F. Kennedy International Airport, Kennedy Airport.*

But do not make up airport names. Instead, opt for more conversational constructions, such as the possessive.

Logan Airport in Boston may be called *Boston's airport,* but it should not be called *Boston Airport.*

• AIR-TIGHT

• AIRWAYS

The system of routes that the federal government has established for airplane traffic.

See the **AIRLINE, AIRLINES** entry for its use in carriers' names.

• ALASKA

It contains the largest land area of the 50 states: *586-thousand, 432 square miles.*

• ALASKA-HAWAII STANDARD TIME

The time zone used in Hawaii and most of Alaska.

There is an *Alaska Daylight Time,* but there is no daylight time in Hawaii.

Bering time applies in some far western sections of Alaska. *Yukon time* is used in a small section south of the Yukon border. *Pacific time* applies in most of the area that borders British Columbia, including the city of Juneau.

See **TIME ZONES.**

• ALBINO, ALBINOS

• "ALCOA"

The acronym is acceptable in all references to the Aluminum Company of America.

• ALCOHOLIC

Use *recovered,* not *reformed,* in referring to those previously afflicted with the disease of alcoholism. Do not use *former.*

• ALDERMAN

See **LEGISLATIVE TITLES.**

• ALERT

See **WEATHER TERMS.**

• AL FATAH (AL FAH-TAH')

A Palestinian guerrilla organization. Drop the article *Al* if preceded by an English article: *The Fatah statement, a Fatah leader.*

• ALIGN

• ALITALIA (AHL-IH-TAHL'-YAH) **AIRLINES**

Headquarters is in Rome.

• ALL-

Use a hypen:

ALL-AROUND (not ALL-ROUND)	ALL-CLEAR
	ALL-OUT
	ALL-STAR

See **ALL RIGHT** and the **ALL TIME, ALL-TIME** entry.

• ALL-AMERICA, ALL-AMERICAN

The Associated Press recognizes only one All-America football team. This is Walter Camp's selection through 1924, and AP selections after that. Do not call anyone an *All-America player* unless he is listed on either the Camp or AP roster.

Similarly do not call anyone an *All-America basketball player* unless an AP selection. The first All-America basketball team was chosen in 1948.

An individual team member may be called an *All-American,* but use *All-America* in all other uses: *He is an All-American. He is an All-America player.*

The same rules apply to the Little All-America teams in both football and basketball.

• ALLEGE

The word must be used with great care.

Some guidelines:

—Avoid any suggestion that the writer is making an allegation.

—Specify the source of an allegation. In a criminal case, it should be an arrest record, an indictment or the statement of a public official connected with the case.

—Use *alleged bribe* or similar phrase when necessary to make it clear that an unproved action is not being treated as fact. Be sure that the source of the charge is specified elsewhere in the story.

—Avoid redundant uses of *alleged.* It is proper to say: *The district attorney alleged that she took a bribe.* Or: *The district attorney accused her of taking a bribe.* But not: *The district attorney accused her of allegedly taking a bribe.*

—Do not use *alleged* before an event that is known to have occurred when the dispute is over who participated in it. Do not say: *He attended the alleged meeting* when what you mean is: *He allegedly attended the meeting.*

—Do not use *alleged* as a routine qualifier. Instead, where appropriate, use words such as *apparent, reputed, suspected, reported,* or *accused.*

For guidelines on related words, see **ACCUSE; ARREST;** and **INDICT.**

• ALLEGHENY AIRLINES

See **U-S-AIR.**

• ALLEGHENY MOUNTAINS

Or simply: *the Alleghenies.*

• ALLOT, ALLOTTED, ALLOTTING

• ALL RIGHT (adv.)

Never *alright.* Hyphenate only if used colloquially as a compound modifer: *He is an all-right guy.*

• ALL TIME, ALL-TIME

An all-time high, but *the greatest runner of all time.*

Avoid the redundant phrase *all-time record.*

• ALLUDE, REFER

To allude to something is to speak of it without specifically mentioning it.

To refer is to mention it directly.

• ALLUSION, ILLUSION
Allusion means an indirect reference: *The allusion was to his opponent's war record.*
Illusion means an unreal or false impression: *The scenic director created the illusion of choppy seas.*

• ALMOST NEVER
Do not use the phrase. Instead use *seldom* or *hardly ever.*

• ALSO-RAN (n.)

• ALTAR, ALTER
An *altar* is a tablelike platform used in a church service.
To alter is to change.

• ALUMINUM COMPANY OF AMERICA
"ALCOA" is acceptable in all references.
Headquarters is in Pittsburgh.

• ALUMNUS, ALUMNI ALUMNA, ALUMNAE
Use *alumnus* (*alumni* in the plural) when referring to a man who has attended a school.
Use *alumna* (*alumnae* in the plural) for similar references to a woman.
Use *alumni* when referring to a group of men and women.

• A-M
Acceptable in all references for the *amplitude modulation* system of radio transmission.

• A-M, P-M
Note hyphens. Avoid the redundant *10 a-m in the morning.* see **MIDNIGHT** and the various **TIME** entries.

• AMALGAMATED CLOTHING AND TEXTILE WORKERS UNION OF AMERICA
The shortened forms *Amalgamated Clothing Workers* and *Clothing Workers union* are acceptable in all references.
Headquarters is in New York.

• AMALGAMATED TRANSIT UNION
Use this full name in the first reference. Do not use the abbreviation *A-T-U* in any reference. Instead, use *the union.*
Headquarters is in Washington.

• AMBASSADOR
Use for both men and women.
See **TITLES.**

• AMBASSADOR-AT-LARGE
But: *ambassador extraordinary, ambassador plenipotentiary.*

• AMENDMENTS TO THE CONSTITUTION
Colloquial references to the Fifth Amendment's protection against self-incrimination are best avoided, but where appropriate: *He took the Fifth seven times.*
Otherwise, use *First Amendment, Tenth Amendment,* etc.

• AMERICAN AIRLINES
Headquarters is in Dallas.

• AMERICAN AUTOMOBILE ASSOCIATION
Triple-A or *A-A-A* is acceptable in all references, as is *the automobile association.*
Headquarters is in New York.

• AMERICAN BAPTIST ASSOCIATION
See **BAPTIST CHURCHES.**

• AMERICAN BAPTIST CHURCHES IN THE U-S-A
See **BAPTIST CHURCHES.**

• AMERICAN BAR ASSOCIATION
A-B-A is also acceptable, as is *the bar association.*
Headquarters is in Chicago.

• AMERICAN BROADCASTING COMPANIES
See **A-B-C.**

• AMERICAN CIVIL LIBERTIES UNION
A-C-L-U is acceptable on second reference.
Headquarters is in New York.

• AMERICAN FEDERATION OF GOVERNMENT EMPLOYEES
Use this full name on first reference to prevent confusion with other unions that represent government workers. Do not abbreviate.
Headquarters is in Washington.

• AMERICAN FEDERATION OF LABOR AND CONGRESS OF INDUSTRIAL ORGANIZATIONS
AFL-CIO is acceptable in all references.
Headquarters is in Washington.

• AMERICAN FEDERATION OF MUSICIANS
Use this full name on first reference.
The shortened form *Musicians union* is acceptable on second reference.
Headquarters is in New York.

• AMERICAN FEDERATION OF STATE, COUNTY AND MUNICIPAL EMPLOYEES
Use this full name on first reference to prevent confusion with other unions that represent government workers.
Headquarters is in Washington.
Do not use the acronym *"AFSCME."*

• AMERICAN FEDERATION OF TEACHERS
Use this full name on first reference to prevent confusion with other unions that represent teachers. *A-F-T* is acceptable on second reference.
Headquarters is in Washington.

• AMERICAN FEDERATION OF TELEVISION AND RADIO ARTISTS
"AFTRA" is acceptable on second reference.
Headquarters is in New York.

• AMERICAN HOSPITAL ASSOCIATION
Do not abbreviate.
Headquarters is in Chicago.

• AMERICANISMS
Words and phrases that have become part of the English language as spoken in the United States are listed in Webster's New World Dictionary with a star ★.
Most Americanisms are acceptable in news stories, but let the context be the guide.
See **WORD SELECTION.**

• AMERICAN LEGION
Members are *legionnaires,* just as members of the Lions Club are *Lions.*
A *legion* is a large group of soldiers or, by derivation, a large number of items: *His friends are legion.* It is best to avoid this usage.

• AMERICAN MEDICAL ASSOCIATION
A-M-A is acceptable on second reference.
Headquarters is in Chicago.

• AMERICAN MOTORS CORPORATION
A-M-C is acceptable on second reference.

Headquarters is in Southfield, Michigan.

● **AMERICAN NEWSPAPER PUBLISHERS ASSOCIATION**

The publishers association is acceptable on the second reference. Do not use the abbreviation *A-N-P-A.*

Headquarters is in Reston, Virginia.

● **AMERICAN PETROLEUM INSTITUTE**

An industry promotional group. Do not use the abbreviation *A-P-I.*

Headquarters is in Washington.

● **AMERICAN POSTAL WORKERS UNION**

This union represents clerks and similar employees who work inside post offices.

Use the full name on first reference to prevent confusion with the National Association of Letter Carriers. The shortened form *Postal Workers union* is acceptable on second reference. Do not abbreviate.

Headquarters is in Washington.

● **AMERICAN PRESS INSTITUTE**

Do not use *A-P-I* on any reference.

Headquarters is in Reston, Virginia.

● **AMERICAN SOCIETY FOR THE PREVENTION OF CRUELTY TO ANIMALS**

This organization is limited to the five boroughs of New York City. *A-S-P-C-A* is acceptable on second reference.

See **SOCIETY FOR THE PREVENTION OF CRUELTY TO ANIMALS.**

● **AMERICAN SOCIETY OF COMPOSERS, AUTHORS AND PUBLISHERS**

"ASCAP" is acceptable on second reference.

Headquarters is in New York.

● **AMERICAN STOCK EXCHANGE**

"AMEX" is acceptable on the second reference.

● **AMERICAN TELEPHONE AND TELEGRAPH COMPANY**

A-T-and-T or *A-T-T* are acceptable on second reference.

A-T-and-T has adopted the proper name *Bell System* (not *Bell Telephone Company*) to describe the corporate complex composed of itself, Western Electric Company (its manufacturing unit), Bell Laboratories (its research and development unit) and the telephone companies it owns in whole or in part.

Headquarters is in New York.

● **AMERICAN VETERANS OF WORLD WAR TWO, KOREA AND VIETNAM**

"AMVETS" is acceptable in second reference.

Headquarters is in Washington.

● **AMERICAS CUP** (Golf)
AMERICA'S CUP (Yachting)

● **"AMEX"** (A'-MEX)

See **AMERICAN STOCK EXCHANGE.**

● **AMID**

Not *amidst.*

● **AMIDSHIPS**

● **AMNESTY**

See the entry that reads **PARDON, PAROLE, PROBATION.**

● **AMOK**

Not *amuck.*

● **AMONG, BETWEEN**

The maxim that *between* introduces two items and *among* introduces more than two covers most questions about how to use these words: *The funds were divided among Ford, Carter and McCarthy.*

However, *between* is the correct word when expressing the relationships of three or more items considered one pair at a time: *Negotiations on a debate format are under way between the network and the Ford, Carter and McCarthy committees.*

As with all prepositions, any pronouns that follow these words must be in the objective case: *among us, between him and her, between you and me.*

• "AMTRAK"

This acronym, drawn from the words *American travel by track,* may be used in all references to the *National Railroad Passenger Corporation. Not "Amtrack."*

The corporation was established by Congress in 1970 to take over intercity passenger operations from railroads that wanted to drop passenger service. All except Southern Railway, Denver and Rio Grande Western Railroad, and the Chicago, Rock Island and Pacific Railroad elected to do so. Amtrak contracts with railroads for the use of their tracks and of certain other operating equipment and crews.

Amtrak is subsidized in part by federal funds appropriated yearly by Congress and administered through the Department of Transportation.

Amtrak should not be confused with *Conrail* (see separate entry). However, the legislation that established Conrail provided for Amtrak to gradually take over ownership of certain trackage in the Boston-Washington corridor and from Philadelphia to Harrisburg.

Amtrak headquarters is in Washington.

• ANEMIA, ANEMIC

• ANESTHETIC

• ANGLICAN COMMUNION

This is the name for the worldwide association of the 22 separate national Anglican churches.

Each national church is independent. A special position of honor is accorded to the archbishop of Canterbury, as the pre-eminent officer in the original Anglican body, the Church of England.

The test of membership in the Anglican Communion traditionally has been whether a church is in communion with the See of Canterbury. No legislative or juridical ties exist, however.

Beliefs: Anglicans believe in the Trinity, the humanity and divinity of Christ, the virginity of Mary, salvation through Christ, and everlasting heaven and hell.

Baptism and the Lord's Supper are recognized as sacraments, although belief in the degree to which Christ is present in the Eucharist may vary.

Together with Scripture, the Book of Common Prayer serves as the principal guide to belief and practice.

A principal difference between Roman Catholics and Anglicans is still the dispute that led to the formation of the Church of England—refusal to acknowledge that the pope, as bishop of Rome, has ruling authority over other bishops.

The communion also contends that its clergy have a direct link to Christ's apostles that is traceable through an unbroken series of ceremonies in which authority was passed down by a laying-on of hands. The Roman Catholic Church, which claims the same type of historic succession for its clergy, has held that 16th century

Anglican practice broke the continuity of apostolic succession among its clergy.

Among individual Anglican (or *Episcopal* in the United States) parishes, practices fall into one of three categories—high, broad or low. A high parish stresses the sacraments and extensive ritual in worship. A low parish favors simpler services and emphasizes the preaching of the Gospel. A broad parish embraces portions of high and low worship practices while tending to be activist on social questions and flexible in matters of church government.

The term *Anglo-Catholic* occasionally is used to describe high Anglican practice. See **CATHOLIC, CATHOLICISM.**

Anglican Churches: Members of the Anglican Communion, in addition to the Church of England, include the Scottish Episcopal Church, the Anglican Church of Canada and, in the United States, the Protestant Episcopal Church.

See **EPISCOPAL CHURCH.**

• ANGLO-

Hyphenate in cases where the word that follows is a proper noun:

ANGLO-AMERICAN
ANGLO-SAXON

Otherwise, no hyphen.

Anglo is used in some parts of the country to refer to a white person. It should be used in that way only in a direct quotation.

• ANGRY

At someone or *with* someone.

• ANIMALS

Do not apply a personal pronoun to an animal unless its sex has been established or the animal has a name:

The dog was scared; it barked. Rover was scared; he barked. The cat, which was scared, ran to its basket. Susie the cat, who was scared, ran to her basket. The bull tosses his horns.

• ANNUAL

An event cannot be described as *annual* until it has been held in at least two successive years.

Do not use the term *first annual.* Instead, note that sponsors plan to hold an event *annually.*

• ANOINT

• ANOTHER

Another is not a synonym for *additional;* it refers to an element that somehow duplicates a previously stated quantity.

Right: *Ten women passed, another ten failed.*

Wrong: *Ten women passed, another six failed.*

Right: *Ten women passed, six others failed.*

• ANTARCTIC, ANTARCTICA, ANTARCTIC OCEAN

Refer to the area near the South Pole.

• ANTE-

The rules in **PREFIXES** apply, but in general, no hyphen. Some examples:

ANTEBELLUM
ANTEDATE

• ANTI-

Hyphenate all except the following words, which have specific meanings of their own:

ANTIBIOTIC	ANTICLIMAX
ANTIBODY	ANTIDOTE

(continued)

(continued)

ANTIFREEZE	ANTIPHON
ANTIGEN	ANTIPHONY
ANTIHISTAMINE	ANTISEPTIC
ANTIKNOCK	ANTISERUM
ANTIMATTER	ANTITHESIS
ANTIMONY	ANTITOXIN
ANTIPARTICLE	ANTITRUST
ANTIPASTO	ANTITUSSIVE
ANTIPERSPIRANT	

(And similar terms in physics such as ANTIPROTON)

This approach has been adopted in the interests of readability and easily remembered consistency.

Hyphenated words, many of them exceptions to Webster's New World, include:

ANTI-AIRCRAFT	ANTI-LABOR
ANTI-BIAS	ANTI-SLAVERY
ANTI-INFLATION	ANTI-SOCIAL
ANTI-INTELLEC-TUAL	ANTI-WAR

See **ANTICHRIST, ANTI-CHRIST.**

• ANTICHRIST, ANTI-CHRIST

Antichrist is the proper name of the individual the Bible says will challenge Jesus Christ.

The adjective *anti-Christ* refers to anyone or anything opposed to Christ.

• ANTICIPATE, EXPECT

To *anticipate* means to expect *and prepare* for something; *expecting* something does not include the notion of preparation:

They expected a record crowd.

They have anticipated it by adding more seats to the auditorium.

• ANTIOCHIAN (AN-TEE-OH'-KEE-UHN) ORTHODOX CHRISTIAN ARCHDIOCESE OF NORTH AMERICA

Formed in 1975 by the merger of the Antiochian Orthodox Christian Archdiocese of New York and all North America and the Antiochian Orthodox Archdiocese of Toledo, Ohio and Dependencies in North America.

It is under the jurisdiction of the patriarch of Antioch.

See **EASTERN ORTHODOX CHURCHES.**

• ANYBODY, ANY BODY, ANYONE, ANY ONE

One word for an indefinite reference: *Anyone can do it.*

But use two words when the emphasis is on singling out one element of a group: *Any one of them may speak up.*

• A-P

Acceptable on second reference to the *The Associated Press.* Hyphenated only when included in a story to be read on the air. Otherwise, *AP.*

Headquarters is in New York.

• APOSTOLIC DELEGATE, PAPAL NUNCIO

An *apostolic delegate* is a Roman Catholic diplomat chosen by the pope to be his envoy to the church in a nation that does not have formal diplomatic relations with the Vatican.

A *papal nuncio* is the pope's envoy to a nation with which the Vatican has diplomatic relations.

• APOSTROPHE (')

The apostrophe is used to indicate the omission of letters. In using it, strive for readability.

Some guidelines:

Possessives: See the **POSSESSIVES** entry.

Omitted Figures: When indicating a specific year, use an apostrophe: *the* *class of '62*. But when indicating a decade, no apostrophe is needed before the figure: *The roaring 20's.*

Omitted Letters: Use an apostrophe to indicate omitted letters: *I've, it's, rock 'n' roll, 'tis the season. See* CONTRACTIONS.

Plurals: When adding an *s* to letters or figures.

• APPALACHIA (AP-UH-LAYCH'-YA)

In the broadest sense, the word applies to the entire region along the Appalachian Mountains, which extend from Maine into northern Alabama.

In a sense that often suggests economic depression and poverty, the reference is to sections of eastern Tennessee, eastern Kentucky, southeastern Ohio and the western portion of West Virginia.

The Appalachian Regional Commission, established by federal law in 1965, has a mandate to foster development in 397 counties in 13 states—all of West Virginia and continguous parts of Alabama, Georgia, Kentucky, Maryland, Mississippi, New York, North Carolina, Ohio, Pennsylvania, South Carolina, Tennessee and Virginia.

When the word *Appalachia* is used, specify the extent of the area in question.

• APPEALS COURT

See **U-S COURT OF APPEALS** and **JUDICIAL BRANCH.**

• APPROVE

See the entry entitled **ADOPT, APPROVE, ENACT, PASS.**

• APRIL FOOLS' DAY

• ARABIAN AMERICAN OIL COMPANY

The acronym *"ARAMCO"* (uh-ram'-koh) is acceptable on the second reference.

Headquarters is in Dhahran (Dahrahn'), Saudi Arabia.

• ARABIC NAMES

In general, use an English spelling that approximates the way a name sounds in Arabic. And use a pronouncer in any case.

If an individual has a preferred spelling and pronunciation in English, use it. If usage has established a common spelling, and no preferred spelling is available, use that instead.

Arabs commonly are known by two names (*Fuad Butros*) or by three (*Ahmed Zaki Yamani*). Follow the individual's preference on the first reference, and use only the final name in the sequence in subsequent references.

The prefix *al* or *el* should not be used in second references, and only in the first if it is the individual's preference.

• ARABIC NUMERALS

The numerical figures 1 through 10. Generally, they are not used in broadcast writing. In this handbook, they may be referred to as *Arabic numerals* or *figures.*

See **NUMERALS.**

• ARBITRATE, MEDIATE

Both terms are used in reports about labor negotiations, but they should not be interchanged.

One who *arbitrates* hears evidence from all persons concerned, then hands down a decision.

One who *mediates* listens to arguments of both parties and tries by the exercise of reason or persuasion to bring them to an agreement.

• ARCH-
It is best to use a hyphen after this prefix to ease readability, as in:

ARCH-RIVAL
ARCH-CONSERVATIVE
ARCH-ENEMY

But in cases where a hyphen is not commonly used, as in *archbishop,* don't use one.

• ARCTIC, ARCTIC CIRCLE, ARCTIC FOX, ARCTIC OCEAN
They refer to the area near the North Pole.

• ARE (AYR)
A unit of surface measure in the metric system equal to 100 square meters.
An are is equal to about one-thousand, 76-point-four square feet, or 119-point-six square yards.
See **HECTARE** and **METRIC SYSTEM.**

• ARMENIAN CHURCH OF AMERICA
The term encompasses two independent dioceses that cooperate in some activities: the Eastern Diocese of the Armenian Church of America, covering areas outside of California, and that state's Western Diocese of the Armenian Church of America.
See **EASTERN ORTHODOX CHURCHES.**

• ARMISTICE DAY
See **VETERANS DAY.**

• ARREST
To avoid any suggestion that someone is being judged before a trial, do not use a phrase such as *arrested for murder.* Instead, use *arrested in connection with the killing,* or *arrested at the scene of the killing,* or similar phrases.
For guidelines on related words, see **ACCUSED; ALLEGE;** and **INDICT.**

• AS
See **LIKE, AS.**

• ASHCAN, ASHTRAY

• ASH WEDNESDAY
The first day of Lent, 46 days before Easter.
See **EASTER** and **LENT.**

• ASIAN, ASIATIC
Use *Asian* or *Asians* when referring to people.
Some Asians regard *Asiatic* as offensive when applied to people.

• ASIAN SUBCONTINENT
In popular usage the term applies to Bangladesh, Bhutan, India, Nepal, Sikkim and the island nation of Sri Lanka (formerly Ceylon) at the southeastern tip of India.
For definitions of terms that apply to other parts of Asia, see **FAR EAST; MIDDLE EAST;** and **SOUTHEAST ASIA.**

• AS IF
The preferred form, but *as though* is acceptable.

• ASSASSIN, KILLER, MURDERER
An *assassin* is a politically motivated killer.
A *killer* is anyone who kills with a motive of any kind.
A *murderer* is one who is convicted of murder in a court of law.
See **EXECUTE** and the **HOMICIDE, MURDER, MANSLAUGHTER** entry.

• ASSASSINATION, DATE OF

A prominent person is shot one day and dies the next. Which day was he assassinated? The day he was attacked.

• ASSAULT, BATTERY

Popularly, *assault* almost always implies physical contact and sudden, intense violence.

Legally, however, *assault* means simply to threaten violence, as in pointing a pistol at an individual without firing it. *Assault and battery* is the legal term when the victim was touched by the assaulter or something the assaulter put in motion.

• ASSEMBLYMAN, ASSEMBLYWOMAN

See **LEGISLATIVE TITLES.**

• ASSETS

Everything a company or individual owns or is owed.

Assets may be categorized further as:

Current Assets: cash, investments, money due to a corporation, unused raw materials and inventories of finished but unsold products.

Fixed Assets: buildings, equipment and land.

Intangible Assets: patents and good will.

• ASSOCIATED PRESS, THE

A newsgathering cooperative dating from 1848. Use *The Associated Press* on the first reference and *the A-P* thereafter.

The address is 50 Rockefeller Plaza, New York, N.Y. 10020. The telephone number is (212) 621-1500.

• ASTROTURF

A trademark for a type of artificial grass. *Artificial grass* or *artificial surface* are preferred when referring to the generic type.

• ATCHISON, TOPEKA AND SANTA FE RAILWAY

Headquarters is in Chicago.

A subsidiary of Santa Fe Industries.

• ATHEIST

See **AGNOSTIC, ATHEIST.**

• ATHLETE'S FOOT, ATHLETE'S HEART

Note apostrophes.

• ATLANTA

The city in Georgia stands alone in datelines.

• ATLANTIC COAST CONFERENCE

Clemson, Duke, Maryland, North Carolina, North Carolina State, Virginia, Wake Forest.

• ATLANTIC RICHFIELD COMPANY

"ARCO" is acceptable on second references.

Headquarters is in Los Angeles.

• ATLANTIC STANDARD TIME, ATLANTIC DAYLIGHT TIME

Used in the Maritime Provinces of Canada and in Puerto Rico.

See **TIME ZONES.**

• AT LARGE

Usually two words for an individual representing more than a single district: *congressman at large, councilman at large.*

But it is *ambassador-at-large,* for an ambassador assigned to no particular country.

• **ATOMIC AGE**

Began on December second, 1942, at the University of Chicago, with the creation of the first self-sustaining nuclear chain reaction.

• **ATOMIC ENERGY COMMISSION**

No longer exists.

See **NUCLEAR REGULATORY COMMISSION.**

• **ATTORNEY, LAWYER**

In common usage the words are interchangeable.

Technically, however, an *attorney* is someone (usually, but not necessarily, a lawyer) empowered to act for another. Such an individual occasionally is called an *attorney in fact.*

A *lawyer* is a person admitted to practice in a court system. Such an individual occasionally is called an *attorney at law.*

Do not abbreviate.

See **LAWYER.**

• **ATTORNEY GENERAL, ATTORNEYS GENERAL**

Never abbreviate.

• **AUGUR**

A transitive verb meaning foretell. It should not be followed with the preposition *for: The tea leaves augur a time of joy.*

Preferred terms are *foretell, predict, suggest* and *forecast.*

• **AUTHOR**

As a noun, it is used for both men and women. Do not use it as a verb; use *write* instead.

• **AUTOMAKER, AUTOMAKERS**

No hyphen.

• **AUTOMATIC**

See **PISTOL** and **WEAPONS** entries.

• **AUTO RACING**

In covering major events in short separate items, report the order of the top finishers as well as the winner's speed.

• **AUTOWORKER, AUTOWORKERS**

One word when used generically.

But *Auto Worker* when referring specifically to the membership and the activities of the United Automobile, Aerospace and Agricultural Implement Workers of America.

• **AVERAGE, MEAN, MEDIAN, NORM**

Average refers to the result obtained by dividing a sum by the number of quatities added together: the average of seven, nine, and 17 is 33—their sum—divided by three—the number of factors. The average is eleven.

Mean commonly designates a figure intermediate between two extremes: The mean temperature of the day with a high of 56 and a low of 34 is 45.

Median is the middle number of points in a series arranged in order of size: The median grade in the group of 50, 55, 85, 88, 92 is 85. The average is 74.

Norm implies a standard of average performance for a given group: *The child was below the norm for his age in reading comprehension.*

• **AVERAGE OF**

The phrase takes a plural verb in a construction such as: *An average of 100 new jobs are created daily.*

• **AVERSE**

See **ADVERSE, AVERSE.**

- **AVIANCA** (AH-VEE-AHN'-KAH)
The headquarters of this airline is in Bogota, Colombia.

- **AVIATOR**
Use for both men and women.

- **AWARDS AND DECORATIONS**
See **NOBEL PRIZE** and **PULITZER PRIZE.**

- **AWE-STRUCK**

- **AWHILE, A WHILE**
He plans to stay awhile.
He plans to say for a while.

- **AX**
Not *axe.*
The verb forms: *ax, axed, axing.*

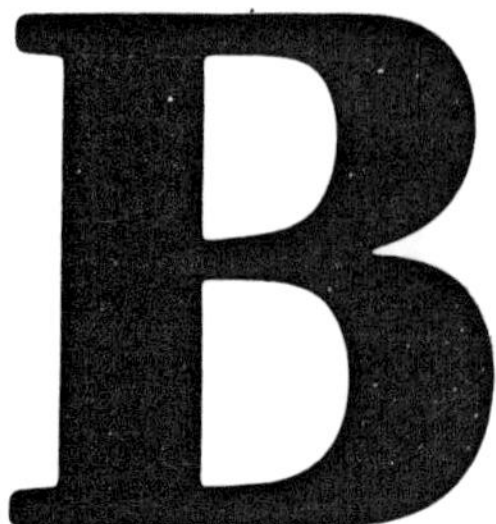

- **BABY-SIT, BABY-SITTING, BABY SITTER**

- **BACCALAUREATE**

- **BACHELOR OF ARTS, BACHELOR OF SCIENCE**

A *bachelor's degree* or *bachelor's* is acceptable in any reference.

- **BACKWARD**

Not *backwards.*

- **BACKBOARD, BACKCOURT, BACKFIELD, BACKHAND, BACKSPIN, BACKSTOP, BACKSTRETCH, BACKSTROKE**

Some are exceptions to Webster's New World, made for consistency in handling sports stories.

- **BACK UP** (v.)
BACK-UP (n., adj.)

- **BACK YARD** (n.)
BACK-YARD (adj.)

- **B-A-C ONE-ELEVEN**

The less cumbersome *Tristar Jet* is preferable.

- **BAD, BADLY**

Bad should not be used as an adverb. It does not lose its status as an adjective, however, in a sentence such as *I feel bad.* Such a statement is the idiomatic equivalent of *I am in bad health.* An alternative, *I feel badly,* could be interpreted as meaning that your sense of touch was bad.

See the GOOD, WELL entry.

- **BAHAMAS**

In datelines, give the name of the city or town followed by *Bahamas:*

(NASSAU, BAHAMAS) --

In stories, use *Bahamas, the Bahamas* or *the Bahama Islands* as the construction of a sentence dictates.

Identify a specific island in the text if relevant.

- **BAIL**

Bail is money or property that will be forfeited to the court if an accused individual fails to appear for trial. It may be posted as follows:

—The accused may deposit with the court the full amount or its equivalent in collateral such as a deed to property.

—A friend or relative may make such a deposit with the court.

—The accused may pay a professional bail bondsman a percentage of the total figure. The bondsman, in turn, guarantees the court that it will receive from him the full amount in the event the individual fails to appear for trial.

It is correct in all cases to say that an accused *posted bail* or *posted a bail bond* (the money held by the court is a form of *bond*). When a distinction is desired, say that the individual *posted his own bail,* that *bail was posted by a friend or relative,* or that *bail was obtained through a bondsman.*

- **BAKER'S DOZEN**

It means 13.

• BAKERY AND CONFECTIONARY WORKERS' INTERNATIONAL UNION OF AMERICA
The shortened form *Bakery Workers union* is acceptable in all references.
Headquarters is in Washington.

• BALANCE OF PAYMENTS, BALANCE OF TRADE
The *balance of payments* is the difference between the amount of money that leaves a nation and the amount that enters it during a period of time.
The balance of payments is determined by computing the amount of money a nation and its citizens send abroad for all purposes—including goods and services purchased, travel, loans and foreign aid—and subtracting from it the amount that foreign nations send into the nation for similar purposes.
The *balance of trade* is the difference between the monetary value of the goods a nation imports and the goods it exports.
An example illustrating the difference between the two:
The United States and its citizens might send ten (b) billion dollars abroad—five (b) billion for goods, three for loans and foreign aid, one for services and one for tourism and other purposes.
Other nations might send nine (b) billion into the United States—six (b) billion for goods, two for services and one for tourism.
The United States would then have a *balance-of-payments deficit* of one (b) billion dollars, but a *balance-of-trade surplus* of one (b) billion.

• BALLCLUB, BALLPARK, BALLPLAYER, BALLROOM
But *ball carrier.*

• BALL-POINT PEN

• BALONEY
Foolish or exaggerated talk.
The sausage or luncheon meat is *bologna.*

• BALTIMORE
The city in Maryland stands alone in datelines.

• BANK OF AMERICA
Acceptable in all references to the *Bank of America National Trust and Savings Association.* As of 1981, this was the largest bank in the United States.
The parent company is Bank America Corporation of San Francisco.

• BANKRUPTCY
The legal sense of the word applies only if a court has told an individual or organization to liquidate assets and distribute the proceeds to creditors.
The action may be involuntary, as the result of a suit by creditors, or it may be a voluntary effort to deal with bills that cannot be paid.
Often a company with financial problems announces that it is seeking to reorganize under federal bankruptcy laws. In such a case, it is incorrect to describe the company as *bankrupt.*
A story that announces such a filing should specify the chapter of the Federal Bankruptcy Act under which the reorganization is sought and describe the basic provisions.
Under Chapter Eleven, the most frequently used, a company obtains a federal court order that frees it from the threat of creditors' lawsuits until it can develop a plan to put its finances in order. While the reorganization proceeds, the activities of management must be approved by the court. The

ulitmate reorganization plan must be accepted by a majority of the creditors. It may involve various options, including a full or partial payment of debts.

Chapter Ten, which is used occasionally, takes away management from the existing officers and turns it over to an independent trustee. Under a Chapter Ten reorganization, stockholders could lose their entire investment. By contrast, under Chapter Eleven, it is possible for stockholders to retain something even if creditors are not paid in full.

Some other chapters apply to specific types of companies or situations.

If a reorganization plan fails, a company may be forced into bankruptcy.

• BAPTISM

See **SACRAMENTS.**

• BAPTIST CHURCHES

It is incorrect to apply the term *church* to any Baptist unit except the local church.

The ultimate governing power rests with members of the local congregation. Majority rule prevails.

This emphasis on the authority of the individual churches helps account for the existence of more than 20 Baptist bodies in the United States.

The largest, the Southern Baptist convention, has more than 12 (m) million members, most of them in the South, although it has churches in 50 states.

The largest northern body is American Baptist Churches in the U-S-A, with about one and a-half (m) million members.

Black predominate in three other large Baptist bodies, the National Baptist Convention of America, the National Baptist Convention U-S-A and the Progressive National Baptist Convention.

The roster of Baptist bodies in the United States also includes the Baptist General Conference, the Conserevative Baptist Association of America, the General Association of Regular Baptist Churches, the General Association of General Baptists, and the North American Baptist General Conference.

The Baptist World Alliance, a voluntary association of Baptist bodies throughout the world, fosters communication among its members, provides a forum for discussion of doctrine and practice, and organizes the Baptist World Congress meetings generally held every five years. Headquarters is in Washington.

Beliefs: Baptists are free to interpret Scripture as their consciences dictate.

In general, however, Baptists believe that no one can be validly baptized without first giving a personal confession of faith in Christ as his savior. They also believe that the baptism should be by immersion.

In addition to belief in original sin and the need of redemption, Baptists generally believe in the Trinity, the humanity and divinity of Christ, salvation through Christ, and everlasting heaven and hell.

Clergy: All members of the Baptist clergy may be referred to as *ministers. Pastor* applies if a minister leads a congregation.

On first reference, use *the Reverend* before the name of a man or woman. On second reference, use only the last name of a man; use *Miss, Mrs. or Ms.* before the last name of a woman depending on her preference.

See **RELIGIOUS TITLES.**

See **RELIGIOUS MOVEMENTS** for definitions of some descriptive terms that often apply to Baptists but are not limited to them.

• BAR MITZVAH

The Jewish religious ritual and family celebration that marks a boy's 13th birthday. Judaism regards the age of 13 as the benchmark of relgious maturity. *Bar mitzvah* translates as "one who is responsible for the Commandments."

Conservative congregations have instituted the *bas mitzvah* or *bat mitzvah,* a similar ceremony for girls.

• BARREL

A standard barrel in American measure contains 31 and a-half gallons.

A standard barrel in British and Canadian measure contains 36 Imperial gallons.

In international dealings with crude oil, a standard barrel contains 42 American gallons or 35 Imperial gallons.

See the **OIL** entry for guidelines on computing the volume and weight of petroleum products.

• BARRISTER

See **LAWYER.**

• BARROOM

• BASEBALL

The spellings for some frequently used words and phrases:

BACKSTOP
BALLCLUB
BALLPARK
BALLPLAYER
BASE LINE
BULLPEN
CENTER FIELD
CENTER FIELDER
DESIGNATED HITTER
DOUBLE-HEADER
DOUBLE PLAY
FAIR BALL
FASTBALL
FIRST BASEMAN
FOUL BALL
FOUL LINE
FOUL TIP
GROUND-RULE DOUBLE
HOME PLATE
HOME RUN
LEFT-HANDER
LINE DRIVE
LINE UP (v.)
LINEUP (n.)
MAJOR LEAGUE(S) (n.)
MAJOR-LEAGUE (adj.)
MAJOR-LEAGUER (n.)
OUTFIELDER
PASSED BALL
PUT OUT (v.)
PUTOUT (n.)
PINCH HIT (v.)
PINCH-HIT (n., adj.)13
PINCH HITTER (n.)
PITCHOUT
PLAY OFF (v.)
PLAYOFF (n., adj.)
R-B-I, R-B-I's
RUNDOWN (n.)
SACRIFICE
SACRIFICE FLY
SACRIFICE HIT
SHOESTRING CATCH
SHORTSTOP
SHUT OUT (v.)
SHUTOUT (n., adj.)
SLUGGER
SQUEEZE PLAY
STRIKE
STRIKE ZONE
TEXAS LEAGUER
TRIPLE PLAY
TWI-NIGHT DOUBLEHEADER
WILD PITCH

Numbers: Follow the rules for **NUMERALS,** except in tabular material and in reporting scores in the body of a story. In reporting scores, use figures, hyphens, and *to: The Reds won 2-to-1. The Giants posted a 5-to-4 victory over the Cardinals.*

Scores: Partial scores are sent after the third and sixth innings, and contain the league designation, the score, and the inning:

AL
BOSTON 7 KANSAS CITY 2 (6)

In addition, partial scores are rounded up once an hour, and are slugged *here is the latest from the ballparks.*

HERE IS THE LATEST FROM THE BALLPARKS:

NATIONAL
FINAL 1ST GAME N.Y. METS 3 L.A. 2
2ND GAME N.Y. METS 2 L.A. 0 (2)
STARTERS TOM SEAVER N.Y. METS
SANDY KOUFAX L.A.

HOUSTON 2 PHILADELPHIA 2 (6 1-2)
TUG MCGRAW PTG PHILADELPHIA 7TH

AMERICAN
MINNESOTA 2 N.Y. YANKEES 1 (3)
CLEVELAND AND SEATTLE PPD., RAIN

Final scores are sent on a spot basis, using this form:

NL
FINAL 1ST GAME N.Y. METS 3 L.A. 2

They are followed by final linescores, using this form:

NATIONAL (1ST GAME)
CINCINNATI 000 010 002 -- 3 7 0
MONTREAL 011 000 000 -- 2 7 1
LACOSS, BAIR (7), HUME (9)
LEA, SOSA (9)
WP: BAIR (1-4)
LP: LEA (2-5)

The visiting team is always listed first, the home team second.

Use the first game designation only if it is the first game of a doubleheader.

In linescores, the visiting team's pitchers are listed first under the scores, with the inning of change indicated in parentheses. The home team's pitchers follow on the next line.

In the listing of winning and losing pitchers, the pitcher's updated record follows his name in parentheses.

League Standings: The form:

NATIONAL LEAGUE
EAST

	W	L	PCT.	GB
PITTSBURGH	92	69	.571	—
PHILADELPHIA	85	75	.531	6½
ETC.				

WEST

CINCINNATI	108	54	.667	—
LOS ANGELES	88	74	.543	20
ETC.				

• BASKETBALL

The spellings of some frequently used words and phrases:

BACKBOARD	GOALTENDING
BACKCOURT	HALF-COURT PASS
BACKCOURTMAN	HALFTIME
BASELINE	HOOK SHOT
FIELD GOAL	JUMP BALL
FOUL LINE	JUMP SHOT
FOUL SHOT	LAYUP
FREE THROW	MAN-TO-MAN
FREE-THROW LINE	MIDCOURT
FRONTCOURT	PIVOTMAN
FULL-COURT PRESS	PLAY OFF (v.)
	PLAYOFF (n., adj.)
	ZONE

Numbers: Follow the rules for **NUMERALS** except in reporting scores in the body of the story. In those cases use figures, hyphens and *to: the '76ers posted a 95-to-93 victory of the Lakers. It was the Knicks 102, the Nets 100.*

Scores: Period scores are sent as they become available, and take this format:

NBA
FIRST BUFFALO 34 LOS ANGELES 32

In addition, they are rounded up hourly, and take this form:

HERE IS THE LATEST FROM PRO BASKETBALL:

FINAL BOSTON 108 SAN ANTONIO 99

THIRD N.J. NETS 67 MILWAUKEE 58
THIRD N.Y. KNICKS 88 CLEVELAND 87

FIRST PHILADELPHIA 15 LOS ANGELES 12

Final scores are moved on a spot basis:

NBA
FINAL N.Y. KNICKS 102 SAN ANTONIO 100

Standings: The format:

NBA				
EASTERN CONFERENCE				
ATLANTIC DIVISION				
	W	*L*	*PCT.*	*GB*
BOSTON	*43*	*22*	*.662*	*--*
PHILADELPHIA	*40*	*30*	*.571*	*5½*
ETC.				

● **BATTALION**

● **BATTLEFIELD**
Also: *battlefront, battleground, battleship.* But *battle station.*

● **BAZAAR**
A fair. *Bizarre* means unusual.

● **B-C**
Acceptable in all references to a calendar year in the period *Before Christ.*

Because the full phrase would be *in the year 43 before Christ,* the abbreviation *B-C* is placed after the figure for year: *43 B-C.*

See **A-D**

● **BECAUSE, SINCE**
Use *because* to denote a specific cause-effect relationship: *He went because he was told.*

Since is acceptable in a causal sense when the first event in a sequence led logically to the second but was not its direct cause. *He went to the game, since he had been given the tickets.*

● **BELIZE** (BAY-LEEZ')
The former British Honduras.

● **BELL SYSTEM**
See **AMERICAN TELEPHONE AND TELEGRAPH COMPANY.**

● **BELLWETHER**

● **BENEFIT, BENEFITED BENEFITING**

● **BENELUX** (BEH'-NEH-LUHKS)
Belgium, the Netherlands and Luxembourg.

If *Benelux* is used, explain that it is an inclusive word for these three nations.

● **BEN-GURION INTERNATIONAL AIRPORT**
Located in Lod (Lohd), Israel, about ten miles south of Tel Aviv.

● **BENZEDRINE**
A trademark for a type of pep pill or stimulant.

● **BERING STANDARD TIME, BERING DAYLIGHT TIME**
Used in the far western section of Alaska, including Nome.

See **TIME ZONES.**

● **BERLIN**
Stands alone in datelines.

When a distinction must be made between sections of the city, do so in the body of the story—not in the dateline.

Acceptable terms include *East Berlin, West Berlin, the Communist sector, the western sector.*

● **BESIDE, BESIDES**
Beside means at the side of.
Besides means in addition to.

● **BESIEGE**

● **BEST SELLER** (n.)

● **BETTING ODDS**
Use figures, a hyphen, and the word *to: 3-to-2 odds, odds of 3-to-2, the odds were 3-to-2.*

But at the beginning of a sentence,

spell out the figures: *Three-to-two were the odds on Beetlebaum today.*

• BETTOR

A person who bets.

• BETWEEN

See the **AMONG, BETWEEN** entry.

• BI-

The rules in **PREFIXES** apply, but in general, no hyphen. Some examples:

BIFOCAL	BIMONTHLY
BILATERAL	BIPARTISAN
BILINGUAL	

• BIANNUAL, BIENNIAL

Biannual means twice a year and is a synonym for the word *semiannual.*

Biennial means once every two years.

Both terms tend to lead to confusion, and ought to be avoided. Instead, use such phrases as *twice a year* or *every two years.*

• BIBLE

The books of the Old Testament, in order, are: Genesis, Exodus, Leviticus, Numbers, Deuteronomy, Joshua, Judges, Ruth, the first book of Samuel, the second book of Samuel, the first book of Kings, the second book of Kings, the first book of Chronicles, the second book of Chronicles, Ezra, Nehemiah, Esther, Job, Psalms, Proverbs, Ecclesiastes, Song of Solomon, Isaiah, Jeremiah, Lamentations, Ezekiel, Daniel, Hosea, Joel, Amos, Obadiah, Jonah, Micah, Nahum, Habakkuk, Zephaniah, Haggai, Zechariah, Malachi.

The books of the New Testament, in order: Matthew, Mark, Luke, John, Acts, Romans, the first book of Corinthians, the second book of Corinthians, Galatians, Ephesians, Philippians, Colossians, the first book of Thessalonians, the second book of Thessalonians, the first book of Timothy, the second book of Timothy, Titus, Philemon, Hebrews, Epistles of James, first book of Peter, the second book of Peter, the first book of John, the second book of John, the third book of John, Jude, Revelation.

• BIBLE BELT

Those sections of the United States, especially in the South and Middle West, where fundamentalist religious beliefs prevail. Use with care, because in certain contexts it can give offense.

See **RELIGIOUS MOVEMENTS.**

• BICYCLE

• BIG-BANG THEORY

The theory that the universe began with the explosion of a superdense primeval atom and has been expanding ever since.

The **OSCILLATING THEORY,** another hypothesis, maintains that expansion eventually will stop, followed by contraction to a superdense atom, followed by another big bang.

The **STEADY-STATE THEORY,** an alternate hypothesis, maintains that the universe always has existed and that matter constantly is being created to replace matter that constantly is being destroyed.

• BIG BOARD

Acceptable on second reference for the *New York Stock Exchange.*

• BIG EIGHT CONFERENCE

Colorado, Iowa State, Kansas, Kansas State, Missouri, Nebraska, Oklahoma, Oklahoma State.

• BIG TEN CONFERENCE

Illinois, Indiana, Iowa, Michigan, Michigan State, Minnesota, Northwestern, Ohio State, Purdue, Wisconsin.

• **BIG THREE AUTOMAKERS**
General Motors, Ford, Chrysler.
The Big Four: The Big Three plus American Motors.

• **BIGWIG**

• **(B) BILLION**
A thousand (m) million. It should always be spelled out.
See **(M) MILLIONS, (B) BILLIONS.**

• **BILL OF RIGHTS**
The first ten amendments to the Constitution.

• **BIMONTHLY**
Means every other month. *Semimonthly* means twice a month. Try to avoid using either in broadcast copy. Use phrases such as: *The magazine is published twice monthly.*

• **BISHOP**
See **RELIGIOUS TITLES** and the entry for the denomination in question.

• **BIWEEKLY**
Means every other week. *Semiweekly* means twice a week. Try to avoid using either in broadcast copy. Say: *The newspaper is published twice weekly.*

• **BIZARRE**
Unusual. A fair is a *bazaar.*

• **BLACK**
Acceptable in all references for *Negro.*
Do not use *colored* as a synonym. See the **COLORED** or **AFRICAN** entries.

• **BLACK MUSLIMS**
See **MOSLEM.**

• **BLACKOUT, BROWNOUT**
A *blackout* is a total power failure over a large area or the concealing of lights that might be visible to enemy raiders.
The term *rotating blackout* is used by electric companies to describe a situation in which electric power to some sections temporarily is cut off on a rotating basis to assure that voltage will meet minimum standards in other sections.
A *brownout* is a small, temporary voltage reduction, usually from two to eight percent, implemented to conserve electric power.

• **BLAST OFF** (v.)
BLASTOFF (n. and adj.)

• **BLIZZARD**
See **WEATHER TERMS.**

• **BLOC, BLOCK**
A *bloc* is a coalition of people, groups or nations with the same purpose or goal.
Block has more than a dozen definitions, but a political alliance is not one of them.

• **BLOND, BLONDE**
Use *blond* as a noun for males and as the adjective for all applications: *She has blond hair.*
Use *blonde* as a noun for females.

• **BLUE-CHIP STOCK**
Stock in a company known for its long-established record of making money and paying dividends.

• **B'NAI B'RITH** (BUH-NAY' BRITH)
A Jewish fraternal and service organization.

• **BOARD OF ALDERMEN**
See **CITY COUNCIL.**

• **BOARD OF SUPERVISORS**
See **CITY COUNCIL.**

• BOAT, SHIP

A *boat* is a watercraft of any size. A *ship* is a large, sea-going vessel that is large enough to carry smaller boats.

The term *boat* is, however, used in some phrases that apply to larger craft: *ferryboat, P-T boat, gunboat.*

The names of boats and ships should be put in quotation marks. Follow the rules for **QUOTATION MARKS; NUMERALS;** and **HYPHEN.** Some examples:

The "Queen Elizabeth Two," the "Q-E-Two," the U-S-S "Enterprise."

The reference for military ships is "Jane's Fighting Ships"; for non-military ships, "Lloyd's Register of Shipping".

• BOEING COMPANY

Formerly Boeing Aircraft Company. Headquarters is in Seattle.

• BOLOGNA

The sausage. *Baloney* is foolish or exaggerated talk.

• BONA FIDE (BOH'-NUH FYD)

Genuine.

• BOND RATINGS

The two most popular are prepared by Moody's Investors Service and Standard and Poor's Corporation.

Moody's uses nine ratings. The range, from the designation for top-quality issues to the one for those judged the greatest risk: *Triple-A, Double-A, A, B-Double-A, B-A, B, C-Double-A, C-A, and C.*

Standard and Poor's uses seven basic grades. The range, from top to bottom: *Triple-A, Double-A, A, Triple-B, Double-B, B, and D.* Sometimes it adds a plus or minus sign on grades *Double A* through *Double-B: A-Plus, Double-A-Minus.*

• BONDS

See **LOAN TERMINOLOGY.**

• B-ONE BOMBER

• BOOK TITLES

See **COMPOSITION TITLES.**

• BOOK VALUE

The difference between a company's assets and liabilities.

The *book value per share of common stock* is the figure obtained by dividing the total number of common shares outstanding into the book value of the company as a whole.

The book value of a stock may have little or no significant relationship to the selling price.

• BORSCHT (BAWRSHT)

Beet soup. This spelling is an exception to Webster's New World.

• BOSPORUS, THE

Not *the Bosporus Strait.*

• BOSTON

The city in Massachusetts stands alone in datelines.

• BOULEVARD

See **ADDRESSES.**

• BOUNDARY

• BOW-LEGGED

• BOXING

Some frequently used terms and their definitions:

The Weight Classes:

Flyweight: A boxer weighing no more than 112 pounds.

Bantamweight: 113 to 118 pounds.

Featherweight: 119 to 126 pounds.

Lightweight: 127 to 135 pounds.
Welterweight: 136 to 147 pounds.
Middleweight: 148 to 160 pounds.
Light heavyweight: 161 to 175 pounds.
Heavyweight: 176 or more pounds.

Some Other Terms:

Kidney Punch: A punch to an opponent's kidney when the puncher has only one hand free. An illegal punch. If the puncher has both hands free, a punch to the opponent's kidney is legal.

Knock Out (v.) *Knockout* (n. and adj.): A fighter is *knocked out* if he takes a ten count.

If a match ends early because one fighter is unable to continue, say that the winner *stopped* the loser. In most boxing jurisdictions there is no such thing as a *technical knockout.*

Outpointed: Not *outdecisioned.*

Rabbit Punch: A punch behind an opponent's neck. It is illegal.

• BOX OFFICE (n.) BOX-OFFICE (adj.)

• BOY

Applicable until 18th birthday is reached. Use *man* or *young man* afterward. Avoid redundancy in reference to boys; do not write *young boy,* for example. To convey his relative youth, note his age.

• BOYCOTT, EMBARGO

A *boycott* is an organized refusal to buy a particular product or service, or to deal with a particular merchant or group of merchants.

An *embargo* is a legal restriction against trade. It usually prohibits goods from entering or leaving a country.

• BOYFRIEND, GIRLFRIEND

• BOY SCOUTS

The full name of the national organization is *Boy Scouts of America.* It also uses the name *Scouting-U-S-A.* Headquarters is in Irving, Texas.

Cub Scouting is for boys eight through ten. Members are *Cub Scouts* or *Cubs.*

Boy Scouting is for boys eleven through 17. Members are *Boy Scouts* or *Scouts.*

Exploring is a separate program open to boys and girls from high school age through 20. Members are *Explorers,* not *Explorer Scouts.* Some units stress nautical programs; members are *Sea Explorers.*

See **GIRL SCOUTS** for programs that a separate organization runs for girls.

• BRA

Acceptable in all references for *brassiere.*

• BRACKETS

They cannot be transmitted over news wires.

See **PARENTHESES.**

• BRAND NAMES

Brand names normally should be used only if they are essential to a story.

Sometimes, however, the use of a brand name may not be essential but is acceptable because it lends an air of reality to a story: *He fished a Camel from his shirt pocket* may be preferable to the less specific *cigarette.*

Brand name is a non-legal term for *service mark* or *trademark.* See entries under those words.

• BRAND-NEW (adj.)

• BRANIFF AIRWAYS

Headquarters is in Dallas.

• BREAK

A break is used in air-ready copy to indicate a place where a spot may be inserted. Generally, the copy above the break sets up the copy below; the copy below must also stand alone.

A break also may be used to indicate places in which local material may be added—as, for example, in a national farm script in which local market figures may be added.

A break should be surrounded by double hyphens:

--BREAK--

• BREAK IN (v.)
BREAK-IN (n. and adj.)

• BREAK UP (v.)
BREAK-UP (n. and adj.)

• BRICKLAYERS, MASONS AND PLASTERERS INTERNATIONAL UNION OF AMERICA

The shortened form *Bricklayers union* is acceptable in all references.

Headquarters is in Washington.

• BRIDE, BRIDEGROOM, BRIDESMAID

Bride is appropriate in wedding stories, but use *wife* or *spouse* in other circumstances.

• BRIGHT'S DISEASE

After Dr. Richard Bright, the London physician who first diagnosed this form of kidney disease.

• BRILL'S DISEASE

It is a form of epidemic typhus fever in which the disease recurs years after the original infection. It is named after Nathan Brill, an American physician.

• BRITISH BROADCASTING CORPORATION

B-B-C is acceptable on all references within contexts such as a television or radio story. Otherwise, spell it out on the first reference.

• BRITISH COLUMBIA

The Canadian province bounded on the west by the Pacific Ocean. Do not abbreviate.

See **DATELINES.**

• BRITISH COMMONWEALTH

See **COMMONWEALTH, THE.**

• BRITAIN

Acceptable in all references for *Great Britain,* which consists of England, Scotland and Wales.

See **UNITED KINGDOM.**

• BRITISH, BRITON(S)

The people of Great Britain: *the English, the Scottish, the Welsh.*

• BRITISH AIRWAYS

The successor to British European Airways and British Overseas Airways Corporation.

Headquarters is in Hounslow, England.

• BRITISH THERMAL UNIT

The amount of heat required to increase the temperature of one pound of water one degree Fahrenheit.

B-T-U or *B-T-U's* is acceptable on the second reference.

• BRITISH TON

See **TON.**

• BRITISH VIRGIN ISLANDS

Use with a community name in datelines on stories from these islands.

Specify an individual island in the text if relevant.

See **DATELINES.**

• BROADCAST

The past tense also is *broadcast,* not *broadcasted.*

• BROADWAY, OFF-BROADWAY, OFF-OFF-BROADWAY

When applied to stage productions, these terms refer to distinctions made by union contracts, not to the location of a theater.

Actors Equity Association and unions representing craft workers have one set of pay scales for *Broadway* productions (generally those in New York City theaters of 300 or more seats) and a lower scale for smaller theaters, classified as *off-Broadway* houses.

The term *off-off-Broadway* refers to workshop productions that may use Equity members for a limited time at substandard pay. Other unions maintain a hands-off policy, agreeing with the Equity attitude that actors should have an opportunity to whet their talents in offbeat roles without losing their Equity memberships.

• BROCCOLI

• BRONZE AGE

The age characterized by the development of bronze tools and weapons, from 3500 to 1000 B-C. Regarded as coming between the Stone Age and the Iron Age.

• BROTHERHOOD OF RAILWAY, AIRLINE AND STEAMSHIP CLERKS, FREIGHT HANDLERS, EXPRESS AND STATION EMPLOYEES

The shortened form *Railway Employees union* is acceptable in all references.

Headquarters is in Rosemont, Illinois.

• BROWNOUT

See the **BLACKOUT, BROWNOUT** entry.

• BRUNET, BRUNETTE

Use *brunet* as a noun for males, and as the adjective for both sexes.

Use *brunette* as a noun for females.

• BRUSSELS SPROUTS

• B-T-U, B-T-U'S

See **BRITISH THERMAL UNIT.**

• BUDAPEST

The capital of Hungary. In datelines, follow it with *Hungary.*

Do not confuse it with *Bucharest,* which is the capital of *Romania.*

• BUDDHA, BUDDHISM

• BUG, TAP

A concealed listening device designed to pick up sounds in a room, an automobile and so on, is a *bug.*

A *tap* is a device attached to a telephone circuit to pick up conversations on the line.

• BUILD UP (v.) BUILDUP (n. and adj.)

• BULLET

See **WEAPONS.**

• BULLETIN

A one-sentence story of an extremely urgent nature. It is not merely a very important story. It should be an item of special interest and immediate urgency.

Bulletins are air-ready, and should be followed by longer, more detailed takes. Generally, a bulletin series should be followed by an *URGENT (TOPS)* or *(DETAILS)* piece.

The form:

B U L L E T I N (AP)
(NEW YORK) -- PRESIDENT REAGAN ...

Bulletins carry five bells.

• BULLFIGHT, BULLFIGHTER, BULLFIGHTING

• BULLPEN

One word, for the place where baseball pitchers warm up, and for a pen that holds cattle.

• BULL'S-EYE

• BUREAU, BUREAUCRAT, BUREAUCRACY

• BURGLARY, LARCENY, ROBBERY, THEFT

Legal definitions of *burglary* vary, but in general a *burglary* involves entering a building (not necessarily by breaking in) and remaining unlawfully with the intention of committing a crime.

Larceny is the legal term for the wrongful taking of property. Its nonlegal equivalents are *stealing* or *theft.*

Robbery in the legal sense involves the use of violence or threat in committing larceny. In a wider sense it means to plunder or rifle, and may thus be used even if a person was not present: *His house was robbed while he was away.*

Theft describes a larceny that did not involve threat, violence or plundering.

Usage Note: You *rob* a person, bank, house, etc., but you *steal* the money or the jewels.

• BUS, BUSES

Transportation vehicles. The verb forms: *bus, bused, busing.*

See **BUSS.**

• BUSHEL

Equal to four pecks or 32 dry quarts, it is the principal unit of measure used by farmers. The metric equivalent is 32-point-two liters.

To convert bushels to liters, multiply by 35-point-two (five bushels times 35-point-two equals 176 liters).

In stories involving farm exports, always convert the tonnage figure (usually given in metric tons) into bushels. The conversion factor varies.

There are 39-point-four bushels to every metric ton of corn. To convert to bushels, multiply the number of metric tons by 39-point-four.

There are 36-point-seven bushels of wheat to every metric ton. To convert to bushels, multiply the number of metric tons by 36-point-seven.

• BUSS, BUSSES

Kisses. The verb forms: *buss, bussed, bussing.*

See **BUS.**

• BY-

The rules in **PREFIXES** apply, but in general, no hyphen. Some examples:

BYLINE	BYPRODUCT
BYPASS	BYSTREET

• BYLAW

• BYLINES

Used in broadcast copy indicate the writer—as opposed to the reporter—of a story, script or news summary. Generally, the byline is placed at the top of the copy, under the title. The exception is the news summary, in which the byline follows a dash after the final item.

- **CABINET**

Each member of the president's cabinet heads a department within the executive branch. See **DEPARTMENT** for a listing of all U-S cabinet departments.

- **CABINET TITLES**

To avoid stumbling blocks in the copy, informalize titles whenever possible: *Agriculture Secretary Bob Bergland, Housing Secretary Patricia Harris.* But always use the first name of the official in the first reference.

See **TITLES.**

- **CACTUS, CACTUSES**

- **CADET**

See **MILITARY ACADEMIES.**

- **CAESAREAN SECTION**

- **CALIBER**

The form: *38-caliber pistol.*

Follow the rules in **NUMERALS.**

See **WEAPONS.**

- **CALL LETTERS**

Use hyphens to separate the letters of a broadcast station: *W-A-B-C, W-B-Z, K-N-X.* But do not use a hyphen between the call letters and the type of station: *W-N-B-C T-V, K-C-B-S Radio.*

Avoid the use of long strings of letters and numbers in stories referring to citizens band licenses or amateur radio unless the call is vital to the story.

- **CALL UP** (v.)
CALL-UP (n. and adj.)

- **CAMBODIA**

Use this name rather than *Democratic Kampuchea (kam-poo-chee'-uh)* in datelines. When *Kampuchea* is used in the story, it should be identified as the formal name of the nation.

- **CAMEROON** (KAM-UH-ROON')

Not *Camerouns* or *Cameroun.*

See **GEOGRAPHIC NAMES.**

- **CANADA**

Montreal, Ottawa, Quebec and *Toronto* stand alone in datelines. For all other datelines, use the city name and the name of the province or territory spelled out.

The ten provinces of Canada are Alberta, British Columbia, Manitoba, New Brunswick, Newfoundland (includes Labrador), Nova Scotia, Ontario, Prince Edward Island, Quebec and Saskatchewan.

The two territories are the Yukon and the Northwest Territories.

The provinces have substantial autonomy from the federal government.

The territories are administered by the federal government, although residents of the territories do elect their own legislators and representatives to Parliament.

See **DATELINES.**

- **CANADA GOOSE**

Not *Canadian goose.*

- **CANADIAN BROADCASTING CORPORATION**

C-B-C is acceptable on the second reference.

• **CANAL ZONE**
See **PANAMA CANAL ZONE.**

• **CANCEL, CANCELED, CANCELING, CANCELLATION**

• **CANNON, CANON**
A *cannon* is a weapon. See the **WEAPONS** entry.
A *canon* is a law or rule, particularly of a church.

• **CANNOT**
One word. *Can't* is just as good.

• **CAN'T HARDLY**
A double negative is implied. Better is: *can hardly.*

• **CANUCK** (CAN-UK')
It means a French Canadian, and often is considered a derogatory racial label. Avoid the word except in formal names (*the Vancouver Canucks,* a professional hockey team) or in quoted matter.
See the **NATIONALITIES AND RACES** entry.

• **CANVAS, CANVASS**
Canvas is heavy cloth.
Canvass is a noun and verb denoting a survey.

• **CAPE CANAVERAL, FLORIDA**
Formerly Cape Kennedy. It is the name of the cape on which the Kennedy Space Center is located.
See **JOHN F. KENNEDY SPACE CENTER** and **LYNDON B. JOHNSON SPACE CENTER.**

• **CAPITAL**
The city where a seat of government is located. See **CAPITOL.**
When used in a financial sense, *capital* describes money, equipment or property used in a business by a person or corporation.

• **CAPITAL GAIN, CAPITAL LOSS**
The difference between a capital asset cost and the price it brought when sold.

• **CAPITAL INVESTMENT**
The process of using money to buy goods, tools, equipment or real estate: major investments that are paid off over a period of time.

• **CAPITALIZATION**
For readability, broadcast copy is typed or printed in a completely upper-case format. There are, therefore, no capitalization rules.
Wire printers are designed to accommodate this format, and type out upper-case letters only—even if the character was lower-cased on the writing terminal.

• **CAPITOL**
The building in Washington: *The meeting was held on Capitol Hill, in the west wing of the Capitol Building.*
It can also refer to the building that houses state governments: *The Virginia Capitol,* as opposed to *Albany is the capital of New York.*
See **CAPITAL.**

• **CARAT, CARET, KARAT**
The weight of precious stones, especially diamonds, is expressed in *carats.* A carat is equal to 200 milligrams or about three grains.
A *caret* is a writer's and proofreader's mark.
The proportion of pure gold used with an alloy is expressed in *karats.*

• **CARBINE**
See **WEAPONS.**

• "CARE"

Acceptable in all references to *Co-operative for American Relief Everywhere, Incorporated.*

Headquarters is in New York.

• CAREFREE

• CARETAKER

• CARIBBEAN (KUH-RIB'-BEE-UHN)

See **WESTERN HEMISPHERE.**

• CARMAKER, CARMAKERS

• CAR POOL

• CARRY-OVER (n. and adj.)

• CASH ON DELIVERY

C-O-D is preferred in all references.

• CASTER, CASTOR

Caster is a roller.

Castor is the spelling for the oil and the bean from which it is derived.

• CATALOG, CATALOGED, CATALOGER, CATALOGING, CATALOGIST

• CATERPILLAR

The worm-like larva of various insects. Also a trademark for a brand of crawler tractor.

• CATHOLIC, CATHOLICISM

Use *Roman Catholic Church, Roman Catholic* or *Roman Catholicism* in first references to those who believe that the pope, as bishop of Rome, has the ultimate authority in administering an earthly organization founded by Jesus Christ.

Most subsequent references may be condensed to *Catholic Church, Catholic* or *Catholicism. Roman Catholic* should continue to be used, however, if the context requires a distinction between Roman Catholics and members of other denominations who often describe themselves as Catholic. They include some high church Episcopalians (who often call themselves *Anglo-Catholics*), members of Eastern Orthodox churches, and members of some national Catholic churches that have broken with Rome. Among churches in this last category are the Polish National Catholic Church and the Lithuanian National Catholic Church.

Those who use *Catholic* in a religious sense are indicating their belief that they are members of a universal church that Jesus Christ left on Earth.

• CAUCASIAN

• CAVE IN (v.)
CAVE-IN (n. and adj.)

• C-B-S

Acceptable in all references for *C-B-S Incorporated,* the former Columbia Broadcasting System.

Divisions include C-B-S News, C-B-S Radio and C-B-S T-V.

Headquarters is in New York.

• CEASE-FIRE, CEASE-FIRES (n. and adj.)

The verb form is *cease fire.*

• CELEBRANT, CELEBRATOR

Reserve *celebrant* for someone who conducts a religious rite: *He was the celebrant of the Mass.*

Use *celebrator* for someone having a good time: *The celebrators kept the party going until 3 a.m.*

• CELLOPHANE

Formerly a trademark, now a generic term.

• CELSIUS (SEL'-SEE-UHS)

Use this term rather than *centigrade* for the temperature scale that is part of the metric system.

The Celsius scale is named for Anders Celsius, a Swedish astronomer who designed it. In it, zero represents the freezing point of water, and 100 degrees is the boiling point (at sea level).

To convert to Fahrenheit, multiply a Celsius temperature by nine, divide the result by five, and add 32 (25 degrees celsius times nine equals 225, divided by five equals 45, plus 32 equals 77 degrees Fahrenheit).

When giving a Celsius temperature, use this form: *40 degrees celsius.* Do not abbreviate *celsius.*

See **FAHRENHEIT** and **METRIC SYSTEM** entries.

• CEMENT

Cement is the powder mixed with water and sand or gravel to make concrete. The proper term is *concrete* (not *cement*) *pavement, blocks and driveways.*

• CENSER, CENSOR, CENSURE

A *censer* is a container in which incense is burned.

To *censor* is to prohibit or restrict the use of something.

To *censure* is to condemn.

• CENTERFOLD

• CENTERS FOR DISEASE CONTROL

The centers, located in Atlanta, form the U-S Public Health Service's National agency for control of infectious and other preventable diseases. It works with state health departments to provide specialized services that they are unable to maintain on an everyday basis.

The normal form for first reference is *the National Centers for Disease Control. C-D-C* is acceptable on the second reference.

• CENTI-

A prefix denoting 100th of a unit. Thus, a centimeter is one 100th of a meter. To convert to the basic unit, move the decimal point two places to the left: 155-point-six centimeters equals one-point-55 meters.

• CENTIGRADE

See **CELSIUS.**

• CENTIMETER

One-hundredth of a meter.

There are ten milimeters in a centimeter. A centimenter is approximately the width of a large paper clip.

To convert to inches, multiply by four-tenths. For example, five centimeters times four-tenths equals two inches.

See **METER; METRIC SYSTEM** and **INCH.**

• CENTRAL AMERICA

See **WESTERN HEMISPHERE.**

• CENTRAL CONFERENCE OF AMERICAN RABBIS

See **JEWISH CONGREGATIONS.**

• CENTRAL INTELLIGENCE AGENCY

C-I-A is acceptable in all references.

The formal title for the individual who heads the agency is *Director of Central Intelligence.* But a preferable reference is simply *C-I-A Director.*

• CENTRAL STANDARD TIME (C-S-T), CENTRAL DAYLIGHT TIME (C-D-T)

See **TIME ZONES.**

• CENTS
See **MONETARY FIGURES.**

• CEYLON (SAY-LAHN')
It is now *Sri Lanka,* which should be used in datelines and other references to the nation.
The people may be referred to as *Ceylonese* (n. or adj.) or *Sri Lankans.* The language is *Sinhalese.*

• CHAIRMAN, CHAIRWOMAN
Do not use the more cumbersome *chairperson* unless it is an organization's formal title for an office.

• CHAMBER OF DEPUTIES
See **FOREIGN LEGISLATIVE BODIES.**

• CHANCELLOR
The translation to English for the first minister in the governments of West Germany and Austria.
See the **PREMIER, PRIME MINISTER** entry and **TITLES.**

• CHANGEABLE

• CHANGEOVER

• CHANGE UP (v.)
CHANGE-UP (n. and adj.)

• CHARACTER, REPUTATION
Character refers to moral qualities.
Reputation refers to the way a person is regarded by others.

• CHARISMATIC GROUPS
See **RELIGIOUS MOVEMENTS.**

• CHARLESTON, CHARLESTOWN, CHARLES TOWN
Charleston is the name of the capital of West Virginia and of a port city in South Carolina.
Charlestown is a section of Boston.
Charles Town is the name of a small city in West Virginia.

• CHAUFFEUR

• CHAUVINISM (SHOH'-VAN-ISM), **CHAUVINIST**
It means unreasoning devotion to a characteristic or thing, such as one's race, sex, or country, with contempt for other races, sexes or countries.
The terms come from Nicolas Chauvin, a soldier of Napoleon the First, who was famous for his devotion to the lost cause.

• CHECK UP (v.)
CHECKUP (n.)

• CHEMICAL MACE
A trademark, usually shortened to *Mace,* for a brand of tear gas that is packaged in an aerosol cannister and temporarily stuns its victims.

• CHEVY
Not *Chevie* or *Chevvy.* This nickname for *Chevrolet* should be used only in automobile features or in quoted matter.

• CHICAGO
The city in Illinois stands alone in datelines.

• CHICANO (CHEE-KAHN'-OH)
Although not always derogatory, *Chicano* should be avoided as a routine description for American citizens or residents of Mexican descent. *Mexican-Americans* is preferred.
Some say *Chicano* resulted from Indian attempts to pronounce *Mexicano.* Others say its origin is a derisive description that Mexicans used for what they regarded as the chicanery of bureaucrats during the French rule of Mexico.

Chicano has been adopted by some social activists of Mexican descent, and may be used when activists use it to describe themselves. To apply it to all Spanish-surnamed citizens would be roughly the same as calling all blacks Muslims.

See the **NATIONALITIES AND RACES** entry.

• CHIEF JUSTICE

The office-holder is the *chief justice of the United States,* not of the Supreme Court.

The other justices are *associate justices,* but may be called simply *justices* in all references.

See **JUDGE.**

• CHIEF PETTY OFFICER

See **MILITARY TITLES.**

• CHIEF WARRANT OFFICER

See **MILITARY TITLES.**

• CHILE

The nation.

• CHILI, CHILIES

The peppers.

• CHILLY

Moderately cold.

• CHINA

When used alone, it refers to the mainland nation. Use it in datelines and other routine references.

Use *People's Republic of China, Communist China, mainland China* or *Red China* only in direct quotations or when needed to distinguish the mainland and its government from Taiwan.

For datelines on stories from the island of Taiwan, use the name of a community and *Taiwan.* In the body of a story, use *Nationalist China* or *Taiwan* for references to the government based on the island. Use the formal name of the government, *the Republic of China,* when required for legal precision.

• CHINAMAN

A patronizing term. Confine it to quoted matter.

• CHINESE NAMES

Drop the apostrophes sometimes used: *Chiang Kai-shek,* not *K'ai-shek.*

The family name usually comes first: *Mao* in second reference to *Mao Tse-tung.* If you are unsure which is the family name, a good rule of thumb is that surnames are never hyphenated, while given names often are.

Some Chinese have westernized the names, putting their given names or the initials for them first: *P.Y. Chen, Jack Wang.*

When translating a name into English, use letters that yield the closest phonetic equivalent in English. If an individual has a preferred English spelling, use it. Always use pronouncers.

• CHRISTIAN CHURCH (DISCIPLES OF CHRIST)

The parentheses and the words they surround are part of the formal name.

The body owes its origins to an early 19th century frontier movement to unify Christians.

The Disciples, led by Alexander Campbell in western Pennsylvania, and the Christians, led by Barton Stone in Kentucky, merged in 1832.

The local church is the basic organizational unit.

National policies are developed by the General Assembly, made up of representatives chosen by local churches and regional organizations. The regional units certify the standing of ministers and provide help and counsel to ministers and congregations.

The church lists more than one (m) million members.

Beliefs: The church allows for varied opinions and stresses freedom of interpretation, based on the historic conviction that there is no creed but Christ and no saving doctrines except those of the New Testament.

Clergy: All members of the clergy may be referred to as *ministers. Pastor* applies if a minister leads a congregation.

On first reference, use *the Reverend* before the name of a man or woman. On second reference, use only the last name of a man; use *Miss, Mrs.* or *Ms.* before the last name of a woman depending on her preference.

See **RELIGIOUS TITLES.**

• CHRISTIAN METHODIST EPISCOPAL CHURCH

See **METHODIST CHURCHES.**

• CHRISTIAN SCIENCE CHURCH

See **CHURCH OF CHRIST, SCIENTIST.**

• CHRISTMAS, CHRISTMAS DAY

December 25th. The federal legal holiday is observed on Friday if December 25th falls on a Saturday, on Monday if it falls on a Sunday.

Never abbreviate *Christmas* to *Xmas* or any other form.

• CHURCHES OF CHRIST

Approximately 18-thousand independent congregations, with a total American membership of more than two (m) million, cooperate under this name. They sponsor numerous educational activities, primarily radio and television programs.

Each local church is autonomous and operates under a governing board of elders. The minister is an evangelist, addressed by members as *Brother.* The ministers do not use clergy titles. Do not precede their names by a title.

The churches do not regard themselves as a denomination. Rather, they stress a non-denominational effort to preach what they consider basic Bible teachings. The churches also teach that baptism is an essential part of the salvation process.

See **RELIGIOUS MOVEMENTS.**

• CHURCH OF CHRIST, SCIENTIST

This denomination was founded in 1879 by Mary Baker Eddy, who attributed her recovery from an illness to insights she gained from reading Scripture.

The Mother Church in Boston is the international headquarters. Its board of directors guides all the approximately 32-hundred churches throughout the world.

A branch church, governed by its own democratically chosen board, is named First Church of Christ, Scientist, or Second Church, according to the order of its establishment in a community.

The terms *Christian Science Church* or *Churches of Christ, Scientist,* are acceptable in all references to the denomination.

Beliefs: Christian Science describes God as the source of all real being, so that nothing except what he has created can ultimately be real. Death, disease and sin are regarded as having no real existence because they are not created by God. Scripture is cited as evidence that a true understanding of God heals sickness as well as sin.

The principal beliefs are contained in "Science and Health With Key to the Scriptures," the denominational textbook written by Mrs. Eddy.

The word *Christian* is used because New Testament writings are an integral element of the denomination's teachings. The word *science* denotes the concept that reality can be understood and proved in Christian experience.

A distinction is made between Christ, regarded as the divine nature or godliness of Jesus, and Jesus, regarded as the human Wayshower and Exemplar of man's sonship with God.

Clergy: The church is composed entirely of lay members and does not have clergy in the usual sense. Either men or women may hold the three principal offices—*reader, practitioner* or *lecturer.*

The terms *Pastor* and *Minister* are not applicable. Do not use *The Reverend* in any reference.

• CHURCH OF ENGLAND

See ANGLICAN COMMUNION.

• CHURCH OF JESUS CHRIST OF LATTER-DAY SAINTS

Note the punctuation of *Latter-day. Mormon Church* is acceptable in all references.

The church is based on revelations that Joseph Smith said were brought to him in the 1820's by heavenly messengers.

After Smith's death in 1844, his followers split into factions, the largest of them the Church of Jesus Christ of Latter-day Saints. Led West by Brigham Young, they founded Salt Lake City, Utah in 1847.

Today, the church headquarters there directs more than 65-hundred congregations with more than three (m) million members worldwide.

Church hierarchy is composed of men known as general authorities. Among them, the policy-making body is the First Presidency, made up of a president and two or more counselors. It has final authority in all spiritual and worldly matters.

The Council of the Twelve Apostles, primarily an advisory body, helps the First Presidency direct church activities. When the church president dies, the First Presidency is dissolved and the Council of the Twelve Apostles selects a new president, traditionally the man who is the senior apostle in the council. He then chooses his counselors.

Other general authorities include the church patriarch, a spiritual adviser; a three-member Presiding Bishopric, which administers temporal affairs; and the First Quorum of Seventy, in charge of missionary work. Women may not become general authorities.

The church's basic geographical units are called stakes. They are governed by a stake presidency, made up of a president and two counselors, and a stake high council. Individual congregations within a stake are called wards. Missions, which oversee members where there are no stakes, are headed by a president and may include one or more congregations known as branches.

Beliefs: Mormons believe that Jesus Christ established one church on earth, that it was taken away upon his death and not restored until the revelations to Smith. They believe that Jesus came to America after his Resurrection, visiting its people, who had immigrated to the continent in ancient times.

Among the revelations were directions to gold plates that Smith said he found on Hill Cumorah, near Palmyra, New York. He taught that the plates, left by a prophet who lived some time after Jesus, contained the records of the people Jesus had visited in America and the true word of God.

The "Book of Mormon," written by Smith, contains what members believe are his translation of the hieroglyphics on the plates. The plates were later returned to Moroni, the heavenly messenger who led Smith to them. Smith also wrote the "Book of Doctrine and Covenants" and the "Pearl of Great Price." These three books and the Bible are the key church documents, although revelation is considered to continue today through members of the First Presidency.

Clergy: All faithful male members over the age of eleven are members of the priesthood and may attain positions of leadership in the all-lay clergy. Younger members go through a series of ranks from deacon to teacher to priest before becoming elders sometime after their 18th birthdays. They may later become seventies or high priests. A high priest may become a bishop or one of two bishop's counselors, who lead local congregations.

The only formal titles are *president* (for the head of the First Presidency), *bishop* (for members of the Presiding Bishopric and for local bishops) and *elder* (for other general authorities and church missionaries).

The terms *minister* or *the Reverend* are not used.

See **RELIGIOUS TITLES.**

Splinter Groups: The term *Mormon* is not properly applied to the other Latter Day Saints churches that resulted from the split after Smith's death.

The largest is the Reorganized Church of Jesus Christ of Latter Day Saints (note the lack of a hyphen), with headquarters in Independence, Missouri. It was founded by Smith's son Joseph the Third, and claims to be the continuation of the original church. It has about one-thousand churches and 150-thousand members.

• C-I-A

Acceptable in all references for *Central Intelligence Agency.*

• CIGARETTE

• CINCINNATI

The city in Ohio stands alone in datelines.

• CITIBANK

The former First National City Bank. The parent holding company is Citicorp of New York.

It is the second-largest bank in the nation.

• CITIES AND TOWNS

There are legal, political and legislative differences between cities, towns and villages. When in doubt, check a gazeteer.

Community is acceptable on second reference for any of these terms.

See **DATELINES** for guidelines on when they should be followed by a state or county name.

Spell out the names of cities unless in direct quotes: *A trip to Los Angeles,* but: *"We're going to L-A."*

• CITIZEN, RESIDENT, SUBJECT, NATIONAL, NATIVE

A *citizen* is a person who has acquired the full civil rights of a nation either by birth or naturalization. Cities and states in the United States do not confer citizenship. To avoid confusion, use *resident,* not *citizen,* in referring to inhabitants of states and cities.

Subject is the term used when the government is headed by a monarch or other sovereign.

National is applied to a person residing away from the nation of which he is a citizen, or to a person under the protection of a specified nation.

Native is the term denoting that an individual was born in a given location.

• CITIZENS BAND

No apostrophe after the *s. C-B* is acceptable on second reference.

The term describes a group of frequencies set aside by the Federal Communications Commission for local use at low power by individuals or businesses.

• CITY COMMISSION

See the next entry.

• CITY COUNCIL

Generally, the basic governing body of a city. But use the proper name if the body is not known as a city council: *The Miami City Commission, the commission, the city commission, the Louisville Board of Aldermen, the Board of Aldermen, the board, the aldermen.*

But use *city council* in the generic sense for plural references: *the city councils of Boston, Miami and Louisville.*

• CIVIL AERONAUTICS BOARD

C-A-B is acceptable on second reference.

See **FEDERAL AVIATION ADMINISTRATION**

• CIVIL CASES, CRIMINAL CASES

A *civil case* is one in which an individual, business or agency of government seeks damages or relief from another individual, business or agency of government. Civil actions generally involve a charge that a contract has been breached or that someone has been wronged or injured.

A *criminal case* is one that a state or the federal government brings against an individual charged with committing a crime.

• CLEAN UP (v.)
CLEANUP (n. and adj.)

• CLEVELAND

The city in Ohio stands alone in datelines.

• CLOSED SHOP

A *closed shop* is an agreement between a union and an employer that requires workers to be members of the union before they may be employed.

A *union shop* requires workers to join the union within a specified period after they are employed.

An *agency shop* requires that the workers who do not want to join the union pay the union a fee instead of union dues.

A *guild shop,* a term often used when the union is The Newspaper Guild, is the same as a *union shop.*

See the **RIGHT-TO-WORK** entry for an explanation of how some states prohibit contracts that require workers to join unions.

• CLOSE-UP (n. and adj.)

• CLOTURE

Not *closure,* for the parliamentary procedure for closing debate.

Whenever practical, use a phrase such as *closing debate* or *ending debate* instead of the technical term.

• CO-

Retain the hyphen when forming nouns, adjectives and verbs that indicate occupation or status:

CO-AUTHOR
CO-CHAIRMAN
CO-DEFENDANT
CO-HOST
CO-OWNER
CO-PARTNER
CO-PILOT
CO-RESPONDENT (in a divorce suit)
CO-SIGNER
CO-STAR
CO-WORKER

(Several are exceptions to Webster's New World in the interests of consistency.)

Use no hyphen in other combinations:

COEDUCATIONAL
COEQUAL
COEXIST
COEXISTENCE
COOPERATE
COOPERATIVE
COORDINATE
COORDINATION

Cooperate, coordinate and related words are exceptions to the rule that a hyphen is used if a prefix ends in a vowel and the word that follows begins with the same vowel.

• COASTAL WATERS

See **WEATHER TERMS**.

• COAST GUARDSMAN

Note spelling.

• COASTLINE

• COCAINE

The slang term *coke* should appear only in quoted matter.

Cocaine is *taken, inhaled or used.* Use the slang term *snorted* only in quoted matter.

• C-O-D

Acceptable in all references for *cash on delivery* or *collect on delivery.*

• COLLATERAL

Stock or other property that a borrower is obliged to turn over to a lender if unable to repay a loan.

See **LOAN TERMINOLOGY.**

• COLLECTIVE NOUNS

Nouns that denote a unit take singular verbs and pronouns: *class, committee, crowd, family, group, herd, jury, orchestra, team.*

Some usage examples: *The committee is meeting to set its agenda. The jury reached its verdict. A herd of cattle was sold.*

Plural in Form: Some words that are plural in form become collective nouns and take singular verbs when the group or quantity is regarded as a unit.

Right: *A thousand bushels is a good yield.* (A unit.)

Right: *A thousand bushels were created.* (Individual items.)

Right: *The data is sound.* (A unit.)

Right: *The data have been carefully collected.* (Individual items.)

• COLLECTORS' ITEM

• COLLEGE

A *university* consists of several *colleges.* But the term *college* can be used in the generic sense to refer to higher education: *More people are going to college this year than last.*

Consult special sections of the Webster's New World Dictionary for lists of junior colleges, colleges and universities in the United States.

• COLLEGE OF CARDINALS

See **ROMAN CATHOLIC CHURCH.**

• COLLIDE, COLLISION

Two objects must be in motion before they can *collide.* An automobile cannot *collide* with a utility pole, for example; it simply *hits* it.

• COLLOQUIALISMS

Because of the conversational tone of most broadcast writing, many colloquialisms are acceptable in most contexts. In all instances, the tone and subject of the story should be the ultimate guide: the lighter the story, the more acceptable colloquialisms will be.

The term itself describes the informal—but not necessarily substandard—use of language.

Webster's New World lists some colloquialisms as substandard; these should not be used.

Sometimes, colloquialisms are particularly useful in the lead of a story, to catch the mood or essence of the event. In such cases, the lead must be supported by a full exposition of the event.

See the **DIALECT** and **WORD SELECTION** entries.

• COLON

A colon is used at the end of a phrase or sentence to introduce material that is directly related. The most frequent use of the colon is to introduce lists, texts and quotations.

Emphasis: The colon can be effective in giving emphasis: *He had only one hobby: eating.*

Introducing Quotations: Use a comma to introduce a direct quotation of one sentence that remains within a paragraph. Use a colon to introduce longer quotations within a paragraph and to end all paragraphs that introduce a paragraph of quoted material.

Placement with Quotation Marks: Colons go outside quotation marks unless they are part of the quotation itself.

Times: Use colons in direct clock readings: *1:30 this morning.* See the **TIMES** entry.

Miscellaneous: Do not combine a dash and a colon.

• COLORED

In some societies, including the United States, the word is considered derogatory and should not be used.

In some countries of Africa, it is used to denote individuals of mixed racial ancestry. Whenever the word is used, place it in quotation marks and provide an explanation of its meaning.

See **AFRICAN.**

• COLUMBIA BROADCASTING SYSTEM

Legally speaking, it no longer exists. See **C-B-S.**

• COLUMBIA LIPPINCOTT GAZETTEER OF THE WORLD, THE

The reference, after Webster's New World Dictionary, for geographic names not covered in this book.

• COLUMBUS DAY

October 12th. The federal legal holiday is the second Monday in October.

• COMBAT, COMBATED, COMBATING

• COMEDIAN

Use for both men and women.

• COMMA

The following guidelines treat some of the most frequent questions about the use of commas. Additional guidelines on specialized uses are provided in separate entries.

For more detailed guidance, consult "The Comma" and "Misused and Unnecessary Commas" in the Guide to Punctuation section in the back of Webster's New World Dictionary.

In a Series: Use commas to separate element in a series, but do not put a comma before the conjunction in a simple series: *The flag is red, white and blue. He would nominate Tom, Dick or Harry.*

Put a comma before the concluding conjunction in a series, however, if an integral element of the series requires a conjunction: *I had orange juice, toast, and ham and eggs for breakfast.*

Use a comma also before the concluding conjunction in a complex series of phrases: *The main points to consider are whether the athletes are skillful enough to compete, whether they have the stamina to endure the training, and whether they have the proper mental attitude.*

See the **DOUBLE DASH** and **SEMICOLON** entries for cases when elements of a series contain internal commas.

With Equal Adjectives: Use commas to separate a series of adjectives equal in rank. If the commas could be replaced by the word *and* without changing the sense, the adjectives are equal: *a thoughtful, precise manner; a dark, dangerous street.*

Use no comma when the last adjective before a noun outranks its predecessors because it is an integral element of a noun phrase, which is the equivalent of a single noun: *a cheap fur coat* (the noun phrase is *fur coat*); *the old oaken bucket; a new, blue spring bonnet.*

With Non-Essential Clauses: See the **ESSENTIAL CLAUSES, NON-ESSENTIAL CLAUSES** entry.

With Non-Essential Phrases: See the **ESSENTIAL PHRASES, NON-ESSENTIAL PHRASES** entry.

With Introductory Clauses and Phrases: A comma normally is used to separate an introductory clause or phrase from a main clause: *When he had tired of the mad pace of New York, he moved to Dubuque.*

The comma may be omitted after short introductory phrases if no ambiguity would result: *During the night he heard many noises.*

But use the comma if its omission would slow comprehension: *On the street below, the curious gathered.*

With Conjunctions: When a conjunction such as *and, but* or *for* links two clauses that could stand alone as separate sentences, use a comma before the conjunction in most cases: *She was glad she had looked, for a man was approaching the house.*

As a rule of thumb, use a comma if the subject of each clause is expressely stated: *We are visiting Washington, and we also plan a side trip to Williamsburg. We visited Washington, and our senator greeted us personally.* But no comma when the subject of the two clauses is the same and is not repeated in the second: *We are visiting Washington and plan to see the White House.*

The comma may be dropped if two clauses with expressly stated subjects are short. In general, however, favor use of a comma unless a particular literary effect is desired or it would distort the sense of a sentence.

Introducing Direct Quotes: Use a comma to introduce a complete, one-sentence quotation within a paragraph: *Wallace said, "She spent six months in Argentina and came back speaking English with a Spanish accent."* But use a colon to introduce quotations of more than one sentence. See **COLON.**

Do not use a comma at the start of an indirect or partial quotation: *He said his victory put him "firmly on the road to a first-ballot nomination."*

Before Attribution: Use a comma instead of a period at the end of a quote that is followed by attribution: *"Rub my shoulders," Miss Cawley suggested.* Such "hanging attribution" should be used only in special instances.

With Hometowns and Ages: Do not use commas to set off ages or hometowns instead of the words *who is* or *of.*

Wrong: *Mary Richards, 48, was there.*

Right: *Mary Richards, who is 48, was there.*

Wrong: *Mary Richards, New York, was there.*

Right: *Mary Richards of New York was there,* or *Mary Richards, who is from New York, was there.*

Names of States and Nations Used with City Names: *His journey will take him from Dublin, Ireland, to Fargo, North Dakota, and back.*

With Yes and No: *Yes, I will be there.*

In Direct Address: *Mother, I will be home late. No, sir, we have no bananas.*

Separating Similar Words: In those rare instances when duplicate words occur next to each other, use a comma to separate them: *The question is, is there life on Mars?* These constructions are, however, best avoided.

Placement with Quotes: Commas always go inside quotation marks.

See **SEMICOLON.**

• COMMITMENT

• COMMODITY

When used in a financial sense, the word describes the products of mining and agriculture before they have undergone extensive processing.

• COMMON MARKET

Acceptable in all references for *European Economic Community.*

The nine members, as of 1981: Belgium, France, West Germany, Italy, Luxembourg, Netherlands (the original six), Denmark, Ireland, United Kingdom.

• COMMON STOCK, PREFERRED STOCK

An ownership interest in a corporation.

If other classes of stock are outstanding, the holders of common stock are the last to receive dividends and the last to receive payments if a corporation is dissolved. The company may raise or lower common stock dividends as its earnings rise or fall.

When preferred stock is outstanding and company earnings are sufficient, a fixed dividend is paid. If a company is liquidated, holders of preferred stock receive payments up to a set amount before any money is distributed to holders of common stock.

• COMMONWEALTH

A group of people united by their common interests.

See **STATE.**

• COMMONWEALTH, THE

Formerly, the British Commonwealth. The members of this free association of sovereign states recognize the British sovereign as head of the Commonwealth. Some also recognize the sovereign as head of their states; others do not.

The members are: Australia, Bahamas, Bangledesh, Barbados, Botswana, Canada, Cyprus, Fiji, Gambia, Ghana, Grenada, Guyana, India, Jamaica, Kenya, Lesotho, Malawi, Malaysia, Malta, Mauritius, New Zealand, Nigeria, Papua New Guinea, St. Lucia, Seychelles, Sierra Leone, Singapore, Sri Lanka, Swaziland, Tanzania, Tonga, Trinidad and Tobago, Uganda, United Kingdom, Western Samoa and Zambia. Nauru, a special member, participates in activities but not in meetings of government heads.

• COMMUNICABLE DISEASE CENTER

The former name of the *Centers for Disease Control.* See entry under that name.

• COMMUNICATIONS SATELLITE CORPORATION

"Comsat" is acceptable on second reference. Headquarters is in Washington.

• COMMUNICATIONS WORKERS OF AMERICA

The shortened form *Communications Workers Union* is acceptable in all references. But do not use the abbreviation *C-W-A.*

Headquarters is in Washington.

• COMMUNISM, COMMUNIST

See the **POLITICAL PARTIES AND PHILOSOPHIES** entry.

• COMMUTATION

See the **PARDON, PAROLE, PROBATION** entry.

• COMPANY NAMES

Consult the company or *"Standard and Poor's Register of Corporations"* if in doubt about a formal name.

Do not use a comma before *incorporated* or *limited,* and do not abbreviate those terms or *company* or *corporation.*

• COMPARED TO, COMPARED WITH

Use *compared to* when the intent is to assert, without the need for elaboration, that two or more items are similar: *She compared her work for women's rights to Susan B. Anthony's campaign for women's suffrage.*

Use *compared with* when juxtaposing two or more items to illustrate similarities and-or differences: *His time was two hours, eleven minutes and ten seconds, compared with two hours, 14 minutes for his closest competitor.*

• COMPATIBLE

• COMPLACENT, COMPLAISANT

Complacent means self-satisfied.

Complaisant means eager to please. Don't use it.

• COMPLEMENT, COMPLIMENT

Complement is a noun and verb denoting completeness or the process of supplementing something: *The ship has a complement of 200 sailors and 20 officers. The hat complements her dress.*

Compliment is a noun or verb that denotes praise or the expression of courtesy: *The captain complimented the sailors. She was flattered by the compliments on her outfit.*

• COMPLEMENTARY, COMPLIMENTARY

The husband and wife have complementary careers.

She received complimentary tickets to the show.

• COMPOSE, COMPRISE, CONSTITUTE

Compose means to create or put together. It commonly is used in both the active and passive voices: *He composed a song. The United States is composed of 50 states. The zoo is composed of many animals.*

Comprise means to contain, to include all or embrace. It is best used only in the active voice, followed by a direct object. *The United States comprises 50 states. The jury comprises five men and seven women. The zoo comprises many animals.*

Constitute, in the sense of form or make up, may be the best word if neither *compose* nor *comprise* seems to fit: *Fifty states constitute the United States. Five men and seven women constitute the jury. A collection of animals can constitute a zoo.*

Use *include* when what follows is only part of the total: *The price includes breakfast. The zoo includes lions and tigers.*

• COMPOSITION TITLES

Apply the guidelines listed here to book titles, movie titles, opera titles, play titles, poem titles, song titles, television program titles, and the titles of lectures, speeches and works of art.

—Put quotation marks around the names of all such works except the Bible.

—Translate a foreign title into English unless the work is widely known in the United States under its foreign name.

Examples:

"The Star-Spangled Banner," "Webster's New World Dictionary," "Gone With The Wind," "The C-B-S Evening News," The N-B-C T-V "Today" Program.

• COMPOUND ADJECTIVES

See the **HYPHEN** entry.

• COMPTROLLER, CONTROLLER

Comptroller generally is the accurate word for government financial officers.

The U-S comptroller of the currency is an appointed official in the Treasury Department who is responsible for the chartering, supervising and liquidation of banks organized under the federal government's National Bank Act.

Controller generally is the proper word for financial officers of businesses and for other positions such as aircraft controller.

There is no difference in pronunciation.

• CONCLAVE

A private or secret meeting. In the Roman Catholic Church it describes the private meeting of cardinals to elect a pope.

• CONCRETE

See **CEMENT.**

• CONFEDERATE STATES OF AMERICA

The formal name for the states that seceded during the Civil War. The shortened form *the Confederacy* is acceptable in all references.

• CONFESS, CONFESSED

In some contexts the words may be erroneous.

See **ADMIT.**

• CONFIRMATION

See **SACRAMENTS.**

• CONGLOMERATE

A corporation that has diversified its operations, usually by acquiring enterprises in widely varied industries.

• CONGO

In datelines, give the name of the city followed by *The Congo:*

(BRAZZAVILLE, THE CONGO) --

Similarly, in stories, make it *the Congo.*

• CONGREGATIONALIST CHURCHES

The word *Congregational* still is used by some individual congregations. The principal national body that used the term dropped it in 1961 when the Evangelical and Reformed Church merged with the Congregational Christian Churches to form the United Church of Christ. It has some one (m) million, 800-thousand members.

The word *church* is correctly applied only to an individual local church. Each such church is responsible for the doctrine, ministry and ritual of its congregation.

The local churches also appoint delegates to associations. Their functions include recognizing local churches, promoting cooperation among the churches, and the licensing, ordination, installation and dismissal of ministers.

Conferences, generally organized along state lines, recognize associations and specialize in missionary and educational work.

A general synod, made up of delegates elected by associations and conferences, is designed primarily to discuss questions of concern to all the churches and to handle communications with other denominations.

A small body of churches that did not enter the United Church of Christ is known as the National Association of Congregational Churches. Churches in the association have more than 100-thousand members.

Beliefs: Jesus is regarded as man's savior, but no subscription to a set creed is required for membership. Emphasis is placed on the value of having persons band together for common worship and to help each other lead religious lives.

Clergy: Members of the clergy are known as *ministers. Pastor* applies if a minister leads a congregation.

On first reference, use *the Reverend* before the name of a man or woman. Do not carry the title through on subsequent references.

• CONGRESS

Although *Congress* sometimes is used as a substitute for the House, it properly is reserved for reference to both the Senate and House. However, *congressman* is acceptable for members of the House. See that entry.

• "CONGRESSIONAL DIRECTORY"

Use this as the reference source for questions about the federal government that are not covered in this handbook.

• "CONGRESSIONAL RECORD"

A daily publication of the proceedings of Congress including a complete stenographic report of all remarks and debates.

• CONGRESSMAN, CONGRESSWOMAN

Use only in references to members of the House of Representatives.

See **LEGISLATIVE TITLES.**

• CONGRESS OF RACIAL EQUALITY

"CORE" is acceptable on second reference.

Headquarters is in New York.

• CONNOTE, DENOTE

Connote means to suggest or imply something beyond the explicit meaning: *To some persons, the word marriage connotes too much restriction.*

Denote means to be explicit about the meaning: *The word demolish denotes destruction.*

• "CONRAIL"

This acronym is acceptable in all references to *Consolidated Rail Corporation.*

A private, for-profit corporation, Conrail was set up by Congress in 1976 to reorganize and consolidate six bankrupt Northeast railroads—the Penn Central, the Erie Lackawanna, Reading, Central of New Jersey, Lehigh Valley, and Lehigh and Hudson River.

The legislation provided for a two (b) billion dollar federal loan to the corporation and set a phased schedule of repayments. A total of 25 (m) million shares of common stock were created, but the shares were not made available for public trading. Instead, the shares were issued in the names of voting trustees chosen to represent the individuals designated as the ultimate recipients after the settlement of litigation over the value of the property that Conrail took over.

Do not confuse *"Conrail"* with *"Amtrak"* (see separate entry). However, the legislation that set up Conrail also provided for Amtrak to gradually acquire from Conrail some of the property that had been owned by the bankrupt railroads.

Headquarters is in Philadelphia.

• CONSENSUS

• CONSERVATIVE
See the **POLITICAL PARTIES AND PHILOSOPHIES** entry.

• CONSERVATIVE JUDAISM
See **JEWISH CONGREGATIONS.**

• CONSTITUTE
See the **COMPOSE, COMPRISE, CONSTITUTE** entry.

• CONSUL, CONSUL GENERAL, CONSULS GENERAL

• CONSULATE
A *consulate* is the residence of a consul in a foreign city. It handles the commercial affairs and personal needs of citizens of the appointing country.

See **EMBASSY** for the distinction between a consulate and an embassy.

• CONSUMER PRICE INDEX
A measurement of changes in the retail prices of a constant marketbasket of goods and services. It is computed by comparing the cost of the marketbasket at a fixed time with its cost at subsequent or prior intervals.

The U-S Consumer Price Index is issued monthly by the Bureau of Labor Statistics, an agency of the labor department. It should not be referred to as a *cost-of-living index*, since it does not include the impact of taxes or the changes in buying patterns that result from inflation. It is, however, the basis for computing cost-of-living raises in many union contracts.

Use *index* on second reference; avoid using the abbreviation *C-P-I.*

• CONSUMER PRODUCT SAFETY COMMISSION
Do not use the abbreviation *C-P-S-C.*

• CONTAGIOUS

• CONTEMPTIBLE

• CONTINENT
The seven continents, in order of their land size: Asia, Africa, North America, South America, Europe, Antarctica and Australia.

• CONTINENTAL AIRLINES
Headquarters is in Los Angeles.

• CONTINENTAL DIVIDE
The ridge along the Rocky Mountains that separates rivers flowing east from those that flow west.

• CONTINENTAL SHELF, CONTINENTAL SLOPE
The *shelf* is the part of a continent

that is submerged in relatively shallow sea at gradually increasing depths, generally up to about 600 feet below sea level.

The *continental slope* begins at the point where the descent to the ocean bottom becomes very steep.

• CONTINUAL, CONTINUOUS

Continual means a steady repetition, over and over again: *The merger has been the source of continual litigation.*

Continuous means uninterrupted, steady, unbroken: *All she saw ahead of her was a continuous stretch of desert.*

• CONTRACTIONS

Contractions reflect informal speech and writing, and therefore are appropriate to many broadcast stories, depending upon the subject and tone.

The most commonly used contractions are *isn't, aren't* and those formed with the word *is* and *not*: *He's going to school, they won't stop him.*

The best rule of thumb is: Use contractions in circumstances where they reflect the way a phrase commonly occurs in speech.

See **AMERICANISMS; COLLOQUIALISMS; QUOTATIONS IN THE NEWS;** and **WORD SELECTION.**

• CONTRASTED TO, CONTRASTED WITH

Use *contrasted to* when the intent is to assert, without the need for elaboration, that two items have opposite characteristics: *He contrasted the appearance of the house today to its ramshackle look last year.*

Use *contrasted with* when juxtaposing two or more items to illustrate similarities and/or differences: *He contrasted the Republican platform with the Democratic platform.*

Memory Aid: See the **COMPARED TO, COMPARED WITH** entry. The same principal applies here.

• CONTROL, CONTROLLED CONTROLLING

• CONTROLLER

See the **COMPTROLLER, CONTROLLER** entry.

• CONTROVERSIAL

An overused word; avoid it. See **NON-CONTROVERSIAL.**

• CONVERTIBLE BOND

See **LOAN TERMINOLOGY.**

• CONVICT (v.)

Follow with the preposition *of*, not *for*: *He was convicted of murder.*

• CONVINCE, PERSUADE

You may be *convinced that* something or *of* something. You must be persuaded *to do* something.

Right: *The robbers persuaded him to open the vault.*

Wrong: *The robbers convinced him to open the vault.*

Right: *The robbers convinced him that it was the right thing to do.*

Wrong: *The robbers persuaded him that it was the right thing to do.*

• COOKIE, COOKIES

• COOPERATE, COOPERATIVE

But *co-op* as a short form of *cooperative*, to distinguish it from *coop*, a cage for animals.

• COORDINATE, COORDINATION

• COP

Often a derogatory term for *police officer*. Confine it to quoted matter.

• COPTER

Acceptable shortening of *helicoper.* But use it only as a noun or adjective. It is not a verb.

• COPYRIGHT (n., v. and adj.)

The disclosure was made in a copyright story.

Use *copyrighted* only as the past tense of the verb: *He copyrighted the article.*

• CO-RESPONDENT

In a divorce suit.

• CORN BELT

The region in the north central Midwest where much corn and corn-fed livestock are raised. It extends from western Ohio to eastern Nebraska and northeastern Kansas.

• CORPORATION

An entity that is treated as a person in the eyes of the law. It is able to own property, incur debts, sue, and be sued.

Do not use the abbreviation *corp.* in any context.

• CORPS

The possessive form is *corps'* for both singular and plural: *one corps' location, two corps' assignments.*

• CORRAL, CORRALLED, CORRALLING

• CORRECTIONAL INSTITUTION

See the **PRISON, JAIL** entry.

• CORRECTION

The function of a wire correction is to enable the broadcaster to easily identify the offending story and fix the error invloved.

Because of the very short deadlines in radio, all wire corrections must move with great speed—and provide substitute sentences, paragraphs or stories.

The proper form for a correction:

C O R R E C T I O N

IN THE FIFTH SUMMARY, SECOND TAKE, THIRD ITEM, READ SECOND SENTENCE X X X THE PRESIDENT SAYS HE WILL NOT ABANDON HIS SUPPORT OF THE TREATY., ETC. X X X (RESTORING DROPPED WORD "ABANDON").

THE AP

See **SUBS.**

• CORSICA (KAWR'-SIH-KUH)

Use instead of *France* in datelines on stories from communities on this island.

• CORTES (KAWR'-TEHS)

The Spanish parliament.

See **FOREIGN LEGISLATIVE BODIES.**

• COSMONAUT

The applicable occupational term for Soviet astronauts.

• CO-STAR

• COST OF LIVING

The amount of money needed to pay taxes and to buy the goods and services deemed necessary to make up a given standard of living, taking into account changes that may occur in tastes and buying patterns.

The term often is treated incorrectly as a synonym for the *Consumer Price Index*, which does not take taxes into account and measures only price changes, keeping the quantities constant over time.

Hyphenate when used as an compound modifier: *The cost of living went up, but he did not receive a cost-of-living raise.*

See the **CONSUMER PRICE INDEX** and **INFLATION** entries.

• COST-PLUS

• COTTON BELT

The region in the South and Southeastern sections of the United States where much cotton is grown.

• COUNCIL, COUNCILOR, COUNCILMAN, CONUCILWOMAN

A deliberative body and those who are members of it.

See the **COUNSEL** entry and **LEGISLATIVE TITLES.**

• COUNCIL OF ECONOMIC ADVISERS

A group of advisers who help the president prepare his annual economic report to Congress and recommend economic measures to him throughout the year.

• COUNSEL, COUNSELED, COUNSELING, COUNSELOR, COUNSELOR AT LAW

To counsel is to advise. A *counselor* is one who advises.

A *counselor at law* (no hyphens for consistency with *attorney at law*) is a lawyer. See **LAWYER.**

• COUNTER-

The rules in **PREFIXES** apply, but in general, no hyphen. Some examples:

COUNTERACT	COUNTER-PROPOSAL
COUNTERCHARGE	COUNTERSPY
COUNTERFOIL	

• COUNTY

See **GOVERNMENTAL BODIES.**

• COUNTY COURT

In some states, it is not a court, but the administrative body of a county. In most cases, the "court" is presided over by a "county judge," who is not really a judge in the traditional sense, but is instead the chief administrative officer of the county.

The terms should be explained if they are not clear in the context.

Do not use *judge* alone before a name except in direct quotations when an administrative rather than judicial official is involved.

Examples:

(SEVIERVILLE, TENNESSEE) -- A reluctant county court approved a school budget today that calls for a 15-percent tax increase for property owners.

The chief administrative officer, County Judge Ray Reagan, says ...

• COUP D'ETAT (KOO DAY TAH)

The word *coup* usually is sufficient for the overthrow of a government.

• COUPLE

When used in the sense of two persons, the word takes plural verbs and pronouns: *The couple were married Saturday and left Sunday on their honeymoon. They will return in two weeks.*

In the sense of a single unit, use a singular verb: Each couple was asked to give ten dollars.

• COUPLE OF

The *of* is necessary. Never use *a couple tomatoes* or a similar phrase.

The phrase takes a plural verb in constructions such as: *A couple of tomatoes were stolen.*

• COURT DECISIONS

Use figures, hyphens, and the word *to*: *The Supreme Court ruled 5-to-4 that schools be desegregated.*

• COURT DISTRICTS

See **COURT NAMES.**

• COURTESY TITLES
The rule is readability: Use whichever construction is clearest.

In general, do not use the courtesy titles *Miss, Mr., Mrs. or Ms.* in the first reference. Instead, use the first and last names of the person: *Betty Ford, Jimmy Carter.*

Do not use courtesy titles in other references unless needed to distinguish among people with the same last name.

If a woman's courtesy titles is used, go with the person's expressed preference: *Miss, Mrs., Ms.*

• COURTHOUSE
One word, except in the proper names of some communities: *Appomattox Court House, Virginia.*

• COURT-MARTIAL, COURT-MARTIALED, COURTS-MARTIAL

• COURT NAMES
See **JUDICIAL BRANCH** and separate listings under *U-S* and the court name.

See **JUDGE** for guidelines on titles before the names of judges.

• COURT OF ST. JAMES'S
Note the *'s.* The formal name for the royal court of the British sovereign. Derived from St. James's Palace, the former scene of royal receptions.

• COURTROOM

• COVER UP (v.)
COVER-UP (n. and adj.)
He tried to cover up the scandal. He was prosecuted for the cover-up.

• CRACK UP (v.)
CRACK-UP (n. and adj.)

• CRAWFISH
Not *crayfish.* An exception to Webster's New World based on the dominant spelling in Louisiana, where it is a popular delicacy.

• CRIMINAL CASES
See the **CIVIL CASES, CRIMINAL CASES** entry.

• CRISIS, CRISES

• CRISS-CROSS

• CRITERION, CRITERIA

• CROSS COUNTRY
No hyphen, an exception to Webster's New World based on the practices of American and international governing bodies for this sport.

• CROSS-EXAMINE, CROSS-EXAMINATION

• CROSS-EYE (n.)
CROSS-EYED (adj.)

• CROSS-FIRE

• CROSSOVER (n. and adj.)

• CROSS SECTION (n.)
CROSS-SECTION (v.)

• CUB SCOUTS
See **BOY SCOUTS.**

• CUCKOO CLOCK

• CUP
Equal to eight fluid ounces. The approximate metric equivalents are 240 milliliters or 24-hundredths of a liter.

To convert to liters, multiply the number of cups by point-two-four (14 cups times 24-hundredths equals three-point-three-six liters).

See **LITER.**

- **CUPFUL, CUPFULS**
Not *cupsful.*

- **CURE-ALL**

- **CURRENCY DEPRECIATION, CURRENCY DEVALUATION**
A nation's money *depreciates* when its value falls in relation to the currency of other nations or in relation to its own prior value.
A nation's money *is devalued* when its government deliberately reduces its value in relation to the currency of other nations.
When a nation devalues its currency, the goods it imports tend to become more expensive. Its exports tend to become less expensive in other nations and thus more competitive.

- **CURTAIN-RAISER**

- **CUT BACK** (v.)
CUTBACK (n. and adj.)
He cut back spending. The cutback will require frugality.

- **CUT OFF** (v.)
CUTOFF (n. and adj.)
He cut off his son's allowance. The cutoff date for applications is Monday.

- **CYCLONE**
See WEATHER TERMS.
It also is the trademark for a brand of chain-link fence.

- **CYNIC, SKEPTIC**
A *skeptic* is a doubter.
A *cynic* is a disbeliever.

- **CZAR**
Not *tsar.* It was a formal title only for the ruler of Russia and some other Slavic nations.

• DACRON

A trademark for a branch of polyester fiber.

• DALAI LAMA (DAH'-LEE LAH-MAH)

The traditional high priest of Lamaism, a form of Buddhism practiced in Tibet and Mongolia. *Dalai Lama* is a title rather than a name, but it is all that is used when referring to that person.

• DALLAS

The city in Texas stands alone in datelines.

• DALLES, THE

A city in Oregon.

• DAMAGE, DAMAGES

Damage is destruction: *Officials say damage from the storm will total more than a (b) billion dollars.*

Damages are awarded by a court as the compensation for injury or loss: *The woman received 25-thousand dollars in damages.*

• DAMN IT

Use instead of *dammit,* but like other profanity it should be avoided unless there is a compelling reason.

See the **OBSCENITIES, PROFANITIES, VULGARITIES** entry.

• DANGLING MODIFIERS

Avoid modifiers that do not refer clearly and logically to some word in the sentence.

Dangling: *Taking our seats, the game started.* (*Taking* does not refer to the subject, *game,* nor to any other word in the sentence.)

Correct: *Taking our seats, we watched the opening of the game.* (*Taking* refers to *we,* the subject of the sentence.)

• DARK AGES

The period beginning with the sack of Rome and ending with the early Renaissance (476 to about 1450). The term is derived from the idea that this period in Europe was characterized by intellectual stagnation, widespread ignorance and poverty.

• DASH

A dash (--*dash*--) is used to indicate a place where a story may be wrapped up without the loss of any essential information. Matter below the dash is expendable, but provides background and detail for those broadcasters needing it.

The copy above a dash must stand alone. Always put a dash on a separate line, indented.

For the punctuation mark (--), see **DOUBLE DASH.**

• DATA

A plural noun, it normally takes plural verbs and pronouns.

See the **COLLECTIVE NOUNS** entry, however, for an example of when *data* may take singular verbs and pronouns.

• DATE LINE

Two words for the imaginary line that separates one day from another.

See the **INTERNATIONAL DATE LINE** entry.

• DATELINES

Datelines on the Radio Wire serve a different function than on the print wires. When printed in a newspaper, a dateline immediately tells the reader where the story came from, making it unnecessaary to repeat that information in the body of the story:

NEW ORLEANS (AP)—An oil-drilling platform exploded in flames 60 miles south of here in the Gulf of Mexico Sunday night.

But datelines don't work that way on the Radio Wire, because broadcasters do not read the datelines aloud. Therefore, the location of the event *must* be included in the body of the text.

(NEW ORLEANS) -- An oil-drilling platform exploded in flames tonight, about 60 miles south of New Orleans in the Gulf of Mexico.

Never use "here" in a Radio Wire story. And always remember to say where the event occurred, whether there's a dateline on the story or not.

Note also the different form used for datelines on the Radio Wire. They are in parentheses, with no AP logo, followed by a double dash.

Datelines are being steadily phased out of the AP broadcast report. In 1980, they were dropped entirely from the national News Watch summaries. However, they are still used in state summaries in many areas because of local member preferences.

They are still used on most separates filed by the national Broadcast Desk.

Domestic Datelines: A list of domestic cities that stand alone in datelines follows. The norms that influenced the selection were the population of the city, the population of its metropolitan region, the frequency of the city's appearance in the news, the uniqueness of its name, and experience that has shown the name to be almost synonymous with the state or nation where it is located.

No state with the following:

ATLANTA	MIAMI
BALTIMORE	MILWAUKEE
BOSTON	MINNEAPOLIS
CHICAGO	NEW ORLEANS
CINCINNATI	NEW YORK
CLEVELAND	OKLAHOMA CITY
DALLAS	PHILADELPHIA
DENVER	PITTSBURGH
DETROIT	ST. LOUIS
HONOLULU	SALT LAKE CITY
HOUSTON	SAN DIEGO
INDIANAPOLIS	SAN FRANCISCO
KANSAS CITY	SEATTLE
LOS ANGELES	WASHINGTON

Also HOLLYWOOD, when used instead of LOS ANGELES on stories about films and the film industry.

Stories from all other American cities should have both the city and the state name in the dateline.

Regional Circuits: On state wires, it is generally assumed that a city which stands alone is in the state in question.

(SPRINGFIELD) -- Governor Jim Thompson today signed a bill giving Illinois State Troopers the right to retire after 20 years of service.

(LA JUNTA) -- A Denver man and his son were injured today when a boulder fell on them while they were skiing on a cross-country trail.

However, state broadcast editors should be sure to add the state to the dateline when sending a story to adjacent states, even if the story is sent as part of a summary.

Springfield, Quincy, Columbia, Washington, Lincoln, etc., are extremely common names; it is essential to add the state identification to all but the largest cities when sending stories out of state.

Foreign Cities: These foreign locations stand alone in datelines:

BERLIN	MONTREAL
GIBRALTAR	MOSCOW
GUATEMALA CITY	OTTAWA
HAVANA	PARIS
HONG KONG	PEKING
JERUSALEM	QUEBEC
KUWAIT	ROME
LONDON	SAN MARINO
LUXEMBOURG	SINGAPORE
MACAO	TOKYO
MEXICO CITY	TORONTO
MONACO	VATICAN CITY

In addition, use UNITED NATIONS alone in stories from U.N. headquarters.

Canadian Datelines: Datelines on stories from Canadian cities other than Montreal, Ottawa, Quebec and Toronto should contain the name of the city followed by the name of the province. Do not abbreviate any province or territory name.

Soviet Datelines: Datelines on stories from Soviet cities other than Moscow should contain the name of the city followed by *Soviet Union.*

Other Foreign Nations: Stories from other foreign cities that do not stand alone in datelines should contain the name of the country or territory (see the next section) spelled out.

Island Nations and Territories: When reporting from nations and territories that are made up primarily of islands but commonly are linked under one name, use the city name and the general name in the dateline. Identify an individual island, if needed, in the text.

Examples:

BRITISH VIRGIN ISLANDS
INDONESIA
NETHERLANDS ANTILLES
PHILIPPINES

Overseas Territories: Some overseas territories, colonies and other areas that are not independent nations commonly have accepted separate identities based on their geographic character or special status under treaties. In these cases, use the commonly accepted territory name after a city name in a dateline.

Examples:

BERMUDA	GUAM
CANAL ZONE	MARTINIQUE
CORSICA	PUERTO RICO
FAEROE ISLANDS	SARDINIA
GREENLAND	SICILY
GRENADA	SIKKIM
GUADELOUPE	TIBET

Spelling and Choice of Names: In most cases, the name of the nation in a dateline is the conventionally accepted short form of its official name: *Argentina,* for example, rather than *Republic of Argentina.* (If in doubt, look for an entry in this book. If none is found, follow Webster's New World Dictionary.)

Note these special cases:

—Instead of *United Kingdom,* use *England, Northern Ireland, Scotland* or *Wales.*

—For divided nations, use the commonly accepted names based on geographic distinctions: *East Germany, West Germany, North Korea, South Korea.*

—Use an article only with *El Salvador.* For all others, use just a country name—*Gambia, Netherlands, Philippines,* etc.

See **GEOGRAPHIC NAMES** for guidelines on spelling the names of foreign cities and nations not listed here or in separate entries.

• DATELINE SELECTION

A dateline should indicate the city in which the basic information for the story was gathered.

For example, a story filed by the Washington AP bureau takes a Washington dateline. But if a local radio station in Chicago carries a report by its Washington correspondent, the story should carry a Chicago dateline when it is picked up by the AP.

Any story contributed by a broadcast member should carry the dateline of the city where the member gathered the story, if he was physically present there.

For example, if a station in Springfield, Missouri, contributes a Joplin story which it covered by phone, the story takes a Springfield dateline. If the Springfield station sent a reporter to Joplin, and he personally covered the event, the story then takes a Joplin dateline.

A foreign dateline should be used only if the information in a story was obtained by a full- or part-time correspondent who was physically present in the dateline community.

If a foreign radio broadcast monitored in another city was the source of information, use the dateline of the city where the monitoring took place and mention that fact in the story.

When a story has been assembled from sources in widely separated areas, use no dateline.

For example, if the Atlanta bureau does a round-up of storm damage in the South, it should carry no dateline.

Pronouncers: If a city or nation in a dateline needs a pronouncer, put the pronouncer in the body of the story, at the first reference to the place name. Do not put it in the dateline.

• DATES

The guidelines are similar to those for NUMERALS:

—For the *first* through the *eleventh* of the month, spell out the date.

—For the *12th* through the *31st,* use arabic figures and the appropriate suffix.

See MONTHS for examples and punctuation guidelines.

• DAUGHTER-IN-LAW, DAUGHTERS-IN-LAW

• DAUGHTERS OF THE AMERICAN REVOLUTION

D-A-R is acceptable on the second reference.

Headquarters is in Washington.

• DAYLIGHT-SAVING TIME

Not *savings.* Note the hyphen.

When linking the term with the name of a time zone, use only the word *daylight: Eastern Daylight Time.*

A federal law, administered by the Transportation Department, specifies that daylight time applies from 2 a-m on the last Sunday of April to 2 a-m on the last Sunday of October in areas that do not specifically exempt themselves.

See TIME ZONES.

• DAY-LONG

• DAYS OF THE WEEK

Do not abbreviate them.

See TIME ELEMENT.

• DAYTIME

• DAY TO DAY, DAY-TO-DAY

Hyphenate when used as a compound modifier: *They have extended the contract on a day-to-day basis.*

• D-C-TEN

• D-DAY

June sixth, 1944, the day the Allies invaded Europe in World War Two.

• D-D-T

Preferred in all references to the insecticide *dichlorodiphenyltrichloro-*

ethane (dy-klaw'-roh-dy-fee'-nil-try'-klaw-roh-eh-thayn).

• **DE-**
See **FOREIGN PARTICLES.**

• **DEAD END** (n.)
DEAD-END (adj.)
She reached a dead end. He has a dead-end job.

• **DEAF-MUTE**
This term may be used, but the preferred form is to say that an individual cannot hear or speak. A *mute* person may be deaf or may be able to hear.

Do not use *deaf and dumb.* Do not use *hearing-impaired.*

• **DEATHBED** (n. and adj.)

• **DEBENTURE**
See **LOAN TERMINOLOGY.**

• **DECADES**
Use Arabic figures to indicate decades of history.

For the 20th Century, only the decade itself is needed. Do not use an apostrophe to the left of the figures, but do use one to the right—along with an *s: The Roaring 20's, the 50's.*

For all previous centuries, use the century as well as the decade number: *The 1890's, the 1760's.*

In special references, which are widely known, the century may be dropped, as in *The Gay 90's.*

• **DECI-**
A prefix denoting one-tenth of a unit.

Move the decimal point one place to the left in converting to the basic unit: 15-point-five decigrams equals one-point-55 grams.

• **DECIMAL UNITS**
All decimal amounts should be spelled out, following the guidelines in **NUMERALS.**

Spell out the word *point* and surround it with hyphens: *five-point-three, point-two, point-oh-one.*

Decimalization should not exceed two places in textual material unless there are special circumstances.

For clarity, decimals also can be expressed in terms of tenths: *three-point-two equals three and two-tenths.* In these cases, hyphenate the number of tenths: *two-tenths of an inch, four and a-tenth meters.*

See **FRACTIONS** and **MONETARY FIGURES.**

• **DEEP-SEA** (adj.)

• **DEEP SOUTH**
The region consists of Alabama, Georgia, Louisiana, Mississippi and South Carolina.

• **DEEP WATER** (n.)
DEEP-WATER (adj.)
The creature swam in deep water. The ship needs a deep-water port.

• **DEFAULT**
See **LOAN TERMINOLOGY.**

• **DEFENDANT**

• **DEFENSE**
Do not use it as a verb.

• **DEFENSE SPENDING**
Military spending usually is the more precise term.

• **DEFINITELY**
Overused as a vague intensifier. Avoid it.

• **DEGREE-DAY**
See **WEATHER TERMS.**

• DEGREES
See **ACADEMIC DEGREES**.

• DEK-, DEKA-
A prefix denoting ten units of a measure. Use *dek-* before words starting with a vowel and *deka-* before words starting with a consonant.

Move a decimal point one place to the right to convert to the basic unit: 15-point-six dekameters equals 156 meters.

• DELAWARE
Has a land area of two-thousand, 57 square miles. Only Rhode Island is smaller in area, with one-thousand, 49 square miles.

• DELEGATE
The formal title for members of the lower houses of some legislatures.

See **LEGISLATIVE TITLES**.

• DELTA AIR LINES
Headquarters is in Atlanta.

• DEMAGOGUE, DEMAGOUGUERY
Not *demagog*.

• DEMOCRAT, DEMOCRATIC, DEMOCRATIC PARTY

• DEMOCRATIC GOVERNORS' CONFERENCE
Note the apostrophe.

• DEMOLISH, DESTROY
Both mean to do away with something completely. Something cannot be *partially demolished or destroyed*. It is redundant to say *totally demolished* or *totally destroyed*.

• DENOTE
See the **CONNOTE, DENOTE** entry.

• DENVER
The city in Colorado stands alone in datelines.

• DEPART
Follow it with a preposition: *He will depart from LaGuardia. She will depart at 11:30 a-m.*

Do not drop the preposition as some airline dispatchers do.

• DEPARTMENTS OF: AGRICULTURE, COMMERCE, DEFENSE, EDUCATION, ENERGY, HEALTH AND HUMAN SERVICES, HOUSING AND URBAN DEVELOPMENT, THE INTERIOR, JUSTICE, LABOR, STATE, TRANSPORTATION, THE TREASURY
The basic governmental departments in the executive branch. Each one is headed by a Cabinet secretary.

Informalize the names on all references: *the agriculture department, the housing department.*

Do not abbreviate any department names except *Housing and Urban Development:* the acronym *"HUD"* is acceptable as an adjective: *The "HUD" grants will total 50 (m) million dollars.*

See **CABINET TITLES**.

• DEPENDENT (n. and adj.)
Not *dependant*.

• DEPRECIATION
The reduction in the value of capital goods due to wear and tear or obsolescence.

Estimated depreciation may be deducted from income each year as one of the costs of doing business.

• DEPRESSION

A severe decline in economic conditions, generally characterized by extremely high unemployment and a falloff in business activity.

The *Great Depression* refers to the worldwide economic hard times generally regarded as having begun with the stock market collapse of October 28th and 29th, 1929.

• DEROGATORY TERMS

Do not use derogatory terms such as *krauts* (for Germans) or *niggers* (for Negroes) except in direct quotes, and then only when their use is an integral, essential part of the story.

See the **OBSCENITIES, PROFANITIES, VULGARITIES** entry and **WORD SELECTION.**

• -DESIGNATE

Hyphenate: *chairman-designate, secretary-designate.*

Avoid this usage whenever possible. Instead, use a phrase such as, *the man expected to be named chairman, the president's choice for the secretary's job.*

• DESTROY

See the **DEMOLISH, DESTROY** entry.

• DETAILS

A *details piece* is a separate that runs no more than 40 seconds and provides background and depth to a spot news item.

Details pieces are datelined, and take a story and details slug:

HOSTAGES (DETAILS)

• DETENTE (DAY-TAHNT')

• DETENTION CENTER

See the **PRISON, JAIL** entry.

• DETROIT

The city in Michigan stands alone in datelines.

• DEVALUATION

See the **CURRENCY DEPRECIATION, CURRENCY DEVALUATION** entry.

• DEXEDRINE

A trademark for a brand of appetite suppressant. It also may be called *dextroamphetamine sulfate.*

• DIALECT

The form of language peculiar to a region or a group, usually in matters of pronunciation or syntax.

Dialect should be avoided at all costs, especially on broadcast circuits. It can be referred to but should not be quoted: *Jimmy Carter's soft Southern drawl was a marked change from the flat Midwestern accent of his predecessor.*

Remember: Everyone has an accent, whether he knows it or not. Do not make gratuitous references to a person's regionalisms, unless they are absolutely necessary to the story.

Atlanta police say the ransom demand came from a caller with a New England accent.

See **AMERICANISMS; COLLOQUIALISMS; QUOTES IN THE NEWS;** and **WORD SELECTION.**

• DIALOGUE (n.)

Never use it as a verb.

• DIARRHEA

• DICTAPHONE

A trademark for a brand of dictation recorder.

Dictation machine is the generic term.

DICTIONARIES

For spelling, style and usage questions not covered in this handbook, consult Webster's New World Dictionary of the American Language, second college edition.

Use the first spelling listed in Webster's New World unless a specific exception is listed in this book. Keep in mind that most of the exceptions listed here are tailored for the requirements of broadcast copy.

If Webster's provides different spellings in separate entries, use the spelling that is followed by a full definition.

If there is no listing in either this book or Webster's New World, the backup dictionary, with more listings, is Webster's Third New International Dictionary.

Webster's New World also is the first reference for geographical names not covered in the handbook.

See **GEOGRAPHIC NAMES.**

DIE-HARD (n. and adj.)

DIET

The Japanese parliament.

See **FOREIGN LEGISLATIVE BODIES.**

DIETITIAN

Not *dietician.*

DIFFERENT

Takes the preposition *from,* not *than.*

DIFFER FROM, DIFFER WITH

To differ from means to be unlike.

To differ with means to disagree.

DILEMMA

It means more than a problem. It implies a choice between two unattractive alternatives.

DIMENSIONS

Spell out such measurements as *inches, feet, yards, meters and millimeters* to indicate depth, height, length and width. Follow the rules for **NUMERALS,** and hyphenate only the adjectival forms before nouns. Use commas to separate units.

Examples:

He is five feet, six inches tall. The five-foot-six man. The new center is a seven-footer.

The storm left five inches of snow. It was a 150-mile trip.

DIOCESE

See **EPISCOPAL CHURCH** and **ROMAN CATHOLIC CHURCH.**

DIS-

The rules in **PREFIXES** apply, but in general, no hyphen. Some examples:

DISMEMBER	DISSERVICE
DISSEMBLE	DISSUADE

DISC JOCKEY

This term has fallen into disrepute in many circles. Most performers who host music programs prefer to be called *air personalities* or just *announcers.*

Never use it to refer to broadcast journalists. Call them *newsmen* or *newswomen,* or just *reporters.*

Most news advisories on the Radio Wire should be directed to the *News Director,* who is generally the person in charge of the station's news department.

The person in charge of the station is usually the *General Manager.*

The *Program Director* is in charge of programming, sometimes including news, sometimes specifically excluding news.

• **DISCREET, DISCRETE**

Discreet means prudent, circumspect: *"I'm afraid I was not very discreet," she wrote.*

Discrete means detached, separate: *There are four discrete sounds from a quadraphonic system.*

• **DISCUS**

The disk thrown in track and field events.

• **DISSOCIATE**

Not *disassociate.*

• **DISTANCES**

Follow the rules in **NUMERALS.**

See also **DIMENSIONS.**

• **DISTANT EARLY WARNING LINE**

A series of radar stations near the 70th parallel in North America.

On second reference, *the "DEW" line.*

• **DISINTERESTED, UNINTERESTED**

Disinterested means impartial, which is usually the better word to convey the thought.

Uninterested means that someone lacks interest.

• **DISPEL, DISPELLED, DISPELLING**

• **DISPOSABLE PERSONAL INCOME**

The income that a person retains after deductions for income taxes, Social Security taxes, property taxes and for other payments such as fines and penalties to various levels of government.

• **DISTRICT ATTORNEY**

The prosecutor in many jurisdictions. Sometimes called the *County Attorney* or *State's Attorney.*

D-A is acceptable on second reference.

• **DISTRICT COURT**

See **COURT NAMES.**

• **DISTRICT OF COLUMBIA**

Abbreviate as D-C when the context requires that it be used in conjunction with *Washington.* In such cases, it does not take a comma.

The term should be spelled out when it is used alone: *the District of Columbia has a unique form of government.*

In both cases, *the District,* rather than *D-C,* should be used in subsequent references.

• **DIVE, DIVED, DIVING**

Not *dove* for the past tense.

• **DIVIDED NATIONS**

See **DATELINES** and entries under the names of nations such as **EAST GERMANY** and **SOUTH KOREA.**

• **DIVIDEND**

In a financial sense, the word describes the payment per share that a corporation distributes to its stockholders as their return on the money they have invested in its stock.

See **PROFIT TERMINOLOGY.**

• **DIVISION**

See the **ORGANIZATIONS AND INSTITUTIONS** entry; **MILITARY UNITS;** and **POLITICAL DIVISIONS.**

• **DIVORCEE** (DUH-VAWR-SAY')

The fact that a woman has been divorced should be mentioned only if a similar story about a man would mention his marital status.

When the woman's marital status is relevant, it seldom belongs in the lead. Avoid stories that begin: *A 35-year-old divorcee ...*

The perferred form is to say in the body of the story that a woman is divorced.

• DOCTOR

Always use the term on the first reference to a person who holds a doctor of medicine degree. If appropriate to the context, it may also be used on the first reference to an individual who holds another type of doctoral degree. But because the public frequently associates the title *doctor* with physicians, care should be taken to assure that the individual's specialty is stated close to the reference.

Do not use *doctor* in subsequent references.

• DOLLARS

Always spell out, following the guidelines in **MONETARY FIGURES.**

For specified amounts, the word takes a singular verb: *he said 500-thousand dollars is what they want.*

• DOMINO, DOMINOES

• DOOR TO DOOR, DOOR-TO-DOOR

Hyphenate when used as a compound modifier: *He is a door-to-door salesman.*

But: *He went from door to door.*

• DOUBLE DASH (--)

Single hyphens are used to connect two or more letters or words. Double dashes are used to imply an abrupt change in thought, and as a visual symbol to set off datelines, dashes and breaks.

Follow these guidelines:

Abrupt Changes: Use a double dash to denote an abrupt change in thought in a sentence. It gives the broadcaster the visual clue that an emphatic pause is called for: *We will fly to Paris in June -- if I get a raise. Smith offered a plan -- an unprecedented one -- to raise revenues.*

Series within a Phrase: When a phrase that otherwise would be set off with commas contains a series of words that must be separated by commas, use double dashes to set off the full phrase: *He listed the qualities -- intelligence, charm, wit -- that he liked in women.*

In Lists: Double dashes should be used to introduce individual sections of a list. Each of the sections must be full sentences.

Example:

Jones gave the following reasons:
-- He never ordered the package.
-- If he did, it didn't come.
-- If it did, he sent it back.

With Spaces: Put a space on both sides of a double dash in all uses except at the start of a paragraph.

In datelines:

(*NEW YORK*) --

In breaks and dashes:

--BREAK--

--DASH--

Location on Keyboard: On most typewriters, the double dash is indicated by typing two hyphens. On most video display terminals, it may be done the same way—or by the single keystroke of the double-dash key.

• DOUGHNUT

Not *donut.*

• DOW JONES AND COMPANY

The company publishes the "Wall Street Journal" and "Barron's National Business and Financial Weekly." It also operates the Dow Jones News Service.

For stock market watchers, it provides the Dow Jones industrial average, the Dow Jones transportation average, the Dow Jones utility average, and the Dow Jones composite average.

Headquarters is in New York.

No hyphens.

• DOWN-

The rules in **PREFIXES** apply, but in general, no hyphen. Some examples:

DOWNGRADE
DOWNTOWN

• -DOWN

Follow Webster's New World. Some examples, all nouns and/or adjectives:

BREAKDOWN	RUNDOWN
COUNTDOWN	SIT-DOWN

All are two words when used as verbs.

• DOWN EAST

Use only in reference to Maine.

• DOWN UNDER

Australia, New Zealand and environs.

• DRAFT BEER

Not *draught beer.*

• DRAMAMINE (DRAM'-UH-MEEN)

A trademark for a brand of motion sickness remedy.

• DRESSING ROOM

• DRIVE-IN (n.)

• DROP OUT (v.)
DROPOUT (n.)

• DROUGHT (DROWT)

• DROWNED, WAS DROWNED

If a person suffocates in water or other fluid, the proper statement is that the individual *drowned.* To say that someone *was drowned* implies that another person caused the death by holding the victim's head under the water.

• DRUGS

Because the word *drugs* has come to be used as a synonym for narcotics in recent years, *medicine* is frequently the better word to specify that an individual is taking medication.

• DRUNK, DRUNKEN

Drunk is the spelling of the adjective used after a form of the verb *to be. He was drunk.*

Drunken is the spelling of the adjective used before nouns: *a drunken driver, drunken driving.*

• DRUNKENNESS

• DUEL

A contest between two people. Three people cannot duel.

• DUFFEL

Not *duffle.*

• DU PONT, E.I.

Note that the second name of the French-born American industrialist is two words.

The company named after him is *E.I. Du Pont de Nemours and Company* of Wilmington, Delaware, The shortened reference *Du Pont* is acceptable on all references.

See **FOREIGN PARTICLES.**

• DUST STORM

See **WEATHER TERMS.**

• DYED-IN-THE-WOOL (adj.)

• DYEING, DYING

Dyeing refers to changing colors.
Dying refers to death.

- **EACH**

Takes a singular verb.

- **EACH OTHER, ONE ANOTHER**

Two persons look at *each other.* *More than two look at one another.*

Either phrase may be used when the number is indefinite: *We help each other. We help one another.*

- **EARL, COUNTESS**

See **NOBILITY.**

- **EARMARK**

- **EARNINGS PER SHARE**

See **PROFIT TERMINOLOGY.**

- **EARTHQUAKES**

Hundreds of earthquakes occur each year. Most are so small they cannot be felt.

First reports on major earthquakes often come from the National Earthquake Information Service operated by the U-S Geological Survey in Golden, Colorado, or the Uppsala Seismological Institute in Uppsala, Sweden.

There are two important scales in measuring earthquakes, the Richter scale and the Mercalli scale.

The difference between them is what they measure. The Richter scale, the more common, provides information on the magnitude—the inherent strength—of a quake. The Mercalli scale describes the intensity of a quake—the degree to which it is felt in a given area.

Dr. Charles Richter, whose work in the 1930's led to the scale that bears his name, illustrates the difference by comparing a quake to a radio signal: The magnitude of the signal is the same no matter where you are. Its intensity varies depending on your distance from the transmitter.

Richter Scale: The Richter scale is a gauge of the energy released by an earthquake, as measured by the ground motion recorded on a seismograph.

Every increase of one number, say from magnitude five-point-five to six-point-five, means that the ground motion is ten times greater. Some experts say the actual amount of energy released may be 30 times greater.

Theoretically, there is no upper limit to the scale, although it is often erroneously reported to be ten. Readings of eight-point-nine, the highest on record, were computed from seismographic records of a quake off the coast of Ecuador in 1906 and from a quake off the coast of Japan in 1933.

A quake of magnitude two is the smallest normally felt by humans.

The relationship between a Richter reading and the potential for damage in populated areas is as follows:

—A quake of magnitude three-point-five can cause slight damage.

—Magnitude four: can cause moderate damage.

—Magnitude five: can cause considerable damage.

—Magnitude six: can cause severe damage.

—Magnitude seven: a major earthquake, capable of widespread and heavy damage.

—Magnitude eight: a "great"

earthquake, capable of causing tremendous damage.

Early in 1977, a group of scientists suggested a new way to compute Richter readings. Officials of the National Earthquake Information Service and similar bodies said they would study the proposal. The method of providing Richter readings would not change, they said, at least until agreement on a new format could be reached through an international conference or similar forum.

Mercalli Scale: The Mercalli scale gauges the intensity of an earthquake as felt in a specific location.

The scale runs from one to 12. A reading of one is "not felt except by a very few, favorably situated." A 12 reading is "damage total, lines of sight disturbed, objects thrown into the air."

Notable Quakes: Earthquakes noted for both their magnitude and the amount of damage they caused include:

—Shensi province of China, January 1556: killed 830-thousand people, the largest number of fatalities on record from an earthquake.

—Tokyo and Yokohama, Japan, September 1923: highest Richter reading was later computed at eight-point-three. The quake and subsequent fires destroyed most of both cities, killing an estimated 200-thousand people. Until the China quake of 1976, this was the highest death toll in the 20th century.

—San Francisco, April 1906: highest Richter reading later computed at eight-point-three. The quake and fires were blamed for an estimated 700 deaths.

—Alaska, March 1964: Highest Richter reading eight-point-five. Killed 114 people.

—Guatemala, February 1976: Highest Richter reading was seven-point-five. Officials reported more than 23-thousand deaths.

—Hopeh province of northern China, July 28th, 1976: Highest Richter reading eight-point-three. A government document later said 655-thousand, 237 people were killed, and 779-thousand were injured. The fatality toll was second only to that of the Shensi quake of 1556.

Other Terms: The word *temblor*—not *tremblor*—is a synonym for *earthquake*. The word *epicenter* means the center of an earthquake.

• EASTER

In the computation used by the Latin rite of the Roman Catholic Church and by Protestant churches, it falls on the first Sunday after the first full moon that occurs on or after March 21st. If the full moon falls on a Sunday, Easter is the next Sunday.

Easter may fall, therefore, between March 22nd and April 25th inclusive.

• EASTERN AIRLINES

Headquarters is in New York.

• EASTERN HEMISPHERE

The half of the earth made up primarily of Africa, Asia, Australia and Europe.

• EASTERN ORTHODOX CHURCHES

The term applies to a group of churches that have roots in the earliest days of Christianity and do not recognize papal authority over their activities.

Churches in this tradition were part of the undivided Christendom that existed until the Great Schism of 1054. At that time, many of the churches in the western half of the old Roman Empire accorded the bishop of Rome supremacy over other bishops. The result was a split between eastern and western churches.

The autonomous churches that constitute Eastern Orthodoxy are organized along mostly national lines. They recognize the patriarch of Constantinople (modern-day Istanbul) as their leader. He convenes councils, but his authority is otherwise that of a "first among equals."

Eastern Orthodox Churches today count about 200 (m) million members. They include the Greek Orthodox Church, the Romanian Orthodox Church and the Russian Orthodox Church.

In the United States, organizational lines are based on the national backgrounds of various ethnic groups. The largest is the Greek Orthodox Archdiocese of North and South America, with about two (m) million members. Next is the Orthodox Church in America, with about one (m) million members, including people of Bulgarian, Romanian, Russian and Syrian descent.

Beliefs: The term *orthodox* (literally "right believing") derives from the adherence of these churches to the teachings of only the seven ecumenical councils held before the Great Schism. The schism was caused, in part, by a Rome-approved change in wording that the Council of Nicea had used in defining the doctrine of the Holy Spirit.

Aside from the question of papal supremacy, beliefs are generally the same as those described in the Roman Catholic Church entry.

Liturgies reflect cultural heritages. The principal worship service is called the Divine Liturgy.

The churches have their own disciplines on matters such as married clergy—a married man may be ordained, but a priest may not marry after ordination.

Clergy: Some of these churches call the archbishop who leads them a *metropolitan*, others use the term *patriarch*. He normally heads the principal archdiocese within a nation. Working with him are other archbishops, bishops, priests and deacons.

Archbishops and bishops frequently follow a monastic tradition in which they are known only by a first name. When no last name is used, repeat the title before the sole name in subsequent references.

Some forms: *Metropolitan Ireney, Archbishop of New York and Metropolitan of America and Canada.* On second reference: *Metropolitan Ireney. Archbishop* may be replaced by *the Most Reverend* on the first reference. *Bishop* may be replaced by *the Right Reverend* on the first reference.

Use *the Reverend* before the name of a priest on the first reference. Use *Deacon* before the name of a deacon on the first reference. Use only last names, customarily available for priests and deacons, in subsequent references.

• EASTERN RITE CHURCHES

The term applies to a group of Roman Catholic churches that are organized along ethnic lines traceable to the churches established during the earliest days of Christianity.

These churches accept the authority of the pope, but they have considerable autonomy in ritual and questions of discipline such as married clergy—a married man may be ordained, but marriage is not permitted after ordination.

Worldwide membership totals more than ten (m) million.

Among the largest Eastern Rite churches are the Greek Catholic Church, the Melchite Church, the Syrian Catholic Church and the Ukranian Catholic Church.

See **ROMAN CATHOLIC CHURCH.**

• EASTERN SHORE

A region on the east side of Chesapeake Bay, including parts of Maryland and Virginia.

Eastern Shore is not a synonym for *East Coast.*

• EASTERN STANDARD TIME (E-S-T), EASTERN DAYLIGHT TIME (E-D-T)

See **TIME ZONES.**

• EAST GERMANY

Use both words, not *Germany* alone, after cities and towns in the German Democratic Republic.

See **BERLIN** and **WEST GERMANY.**

• ECOLOGY

The study of the relationship between organisms and their surroundings. It is not synonymous with *environment.*

Right: *The laboratory is studying the ecology of man and the desert.*

Wrong: *Even so simple an undertaking as maintaining a lawn affects ecology.* (Use *environment* instead.)

An *ecologist* is a scientist who studies the interactions among plants, animals and their environments. An *environmentalist* is a person who works to protect man's surroundings.

To be called an *ecologist,* one must have studied interrelated disciplines including biology, zoology, botany, etc.

There are no academic requirements for the person who calls himself an *environmentalist.*

• EDITOR-IN-CHIEF

• EFFECT

See the **AFFECT, EFFECT** entry.

• EGLIN (EG'-LIN) AIR FORCE BASE, FLORIDA

Not *Elgin.*

• EITHER

Use it to mean *one or the other,* not *both.*

Right: *She said to use either door.*

Wrong: *There were lions on either side of the door.*

Right: *There were lions on each side of the door. There were lions on both sides of the door.*

• EITHER . . . OR, NEITHER . . . NOR

The nouns that follow these words do not constitute a compound subject; they are alternate subjects and require a verb that agrees with the nearer subject:

Neither they nor he is going. Neither he nor they are going.

• EL AL ISRAEL AIRLINES

An *El Al airliner* is acceptable in any reference.

Headquarters is in Tel Aviv.

• ELDER

For its use in religious contexts, see the entry for an individual's denomination.

• ELDERLY

Use this word carefully and sparingly. It is not appropriate in describing anyone under 65 and should not be used casually in referring to anyone beyond that age.

It is appropriate in generic phrases that do not refer to specific individuals: *concern for the elderly, a home for the elderly.*

If the intent is to show that an individual's faculties have deteriorated, cite a graphic example: *His memory fades. She walks with a cane.*

Apply the same principle to terms such as *senior citizen.*

• -ELECT

Always hyphenate: *President-elect Carter.*

• ELECTION DAY

The first Tuesday after the first Monday in November.

• ELECTION RETURNS

Handled differently in stories than in tables.

Election tables carry the exact number of votes, using newspaper style.

REAGAN	*4,356,893*
CARTER	*3,856,098*

But in stories, the numbers are de-emphasized for easy comprehension:

With just about a tenth of the nation's precincts reporting, Reagan has four-point-three (m) million votes, while Carter has three-point-eight (m) million. That gives Reagan about 53 percent of the vote so far.

Always try to simplify.

Instead of this: *Jimmy Carter defeated Gerald Ford 40 (m) million, 827-thousand, 292 to 39 (m) million, 146-thousand, 157 in 1976. . . .*

Use something like this: *Jimmy Carter defeated Gerald Ford by nearly one-point-seven (m) million votes, out of a total of almost 41 (m) million votes cast in the 1976 election.*

• ELECTROCARDIOGRAM

E-K-G is acceptable on second reference.

• ELLIPSIS (. . .)

One of the most over-used forms of punctuation in broadcast writing and one that should be used sparingly.

Technically, the ellipsis indicates that one or more words have been deleted in the process of condensation. Keep in mind, however, that when a statement is condensed for broadcast, the listener cannot see the ellipsis, as can a newspaper or magazine reader.

Example:

"I said that I would not do it, and I meant that I would not do it and I did not want anyone to misunderstand me when I said I would not do it, which is why I said I think I would not do it in the clearest possible way I could think of, and in fact I did not do it, just as I said I would not," the sheriff said.

Condensed for broadcast, this might read:

The sheriff put it this way: "I said that I would not do it, and I meant that I would not do it . . . and in fact I did not do it."

The condensation has taken away the flavor of the original statement, and has done so in such a way that the listener will never know he has missed something.

Many broadcast writers let themselves fall into the trap of using the ellipsis as a substitute for the comma and other standard punctuation marks.

Example:

The City Council took action on a number of matters . . . including sewers . . . the new city budget . . . three zoning protests . . . including one involving a new shopping center proposed for Third and Main . . . the firing of the police chief . . . remodeling of City Hall

... as recommended by a consultant ... and the closing of Fourth Street for a parade on Thanksgiving.

Such careless use of the ellipsis is not only confusing, but also paves the way to sloppy writing.

It is not AP style to substitute the ellipsis for a comma, semi-colon, colon or any other appropriate punctuation mark.

Example:

The City Council took action on a number of matters, including: sewers; the new city budget; three zoning protests, including one involving a new shopping center proposed for Third and Main; the firing of the police chief; remodeling of City Hall, as recommended earlier by a consultant; and, the closing of Fourth Street for a parade on Thanksgiving.

The ellipsis can occasionally be used to indicate hesitation, although the double dash is usually better.

Example:

The president said he would definitely go to Rome ... unless the pope asks him not to.

Preferred:

The president said he will definitely go to Rome -- unless the pope asks him not to.

The double dash is a better signal to the announcer that he should use a rising inflection to indicate that there is more to come.

The one case in which the ellipsis works well is as a signal to the announcer that he should let his voice trail off.

Example:

Are the hostages coming home? The answer could be yes -- but it could also be no ...

--BREAK--

• EL SALVADOR

The use of the article in the name of this nation helps to distinguish it from its capital, *San Salvador.*

Use *Salvadoran(s)* in references to citizens of the nation.

• EMBARGO

See the **BOYCOTT, EMBARGO** entry.

• EMBARGO TIMES

See **RELEASE TIMES.**

• EMBARRASS, EMBARRASSING, EMBARRASSED, EMBARRASSMENT

• EMBASSY

An *embassy* is the official residence of an ambassador in a foreign country and the office that handles the political relations of one nation with another.

A *consulate*, the residence of a consul in a foreign city, handles the commercial affairs and personal needs of citizens of the appointing country.

• EMCEE, EMCEED, EMCEEING

• EMERITUS

This word often is added to formal titles to denote that individuals who have retired retain their rank or title.

When used, place *emeritus* after the formal title, in keeping with the general practice of academic institutions: *Professor Emeritus Samuel Eliot Morison, Dean Emeritus Cortney Brown, Publisher Emeritus Barnard Colby.*

• EMIGRATE, IMMIGRATE

One who leaves a country *emigrates* from it.

One who comes into a country *immigrates.*

The same principle holds for *emigrant* and *immigrant.*

● **EMMY, EMMYS**
The annual awards by the National Academy of Television Arts and Sciences.

● **EMPIRIN** (EM'-PIR-IN)
A trademark for a brand of aspirin compound.

● **EMPLOYEE**
Not *employe.*

● **EMPTY-HANDED**

● **ENACT**
See the **ADOPT, APPROVE, ENACT, PASS** entry.

● **ENCYCLOPEDIA**

● **ENERGY RESEARCH AND DEVELOPMENT ADMINISTRATION**
In 1977, this offshoot of the Atomic Energy Commission was absorbed into the new federal Department of Energy.

● **ENFORCE**
But *reinforce.*

● **ENGINE, MOTOR**
An *engine* develops its own power, usually through internal combustion or the pressure of air, steam or water passing over vanes attached to a wheel: *an airplane engine, an automobile engine, a jet engine, a missile engine, a steam engine, a turbine engine.*
A *motor* receives power from an outside source: *an electric motor, a hydraulic motor.*

● **ENGLAND**
London stands alone in datelines. Use *England* after the names of other English communities in datelines.
See **DATELINES** and **UNITED KINGDOM.**

● **ENOVID** (EN'-OH-VID)
A trademark for a brand of birth control pill.

● **ENROLL, ENROLLED, ENROLLING**

● **EN ROUTE** (AHN-ROOT')
Always two words.

● **ENSURE, INSURE**
Use *ensure* to mean guarantee: *Steps were taken to ensure accuracy.*
Use *insure* for references to insurance: *The policy insures his life.*

● **ENTITLED**
Use it to mean a right to do or have something. Do not use it to mean *titled.*
Right: *She was entitled to the promotion.*
Right: *The book was titled "Gone With the Wind."*

● **ENUMERATIONS**
See examples in the **DOUBLE DASH** and **PERIODS** entries.

● **ENVELOP**
Other verb forms: *enveloping, enveloped.* But: *envelope* (n.)

● **ENVIRONMENT**
See **ECOLOGY.**

● **ENVIRONMENTAL PROTECTION AGENCY**
E-P-A is acceptable on second reference.

● **EPICENTER**
The center of an earthquake. See **EARTHQUAKES.**

● **EPIDEMIOLOGY**
(EH-PIH-DEE-MEE-AH'-LOH-JEE)

• EPISCOPAL, EPISCOPALIAN

Episcopal is the adjective form; use *Episcopalian* only as a noun referring to a member of the Episcopal Church: *She is an Episcopalian.* But: *She is an Episcopal priest.*

• EPISCOPAL CHURCH

Acceptable in all references for the *Protestant Episcopal Church*, the U-S national church that is a member of the Anglican Communion.

The church is governed nationally by two bodies—the permanent National Council and the General Convention, which meets every three years.

After the council, the principal organizational units are, in descending order of size, provinces, dioceses or missionary districts, local parishes and local missions.

The National Council is composed of bishops, priests, laymen and laywomen. One bishop is designated the leader and holds the formal title of presiding bishop. The council is responsible for furthering the missionary, educational and social work of the church.

The General Convention has final authority in matters of policy and doctrine. All acts must pass both of its houses—the House of Bishops and the House of Deputies. The latter is composed of an equal number of clergy and lay delegates from each diocese.

A province is composed of several dioceses. Each has a provincial synod made up of a house of bishops and a house of deputies. The synod's primary duty is to coordinate the work of the church in its area.

Within a diocese, a bishop is the principal official. He is helped by the Diocesan Convention, which consists of all the clergy in the diocese and lay representatives from each parish. The convention adopts a budget, elects a bishop in the case of a vacancy, and elects delegates to the General Convention and the Provincial Synod.

The parish or local church is governed by a vestry, composed of the pastor and lay members elected by the congregation.

Beliefs: See **ANGLICAN COMMUNION.**

Clergy: The clergy consists of bishops, priests, deacons and brothers. A priest who heads a parish is described as a *rector* rather than a *pastor.* The term *minister* seldom is used.

For first reference to bishops, use *Bishop* before the individual's name: *Bishop John M. Allin.* An acceptable alternative in referring to American bishops is *the Right Reverend.* The designation *the Most Reverend* is used only before the name of the Archbishop of Canterbury.

For first references, use *The Reverend* before the name of a priest, *deacon* before the name of a deacon, and *Brother* before the name of a brother.

Do not carry the title through to the second reference.

• EQUAL

An adjective without comparative forms.

When people speak of a *more equal* distribution of wealth, what is meant is *more equitable.*

• EQUAL, EQUALED, EQUALING

• EQUAL EMPLOYMENT OPPORTUNITY COMMISSION

Do not use the cumbersome abbreviation *E-E-O-C. The commission* is preferable on the second reference.

• EQUALLY AS

Do not use the words together; one is sufficient.

Omit the *equally* shown here in parentheses: *She was (equally) as astute as Marilyn.*

Omit the *as* shown here in parentheses: *She and Marilyn were equally (as) astute.*

• EQUAL RIGHTS AMENDMENT

E-R-A is acceptable on second reference.

Ratification requires approval of three-quarters of the 50 states—38—by June 30th, 1982. The original deadline—March 22nd, 1979—was extended by Congress in October of 1978.

The Text:

Section One: Equality of rights under the law shall not be denied or abridged by the United States or by any state on account of sex.

Section Two: The Congress shall have the power to enforce, by appropriate legislation, the provisions of this article.

Section Three: This amendment shall take effect two years after the date of ratification.

• EQUAL TIME, FAIRNESS DOCTRINE

Equal time applies to the Federal Communications Commission regulation that requires a radio or television station to provide a candidate for political office with air time equal to any time that an opponent receives beyond the coverage of news events.

If a station broadcasts material that takes a stand on a controversial issues, the *fairness doctrine* may require it to give advocates of a different position an opportunity to respond.

• EQUITABLE

See EQUAL.

• EQUITY

When used in a financial sense, *equity* means the value of property beyond the amount that is owed on it.

A stockholder's equity in a corporation is the value of the shares he holds.

A *homeowner's equity* is the difference between the value of the house and the amount of the unpaid mortgage.

• E-R-A

Acceptable in all references to baseball's *earned run average.*

Acceptable on second reference for *Equal Rights Amendment.*

• ESCALATOR CLAUSE

A clause in a contract providing for increases or decreases in wages or prices based on fluctuations in the cost of living, production, or expenses.

• ESCAPEE

The preferred words are *escaped convict* or *fugitive.*

• ESSENTIAL CLAUSES, NON-ESSENTIAL CLAUSES

These terms are used in this book instead of *restrictive clause* and *non-restrictive clause* to convey the distinction between the two in a more easily remembered manner.

Both types of clauses provide additional information about a word or phrase in the sentence.

The difference between them is that the essential clause cannot be eliminated without changing the meaning of the sentence—it so "restricts" the meaning of the word or phrase that its absence would lead to a substantially different interpretation of what the author meant.

The non-essential clause, however, can be eliminated without altering the basic meaning of the sentence—it does not "restrict" the meaning so significantly that its absence would radically alter the author's thought.

Punctuation: An essential clause must not be set off from the rest of a sentence by commas. A non-essential clause must be set off by commas.

The presence or absence of commas provides the newscaster with critical information about the writer's intended meaning. Note the following examples:

—*Reporters who do not read the stylebook should not criticize their editors.* (The writer is saying that only one class of reporters, those who do not read the stylebook, should not criticize their editors. If the *who ... stylebook* phrase were deleted, the meaning of the sentence would be changed substantially.)

—*Reporters, who do not read the stylebook, should not criticize their editors.* (The writer is saying that all reporters should not criticize their editors. If the *who ... stylebook* phrase were deleted, this meaning would not be changed.)

Use of Who, That, Which: When an essential or non-essential clause refers to a human being or an animal with a name, it should be introduced by *who* or *whom.* (See the WHO, WHOM entry.)

Do not use commas if the clause is essential to the meaning; use them if it is not.

That is the preferred pronoun to introduce essential clauses that refer to an inanimate object or an animal without a name. *Which* is the only acceptable pronoun to introduce a non-essential clause that refers to an inanimate object or an animal without a name.

The pronoun *which* occasionally may be substituted for *that* in the introduction of an essential clause that refers to an inanimate object or an animal without a name. In general, this use of *which* should appear only when *that* is used as a conjunction in the same sentence: *He said Monday that the part of the army which suffered severe casualties needs reinforcement.*

See THAT (CONJUNCTION) for guidelines on the use of *that* as a conjunction.

• EURASIAN

Of European and Asian descent.

• EURODOLLAR

A dollar on deposit in a European bank, including foreign branches of American banks.

• EUROPEAN ECONOMIC COMMUNITY

Common Market is acceptable in all references. See COMMON MARKET for a listing of members.

Do not use the abbreviation E-E-C.

• EVANGELICAL

See RELIGIOUS MOVEMENTS.

• EVANGELICAL FRIENDS ALLIANCE

See QUAKERS.

• EVANGELISM

See RELIGIOUS MOVEMENTS.

• EVANGELIST

The four Evangelists were *Matthew, Mark, Luke and John.*

Generally, an evangelist is a preacher who makes a profession of seeking conversions.

• EVERY DAY (adv.) EVERYDAY (adj.)

He goes to work every day. She wears everyday shoes.

• EVERY ONE, EVERYONE

Two words when it means each individual item: *Every one of the clues was worthless.*

One word when used as a pronoun meaning all persons: *Everyone wants his life to be happy.* (Note that *everyone* takes singular verbs and pronouns.)

• EX-

Use no hyphen for words that use *ex-* in the sense of *out of:*

EXCOMMUNICATE
EXPROPRIATE

Hyphenate when using *ex-* in the sense of *former:*

EX-CONVICT
EX-PRESIDENT

The prefix modifies the entire term: *ex-New York Governor Nelson Rockefeller;* not *New York ex-Governor.*

Usually *former* is better.

• EXAGGERATE

• EXCEPT

See the **ACCEPT, EXCEPT** entry.

• EXCLAMATION POINTS

Should generally be avoided in broadcast writing.

• EXECUTE

To execute a person is to kill him in compliance with a military order or judicial decision.

See the **ASSASSIN, KILLER, MURDERER** entry and the **HOMOCIDE, MURDER, MANSLAUGHTER** entry.

• EXECUTIVE DIRECTOR

Often the chief operational officer of a business or organization—and so a far better source than the often ceremonial president or chairman.

• EXECUTIVE PROTECTIVE AGENCY

Not *protection.* This agency of the Treasury Department, administered by the Secret Service, is responsible for protecting embassies in Washington.

• EXPLORERS

See **BOY SCOUTS.**

• EXPORT-IMPORT BANK OF THE UNITED STATES

Export-Import Bank is acceptable in all references.

Headquarters is in Washington.

• EXTOL, EXTOLLED, EXTOLLING

• EXTRA-

Do not use a hyphen when *extra-* means *outside of* unless the prefix is followed by a word beginning with *a* or a proper noun:

EXTRALEGAL
EXTRAMARITAL
EXTRATERRESTRIAL
EXTRATERRITORIAL

But:

EXTRA-ALIMENTARY
EXTRA-BRITANNIC

Follow *extra* with a hyphen when it is part of a compound modifier describing a condition beyond the usual size, extent or degree:

EXTRA-BASE HIT
EXTRA-DRY DRINK
EXTRA-LARGE BOOK
EXTRA-MILD TASTE

• EXTRAORDINARY LOSS, EXTRAORDINARY INCOME

See **PROFIT TERMINOLOGY.**

• EXTRASENSORY PERCEPTION
E-S-P is acceptable on second reference.

• EXTREME UNCTION
See SACRAMENTS.

• EXXON CORPORATION
Formerly Standard Oil Comany—the one in New Jersey.
Headquarters is in New York.

• EYE, EYED, EYING

• EYESTRAIN

• EYE TO EYE, EYE-TO-EYE
Hyphenate when used as a compound modifier: *an eye-to-eye confrontation.*

• EYEWITNESS

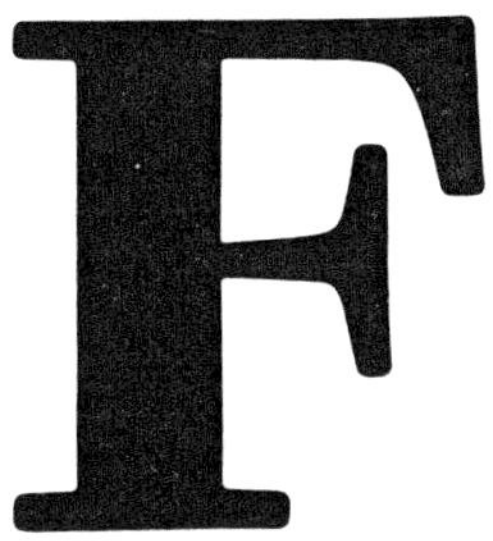

- **FACADE** (FUH-SAHD')

- **FACT-FINDING** (adj.)
  FACT-FINDER (n.)

- **FADE OUT** (v.)
  FADE-OUT (n.)

- **FAHRENHEIT**
  The temperature scale commonly used in the United States.

  The scale is named for Gabriel Daniel Fahrenheit, a German physicist who designed it. In it, the freezing point of water is 32 degrees and the boiling point is 212 degrees.

  To convert to Celsius, subtract 32 from the Fahrenheit figure, multiply by five and divide by nine. For example, 77 minus 32 equals 45, times five equals 225, divided by nine equals 25 degrees Celsuis.

  In cases that require mention of the scale, use this form: *86 degrees Fahrenheit.* Do not abbreviate.

  See **CELSIUS** and **KELVIN.**

  For guidelines on when Celsius temperatures should be used, see the **METRIC SYSTEM** entry.

TEMPERATURE CONVERSION TABLE

Note: Celsius temperatures have been rounded to the nearest whole number.

F	C	F	C	F	C	F	C	F	C
−26	−32	1	−17	28	−2	55	13	82	28
−24	−31	3	−16	30	−1	57	14	84	29
−22	−30	5	−15	32	0	59	15	86	30
−20	−29	7	−14	34	1	61	16	88	31
−18	−28	9	−13	36	2	63	17	90	32
−17	−27	10	−12	37	3	64	18	91	33
−15	−26	12	−11	39	4	66	19	93	34
−13	−25	14	−10	41	5	68	20	95	35
−11	−24	16	− 9	43	6	70	21	97	36
− 9	−23	18	− 8	45	7	72	22	99	37
−8	−22	19	−7	46	8	73	23	100	38
−6	−21	21	−6	48	9	75	24	102	39
−4	−20	23	−5	50	10	77	25	104	40
−2	−19	25	−4	52	11	79	26	106	41
0	−18	27	−3	54	12	81	27	108	42

• FAIRNESS DOCTRINE

See the **EQUAL TIME, FAIRNESS DOCTRINE** entry.

• FALLOUT (n.)

• "FANNIE MAE"

See **FEDERAL NATIONAL MORTGAGE ASSOCIATION.**

• FAR EAST

The easternmost portions of the continent of Asia: China, Japan, North and South Korea, Taiwan, Hong Kong and the eastern portions of the Soviet Union.

Confine *Far East* to this restricted sense, as defined in the Columbia Lippincott Gazetteer. Use the *Far East and Southeast Asia* when referring to a wider portion of eastern Asia.

See the **ASIAN SUBCONTINENT** and **SOUTHEAST ASIA** entries.

• FAR-FLUNG (adj.)

• FAR-OFF (adj.)

• FAR-RANGING (adj.)

• FARSIGHTED

When used in a medical sense, it means that a person can see objects at a distance but has difficulty seeing material at close range.

• FARTHER, FURTHER

Farther refers to physical distance: *He walked farther into the woods.*

Further refers to an extension of time or degree: *She will look further into the mystery.*

• FAR WEST

The region west of the Rocky Mountains.

• FASCISM, FASCIST

• FATHER

Use *Reverend* in first reference before the names of Episcopal, Orthodox and Roman Catholic priests. Use *Father* before a name only in direct quotations.

See **RELIGIOUS TITLES.**

• FATHER-IN-LAW, FATHERS-IN-LAW

• FAZE, PHASE

Faze means to embarrass or disturb: *The snub did not faze her.*

Phase denotes an aspect or stage: *They will phase in a new system.*

• F-B-I

Acceptable in all references for *Federal Bureau of Investigation.*

See **FEDERAL BUREAU OF INVESTIGATION.**

• FEATHER BEDDING, FEATHERBEDDING

Feather bedding is a mattress stuffed with feathers.

Featherbedding is the practice of requiring an employer to hire more workers than needed to handle a job.

• FEDERAL AVIATION ADMINISTRATION

F-A-A is acceptable on the second reference.

The *F-A-A* is responsible for policing the manufacture, operation and maintenance of aircraft as well as the rating and certification of airmen and airports. Its function is to make sure all of these are safe.

The *Civil Aeronautics Board* polices the air carriers, authorizing them to engage in interstate commerce.

The *National Transportation Safety Board* is responsible for investigating transportation safety and recommending improvements to agencies such as the F-A-A.

• FEDERAL BUREAU OF INVESTIGATION

F-B-I is acceptable in all references. To avoid alphabet soup, however, use *the bureau* in some references.

• FEDERAL COMMUNICATIONS COMMISSION

F-C-C if acceptable on second reference.

• FEDERAL COURT

For clarity, it is best to use the proper name of the court in one reference in the story. See entries under U-S and the court name.

For readability, names can be informalized in other references. But be careful not to invent court names such as *Manhattan Federal Court.* Instead, use *a federal court in Manhattan.*

See **JUDICIAL BRANCH.**

• FEDERAL CROP INSURANCE CORPORATION

Do not abbreviate.

• FEDERAL DEPOSIT INSURANCE CORPORATION

F-D-I-C is acceptable on second reference.

• FEDERAL ENERGY ADMINISTRATION

No longer exists. Its functions are now performed by the U-S Department of Energy.

• FEDERAL FARM CREDIT BOARD

Do not abbreviate.

• FEDERAL HIGHWAY ADMINISTRATION

Do not abbreviate. The *F-H-A* abbreviation is reserved for the *Federal Housing Administration.*

• FEDERAL HOME LOAN BANK BOARD

Do not abbreviate.

• FEDERAL HOUSING ADMINISTRATION

F-H-A is acceptable on second reference.

• FEDERAL LEGAL HOLIDAYS

See the **HOLIDAYS AND HOLY DAYS** entry.

• FEDERAL MARITIME COMMISSION

Do not abbreviate.

• FEDERAL MEDIATION AND CONCILIATION SERVICE

Do not abbreviate. Use *the service* on second reference.

• FEDERAL NATIONAL MORTGAGE ASSOCIATION

The nickname for this agency is *"Fannie Mae."* While that is acceptable on the second reference in business copy, it is not to be used in general news copy.

Similarly, the association's bonds may be referred to as *"Fannie Maes"* in business copy only.

• FEDERAL POWER COMMISSION

Do not abbreviate.

• FEDERAL REGISTER

This publication, issued every workday, is the legal medium for recording and communicating the rules and regulations established by the executive branch of the federal government.

Individuals or corporations cannot be held legally responsible for compliance with a regulation unless it has been published in the Register.

In addition, executive agencies are required to publish in advance some types of proposed regulations, particularly when they would impose restrictions on a citizen (require seat belts in cars, for example) or institute a penalty for noncompliance. The advance publication is designed to provide the public with an opportunity to comment.

• FELONY, MISDEMEANOR
A *felony* is a serious crime. A *misdemeanor* is a minor offense against the law.

A fuller definition of what constitutes a felony or misdemeanor depends on the governmental jurisdiction involved.

At the federal level, a *misdemeanor* is a crime that carries a potential penalty of no more than a year in jail. A *felony* is a crime that carries a potential penalty of more than a year in prison. Often, however, a statute gives a judge options such as imposing a fine or probation in addition to or instead of a jail or prison sentence.

A *felon* is a person who has been convicted of a felony, regardless of whether the individual actually spends time in confinement or is given probation or a fine instead.

See the **PRISON, JAIL** entry.

• FERRYBOAT

• FERTILITY RATE
As calculated by the federal government, it is the number of live births per one-thousand females age 15 to 44.

• FEWER, LESS
In general, use *fewer* for individual items and *less* for bulk or quantity:

I have less than 50 dollars in my pocket, but *I have fewer than 50 dollar-bills.*

• F-FOUR

• FIANCE (man)
FIANCEE (woman)
In common usage, both are pronounced (fee-ahn-say').

• FIGURATIVELY, LITERALLY
Figuratively means in an analogous sense, but not in the exact sense: *He bled them white.*

Literally means in an exact sense; do not use it to mean figuratively.

Wrong: *He literally bled them white.* (Unless the blood was drained from their bodies.)

• FIGURE
The symbol for a number.
See **NUMERALS.**

• FILIBUSTER
To filibuster is to make long speeches to obstruct the passage of legislation.

A legislator who uses such methods also is a *filibuster,* not a *filibusterer.*

• FILIPINOS
The people of the Philippines.

• FIORD (FEE-YAWRD')
Not *fjord.*

• FIREFIGHTER, FIREMAN
Both are acceptable in any reference.

Avoid such slang references as *smokeater.*

• FIRM

A business partnership is correctly referred to as a *firm: He joined a law firm.*

Do not use *firm* in reference to an incorporated business entity. Use *the company* or *the corporation* instead.

• FIRST DEGREE, FIRST-DEGREE

Hyphenate when used as a compound modifier: *It was murder in the first degree. He was convicted of first-degree murder.*

• FIRST QUARTER, FIRST-QUARTER

Hyphenate when used as a compound modifier: *He scored in the first quarter. The team took the lead on his first-quarter goal.*

• FISCAL, MONETARY

Fiscal applies to budgetary matters.

Monetary applies to money supply.

• FISCAL YEAR

The 12-month period that a corporation or governmental body uses for bookkeeping purposes.

The federal government's fiscal year starts three months ahead of the calendar year—fiscal 1981, for example, runs from October first, 1980, to September 30th, 1981.

• FITFUL

It means restless, not a condition of being fit.

• FLACK, FLAK

Flack is slang for *press agent.*

Flak is a type of anti-aircraft fire, hence figuratively a barrage of criticism.

• FLAGPOLE, FLAGSHIP

• FLAIL, FLAY

To flail is to swing the arms widely.

To flay is, literally, to strip off the skin by whipping. Figuratively, *to flay* means to tongue-lash a person.

• FLAIR, FLARE

Flair is conspicuous talent.

Flare is a verb meaning to blaze with sudden, bright light or to burst out in anger. It also is a noun meaning a flame.

• FLARE UP (v.)
FLARE-UP (n.)

See the **FLAIR, FLARE** entry.

• FLASH

In wire-service terminology, a Flash is the highest possible story classification. It is reserved for presidential assassinations, atomic confrontations and other transcendent events.

A flash will interrupt anything which is moving on the wire. It often consists of just a few words:

F L A S H
MAN ON MOON.

F L A S H
ROOSEVELT DEAD.

• FLASH FLOOD

See **WEATHER TERMS.**

• FLAUNT, FLOUT

To flaunt is to make an ostentatious or defiant display: *She flaunted her beauty.*

To flout is to show contempt for: *He flouts the law.*

• FLAUTIST

The preferred word is *flutist.*

• FLIER, FLYER

Flier is the preferred term for an aviator or a handbill.

Flyer is the proper name of some trains and buses: *"The Western Flyer."*

• FLOODS, FLOOD STAGE

See **WEATHER TERMS.**

• FLOODWATERS

• FLOOR LEADER

Do not use when a formal title such as *majority leader, minority leader* or *whip* would be the accurate description.

See the **LEGISLATIVE TITLES** and **TITLES** entries.

• FLORIDA KEYS

A chain of small islands extending southwest from the southern tip of mainland Florida.

• FLOUNDER, FOUNDER

A *flounder* is a fish; *to flounder* is to move clumsily or jerkily, to flop about: *The fish floundered on land.*

To founder is to bog down, become disabled or sink: *The ship floundered in the heavy seas for hours, then foundered.*

• FLOUT

See the **FLAUNT, FLOUT** entry.

• FLUID OUNCE

A *fluid ounce* is equal to one-point-eight cubic inches, two tablespoons or six teaspoons. The metric equivalent is about 30 milliliters.

To convert to milliliters, multiply by 30: three ounces times 30 equals 90 milliliters.

See **LITERS.**

• FLUORESCENT

• FLYER

See the **FLIER, FLYER** entry.

• F-M

Acceptable on all references to the *frequency modulation* system of radio transmission.

• F-O-B

Acceptable on first reference for *free on board.* But the concept should be explained in the story—if it is not a business-oriented broadcast: the seller agrees to put an item on a bus, train, truck or ship at no charge, but the transportation costs must be paid by the buyer.

• -FOLD

No hyphen:

TWOFOLD
FOURFOLD

• FOLK SINGER, FOLK SONG

• FOLLOWING

The word usually is a noun, verb or adjective: *He has a large following. He is following his conscience. The following statement was made.*

Although Webster's New World records its use as a preposition, the preferred word is *after: He spoke after dinner.* Not: *He spoke following dinner.*

• FOOD AND AGRICULTURE ORGANIZATION

Not *Agricultural.* Do not abbreviate.

• FOOD AND DRUG ADMINISTRATION

F-D-A is acceptable on second reference.

• FOOT

The basic unit of length in the measuring system that has been used in the United States. Its origin was a calculation that this was the length of the average human foot.

The metric equivalent is exactly 30-point-48 centimeters, which may be rounded to 30 centimeters for most comparisons.

Therefore, for most conversions to centimeters, simply multiply by 30—five feet times 30 equals 150 centimeters. For more precise figures, multiply by 30-point-48: five feet times 30-point-48 equals 152-point-four centimeters.

Similarly, to convert from feet to meters, multiply by three-tenths: five feet times point-three equals one and a-half meters.

See **CENTIMETER, METER** and **DIMENSIONS.**

• FOOTBALL

The spellings of some frequently used words and phrases:

BALL CARRIER	LINE OF SCRIMMAGE
BALLCLUB	OUT OF BOUNDS (adv.)
BLITZ (n.,v.)	OUT-OF-BOUNDS (adj.)
END LINE	PITCHOUT (n.)
END ZONE	PLACE KICK
FAIR CATCH	PLACE-KICKER
FIELD GOAL	PLAY OFF (v.)
FOURTH-AND-ONE (adj.)	PLAYOFF (n., adj.)
FULLBACK	QUARTERBACK
GOAL LINE	RUNBACK (n.)
GOAL-LINE STAND	RUNNING BACK
HALFBACK	SPLIT END
HALFTIME	TAILBACK
HANDOFF	TIGHT END
KICK OFF (v.)	TOUCHBACK
KICKOFF (adj.)	TOUCHDOWN
LEFT GUARD	WIDE RECEIVER
LINEBACKER	
LINEMAN	

Numbers: Follow the rules for **NUMERALS** except when reporting scores in the text of a story and in tabular material. When reporting scores in scripted material, use figures, hyphens, and *to:*

The Bills beat the Giants 24-to-nothing. It was a 54-to-12 defeat.

Scores: Quarter-scores are sent on a spot basis, as are finals, and take this format:

NFL
FIRST GREEN BAY 7 N.Y. JETS 3

Finals take the same format, but with *final* in place of the period number.

Standings: The form for professional standings:

AMERICAN CONFERENCE
EAST

	W	L	T	PCT.	PF	PA
BALTIMORE	10	4	0	.714	395	269
N.Y. JETS	9	5	0	.643	387	275
ETC.						

• FORBID, FORBADE, FORBIDDING

• FORCIBLE RAPE

A redundancy that usually should be avoided. It may be used, however, in stories dealing with both rape and statutory rape, which does not necessarily involve the use of force.

• FORD MOTOR COMPANY

Use *Ford,* not *F-M-C,* on the second reference.

Headquarters is in Dearborn, Michigan.

• FORE-

The rules in **PREFIXES** apply, but in general, no hyphen. Some examples:

FOREBRAIN	FOREGOING
FOREFATHER	FORETOOTH

There are three nautical exceptions based on long-standing practice:

FORE-TOPGALLANT
FORE-TOPMAST
FORE-TOPSAIL

• FORECAST

Use *forecast* also for the past tense, not *forecasted.*

See **WEATHER TERMS.**

• FOREGO, FORGO

To forego means to go before, as in *foregone conclusion.*

To forgo means to abstain from.

• FOREIGN LEGISLATIVE BODIES

The most frequent names in use are *congress, national assembly* and *parliament.*

Parliament is the appropriate generic descriptive for the Diet, the Cortes in Spain, the Knesset in Israel and the Supreme Soviet in the Soviet Union.

Parliaments: Nations in which *parliament* is the name include: Australia, Canada, Denmark, Finland, France, India, Iran, Ireland, Italy, New Zealand, Norway, Poland and the United Kingdom.

National Assemblies: Nations in which *national assembly* is the name include: Bulgaria, Czechoslovakia, Egypt, Hungary, Nepal, Pakistan, Portugal, Tunisia, Uganda, Zaire and Zambia.

In many countries *national assembly* is the name of a unicameral legislative body. In some, such as France, it is the name for the lower house of a legislative body known by some other name such as *parliament.*

• FOREIGN MONEY

Generally, amounts of foreign money mentioned in news stories should be converted to dollars.

The basic monetary units of nations are listed in Webster's New World Dictionary among the M's under "Monetary Units of All Nations." Do not use the exchange rates listed in the dictionary. Instead, use, as appropriate, the official exchange rates, which change from day to day on the world's markets.

• FOREIGN NAMES

For foreign place names, use the primary spelling in Webster's New World Dictionary. If it has no entry, follow the Columbia Lippincott Gazetteer of the World.

For personal names, follow the individual's preference for an English spelling if it can be determined. Otherwise:

—Use the nearest phonetic equivalent in English if one exists: *Alexander Solzhenitsyn,* for example, rather than *Aleksandr,* the spelling that would result from a transliteration of the Russian letters into the English alphabet.

—If a name has no close phonetic equivalent in English, express it with an English spelling that approximates the sound in the original language: *Anwar Sadat.*

Always use a pronouncer.

For additional guidelines, see **ARABIC NAMES; CHINESE NAMES; RUSSIAN NAMES;** and **SPANISH AND PORTUGUESE NAMES.**

When a question arises, the news services will announce a common policy.

• FOREIGN PARTICLES

They are part of the last name but precede it, with a space in between: *Charles de Gaulle, Baron Manfred von Richthofen.*

On the second reference: *de Gaulle, von Richthofen.*

• FOREIGN WORDS

Some foreign words have been accepted universally into the English language: *bon voyage, versus, et cetera.* They may be used without explanation if they are clear in the context.

Many foreign words are not understood universally, although they may be used in special applications such as medical or legal terminology. Such words are marked in Webster's New World by a double dagger (‡). If such a word or phrase is needed in a story, place it in quotation marks and provide an explanation: *"ad astra per aspera," a Latin phrase meaning "to the stars through difficulty."*

Where necessary, use a pronouncer.

• FORMOSA

See **TAIWAN.**

• FORMOSA STRAIT

Not *the Straits of Taiwan.*

• FORMULA, FORMULAS

• FORSAKE, FORSOOK, FORSAKEN

• FORT

Do not abbreviate, for cities or for military installations.

In datelines for cities:

(FORT LAUDERDALE, FLORIDA) --

In datelines for military installations:

(FORT BRAGG, NORTH CAROLINA) --

• FORTNIGHT

The expression *two weeks* is preferred.

• FORTUNE-TELLER, FORTUNE-TELLING

• FORWARD

Not *forwards.*

• FOUL, FOWL

Foul means offensive, out of line.

A *fowl* is a bird, especially the larger domestic birds used as food: chickens, ducks, turkeys.

• FOUNDER

See the **FLOUNDER, FOUNDER** entry.

• FOUR-H CLUB

Members are *Four-H'ers.*

• FOUR-STAR GENERAL

• FOURTH ESTATE

A collective name for journalism and journalists.

The description is attributed to Edmund Burke, who is reported to have called the reporters' gallery in Parliament a "Fourth Estate."

The three estates of early English society were the Lords Spiritual (the clergy), the Lords Temporal (the nobility) and the Commons (the bourgeoisie).

• FOURTH OF JULY, JULY FOURTH

Also: *Independence Day.* The federal legal holiday is observed on Friday if July fourth falls on a Saturday—on Monday if it falls on a Sunday.

• FRACTIONS

Spell them out, using hyphens between units and numerals: *three and a-half, six and two-thirds, one-half of one percent,* but a *half-percent.*

Informalize fractions wherever possible: instead of *one-half of a dollar,* use *a half-dollar.*

See **NUMERALS, DECIMAL UNITS** and **PERCENTAGES.**

• FRAGMENT, FRAGMENTARY

Fragment describes a piece or pieces broken from the whole: *She sang a fragment of the song.*

Fragmentary describes disconnected and incomplete parts: *Early returns were fragmentary.*

• FRAME UP (v.) FRAME-UP (n.)

- **FRANKFURTERS**
  They first were called *hot dogs* in 1906 when a cartoonist, T. A. "Tad" Dorgan, showed a dachshund inside an elongated bun.

- **FREE-FOR-ALL** (n. and adj.)

- **FREE-LANCE** (v. and adj.)
  The noun: *free-lancer.*

- **FREE ON BOARD**
  See **F-O-B.**

- **FREEWHEELING**

- **FREE WORLD**
  An imprecise description. Use only in quoted matter.

- **FREEZE-DRY, FREEZE-DRIED, FREEZE-DRYING**

- **FREEZING DRIZZLE, FREEZING RAIN**
  See **WEATHER TERMS.**

- **FRENCH CANADIAN, FRENCH CANADIANS**
  Without a hyphen. An exception to the normal practice in describing a dual ethnic heritage.

- **FRENCH FOREIGN LEGION**
  Unlike the American Legion's members, members of the French Foreign Legion are active soldiers.

- **FREQUENCY MODULATION**
  F-M is acceptable in all references.

- **FRIENDS GENERAL CONFERENCE, FRIENDS UNITED MEETING**
  See **QUAKERS.**

- **FRONTIER AIRLINES**
  Headquarters is in Denver.

- **FRONT LINE** (n.)
  FRONT LINE (adj.)

- **FRONT PAGE** (n.)
  FRONT-PAGE (adj.)

- **FRONT-RUNNER**

- **FROST**
  See **WEATHER TERMS.**

- **FULFILL, FULFILLED, FULFILLING**

- **FULL-**
  Hyphenate when used to form compound modifiers.

  FULL-DRESS   FULL-PAGE
  FULL-FLEDGED   FULL-SCALE
  FULL-LENGTH

  See the listings that follow and Webster's New World Dictionary for the spelling of other combinations.

- **FULL FAITH AND CREDIT BOND**
  See **LOAN TERMINOLOGY.**

- **FULL HOUSE** (poker)

- **FULL TIME, FULL-TIME**
  Hyphenate when used as a compound modifier: *He works full time. She has a full-time job.*

- **FUND RAISING, FUND-RAISING, FUND-RAISER**
  Fund raising is difficult. They planned a fund-raising campaign. A fund-raiser was hired.

- **FUNDAMENTALIST**
  See **RELIGIOUS MOVEMENTS.**

- **FUNNEL CLOUD**
  See **WEATHER TERMS.**

- **FURLOUGH**

- **FUSELAGE**

- **FUSILLADE**

- **FUTURES CONTRACTS**

A *futures contract* is an agreement to deliver or take delivery of a commodity at a fixed price on a fixed future date. The amount, quality, and other terms of the contract are fixed in the futures agreement—and generally are standardized at major futures trading centers.

In some fields, and especially grain trading, futures prices go far in determining immediate cash market prices.

- **F. W. WOOLWORTH COMPANY**

Woolworth's is acceptable in all references.

Headquarters is in New York.

• G

The *general audience* rating. See **MOVING RATINGS.**

• GAGE, GAUGE

A gage is a security or a pledge.

A *gauge* is a device to measure something.

Gauge is also a term used to designate the size of shotguns. See **WEAPONS.**

• GAIETY

• GALE

See **WEATHER TERMS.**

• GALLON

Equal to 128 fluid ounces. The metric equivalent is roughly three-point-eight liters.

To convert to liters, multiply by three-point-eight: three gallons times three-point-eight equals eleven-point-four liters.

See **IMPERIAL GALLON, LITER** and **METRIC SYSTEM.**

• GALLUP POLL

Prepared by The American Institute of Public Opinion, Princeton, New Jersey.

• GAME PLAN

• GAMUT, GANTLET, GAUNTLET

A *gamut* is a scale of notes or any complete range or extent.

A *gantlet* is a flogging ordeal, literally or figuratively.

A *gauntlet* is a glove. *To throw down the gauntlet* means to issue a challenge. *To take up the gauntlet* means to accept a challenge.

• GAMY, GAMIER, GAMIEST

• GARNISH, GARNISHEE

Garnish means to adorn or decorate.

As a verb, *garnishee* (*garnisheed, garnisheeing*) means to attach a debtor's property or wages to satisfy a debt. As a noun, it identifies the individual whose property was attached.

• GAUGE

See the **GAGE, GAUGE** entry.

• GAY

Do not use as a noun meaning a homosexual unless it appears in the formal name of an organization or in quoted matter.

In a story about homosexuals, *gay* may be used as an adjective meaning homosexual.

• GENERAL ACCOUNTING OFFICE

This federal agency, the investigative arm of Congress, may be referred to as the *G-A-O* in second reference.

• GENERAL ASSEMBLY

Always identify as the *United Nations* or *U-N General Assembly* in one reference.

• GENERAL COURT

Part of the official proper name for the legislatures in Massachusetts and New Hampshire.

But in keeping with accepted practice, *legislature* may be used in all references.

• GENERAL ELECTRIC COMPANY

G-E is acceptable on second reference.

Headquarters is in Fairfield, Connecticut.

• GENERAL MOTORS CORPORATION

G-M is acceptable on second reference.

The company makes a distinction between its corporate headquarters, in New York, and its main office, in Detroit, where the president and chairman of the board are based.

• GENERAL OBLIGATION BOND

See **LOAN TERMINOLOGY.**

• GENERAL SERVICES ADMINISTRATION

G-S-A is acceptable on the second reference for this federal house-keeping and office supply agency.

• GENIE

Not *jinni,* the spelling under which Webster's New World gives the definition.

• GENTILE

Generally, any person not a Jew; often, specifically a Christian. But to Mormons it is anyone not a Mormon.

• GENTLEMAN

Do not use as a synonym for *man.* See **LADY.**

• GEOGRAPHIC NAMES

The basic guidelines:

Domestic: The authority for spelling place names in the 50 United States and territories is The U-S Postal Service Directory of Post Offices, although there are two exceptions:

—Do not use the postal abbreviations.

—*Saint* may be abbreviated *St.,* and *Sainte,* as in *Sault Sainte Marie,* may be abbreviated *Ste.*

Foreign: The first source for the spelling of all foreign place names is Webster's New World Dictionary as follows:

Use the first-listed spelling if an entry gives more than one.

If the dictionary provides different spellings in separate entries, use the spelling that is followed by a full description of the location. There are four exceptions:

1. For divided nations, use the familiar geographic names, instead of the formal titles: *East Germany, West Germany,* instead of *German Democratic Republic* and *Federal Republic of Germany.* See the **DATELINES** entry.

2. Use *Cameroon,* not *Cameroons* or *Cameroun.*

3. Use *Sri Lanka,* not *Ceylon.*

4. The latter three exceptions conform with the United Nations and U-S Board of Geographic Names. Follow those bodies' guidelines on new names.

If the dictionary does not have an entry for the name in question, consult the first-listed spelling in The Columbia Lippincott Gazetteer of the World.

• GERMAN MEASLES

Also known as *rubella.*

• GERMANY

Use *East Germany* in datelines after the names of communities in the German Democratic Republic.

Use *West Germany* after the names

of communities in the Federal Republic of Germany.

Berlin stands alone in datelines. See the **BERLIN** entry.

• GETAWAY (n.)

• GET-TOGETHER (n.)

• GHETTO, GHETTOS

Do not use indiscriminately as a synonym for the sections of cities inhabited by minorities or the poor. *Ghetto* has a connotation that government decree has forced people to live in a certain area.

In most cases, *section, district, slum, area* or *quarter* is the more accurate word. Sometimes a place name alone has connotations that make it best: *Harlem, Watts.*

• G-I, G-I's

Soldier is preferred unless the story contains the term in quoted matter or involves a subject such as the *G-I Bill of Rights.*

• GIBE, JIBE (JYB)

To gibe means to taunt or sneer: *They gibed him about his mistakes.*

Jibe means to shift direction or, colloquially, to agree: *They jibed their ship across the wind. Their stories didn't jibe.*

• GIBRALTAR, STRAIT OF

The British colony on the peninsula that juts into the strait, *Gibraltar,* stands alone in datelines.

• GIGA- (GIG'-UH)

A prefix denoting one (b) billion units of a measure. It is best avoided. Move a decimal point nine places to the right, adding zeros if necessary, to convert to the basic unit: five-point-five gigatons equals five (b) billion, 500 (m) million tons.

• GIRL

Applicable until 18th birthday is reached. Use *woman* or *young woman* afterward. *Young girl* or *little girl* is redundant; simply add her age.

• GIRLFRIEND, BOYFRIEND

• GIRL SCOUTS

The full name of the organization is the *Girl Scouts Of The United States of America.* Headquarters is in New York.

Girls aged six through eight are *Brownie Girl Scouts* or *Brownies.* Girls nine through eleven are *Junior Girl Scouts* or *Juniors.* Girls 12 through 14 are *Cadette Girl Scouts* or *Cadettes.* And those aged 15 through 17 are *Senior Girl Scouts,* or *Seniors.*

See **BOY SCOUTS** for programs run by that separate organization.

• GIZMO

Not *gismo.*

• GLAMOUR

One of the few *our* endings still used in American writing. But the adjective is *glamorous.*

• GLOBE-TROTTER, GLOBE-TROTTING

But the proper name of the basketball team is the *Harlem Globetrotters.*

• G-M-T

For *Greenwich Mean Time.* See **TIME ZONES.**

• GOBBLEDYGOOK

Avoid it.

• GO-BETWEEN (n.)

• GODCHILD, GODDAUGHTER

Also: *godfather, godliness, godmother, godsend, godson, godspeed.*

• GO-GO

• GOLF

Some frequently used terms and some definitions:

Americas Cup: No possessive.

Birdie, Birdies: One stroke under par.

Bogey, Bogeys: One stroke over par. The past tense is *bogeyed.*

Eagle: Two strokes under par.

Fairway.

Masters Tournament: No possessive. Use *the Masters* on second reference.

Tee, Tee Off.

U-S Open Championship: Use *the U-S Open* or *the Open* on second reference.

Numbers: Some sample uses of numbers:

Use figures for handicaps: *He has a 3 handicap; a 3-handicap golfer; a handicap of 3 strokes; a 3-stroke handicap.*

Use figures for par listings: *He had a par 5 to finish 2-up for the round; a par-4 hole; a 7-under-par 64; the par-3 seventh hole.*

Use figures for club ratings: *a No. 5 iron, a 5-iron, a 7-iron shot, a 4-wood.*

Miscellaneous: *the first hole, the ninth hole, the 10th hole, the back nine, the final 18, the third round. He won 3 and 2.*

Associations: In general, spell out *Professional Golfers' Association* (note the apostrophe) on first reference. A phrase such as *P-G-A tournament* may be used on first reference, however, to avoid a cumbersome lead.

The same principle applies to the *Ladies Professional Golf Association* (no apostrophe, in keeping with *L-P-G-A* practice).

• GOOD, WELL

Good is an adjective that means something is as it should be or is better than average.

When used as an adjective, *well* means suitable, proper, healthy. When used as an adverb, *well* means in a satisfactory manner or skillfully.

Good should not be used as an adverb. It does not lose its status as an adjective in a sentence such as *I feel good.* Such a statement is the idiomatic equivalent of *I am in good health.* An alternative, *I feel well,* could be interpreted as meaning that your sense of touch was good.

See **BAD, BADLY** entry and **WELL.**

• GOODBYE

Not *goodby.*

• GOOD FRIDAY

The Friday before Easter.

• GOOD WILL (n.)
GOODWILL (adj.)

• G-O-P

See **GRAND OLD PARTY.**

• GOURMAND, GOURMET

A *gourmand* is a person who likes good food and tends to eat to excess; a glutton.

A *gourmet* is a person who likes fine food and is an excellent judge of food and drink.

• GOVERNMENT, JUNTA, REGIME

A *government* is an established system of political administration: *the U-S government.*

A *junta* is a group or council that often rules after a coup: *A military junta controls the nation.* A junta becomes a government after it establishes a system of political administration.

The word *regime* is a synonym for *political system: a democratic regime, an authoritarian regime.* Do not use *regime* to mean government or junta. For example, use *the Franco government* in referring to the government of

Spain under Francisco Franco, not *Franco regime.* But: *The Franco government was an authoritarian regime.*

An *administration* consists of officials who make up the executive branch of a government: *the Reagan administration.*

• GOVERNOR GENERAL, GOVERNORS GENERAL

The formal title for the British sovereign's representatives in Canada and elsewhere.

Do not abbreviate in any use.

• GRADE, GRADER

Hyphenate both the noun forms (*first-grader, second-grader, tenth-grader*) and the adjectival forms (*a fourth-grade pupil, a 12th-grade pupil*).

• GRADUATE (v.)

Graduate is correctly used in the active voice: *She graduated from the university.* It is correct, but unnecessary, to use the passive voice: *He was graduated from the university.*

Do not, however, drop *from: John Adams graduated from Harvard.* Not: *John Adams graduated Harvard.*

• GRAIN

The smallest unit in the system of weights that has been used in the United States. It originally was defined as the weight of one grain of wheat.

It takes 437 and a-half grains to make an ounce.

See **OUNCE (WEIGHT)** and **POUND.**

• GRAM

The basic unit of weight in the metric system. It is the weight of one cubic centimeter of water at four degrees Celsius.

A gram is roughly equivalent to the weight of a paper clip—about one-28th of an ounce.

To convert to ounces, multiply by 35-thousandths: 86 grams times 35-thousandths equals three ounces.

See **METRIC SYSTEM.**

• GRAMMAR

• GRANDDAD, GRANDDAUGHTER

Also: *grandfather, grandmother, grandson.*

• GRAND OLD PARTY

G-O-P is acceptable as a second-reference synonym for *Republican Party* without first spelling out *Grand Old Party.*

• GRANT-IN-AID, GRANTS-IN-AID

• GRAY

Not *grey.* But *greyhound.*

• GREAT-

Hyphenate *great-grandfather, great-great-grandmother.*

Use *great grandfather* only if the intended meaning is that the grandfather was a great man.

• GREAT ATLANTIC AND PACIFIC TEA COMPANY, INCORPORATED

A-and-P is acceptable in all references.

Headquarters is in Montvale, New Jersey.

• GREAT BRITAIN

It consists of England, Scotland and Wales, but not Northern Ireland.

Britain is acceptable in all references.

See **UNITED KINGDOM.**

• GREAT DEPRESSION

See **DEPRESSION.**

● **GREAT LAKES**
The five, from the largest to the smallest: Lake Superior, Lake Huron, Lake Michigan, Lake Erie, Lake Ontario.

● **GREAT PLAINS**
The prairie lands that extend from North Dakota to Texas, and from the Missouri River to the Rocky Mountains.
Use *northern Plains, southwestern Plains* and the like when referring to a portion of the region.

● **GREEK CATHOLIC CHURCH**
See **EASTERN RITE CHURCHES.**

● **GREEK ORTHODOX ARCHDIOCESE OF NORTH AND SOUTH AMERICA**
See **EASTERN ORTHODOX CHURCHES.**

● **GREEK ORTHODOX CHURCH**
See **EASTERN ORTHODOX CHURCHES.**

● **GREEN REVOLUTION**
The substantial increase in agricultural yields that resulted from the development of new varieties of grains.

● **GREENWICH MEAN TIME**
The abbreviation *G-M-T* is acceptable on the second reference
G-M-T is five hours ahead of Eastern Standard Time and four hours ahead of Eastern Daylight Time.

● **GRINGO**
See the **NATIONALITIES AND RACES** entry.

● **GRISLY, GRIZZLY**
Grisly is horrifying, repugnant.
Grizzly means grayish or is a short form for *grizzly bear.*

● **GRITS**
Ground hominy. The word normally takes plural verbs and pronouns: *Grits are to country ham what Yorkshire pudding is to roast beef.*

● **GROSS NATIONAL PRODUCT**
The total value at retail prices of all the goods and services produced by a nation's economy in a given time period.
As calculated quarterly by the Department of Commerce, the gross national product of the United States is considered the broadest available measure of the nation's economic activity.

● **GROSS PROFIT, GROSS REVENUE**
See **PROFIT TERMINOLOGY.**

● **GROUNDHOG DAY**
February second.

● **GROUNDSKEEPER**

● **GROUNDSWELL**

● **GROUP**
Takes singular verbs and pronouns: *The group is reviewing its position.*

● **GROWN-UP** (n. and adj.)

● **GRUMMAN** (GRUHM'-UHN) **CORPORATION**
Headquarters of this aerospace firm is in Bethpage, New York.

● **GUADALUPE** (GWAD-AH-LOOP'-AY) (Mexico)

● **GUADELOUPE** (GWAD-AH-LOOP') (West Indies)

● **GUAM**
Use in datelines after the name of a community. See **DATELINES.**

• **GUARANTEE**
Preferred to *guaranty*, except in proper names.

• **GUARDSMAN**
See **NATIONAL GUARD** and **COAST GUARDSMAN.**

• **GUATEMALA CITY**
Stands alone in datelines.

• **GUBERNATORIAL**

• **GUERRILLA**
Unorthodox soldiers and their tactics.

• **GUEST**
Do not use as a verb except in quoted matter. (An exception to a use recorded by Webster's New World.)

• **GULF AND WESTERN INDUSTRIES, INCORPORATED**
Headquarters is in New York.

• **GULF OF IRAN**
Use the long-established name, *Persian Gulf*, unless directly quoting the government of Iran.
When *Gulf of Iran* is used, explain in the text that this body of water off the southern coast of Iran is more commonly known as *the Persian Gulf.*

• **GULF OIL CORPORATION**
Headquarters is in Pittsburgh.

• **GULF STREAM**
But the racetrack is *Gulfstream Park.*

• **GUNBATTLE, GUNBOAT, GUNFIGHT, GUNFIRE, GUNPOINT, GUNPOWDER**

• **GUNG-HO**
A colloquialism to be used sparingly.

• **GUNS**
See **WEAPONS.**

• **GURU**

• **GYPSY MOTH**

• HABEAS CORPUS
(HAY'-BEE-UHS KAWR'-PUHS)

A writ or form of petition filed to seek the prompt release of someone in custody. It places the burden of proof on those detaining the person to justify it.

When *habeas corpus* is used in a story, define it.

• HAGUE, THE (HAYG)

Use the article *the* in datelines and all references to the capital of The Netherlands.

• HALF

It is not necessary to use the preposition *of*: *half the time* is correct, but *half of the time* is not wrong.

• HALF-

Follow Webster's New World Dictionary. Hyphenate if not listed there.

Some frequently used words without a hyphen:

HALFBACK	HALFTONE
HALFHEARTED	HALFTRACK

Also: HALFTIME, an exception to the dictionary in keeping with widespread practice in sports copy.

Some frequently used combinations that include a hyphen:

HALF-BAKED	HALF-LIFE
HALF-BLOOD	HALF-MOON
HALF-COCKED	HALF-SOLE (v.)
HALF-HOUR	HALF-TRUTH

• HALF-MAST, HALF-STAFF

On ships and at naval stations ashore, flags are flown at *half-mast.*

Elsewhere ashore, flags are flown at *half-staff.*

• HALLELUJAH

• HALLEY'S COMMET

After Edmund Halley, an English astronomer who predicted the comet's appearance once every 75 years, last seen in 1910.

• HALLOWEEN

• HALO, HALOS

• HANDICAPS

Follow the rules for NUMERALS, hyphenating adjectival forms before a noun: *He has a three handicap, he is a three-handicap golfer.*

• HANDMADE

• HAND-PICKED

• HANDS OFF, HANDS-OFF

Hyphenate when used as a compound modifier: *He kept his hands off the matter. He follows a hands-off policy.*

• HAND TO HAND, HAND-TO-HAND, HAND TO MOUTH, HAND-TO-MOUTH

Hyphenate when used as compound modifiers: *The cup was passed from hand to hand. They live a hand-to-mouth existence.*

• HANG, HANGED, HUNG

One *hangs* a picture, a criminal or oneself.

For past tense or the passive, use *hanged* when referring to executions or suicides, *hung* for other actions.

● **HANGAR, HANGER**
A *hangar* is a building.
A *hanger* is used for clothes.

● **HANGOVER**

● **HANKY-PANKY**

● **HANUKKAH**
The Jewish Feast of Lights, an eight-day commemoration of the re-dedication of the Temple by the Macabees after their victory over the Syrians.

Usually occurs in December but sometimes falls in late November.

● **HARASS, HARASSMENT**

● **HAREBRAINED**

● **HARELIP**

● **HARRIS SURVEY**
Prepared by Louis Harris and Associates of New York.

● **HAVANA**
The city in Cuba stands alone in datelines.

● **HAWAII**
Residents are *Hawaiians.*

The state is comprised of 132 islands, about two-thousand, 400 miles southwest of San Francisco. Collectively, they are the *Hawaiian Islands.*

Eight islands—Hawaii, Hihau (hee-ah'-oo), Kahoolawe (kah-hoo-lah'-weh), Kauai (kah-oo'-eye), Lanai (lah'-ny), Maui (mow'-ee), Molokai (muh-loh'-ky) and Oahu (oh-ah'-hoo)—account for all but three square miles of the six-thousand, 450 in the state.

The largest island in terms of land area is Hawaii. Honolulu and Pearl Harbor are on Oahu, where more than 80 percent of the state's residents live.

Honolulu stands alone in datelines.

Use *Hawaii* after all other cities in datelines. If need be, specify the island in the body of the story.

● **HAWAIIAN AIRLINES**
Headquarters is in Honolulu.

● **H-BOMB**
Use *hydrogen bomb* unless a direct quotation is involved.

● **HEADLONG**

● **HEAD-ON** (adj. and adv.)

● **HEADQUARTERS**
May take a singular or a plural verb.

Do not use *headquarter* as a verb.

● **HEARING EXAMINER**
See ADMINISTRATIVE LAW JUDGE.

● **HEARSAY**

● **HEAVEN**

● **HECT-** (before a vowel)
HECTO- (before a consonant)
A prefix denoting 100 units of a measure. Move a decimal point two places to the right, adding zeros if necessary, to convert to the basic unit: five and a-half (five-point-five) hectometers equals 550 meters.

● **HECTARE**
A unit of surface measure in the metric system equal to 100 ares or ten-thousand square meters.

A hectare equals two-point-47 (roughly two and a-half) acres, 107-thousand, 639-point-one square feet, or eleven thousand, 959-point nine square yards.

To convert to acres, multiply by two-point-47: five hectares times two-point-47 equals 12-point 35 acres.

See ACRE and METRIC SYSTEM.

- **HEIGHTS**
  See **DIMENSIONS**.

- **HELIPORT**

- **HELTER-SKELTER**

- **HEMORRHAGE**

- **HEMORRHOID**

- **HER**
  Do not use this pronoun in reference to nations or ships, except in quoted matter.
  Use *it* instead.

- **HEROIN**
  The narcotic, originally a trademark.

- **HERTZ**
  This term, the same in singular or plural, has been adopted as the international unit of frequency equal to one cycle per second.
  In contexts where it would not be understood by most listeners, it should be explained.
  Do not abbreviate.

- **HIDEAWAY**

- **HIGHWAY DESIGNATIONS**
  Follow the rules for **ABBREVIATIONS; NUMERALS;** and **HYPHENS.**
  Interstate highways should be identified as such on the first reference: *Interstate Route 495* or *Interstate 495.* But on the second reference, the more familiar *I-495* may be used.
  When a letter is appended to a number, hyphenate: *Route One-a.*

- **HIKE**
  People take *hikes* through the woods, but they *increase* prices.

- **HIROSHIMA**
  On August sixth, 1945, the Japanese city and military base were the targets of the first atomic bomb dropped as a weapon. The explosion had the force of 20-thousand tons—20 kilotons—of T-N-T. It destroyed more than four square miles and killed or injured 160-thousand people.

- **HIS, HER**
  Do not presume maleness in constructing a sentence, but use the pronoun *his* when an indefinite antecedent may be male or female: *A reporter attempts to protect his sources.* (Not *his* or *her* sources, but note the use of the word *reporter* rather than *newsman.*)
  Frequently, however, the best choice is a slight revision of the sentence: *Reporters attempt to protect their sources.*

- **HISPANIOLA**
  The island shared by the Dominican Republic and Haiti.
  See **WESTERN HEMISPHERE.**

- **HISTORIC, HISTORICAL**
  A *historic* event is an important occurrence, one that stands out in history.
  Any occurrence in the past is a *historical* event.

- **HISTORY**
  Avoid the redundant *past history.*

- **HIT AND RUN** (v.)
  HIT-AND-RUN (n. and adj.)
  The coach told him to hit and run. He scored on a hit-and-run. She was struck by a hit-and-run driver.

- **HITCHHIKE, HITCHHIKER**

• HOCKEY

The spellings of some frequently used words:

BLUE LINE	PLAYOFF (n., adj.)
CREASE	POWER PLAY
FACE OFF (v.)	POWER-PLAY GOAL
FACEOFF (n., adj.)	RED LINE
GOALIE	SHORT-HANDED
GOAL LINE	SLAP SHOT
GOAL POST	TWO-ON-ONE BREAK
GOALTENDER	
PENALTY BOX	
PLAY OFF (v.)	

The term *hat trick* applies when a player has scored three goals in a game. Use it sparingly, however.

Scores: Period scores and final scores are moved on a spot basis, using this format:

NHL
FIRST BOSTON 2 N.Y. RANGERS 1

Final scores would substitute *final* for the period number.

Standings: The form:

CAMPBELL CONFERENCE
PATRICK DIVISION

	W	L	T	PTS	GF	GA
PHILADELPHIA	47	10	14	108	314	184
N.Y. ISLANDERS	45	17	9	99	310	192

• HOCUS-POCUS

• HODGEPODGE

• HODGKIN'S DISEASE

After Dr. Thomas Hodgkin, the English physician who first described the disease of the lymph nodes.

• HO-HUM

• HOLDING COMPANY

A company whose principal assets are the securities it owns in companies that actually provide goods or services.

The usual reason for forming a holding company is to enable one corporation and its directors to control several companies by holding a majority of their stock.

• HOLD UP (v.) HOLDUP (n. and adj.)

• HOLIDAYS AND HOLY DAYS

The legal holidays in federal law are New Year's, Washington's Birthday, Memorial Day, Independence Day, Labor Day, Columbus Day, Veterans Day, Thanksgiving and Christmas. See individual entries for the official dates and when they are observed if they fall on a weekend.

The designation of a day as a federal legal holiday means that federal employees receive the day off or are paid overtime if they must work. Other requirements that may apply to holidays generally are left to the states. Many follow the federal lead in designating holidays, but they are not required to do so.

• HOLLYWOOD

Stands alone in datelines when used instead of *Los Angeles* on stories about films and the film industry.

• HOLOCAINE

A trademark for a type of local anesthetic.

• HOLY FATHER

The preferred form is to use *the pope* or *the pontiff,* or to give the individual's name.

Use *Holy Father* in direct quotations

or special contexts where a particular literary effect is desired.

• HOLY SEE

The headquarters of the Roman Catholic Church in Vatican City.

• HOLY SPIRIT

Now preferred over *Holy Ghost* in most usage.

• HOLY WEEK

The week before Easter.

• HOME-MADE

• HOMETOWN (n. and adj.)

• HOMICIDE, MURDER, MANSLAUGHTER

Homicide is a legal term for slaying or killing.

Murder is malicious, premeditated homicide. Some states arbitrarily define certain homicides as murder if the killing occurs on the course of armed robbery, rape, and so on.

Manslaughter is homicide without malice or premeditation.

A person should not be described as a *murderer* until convicted of the charge.

Unless authorities say premeditation was obvious, do not say that a victim *was murdered* until someone has been convicted of murder in court. Instead, say that a victim *was killed.*

See **EXECUTE** and the **ASSASSIN, KILLER, MURDERER** entry.

• HONG KONG

Stands alone in datelines.

• HONKY

A term of abuse directed toward whites by blacks. Use it only in quoted matter.

See the **NATIONALITIES AND RACES** entry.

• HONOLULU

The city in Hawaii stands alone in datelines. It is on the island of Oahu.

See **HAWAII.**

• HONORARY DEGREES

All references to honorary degrees should specify that the degree was honorary.

Do not use *doctor* before the name of an individual whose only doctorate is honorary.

• HOOF-AND-MOUTH DISEASE

• HOOKY

Not *hookey.*

• HOPEFULLY

It means in a hopeful manner. Do not use it to mean it is hoped, let us hope or we hope.

Right: *It is hoped that we will complete our work in June.*

Right: *We hope that we will complete our work in June.*

Wrong as a way to express the thought in the previous two sentences: *Hopefully, we will complete our work in June.*

• HORSEPOWER

• HORSE RACING

Some frequently used terms and their definitions:

Colt: A male horse from two to five years old.

Horse: A male horse five years or older.

Gelding: A castrated male horse.

Filly: A female horse two to five years old.

Mare: A female horse five years or older.

Stallion: A male horse used for breeding.

Broodmare: A female horse used for breeding.

Furlong: One-eighth of a mile. Race distances are given in furlongs up through seven furlongs. After that, they are expressed in miles and fractions of a mile, as in *one and a-16th miles.*

Entry: Two or more horses owned by same owner running as a single betting interest. In some states two or more horses trained by same person but having different owners also are coupled in betting.

Mutuel Field: Two or more horses, long shots, that have different owners and trainers. They are coupled as a single betting interest to give the field not more than 12 wagering interests. There cannot be more than 12 betting interests in a race. The bettor wins if either horse finishes in the money.

Half-Mile Pole: The pole on a race track that marks one-half mile from the finish. All distances are measured from the finish line, meaning that when a horse reaches the quarter pole, he is one-quarter mile from the finish.

Bug Boy: An apprentice jockey, so called because of the asterisk beside the individual's name in a program. It means that the jockey's mount gets a five-pound weight allowance.

• HOST

Do not use it as a verb. (Exception to a usage recorded in Webster's New World.)

• HOTEL AND RESTAURANT EMPLOYEES AND BARTENDERS INTERNATIONAL UNION

The shortened forms *Hotel and Restaurant Employees union* and *Bartenders union* are acceptable in all references.

Headquarters is in Cincinnati.

• HOT LINE

The circuit linking the United States and the Soviet Union.

• HOUSEHOLD, HOUSING UNIT

In the sense used by the Census Bureau, a *household* is made up of people who occupy a house, room, group of rooms or an apartment that constitutes a housing unit. A household may contain more than one family or may be used by one person.

A *housing unit*, as defined by the bureau, is a group of rooms or a single room occupied by people who do not live and eat with any other persons in the structure. It must have either direct access from the outside or through a common hall, or have a kitchen or cooking equipment for the exclusive use of the occupants.

• HOUSE OF COMMONS, HOUSE OF LORDS

The two houses of the British Parliament.

On second reference: *Commons* or *the Commons, Lords* or *the Lords.*

• HOUSTON

The city in Texas stands alone in datelines.

• HOVERCRAFT

A trademark for a vehicle that travels on a cushion of air.

• HOWEVER

But is better.

• HOWITZER

See **WEAPONS**.

• HUMAN, HUMAN BEING

Human is preferred, but either is acceptable.

• HURRICANES

Use *it* and *its* in pronoun references to hurricanes.

Weather forecasters assign both masculine and feminine names to the storms. Do not use the presence of a woman's name as an excuse for the use of sexist images in describing the storm's course. Avoid, for example, such sentences as *The fickle Hazel teased the Louisiana coast.*

See **WEATHER TERMS**.

• HUSBAND, WIDOWER

When a wife dies, she is survived by her *husband.* Thereafter, he is a *widower.*

• HYDRO-

The rules in **PREFIXES** apply, but in general, no hyphen. Some examples:

HYDROELECTRIC
HYDROPHOBIA

• HYPER-

The rules in **PREFIXES** apply, but in general, no hyphen. Some examples:

HYPERACTIVE
HYPERCRITICAL

• HYPHEN

Hyphens are joiners. They are used to avoid ambiguity as well as to form a single idea from two or more words. They are also used in broadcast writing to guide the announcer through unusual constructions, long rows of numbers and unusual combinations of letters.

In general, writers are urged to avoid unnecessary hyphenation. But in broadcast writing, it is far better to use an extra hyphen now and then if it makes the copy easier to read aloud.

Some general guidelines:

Avoid Ambiguity: Use a hyphen whenever the thought would be unclear without it. *He is a small-business representative* sounds the same on the air as: *He is a small business representative.* But the announcer knows upon seeing the hyphen that the person in question is a representative of small businesses, not a small person who represents business.

Compound Modifiers: A compound modifier, two or more words expressing a single concept, should be tied together with hyphens when followed by a noun: *a first-quarter touchdown, a bluish-green dress, a full-time job, a know-it-all attitude.*

But it is not necessary to use hyphens to connect the adverb *very* or any adverb ending in *-ly*: *a very good time, an easily remembered rule.*

Two-Thought Compounds: *Socio-economic, serio-comic.*

Compound Proper Nouns and Adjectives: *Italian-American, Mexican-American.*

Prefixes and Suffixes: See the **PREFIXES** and **SUFFIXES** entries for the most frequently used forms.

Break Up Duplicated Vowels, Tripled Consonants: *anti-intellectual, pre-empt, shell-like.*

Numerals: Use a hyphen to link numerals and the word *to* in odds, scores and ratios: *He beat him two-to-*

one; It was a 7-to-5 loss. Also to link compound numerals: *ten-thousand, 500 dollars.*

Do not use hyphens with (m) millions and (b) billions: *ten (m) million dollars.* But: *ten-point-five (m) million dollars.*

With Abbreviations: Use hyphens with abbreviations which should be pronounced letter-by-letter: *U-N, C-B-S, A-B-C, N-B-C, AFL-CIO* (an exception).

Don't use them with acronyms—abbreviations that should be pronounced as a word: *"UNESCO," "WATS."*

See **NUMERALS; ABBREVIATIONS; ACRONYMS;** and **DOUBLE DASH.**

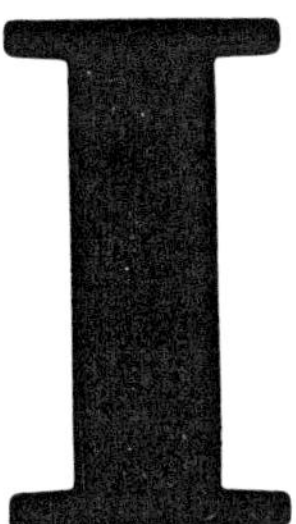

• IBERIA AIR LINES OF SPAIN

An *Iberia airliner* is acceptable in any reference.

Headquarters is in Madrid.

• I-C-B-M, I-C-B-M'S

Acceptable on first reference for *intercontinental ballistic missile*, but the term should be defined in the body of the story.

And avoid the redundant *I-C-B-M missiles.*

• ICE AGE

Denotes not a single period, but any of a series of cold periods marked by glaciation alternating with periods of relative warmth.

Together, the Ice Ages, which began about 600-thousand years ago, make up glacial epochs. During the first, called the *Pleistocene (ply'-stoh-seen),* glaciers covered much of North America and Northwestern Europe.

The present epoch, the *Helocene (heel'-oh-seen)* or *Recent*, began about 12-thousand years ago, with glaciers restricted to Antarctica and Greenland.

• ICELANDIC AIRLINES

Headquarters is in Reykjavik (Ray'-kyuh-vik), Iceland.

• ICE STORM

See **WEATHER TERMS.**

• ILLEGAL

Use *illegal* only to mean a violation of the law. Be especially careful in labor-management disputes, where one side often calls an action by the other side *illegal.* Usually it is a charge that a contract or rule, not a law, has been violated.

• ILLUSION

See the **ALLUSION, ILLUSION** entry.

• IMAM

The leader of a prayer in a Moslem mosque.

Also the formal title for a Moslem leader or ruler.

• IMMIGRATE

See **EMIGRATE, IMMIGRATE** entry.

• IMPASSABLE, IMPASSIBLE, IMPASSIVE

Impassable means that passage is impossible. *The bridge was impassable.*

Impassible and *impassive* describe the lack of sensitivity to pain or suffering. Webster's New World notes, however, that *impassible* suggests an inability to be affected, while *impassive* implies only that no reaction was noticeable: *She was impassive throughout the ordeal.*

• IMPEL, IMPELLED, IMPELLING

• IMPERIAL GALLON

The standard British gallon, equal to 277-point-42 cubic inches or about one-point-two U-S gallons.

The metric equivalent is about four and a-half liters.

See **LITER.**

• IMPERIAL QUART

One-fourth of an imperial gallon.

• IMPLAUSIBLE

• IMPLY, INFER

Writers or speakers *imply* in the words they use.

A listener or reader *infers* something from the words.

• IMPOSTOR

Not *imposter.*

• IMPROMPTU

It means without preparation or advance thought.

• IN, INTO

In indicates location: *He was in the room.*

Into indicates motion: *She walked into the room.*

• "IN"

When employed to indicate that something is in vogue, use quotation marks only if followed by a noun: *It was the "in" thing to do. Racoon coats are in again.*

• IN-

No hyphen when it means not:

INACCURATE
INSUFFERABLE

Often solid in other cases:

INBOUND	INFIGHTING
INDOOR	INPATIENT (n., adj.)
INFIELD	

A few combinations take a hyphen, however:

IN-DEPTH	IN-HOUSE
IN-GROUP	IN-LAW

Follow Webster's New World when in doubt.

• -IN

Precede with a hyphen:

BREAK-IN	WALK-IN
CAVE-IN	WRITE-IN

• INCH

One-12th of a foot.

The metric equivalent is exactly two-point-54 centimeters.

To convert to centimeters, multiply by two-point-54. Six inches times two-point-54 equals 15-point-24 centimeters.

See **CENTIMETER, FOOT,** and **DIMENSIONS.**

• INCLUDE

Use *include* to introduce a series when the items that follow are only part of the total: *The price includes breakfast. The zoo includes lions and tigers.*

Use *comprise* when the full list of individual elements is given: *The zoo comprises 100 types of animals, including lions and tigers.*

See the **COMPOSE, COMPRISE, CONSTITUTE** entry.

• INCOME

See **PROFIT TERMINOLOGY.**

• INCORPORATED

Do not abbreviate.

Generally, it should be used only when referring to the formal title of a corporation: *J. C. Penny Company, Incorporated.* But in most contexts, informalize the name: *J. C. Penney says it is opening a new store.*

• INCREDIBLE, INCREDULOUS

Incredible means unbelievable.

Incredulous means skeptical.

• INCUR, INCURRED, INCURRING

• INDEPENDENCE DAY

July Fourth or *Fourth of July* also are acceptable.

The federal legal holiday is observed on Friday if the Fourth falls on a Saturday, and on Monday if it falls on a Sunday.

• INDEX, INDEXES

• INDEX OF LEADING ECONOMIC INDICATORS
A composite of 12 economic measurements that was developed to help forecast likely shifts in the economy as a whole.

It is compiled by the Commerce Department.

• INDIANAPOLIS
The city in Indiana stands alone in datelines.

• INDIANS
In news stories about American Indians, such words as *wampum, warpath, powwow, tepee, brave, squaw,* can be disparaging and offensive. Avoid them.

• INDICT
Use *indict* only in connection with the legal process of bringing charges against an individual or corporation.

To avoid any suggestion that someone is being judged before a trial, do not use phrases such as *indicted for killing* or *indicted for bribery.* Instead, use *indicted on a charge of killing, indicted on a bribery charge.*

For guidelines on related words, see the entries under ACCUSE; ALLEGE; and ARREST.

• INDISCREET, INDISCRETE
Indiscreet means lacking prudence. Its noun form is *indiscretion.*

Indiscrete means not separated into distinct parts. Its noun form is *indiscreteness.*

• INDISCRIMINATE, INDISCRIMINATELY

• INDISPENSIBLE

• INDO-
Usually hyphenated:

INDO-ARYAN INDO-HITITE
INDO-GERMAN INDO-IRANIAN

But: INDOCHINA.

• INDOCHINA
Formerly French Indochina, now divided into Cambodia, Laos and Vietnam.

• INDOCHINESE PENINSULA
Located here are the nations of Burma, Cambodia, Laos, Thailand and Vietnam.

• INDONESIA
Use after the name of a community in datelines on stories from this nation.

Specify an individual island, if needed, in the text.

• INDOOR (adj.)
INDOORS (adv.)
He plays indoor tennis. He went indoors.

• INFANT
Applicable to children through 12 months old.

• INFANTILE PARALYSIS
The preferred term is *polio.*

• INFLATION
A sustained increase in prices. The result is a decrease in the purchasing power of money.

There are two basic types of inflation:

Cost-push inflation occurs when rising costs are the chief reason for the increased prices.

Demand-pull inflation occurs when the amount of money available exceeds the amount of goods and services available for sale.

• INFRA-

The rules in **PREFIXES** apply, but in general, no hyphen. Some examples:

INFRARED
INFRASTRUCTURE

• INITIALS

Avoid initials whenever possible. This rule applies to all types of writing, but is especially important when writing for broadcast.

Make it *Richard Nixon,* not *Richard M. Nixon.*

Some people insist on using their initials instead of a first name. In that case, use periods and no space; this will ensure that the two initials run on the same line when sent on the wire: *H.L. Mencken.*

Do not use only an initial for a first name unless it is the individual's preference or the first name cannot be learned: *Police identified the victim only as J. Jones, no known address.*

• INJURIES

They are *suffered* or *sustained,* not *received.*

• IN-LAW

• INNOCENT

Use *innocent,* rather than *not guilty,* in describing a defendant's plea or a jury's verdict, to guard against the word *not* being dropped inadvertently.

It is impossible to be too careful when reporting criminal pleas and verdicts. Always check carefully before sending the story.

• INNOCUOUS

• INNUENDO

• INOCULATE

• INQUIRE, INQUIRY

Not *enquire, enquiry.*

• INSIGNIA

Singular and plural.

• IN SPITE OF

Despite means the same thing and is shorter.

• INTELLIGENCE QUOTIENT

I-Q is acceptable in all references.

• INTER-

The rules in **PREFIXES** apply, but in general, no hyphen. Some examples:

INTERAMERICAN
INTERRACIAL
INTERSTATE

• INTERCOLLEGIATE ASSOCIATION OF AMATEUR ATHLETES OF AMERICA

Spell it out on the first reference. After that, use *the association.*

• INTERNAL REVENUE SERVICE

I-R-S is acceptable in all references.

• INTERNATIONAL ASSOCIATION OF MACHINISTS AND AEROSPACE WORKERS

The shortened form *Machinists union* is acceptable in all references.

Headquarters is in Washington.

• INTERNATIONAL BANK FOR RECONSTRUCTION AND DEVELOPMENT
World Bank is acceptable in all references.
Headquarters is in Washington.

• INTERNATIONAL BROTHERHOOD OF ELECTRICAL WORKERS
Use the full name of the first reference to avoid confusion with the United Electrical, Radio and Machine Workers of America.
Do not use the abbreviation *I-B-E-W.* Instead, on second reference, use such terms as *the union* or *the electrical workers.*
Headquarters is in Washington.

• INTERNATIONAL BROTHERHOOD OF PAINTERS AND ALLIED TRADES OF THE UNITED STATES AND CANADA
The shortened form *Painters union* is acceptable in all references.
Headquarters is in Washington.

• INTERNATIONAL BROTHERHOOD OF TEAMSTERS, CHAUFFURS, WAREHOUSEMEN AND HELPERS OF AMERICA
The shortened formed *Teamsters union*—no apostrophe—is acceptable in all references.
Headquarters is in Washington.

• INTERNATIONAL BUSINESS MACHINES CORPORATION
I-B-M is acceptable in all references.
Headquarters is in Armonk, New York.

• INTERNATIONAL COURT OF JUSTICE
The principal judicial organ of the United Nations, established at The Hague in 1945.
The court is not open to individuals. It has jurisdiction over all matters specifically provided for either in the U-N charter or in treaties and conventions in force. It also has jurisdiction over cases referred to it by U-N members and by non-members such as Switzerland that subscribe to the court statute.
The court serves as the successor to the Permanent Court of International Justice of the League of Nations, which also was known as the World Court.
On second reference use *international court* or *world court.* Do not abbreviate.

• INTERNATIONAL CRIMINAL POLICE ORGANIZATION
Interpol is acceptable in all references.
Headquarters is in Paris.

• INTERNATIONAL DATE LINE
Three words. It is the imaginary line drawn north and south through the Pacific Ocean, largely along the 180th meridian.
By international agreement, when it is 12:01 a-m Sunday just west of the line, it is 12:01 a-m Saturday just east of it.
See **TIME ZONES.**

• INTERNATIONAL LABOR ORGANIZATION
Do not abbreviate.
Headquarters is in Geneva, Switzerland.

• INTERNATIONAL LADIES' GARMENT WORKERS UNION
The shortened forms *Ladies' Garment Workers* and *Ladies' Garment*

Workers union are acceptable in all references. But do not abbreviate.

Headquarters is in New York.

• INTERNATIONAL LONGSHOREMEN'S ASSOCIATION

The shortened form *Longshoremen's union* is acceptable in all references. Do not abbreviate.

Headquarters is in New York.

• INTERNATIONAL MONETARY FUND

Do not abbreviate; use *the fund* on the second reference.

Headquarters is in Washington.

• INTERNATIONAL TELECOMMUNICATIONS SATELLITE ORGANIZATION

Intelsat is acceptable on first reference, but the body of the story should identify it as the shortened form of the full name.

(The original name was International Telecommunications Satellite Consortium.)

Headquarters is in Washington.

• INTERNATIONAL TELEPHONE AND TELEGRAPH CORPORATION

I-T-T is acceptable on second reference.

Headquarters is in New York.

• INTERNATIONAL UNION, UNITED AUTOMOBILE, AEROSPACE AND AGRICULTURAL IMPLEMENT WORKERS OF AMERICA

This is the full, formal name for the union known more commonly as the *United Auto Workers*.

See the entry that begins **UNITED AUTOMOBILE.**

• INTERPOL

Acceptable in all references for *International Criminal Police Organization.*

• INTERSTATE COMMERCE COMMISSION

I-C-C is acceptable on second reference.

• INTRA-

The rules in **PREFIXES** apply, but in general, no hyphen. Some examples:

INTRAMURAL
INTRASTATE

It means *within,* as opposed to *inter-,* which means *between* or *among.* Thus, *intrastate commerce* is commerce within a single state, while *interstate commerce* occurs between two or more states.

• INTRAUTERINE DEVICE

I-U-D is acceptable on second reference.

• I-O-U, I-O-U'S

• IRAN

The nation formerly called Persia. It is not an Arab country.

The people are *Iranians,* not *Persians* or *Irani.*

For the language, use *Persian,* the word widely accepted outside Iran. Inside Iran, the language is called *Farsi.*

• IRAQ

The Arab nation coinciding roughly with ancient Mesopotamia.

Its people are *Iraqis.* The dialect of Arabic is *Iraqi.*

• IRELAND

Acceptable in most references to

the independent nation known formerly as the Irish Republic.

Use *Irish Republic* when a distinction must be made between this nation and *Northern Ireland,* a part of the United Kingdom.

• IRISH INTERNATIONAL AIRLINES

The preferred name is *Aer Lingus.* Headquarters is in Dublin, Ireland.

• IRISH REPUBLICAN ARMY

A group that fights to wrest Northern Ireland from British rule and unite it with the Irish Republic.

I-R-A is acceptable on second reference.

• IRON CURTAIN

Use it only in quoted matter.

• IRREGARDLESS

Regardless is correct.

• ISLAM

The Moslem religion. Its deity is Allah. Mohammed is its founder and prophet.

The adjective is *Islamic.*

See **MOSLEM.**

• ISLAND

Some guidelines:

In Domestic Datelines: For communities on islands within the United States, use the community and state names:

(EDGARTOWN, MASSACHUSETTS) --

Honolulu, however, stands alone.

In Foreign Datelines: If an island has an identity of its own—for example, *Bermuda, Puerto Rico,* or *Taiwan*—use it in the dateline:

(HAMILTON, BERMUDA) --

Havana, Hong Kong, Macao and *Singapore* stand alone, however.

If the island is part of a chain, use the chain's name:

(MANILA, THE PHILIPPINES) --

For additional guidelines, see **DATELINES.**

• IT

Use this pronoun, rather than *she,* in references to nations and ships.

• IT'S, ITS

It's is a contraction for *it is* or *it has: It's up to you. It's been a long time.*

Its is the possessive form of the neuter pronoun: *The company lost its assets.*

• IVY LEAGUE

Brown University, Columbia University, Cornell University, Dartmouth College, Harvard University, Princeton University, the University of Pennsylvania and Yale University.

• JAIL

Not interchangeable with *prison*. See the **PRISON, JAIL** entry.

• "JANE'S ALL THE WORLD'S AIRCRAFT," "JANE'S FIGHTING SHIPS"

The reference sources for questions about aircraft and military ships not covered in this book.

The reference for non-military ships is Lloyd's Register of Shipping.

• JAPAN AIR LINES

J-A-L is acceptable on second reference.

Headquarters is in Tokyo.

• JAPAN CURRENT

A warm current flowing from the Philippine Sea east of Taiwan and northeast past Japan.

• JARGON

The special vocabulary and idioms of a particular class or occupational group.

In general, avoid jargon. When it is appropriate in a special context, include an explanation of any words likely to be unfamiliar to most readers.

See **DIALECT** and **WORD SELECTION.**

• JAYCEES

The proper name for the former Junior Chamber of Commerce. The United State Jaycees, the parent domestic organization, is affiliated with the worldwide body, the Jaycees International.

Headquarters is in Tulsa, Oklahoma.

• J.C. PENNEY COMPANY, INCORPORATED

J.C. Penney or *Penney's* is acceptable on all references.

Headquarters is in New York.

• JEHOVAH'S WITNESSES

The denomination was founded in Pittsburgh in 1872 by Charles Taze Russell, a former Congregationalist layman.

Witnesses do most of their work through three legal corporations: the Watch Tower and Trace Society of Pennsylvania, the Watchtower Bible and Tract Society of New York, Incorporated, and, in England, the International Bible Students Association. The principal officers of the corporation elect a director, who becomes the international head of the Jehovah's Witnesses.

American membership is listed at more than 500-thousand.

Beliefs: Witnesses believe that they adhere to the oldest religion on earth, the worship of Almighty God revealed in the Bible as Jehovah.

They regard civil authority as necessary and obey it "as long as its laws do not contradict God's law." Witnesses refuse to bear arms, salute the flag or participate in secular government.

They refuse blood transfusions as being against the Bible, citing the section of Leviticus that reads: "'Whatsoever man . . . eats any manner of blood, I will cut him off from among his people."

Clergy: Witnesses consider themselves a society of ministers. A public ceremony of water immersion sets an individual apart as a minister of Jehovah.

There are no formal titles, but there are four levels of ministry: *publishers* (part-time workers expected to devote 60 hours a month to distributing literature), *general pioneers* and *special pioneers* (terms for part time workers who devote more than 60 hours a month to activities) and *pioneers* (full-time workers).

- **JERUSALEM**

Stands alone in datelines.

- **JESUS**

The central figure of Christianity, he also may be called *Jesus Christ.*

- **JET, JETLINER, JET PLANE**

See **AIRCRAFT TERMS.**

- **JEW**

Use for men and women. Do not use *Jewess.*

- **JEWISH CONGREGATIONS**

A Jewish congregation is autonomous. No synods, assemblies or hierarchies control the activities of an individual synagogue.

In the United States, there are three major expressions of Judaism:

1. Orthodox Judaism. Most of its congregations are represented nationally by the Union of Orthodox Jewish Congregations of America. Most of its rabbis are members of the Rabbinical Council of America.

2. Reform Judaism. Its national representatives are the Union of American Hebrew Congregations and the Central Conference of American Rabbis.

3. Conservative Judaism. Its national representatives are the United Synagogue of America and the Rabbinical Assembly.

These six groups make up the New York-based Synagogue Council of America. It is the vehicle for consultation among the three expressions and coordinates joint activities.

The council estimates that its members represent about three (m) million synagogue-afffiliated American Jews, divided about equally among the three major groupings. The council also estimates that one (m) million American Jews, most of them orthodox, are members of congregations not represented in the council.

Beliefs: Jews generally believe that a divine kingdom will be established on earth, opening a messianic era that will be marked by peace and bliss. They also believe that they have a mandate from God to work toward his kingdom.

The key to beliefs is the Torah, or Law of Moses, which consists of the first five books of the Bible. Jewish Scripture also includes the other books of the Old Testament. Additional elements of Jewish belief are contained in the Talmud, a detailed interpretation of the written and oral law of the faith.

Orthodox Jews expect the coming of the Messiaah, who is to be a descendant of King David. They are strict adherents of the biblical dietary laws, ritual forms and traditional holy days.

Reform Jews believe in the coming of a messianic age, but not a personal Messiah. They regard dietary laws and ritual forms as concessions to the customs of ancient times that may be adapted to the modern needs.

Conservative Jews take a middle position, generally adhering to traditional customs of diet and ritual but stressing that faith is not static and should adapt to the needs of contemporary culture.

Clergy: The only formal titles in use are *rabbi,* for the spiritual leader of a congregation, and *cantor,* for the individual who leads the congregation in song.

• JEWISH HOLY DAYS

See separate listings for Hanukkah, Passover, Purim, Rosh Hashana, Shavuot, Sukkot and Yom Kippur.

The High Holy Days are Rosh Hashana and Yom Kippur.

• JIBE

See the **GIBE, JIBE** entry.

• JOHN F. KENNEDY SPACE CENTER

Located in Cape Canaveral, Florida, it is "NASA's" principal launch site for manned spacecraft.

Kennedy Space Center is acceptable on all references.

For datelines on launch stories: *(CAPE CANAVERAL, FLORIDA)* --

See **CAPE CANAVERAL** and **LYNDON B. JOHNSON SPACE CENTER.**

• JOHNS HOPKINS UNIVERSITY

No apostrophes.

• JOINT CHIEFS OF STAFF

Also: *the Joint Chiefs, the chiefs* or *the chiefs of staff.*

• JUDGE

Do not use the title in the second reference. Do not use *court* as part of the title unless confusion would result without it:

—No *court* in the title: *U-S District Judge John Sirica, District Judge John Sirica, federal Judge John Sirica, Judge John Sirica, U-S Circuit Judge Homer Thornberry, appellate Judge John Blair.*

—*Court* needed in the title: *Juvenile Court Judge John Jones, Criminal Court Judge John Jones, Superior Court Judge Robert Harrison, state Supreme Court Judge William Cushing.*

When the formal title *chief judge* is used, put the court name after the judge's names: *Chief Judge John Sirica of U-S District Court in Washington, Chief Judge Clement Haynesworth of the Fourth Circuit Court of Appeals.* In such cases, it is often best to break the title in two, using the *chief judge* in reference to the person's name in one sentence, and the full court name in another.

Do not pile up long court names before the name of a judge. Make it *Judge John Smith of Allegheny County Common Pleas Court.* Not: *Allegheny County Common Pleas Court Judge John Smith.*

See **ADMINISTRATIVE LAW JUDGE; COURT NAMES; JUDICIAL BRANCH;** and **JUSTICE.**

• JUDGE ADVOCATE

The plural: *judge advocates.* Also: *judge advocate general, judge advocates general.*

See **TITLES.**

• JUDGMENT

Not *judgement.*

• JUDICIAL BRANCH

The federal court system that exists today as the outgrowth of Article Three of the Constitution is composed of the Supreme Court of the United States, the U-S District Courts of Appeals, U-S District Courts, the U-S Court of Claims, the U-S Court of Customs and Patent Appeals, and the U-S Customs Court. There are also four district judges for U-S territories.

The U-S Tax Court and U-S Court of Military Appeals are not part of the judicial branch.

For more detail on federal courts, see separate entries under the names listed above.

• JUDICIAL CONFERENCE OF THE UNITED STATES

This rule-making body for the courts of the judicial branch meets twice a year. Its 25 members are the Chief Justice of the United States, the chief judges of the eleven circuit courts, one district judge from each of the circuits, and the chief judges of the U-S Court of Claims and the U-S Court of Customs and Patent Appeals.

Day-to-day functions are handled by the Administrative Office of U-S Courts.

• JUMBO JET

Any very large jet plane, including the Boeing 747, the D-C-Ten, the L-Ten-Eleven and the C-Five-A.

• JUNIOR, SENIOR

Do not abbreviate, and do not precede by a comma: Joseph Kennedy Junior.

The notation *the second* may be used if it is the person's preference. But note thaat *the second* does not necessarily designaate *junior;* it often is used by a nephew or grandson.

If necessary to distinguish between father and son on the second reference, use phrases such as *the elder Smith* or *the younger Smith.*

See **NAMES.**

• JUNTA

See the **GOVERNMENT, JUNTA, REGIME** entry.

• JURY

The word takes singular verbs and pronouns: *The jury has been sequestered until it reaches a verdict.*

Do not use awkward phrases such as *seven-man, five-woman jury.* Make it: *jury of seven men and five women.*

See **GRAND JURY.**

• JUSTICE

It is the formal title for members of the Supreme Court and for jurists on some state courts. In such cases, do not use *judge* in first or subsequent references.

See **JUDGE; SUPREME COURT OF THE UNITED STATES.**

• JUVENILE DELINQUENT

Juveniles may be declared delinquents in many states for antisocial behavior or for breaking the law. In some states, laws prohibit publishing or broadcasting the names of juvenile delinquents.

Follow the local practice unless there is a compelling reason to the contrary.

- **KANSAS CITY**

Stands alone in datelines from *Kansas City, Missouri.*

But stories from *Kansas City, Kansas* should carry the state name.

- **KARAT**

See the **CARAT, CARET, KARAT** entry.

- **KELVIN SCALE**

A scale of temperatures based on, but different from, the Celsius scale. It is used primarily in science to record very high and very low temperatures. The Kelvin scale starts at zero and indicates the total absence of heat (absolute zero).

Zero on the Kelvin scale is equal to minus 273-point-15 degrees Celsius, or minus 460 degrees Fahrenheit.

The freezing point of water is 273-point-16 degrees Kelvin. The boiling point of water is 373-point-16 degress Kelvin.

See **CELSIUS** and **FAHRENHEIT.**

- **KEROSENE**

Formerly a trademark, now a generic term.

- **KETCHUP**

Not *catchup* or *catsup.*

- **KEYNOTE ADDRESS**

Also: keynote speech.

- **KEYSTONE KOPS**

- **K-G-B**

Acceptable on first reference, but the story should contain a phrase identifying it as the Soviet secret police and intelligence agency.

The initials stand for the Russian words meaning *Committee for State Security.*

- **KIBBUTZ** (KIH-BUTS')

An Israeli collective settlement.

The plural is *kibbutzim (kih-but-seem').*

- **KIDNAP, KIDNAPPED, KIDNAPPING, KIDNAPPER**

- **KIDS**

Use *children* unless you are talking about goats, or the use of *kids* as an informal synonym for *children* is appropriate in the context.

- **KILLER**

See the **ASSASSIN, KILLER, MURDERER** entry.

- **KILO-** (KEE'-LOH)

A prefix denoting one-thousand of a unit. Move a decimal point three places to the right, adding zeroes if necessary, to convert to the basic unit: ten and a-half kilograms equals ten-thousand, 500 grams.

- **KILOCYCLES**

The new term is *kilohertz.*

- **KILOGRAM** (KIL'-OH-GRAM)

The metric term for one-thousand grams.

A kilogram is equal to about two-point-two pounds, or 35 ounces.

To convert to pounds, multiply a kilogram measurement by two and two-tenths: nine kilograms times two-point-two equals 19-point-eight pounds.

See **GRAM; METRIC SYSTEM;** and **POUND.**

• KILOHERTZ (KIL'-OH-HERTS)
One-thousand cycles per second. The term replaces *kilocycles* as the correct term in applications such as broadcast frequencies.
Do not abbreviate.

• KILOMETER (KIL-AHM'-UH-TUHR)
The metric term for one-thousand meters.
A kilometer is equal to about three-thousand, 281 feet—five-eights (point-62) of a mile.
To convert a kilometer measurement to miles, multiply by point-62: five kilometers times point-62 equals three and one-tenth miles.
See **METER; METRIC SYSTEM;** and **MILES.**

• KILOTON (KIH'-LOH-TUHN), **KILOTONNAGE**
The unit used to measure the power of nuclear explosions. One kiloton has the explosive force of one-thousand tons of T-N-T.
The atomic bomb dropped on August sixth, 1945, on the Japanese city of Hiroshima, had an explosive force of 20 kilotons.
A *megaton* has the force of one (m) million tons of T-N-T. A *gigaton* has the force of one (b) billion tons of T-N-T.

• KILOWATT-HOUR
The amount of electricity consumed when one-thousand watts are used for one hour.
Do not abbreviate.

• KINDERGARTEN

• KING
Use in all references that use the king's given name: *King George the Fifth, the King, King George.*

• KLAN IN AMERICA
See **KU KLUX KLAN.**

• K-L-M ROYAL DUTCH AIRLINES
A K-L-M airliner is acceptable in any reference.
Headquarters in is Amsterdam, Netherlands.

• KNESSET (KUH-NES'-ET)
The Israeli parliament. See **FOREIGN LEGISLATIVE BODIES.**

• KNIGHT OF COLUMBUS
K-of-C may be used on second reference.

• KNOT
One nautical mile—six-thousand, 76-point-ten feet—per hour. It is a rate of travel; it is therefore redundant to say *knots-per-hour.*
A knot is computed as the length of one minute of a meridian. To convert knots to approximate statute miles per hour, multiply knots by one-point-15.

• KNOW-HOW

• KODAK
A trademark for cameras and other photographic products made by Eastman Kodak Company of Rochester, New York.

• KORAN (KOH-RAN')
The sacred book of Moslems, who believe that it contains the words of Allah dictated to the Prophet Mohammed through the Angel Gabriel.

• KOWTOW

• KRISS KRINGLE
Not *Kris.*

• KUDOS
It means credit or praise for an achievement.

The word takes plural verbs: *Kudos go to John Jones.*

• KU KLUX KLAN
Not *Klu.* There are 42 separate organizations known as the *Klan in America.*

Some of them do not use the full name *Ku Klux Klan,* but each may be called that, and the *K-K-K* initials may be used for any of them on second reference.

The two largest Klan organizations are the National Knights of the Ku Klux Klan, based in Stone Mountain, Georgia, and the United Klans of America, based in Tuscaloosa, Alabama.

An Imperial Board, composed of leaders from the various groups, meets occasionally to coordinate activities.

Formal titles are: *Imperial Wizard James Venable, Grand Dragon Dale Reusch.* Members are *Klansmen.*

• KUOMINTANG (GWOH'-MIN-TAHNG)
The Chinese Nationalist political party. Do not follow with the word *party. Tang* means party.

• KUWAIT (KOO-WAYT')
Stands alone in datelines.

- **LABOR DAY**

The first Monday in September.

- **LABORERS' INTERNATIONAL UNION OF NORTH AMERICA**

The shortened form *Laborers' union* is acceptable in all references.

Headquarters is in Washington.

- **LABOR PARTY**

Not *Labour,* even if British.

- **LABRADOR**

The mainland portion of the Canadian province of Newfoundland.

Use *Newfoundland* in datelines after the name of a community. Specify in the text that it is in Labrador.

- **LADIES PROFESSIONAL GOLF ASSOCIATION**

No apostrophe after *Ladies.* In general, spell out on first reference.

A phrase such as *L-P-G-A tournament* may be used on first reference to avoid a cumbersome lead. If this is done, provide the full name later in the story.

- **LADY**

Do not use as a synonym for *woman. Lady* may be used when it is a courtesy title or when a specific reference to fine manners is appropriate without patronizing overtones.

See **NOBILITY.**

- **LAETRILE** (LAY'-UH-TRIL)

A trademark for a substance derived from the chemical *amygdalin (uh-mig'-duh-lin),* found naturally in the pits of apricots and peaches and in bitter almonds.

It is believed by some to be an effective cancer treatment. The U-S Food and Drug Administration has said that the substance has not been proved safe and effective as an anti-cancer agent and has banned its interstate transportation. Marketed in some areas under the names *Bee-Seventeen* or *Aprikern.*

- **LAGER** (LAH'-GUHR) (beer)

- **LAME DUCK** (n.)
LAME-DUCK (adj.)

- **LAND-ROVER**

With a hyphen. A trademark for a brand of all-terrain vehicle.

- **LARCENY**

See the **BURGLARY, LARCENY, ROBBERY, THEFT** entry.

- **LAST**

Avoid the use of *last* as a synonym for *latest* if it might imply finality. *The last time it rained, I forgot my umbrella,* is acceptable. But: *The last announcement was made at noon today* may leave the newscaster and listener wondering whether the announcement was the final announcement, or whether others are to follow.

The word *last* is not necessary to convey the notion of most recent when the name of a month or day is used:

Preferred: *It happened Wednesday. It happened in April.* Correct, but redundant: *It happened last Wednesday.*

But: *It happened last week. It happened last month.*

• LATE

Do not use it to describe someone's actions while alive.

Wrong: *Only the late senator opposed this bill.* (He was not dead at that time.)

• LATEX (LAY'-TEX)

A resin-based substance used in making elastic materials and paints.

• LATIN AMERICA

See **WESTERN HEMISPHERE.**

• LATIN RITE

See **ROMAN CATHOLIC CHURCH.**

• LATITUDE AND LONGITUDE

Latitude, the distance north or south of the equator, is designated by parallels. *Longitude,* the distance east or west of Greenwich, England, is designated by meridians.

Following the rules for **NUMERALS,** use these forms to express degrees of latitude or longitude: *New York City lies at 40 degrees, 45 minutes north latitude and 74 degrees, zero minutes west longitude. It also happens to be south of the 41st parallel north, and along the 74th meridian west.*

• LATTER DAY SAINTS, LATTER-DAY SAINTS

See **CHURCH OF JESUS CHRIST OF LATTER-DAY SAINTS.**

• LAUNDROMAT

A trademark for a coin-operated laundry.

• LAW ENFORCEMENT ASSISTANCE ADMINISTRATION

L-E-A-A is acceptable on second reference.

• LAWSUIT

• LAWYER

A generic term for all members of the bar.

An *attorney* is someone legally appointed or empowered to act for another, usually, but not always, a lawyer. An *attorney at law* is a lawyer.

A *barrister* is an English lawyer who is specially trained and appears exclusively as a trial lawyer in higher courts. He is retained by a solicitor, not directly by the client. There is no equivalent term in the United States.

Counselor, when used in a legal sense, means a person who conducts a case in court, usually, but not always, a lawyer. A *counselor at law* is a lawyer. *Counsel* frequently is used collectively for a group of counselors.

A *solicitor* in England is a lawyer who performs legal services for the public. A solicitor appears in lower courts but does not have the right to appear in higher courts, which are reserved to barristers.

A *solicitor* in the United States is a lawyer employed by a governmental body. *Solicitor* is generally a job description, but in some agencies it is a formal title.

Solicitor general is the formal title for a chief law officer (where there is no attorney general) or for the chief assistant to the law officer (when there is an attorney general).

Do not use *lawyer* as a formal title.

See the **ATTORNEY, LAWYER** entry and **TITLES.**

• LAY, LIE

The action word is *lay.* It takes a direct object. *Laid* is the form for its past tense and its past participle. Its present participle is *laying.*

Lie indicates a state of reclining along a horizontal plane. It does not take a direct object. Its past tense is *lay*. Its past participle is *lain*. Its present participle is *lying*.

When *lie* means to make an untrue statement, the verb forms are *lie, lied, lying*.

Some examples:

Present or Future Tenses:

Right: *I will lay the book on the table. The prosecutor tried to lay the blame on him.*

Wrong: *He lays on the beach all day. I will lay down.*

Right: *He lies on the beach all day. I will lie down.*

In the Past Tense:

I laid the book on the table. The prosecutor has laid the blame on him.

He lay on the beach all day. He has lain on the beach all day. I lay down. I have lain down.

With the Present Participle:

I am laying the book on the table. The prosecutor is laying the blame on him.

He is lying on the beach. I am lying down.

• LEATHERNECK

The nickname for a member of the U-S Marine Corps. It is derived from the leather lining that was formerly part of the collar on the Marine uniform.

• LECTERN, PODIUM, PULPIT, ROSTRUM

A speaker stands *behind a lectern, on a podium* or *rostrum*, or *in the pulpit*.

• LEFT HAND (n.) LEFT-HANDED (adj.) LEFT-HANDER (n.)

• LEFTIST, ULTRA-LEFTIST

In general, avoid these terms in favor of a more precise description of an individual's political philosophy.

As popularly used today, particularly abroad, *leftist* often applies to someone who is merely liberal or believes in a form of democratic socialism.

Ultra-leftist suggests an individual who subscribes to a communist view or one holding that liberal or socialist change cannot come within the present form of government.

See **RADICAL** and the **RIGHTIST, ULTRA-RIGHTIST** entry.

• LEFT WING (n.)

But: *left-wing* (adj.), *left-winger* (n.).

• LEGAL HOLIDAY

See the **HOLIDAYS AND HOLY DAYS** entry.

• LEGION, LEGIONNAIRE

See **AMERICAN LEGION** and **FRENCH FOREIGN LEGION.**

• LEGISLATIVE TITLES

Don't abbreviate them when writing for broadcast.

A member of the Senate is a *Senator.*

A member of the House is a *Representative. Congressman* or *Congresswoman* may be used in subsequent descriptions which do not use an individual's name, but they should not be used as formal titles except in a direct quotation.

It is not necessary to add *U-S* or *State* before *Senator* or *Representative* unless it is necessary to avoid confusion: *U-S Senator Herman Talmadge met with state Senator Hugh Carter.*

Other titles commonly encountered include *assemblyman, assemblywoman, city councilman, city councilwoman, alderman, delegate, etc.*

Second Reference: Do not use legislative titles on second reference.

Clutter: Don't try to cram all of the titles and affiliations into the first sentence: *Arizona Republican Senator Barry Goldwater today . . .*

Instead, try: *Barry Goldwater says President Reagan is doing an "outstanding job." The Arizona senator said he and all other Republicans are proud of Reagan.*

With a well-known politician, the title can be worked into the story later.

Organizational Titles: These are the formal titles of the federal legislative leaders:

SENATE MAJORITY LEADER
SENATE MINORITY LEADER
SENATE DEMOCRATIC WHIP
SENATE REPUBLICAN WHIP
PRESIDENT PRO TEM OF THE SENATE

SPEAKER OF THE HOUSE
HOUSE MAJORITY LEADER
HOUSE MINORITY LEADER
HOUSE MAJORITY WHIP
HOUSE MINORITY WHIP

See **PARTY AFFILIATION** and **TITLES.**

• LEGISLATURE

In 49 states, the separate bodies are the state *senate* and the state *assembly* or *house.*

The exception is Nebraska, where the legislature is a unicameral body.

• LENT

The period from Ash Wednesday through Holy Saturday, the day before Easter. The 40-day Lenten period for penance, suggested by Christ's 40 days in the desert, does not include the six Sundays between Ash Wednesday and Easter.

See **EASTER** for the method of computing when Easter occurs.

• LESBIAN, LESBIANISM

See **GAY.**

• LESS

See the **FEWER, LESS** entry.

• LESS

No hyphen before this suffix:

CHILDLESS
TAILLESS
WATERLESS

• LET UP (v.)
LETUP (n. and adj.)

• LEVI'S

A trademark for a brand of jeans.

• LIABILITIES

When used in a financial sense, the word means all the claims against a corporation.

They include accounts payable, wages and salaries due but not paid, dividends declared payable, taxes payable, and fixed or long-term obligations such as bonds, debentures and bank loans.

See **ASSETS.**

• LIAISON (LEE-AY'-ZAHN)

• LIBERAL, LIBERALISM

• LIE

See the **LAY, LIE** entry.

• LIE IN STATE

Only persons who are entitled to a state funeral may formally lie in state. In the United States, this occurs in the rotunda in the Capitol.

Those entitled to a state funeral are a president, a former president, a president-elect or any other person designated by the president.

Members of Congress may lie in state, and a number have done so. The decision is either house's to make, although the formal process normally begins with a request from the president.

Those entitled to an official funeral, but not to lie in state, are the vice president, the chief justice, Cabinet members and other government officials when designated by the president.

• LIEUTENANT
See **MILITARY TITLES.**

• LIFE-SIZE

• LIFESTYLE
An exception to Webster's.

• LIFETIME

• LIGHT, LIGHTED, LIGHTING
Do not use *lit* as the past tense form.

• LIGHTNING
The electrical discharge.

• LIGHT-YEAR
The distance that light travels in one year at the rate of 186-thousand, 282 miles per second (the speed of light). It works out to above five (t) trillion, 878 (b) billion, 612 (m) million, 800 thousand miles.

• LIKABLE
Not *likeable.*

• LIKE, AS
Use *like* as a preposition to compare nouns and pronouns. It requires an object: *Jim blocks like a pro.*

The conjunction *as* is the correct word to introduce clauses: *Jim blocks the linebacker as he should.*

• LIKE-
Follow with a hyphen when used as a prefix meaning similar to:

LIKE-MINDED
LIKE-NATURED

No hyphen in words that have meanings of their own:

LIKELIHOOD
LIKENESS
LIKEWISE

• -LIKE
Do not precede this suffix by a hyphen unless the letter *l* would be tripled:

BILL-LIKE	LIFELIKE
BUSINESSLIKE	SHELL-LIKE

• LIMITED
Do not abbreviate, even when used as part of a formal corporate name: *the Smith Corporation, Limited.*

• LIMOUSINE

• LINAGE, LINEAGE
Linage is the number of lines.
Lineage is ancestry or descent.

• LINCOLN'S BIRTHDAY
It is February 12th. While it is widely celebrated, it is not a federal legal holiday.
See **HOLIDAYS.**

• LIQUEFIED
Not *liquified.*

• LIQUIDATION
When used in a financial sense, the

word means the process of converting stock or other assets into cash.

When a company is liquidated, the cash obtained is first used to pay debts and obligations to holders of bonds and preferred stock. Whatever cash remains is distributed on a per-share basis to the holders of common stock.

• LIQUIDITY

The ease with which assets can be converted to cash without loss in value.

• LITER

The basic unit of volume in the metric system. It is defined as the volume occupied by one kilogram of water at four degrees Celsius. It works out to a total of one-thousand cubic centimeters (one cubic decimeter).

It takes one-thousand milliliters to make a liter.

A liter is equal to about 34 fluid ounces or one-point-zero-six liquid quarts. It also works out to just over nine-tenths (point-91) dry quarts. The metric system makes no distinction between wet and dry volume.

To convert to liquid quarts, multiply by one-point-zero-six (one and six-hundredths): four liters times one-point-oh-six equals four-point-24 liquid quarts.

To convert to dry quarts, multiply by point-91: four liters times point-91 equals three-point-64 dry quarts.

To convert to liquid gallons, multiply by point-26: eight liters times point-26 equals two-point-oh-eight gallons.

See **GALLON; KILOGRAM; METRIC SYSTEM; QUART (DRY)**; and **QUART (FLUID)**.

• LITERALLY

See the **FIGURATIVELY, LITERALLY** entry.

• LIVABLE

Not *liveable.*

• LIVID

It is not a synonym for *fiery, bright, crimson, red* or *flaming.* If a person turns livid with rage, his face becomes ashen or pale. It can mean *blue, bluish gray, gray, dull white, dull purple* or *grayish black.*

• LLOYDS BANK INTERNATIONAL, LIMITED

A prominent bank with headquarters in London.

• LLOYD'S OF LONDON

A prominent insurance company with headquarters in London.

• "LLOYD'S REGISTER OF SHIPPING"

The reference source for questions about non-military ships not covered in this book.

It is published by Lloyd's Register of Shipping Trust Corporation, Limited, in London.

• LOAN TERMINOLOGY

Note the meanings of these terms in describing loans by governments and corporations:

Bond: A certificate issued by a corporation or government stating the amount of a loan, the interest to be paid, the time for repayment and the collateral pledged if payment cannot be made. Repayment generally is not due for a long period, usually seven years or more.

Collateral: Stock or other property that a borrower is obligated to turn over to a lender if unable to repay a loan.

Commercial Paper: A document describing the details of a short-term loan between corporations.

Convertible Bond: A bond carrying the stipulation that it may be exchanged for a specific amount of stock in the company that issued it.

Coupon: A slip of paper attached to a bond that the bondholder clips at specified times and returns to the issuer for payment of the interest due.

Default: A person, corporation or government is in default if it fails to meet the terms for repayment.

Debenture: A certificate stating the amount of a loan, the interest to be paid and the time for repayment, but not providing collateral. It is backed only by the corporation's reputation and promise to pay.

Full Faith and Credit Bond: An alternate term for a *general obligation bond,* often used to contrast such a bond with *a moral obligation bond.*

General Obligation Bond: A bond that has had the formal approval of either the voters or their legislature. The government's promise to repay the principal and pay the interest is constitutionally guaranteed on the strength of its ability to tax the population.

Maturity: The date on which a bond, debenture or note must be repaid.

Moral Obligation Bond: A government bond that has not had the formal approval of either the voters or their legislature. It is backed only by the government's "moral obligation" to repay the principal and interest on time.

Municipal Bond: A general obligation bond issued by a state, county, city, town, village, possession or territory, or a bond issued by an agency or authority set up by one of these governmental units. In general, interest paid on municipal bonds is exempt from federal income taxes. It also usually is exempt from state and local income taxes if held by someone living within the state of issue.

Note: A certificate issued by a corporation or government stating the amount of a loan, the interest to be paid and the collateral pledged in the event payment cannot be made. The date for repayment is generally more than a year after issue but not more than seven or eight years later. The shorter interval for repayment is the principal difference between a note and a bond.

Revenue Bond: A bond backed only by the revenue of the airport, turnpike or other facility that was built with the money it raised.

Treasury Borrowing: A *treasury bill* is a certificate representing a loan to the federal government that matures in three, six or 12 months. A *treasury note* may mature in one to ten years. A *treasury bond* matures in seven years or more.

• LOCAL

Avoid the irrelevant use of the word.

Irrelevant: *The injured were taken to a local hospital.*

Better: *The injured were taken to a hospital.*

• LOCKER ROOM

• LOCKHEED AIRCRAFT CORPORATION

Headquarters is in Burbank, California.

• LONDON

The city in England stands alone in datelines.

• LONG DISTANCE, LONG-DISTANCE

Always a hyphen in reference to telephone calls: *We keep in touch by long-distance. He called long-distance. She took the long-distance call.*

In other uses, hyphenate only when

used as a compound modifier: *She traveled a long distance. She made a long-distance trip.*

• LONGITUDE
See the **LATITUDE AND LONGITUDE** entry.

• LONG TERM, LONG-TERM
Hyphenate when used as a compound modifier: *We will win in the long term. He has a long-term assignment.*

• LONG TIME, LONGTIME
They have known each other a long time. They are longtime partners.

• LONG TON
Also known as a *British ton.* Equal to two-thousand, 240 pounds.
See **TON.**

• LOS ANGELES
The city in California stands alone in datelines.
Confine *L-A* to quoted matter.

• L-O-T POLISH AIRLINES
Headquarters is in Warsaw, Poland.

• LOW COUNTRIES
Belgium, Luxembourg and Netherlands.

• L-S-D
Acceptable in all references for *lysergic acid diethylamide.*

• L-TEN-ELEVEN
Tristar jet is also acceptable.

• LUCITE
A trademark for acrylic plastic.

• LUFTHANSA (LUF-TAHN'-SUH) GERMAN AIRLINES
A *Lufthansa airliner* is acceptable in any reference.

Headquarters is in Cologne (kuh-lohn'), West Germany.

• LUTHERAN CHURCHES
The basic unit of government in Lutheran practice is the congregation. It normally is administered by a council, headed either by the senior pastor or a lay person elected from the membership of the council. The council customarily consists of congregation's clergy and elected lay persons.

National church bodies are made up of congregations and governed by conventions. Congregations are grouped into territorial districts or synods whose functions vary. The term *synod* also is used in the names of some national bodies.

The Lutheran Church in America is the largest of three major Lutheran bodies in the United States. Of the three, it takes the least rigid or literalistic stand on doctrine and Bible interpretation. Formed in 1962 from a merger of four bodies with Danish, Finnish, German and Swedish backgrounds, it has almost three (m) million members.

The Lutheran Church-Missouri Synod, with about two (m) million, 700-thousand members, is regarded as the most conservative of the three bodies. A split has developed within the synod over the question of Bible interpretation and synod leadership. Its background is predominantly German.

The American Lutheran Church, with some two (m) million, 400-thousand members, generally is regarded as middle of the road in doctrinal emphasis. It was formed in 1960 through a merger of four bodies with Danish, German and Norwegian backgrounds.

All three bodies are members of the New York-based Lutheran Council in the U-S-A, which coordinates various joint activities.

Beliefs: Lutheran teachings go back to Martin Luther, a 16th-century Roman Catholic priest whose objections to elements of Roman Catholic practice began the movement known as the Protestant Reformation.

Lutherans believe in the Trinity and emphasize both the divinity and humanity of Christ. There are two sacraments, baptism and the Lord's Supper.

In recent years, the question of Bible interpretation has divided Lutherans into "moderate" and "conservative" camps. Conservatives argue for a literal interpretation of passages others consider symbolic. Moderates argue that some truths in the Bible are expressed in allegories.

Clergy: Members of the clergy are known as *ministers. Pastor* applies if a minister leads a congregation.

On first reference, use *the Reverend* before the name of a man or woman. Do not carry the title through on subsequent references

In the American Lutheran Church, the president and district presidents are often referred to as bishops. Use *Bishop* before such an individual's name on first reference.

Other Officials: Lay members of a church council frequently are designated *elders, deacons* or *trustees.* The preferred form for identifying them is a construction that requires commas to set their names off from these titles.

• LUXEMBOURG

Stands alone in datelines.

• -LY

Do not use a hyphen between adverbs ending in *-ly* and adjectives they modify: *an easily remembered rule, a badly damaged island, a fully informed woman.*

See the compound modifers section of the HYPHEN entry.

• LYNDON B. JOHNSON SPACE CENTER

Formerly the Manned Spacecraft Center. Located in Houston, it is the National Aeronautics and Space Administration's principal control and training center for manned spaceflight.

Johnson Space Center is acceptable in all references.

In datelines:

(SPACE CENTER, HOUSTON) --

See JOHN F. KENNEDY SPACE CENTER.

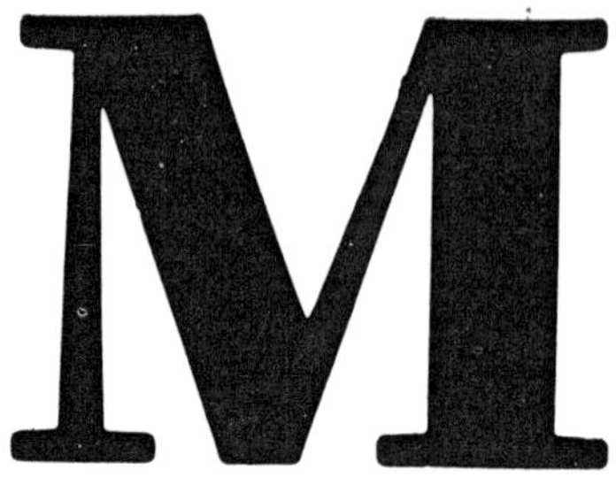

• **MACAO**
Stands alone in datelines.

• **MACE**
A trademark, shortened from *Chemical Mace,* for a brand of tear gas that is packaged in an aerosol canister and temporarily stuns its victims.

• **MACHINE GUN** (n.)
But: *machine-gun* (v. and adj.), *machine-gunner.*
See **WEAPONS.**

• **MACH** (MAHK) **NUMBER**
Named for Ernst Mach, an Austrian physicist, the figure represents the ratio of the speed of an object to the speed of sound in the surrounding medium, such as air.
A rule of thumb for the speed of sound is that it is roughly 750 miles-per-hour at sea level, and about 660 miles-per-hour at 30-thousand feet.
A body traveling at *Mach one* would be traveling at the speed of sound, while one traveling at *Mach two* would be traveling twice as fast.

• **MAFIA, MAFIOSI**
The secret society of criminals and its members. Do not use as a synonym for *organized crime* or the *underworld.*

• **MAGAZINE NAMES**
Put them in quotes on the first reference.
See **QUOTATION MARKS.**

• **MAGNA CHARTA** (KAHR'-TUH)
The charter the English barons forced King John of England to grant at Runnymede in June 1215. It guaranteed certain civil and political liberties.

• **MAILGRAM**
A trademark for a telegram sent to a post office near the recipient's address and delivered to the address by letter carrier.

• **MAILMAN**
Letter carrier is preferable because many women hold this job.

• **MAJORCA** (MAH-YAWR'-KAH)
Use instead of *Spain* in datelines on stories from communities on this island.

• **MAJORITY, PLURALITY**
Majority means more than half.
Plurality means more than the next highest number.
Computing a Majority: To describe how large a majority is, take the winning figure and subtract everything else from it: if 100-thousand votes were cast, and one candidate received 60-thousand while the rest, combined, received 40-thousand, the winner would have majority of 20-thousand votes.
Computing a Plurality: To describe how large a plurality is, take the highest number and subtract it from the next highest number: if, in the example cited above, the second-place finisher had 25-thousand votes, the winner's *plurality* would have been 35-thousand votes.
Suppose, however, that no candidate in this example had a majority. If the first-place finisher had 40-thousand votes and the second-place finisher had 30-thousand, for example, the leader's *plurality* would be ten-thousand votes.

Usage: When *majority* and *plurality* are used alone, they take singluar verbs and pronouns: *The majority has made its decision.*

If a plural word follows an *of* construction, the decision on whether to use a singular or plural verb depends on the sense of the sentence: *A majority of two votes is not adequate to control the committee. The majority of the houses on the block were destroyed.*

• MAJORITY LEADER, MINORITY LEADER

These congressional—and state legislative—leaders are usually selected by caucuses by their parties in their legislative chambers.

See **LEGISLATIVE TITLES.**

• MAKE UP (v.)
MAKEUP (n. and adj.)

• MALDIVES (MAL'-DYVZ)

Use this official name with a community name in a dateline. The body of the story should note that the nation frequently is called *the Maldive Islands.*

• MAN, MANKIND

Either may be used when both men and women are involved and no other term is convenient. In these cases, do not use duplicate phrases such as *a man or a woman* or *mankind and womankind.*

Frequently the best choice is a substitute such as *humanity, a person* or *an individual.*

See **WOMEN.**

• MANAGEABLE

• MANITOBA

A province of central Canada. Do not abbreviate.

See **DATELINES.**

• MANSLAUGHTER

See the **HOMICIDE, MURDER, MANSLAUGHTER** entry.

• MANTEL, MANTLE

A mantel is a shelf. A *mantle* is a cloak.

• MAOISM (MAOIST)

The communist philosophy and policies of Mao Tse-tung.

• MARDI GRAS

Literally "fat Tuesday," the term describes a day of merrymaking on the Tuesday before Ash Wednesday.

In New Orleans and many Roman Catholic countries, the Tuesday celebration is preceded by a week or more of parades and parties.

• MARIJUANA

Not *marihuana.*

• MARINES

It is *the U-S Marines Corps,* or *the Marines.*

Do not use the abbreviation *U-S-M-C.*

• MARITIME PROVINCES

The Canadian provinces of Nova Scotia, New Brunswick and Prince Edward Island.

• MARKETBASKET, MARKETPLACE

• MARSHAL, MARSHALED, MARSHALING, MARSHALL

Marshal is the spelling for both the verb and the noun: *Marilyn will marshal her forces. Erwin Rommel was a field marshal.*

Marshall is used in proper names, *George Marshall, John Marshall, the Marshall Islands.*

• MARSHALL ISLANDS

Named for John Marshall, a British explorer.

In datelines, give the name of a city and *Marshall Islands.* List the name of an individual island in the text.

• MARXISM (MARXIST)

The system of thought developed by Karl Marx and Friedrich Engels.

• MASON-DIXON LINE

The boundary line between Pennsylvania and Maryland, generally regarded as separating the North from the South.

• MASS

It is *celebrated, said* or *sung.*

In Eastern Orthodox churches the correct term is *Divine Liturgy.*

See **ROMAN CATHOLIC CHURCH.**

• MASTER OF ARTS, MASTER OF SCIENCE

A *master's degree* or a *master's* is acceptable in any reference.

See **ACADEMIC DEGREES.**

• MATURITY

In a financial sense, the date on which a bond, debenture or note must be repaid.

See **LOAN TERMINOLOGY.**

• MCDONNELL DOUGLAS CORPORATION

Headquarters is in St. Louis.

• MEAGER

• MEAN

See the **AVERAGE, MEAN, MEDIAN, NORM** entry.

• MEDAL OF FREEDOM

It is now the *Presidential Medal of Freedom.* See entry under that name.

• MEDAL OF HONOR

The nation's highest military honor, given by Congress for risk of life in combat beyond the call of duty.

There is no *Congressional Medal of Honor.*

• MEDIA

In the sense of mass communication, such as magazines, newspapers, the news services, radio and television, the word is plural: *The news media are resisting attempts to limit their freedom.*

• MEDIAN

See the **AVERAGE, MEAN, MEDIAN, NORM** entry.

• MEDIATE

See the **ARBITRATE, MEDIATE** entry.

• MEDICAID

A federal-state program that helps pay for health care for the needy, aged, blind and disabled, and for low-income families with children.

A state determines eligibility and which health services are covered. The federal government reimburses a percentage of the state's expenditures.

• MEDICARE

The federal health care insurance program for people aged 65 and over, and for the disabled. Eligibility is based mainly on eligibility for Social Security.

Medicare helps pay charges for hospitalization, for stays in skilled nursing facilities, for physician's charges and for some associated health costs. There are limitations on the length of stay and type of care.

In Canada, *Medicare* refers to the nation's national health insurance program.

• MEDIEVAL

• MEGA-

A prefix denoting one (m) million units of a measure. Move the decimal point six places to the right, adding zeroes when necessary, to convert to the basic unit: five-point-five megatons equals five (m) million, 500-thousand tons.

• MELCHITE CHURCH

See **EASTERN RITE CHURCHES.**

• MELEE (MAY'-LAY)

• MEMENTO, MEMENTOS

• MEMO, MEMOS

• MEMORIAL DAY

Formerly May 30th. The federal legal holiday is the last Monday in May.

• MENSWEAR

Not *men's wear.*

• MERCALLI SCALE

See **EARTHQUAKES.**

• MERIDIANS

Follow the rules for **NUMERALS** when identifying the imaginary locater lines that ring the globe from north to south through the poles.

They are measured in units of zero to 180 degrees east and west of the *prime meridian,* which runs through Greenwich, England. Examples: *the first meridian west, the 100th meridian east, the 33rd meridian.* Note in the final example that the *east* or *west* designation is not necessary if the location east or west of Greenwich is obvious.

See **LATITUDE AND LONGITUDE.**

• MERRY-GO-ROUND

• METER

The basic unit of length in the metric system. It is defined as being equal to one (m) million, 650-thousand, 763-point-73 wavelengths of the orange-red radiation of an isotope of krypton. That's for reference only. There's no context in which it should be so precisely defined.

It is equal to about 39-point-37 inches, which may be rounded off to 39 and a-half inches in most comparisons.

It takes 100 centimeters to make a meter.

It takes one-thousand meters to make a kilometer.

To convert to inches, multiply the meter measurement by 39-point-37: five meters times 39-point-37 equals 196-point-85 inches.

To convert to yards, multiply by one-point-one: five meters times one-point-one equals five-point-five yards.

See **INCHES; METRIC SYSTEM;** and **YARDS.**

• METHODIST CHURCHES

The term *Methodist* originated as a nickname applied to a group of 18th century Oxford University students known for their methodical application to Scripture study and prayer.

The principal Methodist body in the United States is the United Methodist Church, which also has some member conferences outside the United States. It was formed in 1968 by the merger of the Methodist Church and the Evangelical United Brethren Church. It has about ten (m) million members.

The government of the United Methodist Church follows a stratified pattern from the General Conference through several intermediate conferences down to the local congregation.

The General Conference, which meets every four years, has final authority in all matters. Its members, half lay and half clergy, are elected by the annual conferences.

Jurisdictional conferences covering

major sections of the nation are composed of ministers and lay delegates. Their principal function is to elect bishops.

Annual conferences, generally organized along state lines, elect delegates to higher conferences and make official appointments within their areas.

A Methodist bishop presides over a "church area," which may embrace one or more annual conferences. Bishops have extensive administrative powers, including the authority to place, transfer and remove local church pastors, usually in consultation with district superintendents.

Districts in each conference are responsible for promotion of mission work, support of colleges, hospitals and publications, and examination of candidates for the ministry.

Members of a congregation form a charge conference. It elects officers to a board that assists the pastor.

Methodism in the United States also includes three major black demominations: the African Methodist Episcopal Church, the African Methodist Episcopal Zion Church and the Christian Methodist Episcopal Church.

Beliefs: Methodist teachings emphasize that the Holy Scriptures contain all the knowledge necessary for salvation. Tradition is not acknowledged as a valid source of revelation, although the writings of John Wesley, a leader of the Oxford University group, are regarded as sound interpretations of the Scriptures.

Methodists believe in the Trinity and the humanity and divinity of Christ. There are two sacraments, baptism and the Lord's Supper.

Clergy: Ordained individuals are known as *bishops* and *ministers. Pastor* applies if a minister leads a congregation.

For first references to bishops, use the word: *Bishop Kenneth Goodson of Richmond, Virginia.* The designations *the Most Reverend* or *the Right Reverend* do not apply.

For first references to ministers, use *the Reverend.* Do not use the title on subsequent references.

• METRIC SYSTEM

In general, metric terms should be used only when they are crucial to the story.

Application of this guideline will, of course, change as the use of the metric system of measurement becomes more widespread in the United States.

In all cases, though, the rule is clarity: when a metric term will only confuse the newscaster and listener, convert to the more familiar form of measurement. When the metric term is relevant and clear, use it.

Never mix forms of measurement in a story, unless you are trying to clarify quoted matter:

In the doctor's words, "the bullet missed his heart by two millimeters." That's less than an inch.

An even better way to write it:

The doctor says the bullet stopped less than an inch from his heart.

Don't provide metric or American equivalents in parentheses; that only tends to confuse the newscaster reading the story cold. If an equivalency must be given, do it conversationally:

Officials say it happened about a kilometer away. A kilometer equals about five-eighths of a mile.

In any case, avoid using too many measurements. Use figures only where it serves to clarify the story or make the scene more vivid. And, again: stay with what's most familiar so the story is easy to understand.

Conversion Formulas: A conversion table for frequently used metric terms appears on page 191.

METRIC CONVERSION TABLE

INTO METRIC

Length:

If You Know:	*Multiply by:*	*To Get:*
inches	2.54	centimeters
feet	30	centimeters
yards	0.91	meters
miles	1.6	kilometers

Area:

If You Know:	*Multiply by:*	*To Get:*
sq. inches	6.5	sq. centimeters
sq. feet	0.09	sq. meters
sq. yards	0.8	sq. meters
sq. miles	2.6	sq. kilometers
acres	0.4	hectares

Mass (Weight):

If You Know:	*Multiply by:*	*To Get:*
ounces	28	grams
pounds	0.45	kilograms
short tons	0.9	metric tons

Volume:

If You Know:	*Multiply by:*	*To Get:*
teaspoons	5	milliliters
tablespoons	15	milliliters
fluid ounces	30	milliliters
cups	0.24	liters
pints	0.47	liters
quarts	0.95	liters
gallons	3.8	liters
cubic feet	0.03	cubic meters
cubic yards	0.76	cubic yards

Temperature:

If you know *Fahrenheit,*
subtract 32, then multiply by 0.556,
to get *Celsius.*

OUT OF METRIC

Length:

If You Know:	*Multiply by:*	*To Get:*
millimeters	0.04	inches
centimeters	0.4	inches
meters	3.3	feet
kilometers	0.62	miles

Area:

If You Know:	*Multiply by:*	*To Get:*
sq. centimeters	0.16	sq. inches
sq. meters	1.2	sq. yards
sq. kilometers	0.4	sq. miles
hectares	2.47	acres

Mass (Weight):

If You Know:	*Multiply by:*	*To Get:*
grams	0.035	ounces
kilograms	2.2	pounds
metric tons	1.1	short tons

Volume:

If You Know:	*Multiply by:*	*To Get:*
milliliters	0.03	fluid ounces
liters	2.1	pints
liters	1.06	quarts
liters	0.26	gallons
cubic meters	35	cubic feet
cubic meters	1.3	cubic yards

Temperature:

If you know *Celsius,*
multiply by 1.8 then add 32,
to get *Fahrenheit.*

In addition, separate entries for *gram, meter, liter, Celsius* and other frequently used metric units define them and give examples of how to convert them to equivalents in the terminology that has been used in the United States.

Similarly, entries for *pound, inch, quart, Fahrenheit,* contain examples of how to convert these terms to metric forms.

To avoid the need for long strings of figures, prefixes are added to the metric units to denote fractional elements or large multiples. The prefixes are: *pico-* for one (t) trillionth, *nano-* for one (b) billionth, *micro-* for one (m) millionth, *milli-* for one-thousandth, *centi-* for one-hundredth, *deci-* for one-tenth, *deka-* for ten times, *hecto-* for 100 times, *kilo-* for one-thousand times, *mega-* for one (m) million times, *giga-* for one (b) billion times, and *tera-* for one (t) trillion times.

Entries for each prefix show how to convert a unit preceded by the prefix to the basic unit.

Do not abbreviate any units.

• METRIC TON

A unit of measure equal to two-thousand, 205 pounds. In agricultural stories, metric tonnages should be converted to bushels; see that entry.

• METRO-GOLDWYN-MAYER, INCORPORATED

M-G-M is acceptable in all references.

Headquarters is in Culver City, California.

• METROPOLITAN

See EASTERN ORTHODOX CHURCHES.

• MEXICO CITY

The city in Mexico stands alone in datelines.

• MIAMI

The city in Florida stands alone in datelines.

• MICRO-

A prefix denoting one (m) millionth of a unit. move the decimal point six places to the left in converting to the basic unit: two (m) million micro-seconds equals two seconds.

• MID-

No hyphen unless a proper noun follows:

MID-AMERICA	MIDSEMESTER
MID-ATLANTIC	MIDTERM

But use a hyphen when *mid-* precedes a figure: *mid-30's.*

• MIDDLE AGES

476 A-D to 1450 A-D.

• MIDDLE ATLANTIC STATES

As defined by the Census Bureau, they are New Jersey, New York and Pennsylvania.

Less formal references often consider Delaware part of the group.

See NORTHEAST REGION.

• MIDDLE CLASS, MIDDLE-CLASS

He is a member of the middle class. She has middle-class values.

• MIDDLE EAST

Mideast is just as good, and often more conversational. As defined by the Columbia Lippincott Gazetteer, the term applies to southwest Asia west of Pakistan (Afghanistan, Iran, Iraq, Israel, Kuwait, Jordan, Oman, Qatar, Saudi Arabia, South Yemen, Syria, Turkey, United Arab Emirates and Yemen), northeastern Africa (Egypt and Sudan), and the island of Cyprus.

Popular usage once distinguished between the *Near East* (the westerly nations in the listing) and the *Middle East* (the easterly nations), but the gazetteer advises that the two terms now overlap with current practice favoring *Middle East* for both areas.

Use *Middle East* unless *Near East* is used by a source in a story.

• **MIDDLE INITIALS**

It is more conversational to avoid them whenever possible. They should be used, however, in casualty lists, stories about criminal proceedings and other cases where exact identification is important.

When the middle initial is used, follow it with a period and a space: *John Y. Brown.*

• **MIDDLEMAN**

• **MIDNIGHT**

Do not put a *12* in front of it. It is part of the day that is ending, not the one that is beginning.

To avoid confusion, when there is, for example, a midnight Sunday deadline, write *early Monday morning* or *at 12:01 a-m Monday.*

• **MIDWEST, MIDWESTERN**

See the **DIRECTIONS AND REGIONS** entry.

• **MIG-21**

No quotation marks around the acronym MIG.

• **MILE**

Also called a *statute mile,* it equals five-thousand, 280 feet.

The metric equivalent is about one-point-six kilometers.

To convert to kilometers, multiply the mileage figure by one-point-six: five miles times one-point-six equals eight kilometers.

See **FOOT; KILOMETER; KNOT;** and **NAUTICAL MILE.**

• **MILES-PER-GALLON**

Note hyphens. The abbreviation *M-P-G* is acceptable on second reference.

• **MILES-PER-HOUR**

Note hyphens. Do not use the abbreviation *M-P-H.*

• **MILITARY ACADEMIES**

While the formal titles include the designation *U-S,* it is not needed in any reference except to distinguish the American academy from foreign institutions.

So the *U-S Air Force Academy* may simply be referred to as *the Air Force Academy.*

Cadet is the proper title on first reference for men and women enrolled at the Army and Air Force academies. *Midshipman* is the proper title for men and women enrolled at the Navy and Coast Guard academies.

The title should be used on the first reference only.

• **MILITARY TITLES**

Spell them out.

On first reference, use the appropriate title before the full name of a member of the military.

In subsequent references, do not continue using the title before a name.

In some cases, it may be necessary to explain the significance of a title: *Army Sergeant Major John Jones described the attack. Jones, who holds the Army's highest rank for enlisted men, said it was unprovoked.*

In addition to the ranks listed below, each service has ratings, such as *machinist, radarman, torpedoman,* that are job descriptions. Do not use any of these designations as a title on first reference.

The same guidelines apply to fire and police officers.

Retired Officers: A military rank may be used in first reference before the name of an officer who has retired if it is relevant to a story.

Use *retired* just as *former* would be used before the title of a civilian: *They invited retired Army General John Smith.*

ARMY

Commissioned Officers

GENERAL
LIEUTENANT GENERAL
MAJOR GENERAL
BRIGADIER GENERAL
COLONEL
LIEUTENANT COLONEL
MAJOR
CAPTAIN
FIRST LIEUTENANT
SECOND LIEUTENANT

Warrant Officers

CHIEF WARRANT OFFICER
WARRANT OFFICER

Enlisted Personnel

SERGEANT MAJOR OF THE ARMY
COMMAND SERGEANT MAJOR
STAFF SERGEANT MAJOR
FIRST SERGEANT
MASTER SERGEANT
PLATOON SERGEANT
SERGEANT FIRST CLASS
SPECIALIST SEVEN
STAFF SERGEANT
SPECIALIST SIX
SERGEANT
SPECIALIST FIVE
CORPORAL
SPECIALIST FOUR
PRIVATE FIRST CLASS
PRIVATE TWO
PRIVATE ONE

NAVY, COAST GUARD

Commissioned Officers

ADMIRAL
VICE ADMIRAL
REAR ADMIRAL
COMMODORE
CAPTAIN
COMMANDER
LIEUTENANT COMMANDER
LIEUTENANT
LIEUTENANT JUNIOR GRADE (J-G)
ENSIGN

Warrant Officers

COMMISSIONED WARRANT OFFICER
WARRANT OFFICER

Enlisted Personnel

MASTER CHIEF PETTY OFFICER
SENIOR CHIEF PETTY OFFICER
CHIEF PETTY OFFICER
PETTY OFFICER FIRST CLASS
PETTY OFFICER SECOND CLASS
PETTY OFFICER THIRD CLASS
SEAMAN
SEAMAN APPRENTICE
SEAMAN RECRUIT

MARINE CORPS

Ranks for commissioned officers are the same as those in the Army. Warrant officer ratings follow the same system used in the Navy. There are no specialist ratings.

Others

SERGEANT MAJOR
MASTER GUNNERY SERGEANT
MASTER SERGEANT
FIRST SERGEANT
GUNNERY SERGEANT
STAFF SERGEANT
SERGEANT
CORPORAL
LANCE CORPORAL
PRIVATE FIRST CLASS
PRIVATE

AIR FORCE

Ranks for commissioned officers are the same as those in the Army.

Enlisted Designations

CHIEF MASTER SERGEANT

SENIOR MASTER SERGEANT
MASTER SERGEANT
TECHNICAL SERGEANT
STAFF SERGEANT
SERGEANT
AIRMAN FIRST CLASS
AIRMAN
AIRMAN BASIC

• MILITARY UNITS

Follow the rules for **NUMERALS** in referring to military units: *the First Infantry Division, the Third Division, the Fifth Battalion, the Sixth Army, 395th Field Artillery.*

• MILLI-

A prefix denoting one-thousandth of a unit. Move the decimal point three places to the left to convert to the basic unit: one-thousand millimeters equals one meter.

• MILLIMETER

One-thousandth of a meter.

It takes ten millimeters to make a centimeter.

A millimeter is roughly equal to the thickness of a paper clip.

To convert to inches, multiply by point-oh-four: five millimeters times point-oh-four equals two-tenths of an inch.

Do not abbreviate.

See **METER; METRIC SYSTEM;** and **INCH.**

• (M) MILLIONS, (B) BILLIONS

Should always be spelled out and preceded by the identifying letter in parentheses. This confirms the unit, reducing the chance of typographical error.

Similarly, *(t) trillions.*

Follow the rules for **NUMERALS.** In general, when dealing with (b) billions and fractions of (m) millions, spell out both units: *seven (b) billion, 100 (m) million dollars* is preferable to *seven-point-one (b) billion dollars.*

Note that a hyphen is not used to join the figure and the unit, even in this type of phrase: *The president submitted a 300 (b) billion dollar budget.*

• MILWAUKEE

The city in Wisconsin stands alone in datelines.

• MINI-

The rules in **PREFIXES** apply, but in general, no hyphen. Some examples:

MINIBUS
MINISERIES
MINISKIRT

• MINISTER

It is not a formal title. Do not use it before the name of a member of the clergy.

See **RELIGIOUS TITLES** and the entry for an individual's denomination.

• MINNEAPOLIS

The city in Minnesota stands alone in datelines.

• MINORITY LEADER

Treat the same as *majority leader.*

See that entry and **LEGISLATIVE TITLES.**

• MINUSCULE

Not *miniscule.*

• MINUS SIGN

Don't use it. Use *minus* or *below zero,* as appropriate.

• "MIRV," "MIRVS"

Acceptable on first reference for *multiple independently targetable re-entry vehicle(s).*

Explain in the text that a *"MIRV"* is

an intercontinental ballistic missile with several warheads, each of which can be directed to a different target.

• MISDEMEANOR
See the FELONY, MISDEMEANOR entry.

• MISHAP
A minor misfortune. People are not killed in mishaps.

• MISS
See COURTESY TITLES.

• MISSILE NAMES
See AIRCRAFT NAMES and A-B-M; I-C-B-M, "MIRV" and "SAM."

• MIX UP (v.)
MIX-UP (n. and adj.)

• MOBIL CORPORATION
Headquarters is in New York.
Mobil Oil Corporation is a subsidiary.

• MOCK-UP (n.)

• MOHAMMED
The spelling for the founder of the Moslem religion.

• MONACO
After the Vatican, the world's smallest state.
The *Monaco* section stands alone in datelines. The other two sections, *La Condamine* and *Monte Carlo,* are followed by *Monaco:*
(MONTE CARLO, MONACO) --

• MONDAY MORNING QUARTERBACK
One who second-guesses.

• M-ONE, M-14
See WEAPONS.

• MONETARY
See the FISCAL, MONETARY entry.

• MONETARY FIGURES
Follow the rules in NUMERALS.
All monetary units should be spelled out. Use a comma to separate units, as in *five dollars, ten cents* or *135-thousand, 400 dollars.*
Informalize monetary figures where appropriate: *two dollars, 50 cents* can be expressed as *two and a-half dollars* or *two-50.*
Decimal expressions of (m) millions and (b) billions of dollars should be avoided: *three-point-two (b) billion* is better expressed as *three (b) billion, 200 (m) million dollars,* although the former is acceptable for brevity. Similarly, *five-point-one (m) million dollars* can be expressed as *five (m) million, 100-thousand dollars.*

• MONEYMAKER

• MONTESSORI METHOD
After Maria Montessori, a system of training young children. It emphasizes training of the senses and guidance to encourage self-education.

• MONTH-LONG

• MONTHS
Never abbreviate when writing broadcast. When a phrase lists only a month and a year, do not separate the year with commas: *April 1979 was a pleasant month.*
When the month, day and year are included, set off the year with commas: *November 22nd, 1963, is a day he will always remember.*
Remember to use numerals correctly: *December First, April 14th, August 30th.*
See NUMERALS; DATES; and YEARS.

• MONTREAL
The city in Canada stands alone in datelines.

• MOP UP (v.)
MOP-UP (n. and adj.)

• MORAL OBLIGATION BOND
See **LOAN TERMINOLOGY.**

• MORE THAN
See **OVER.**

• MORMON CHURCH
Acceptable in all references for *Church of Jesus Christ of Latter-day Saints,* but always include the full name in a story dealing primarily with church activities.

See the entry under the formal name.

• MOSCOW
The city in the Soviet Union stands alone in datelines.

• MOSLEMS
The preferred term for describing adherents of Islam.

In the names of certain American organizations, such as the *Black Muslims,* and in references to their members, *Muslims* may be used.

• MOSQUITO, MOSQUITOES

• MOTHER-IN-LAW, MOTHERS-IN-LAW

• MOTHER'S DAY
The second Sunday in May.

• MOTOR
See the **ENGINE, MOTOR** entry.

• MOUNT
Spell out in all uses, including the names of communities and of mountains: *Mount Clemens, Michigan; Mount Everest.*

• MOUNTAIN STANDARD TIME (M-S-T), MOUNTAIN DAYLIGHT TIME (M-D-T)
See **TIME ZONES.**

• MOUNTAIN STATES
As defined by the Census Bureau, the eight are Arizona, Colorado, Idaho, Montana, Nevada, New Mexico, Utah and Wyoming.

• MOVIE RATINGS
The rankings used by the Motion Picture Association of America are:

G For *general audiences.* All ages admitted.

PG For *parental guidance.* Some material may not be suitable for children less than 13 years old.

R For *restricted.* Persons under 17 must be accompanied by a parent or adult guardian.

X For *no one under 17 admitted.* (The age limit may be different in some areas.)

When the ratings are used in news stories or reviews, use these forms as appropriate: *the movie has an X rating, an X-rated movie, the movie is X-rated.*

• M-P-H
Don't use it. Use *miles-per-hour* instead.

• MR., MRS.
See **COURTESY TITLES.**

Avoid constructions which call for the use of the plurals of *Mr.* or *Mrs.*

• MS. (MIZ)
This is the spelling and punctuation for all uses of the courtesy title, including direct quotations.

There is no plural. If several

women who prefer *Ms.* must be listed in a series, repeat *Ms.* before each name.

See **COURTESY TITLES** for guidelines on when to use *Ms.*

• MULTI-

The rules in **PREFIXES** apply, but in general, no hyphen. Some examples:

MULTICOLORED
MULTILATERAL
MULTIMILLION
MULTIMILLIONAIRE

• MUNICIPAL BOND

See **LOAN TERMINOLOGY.**

• MURDER

See the **HOMICIDE, MURDER, MANSLAUGHTER** entry.

• MURDERER

See the **ASSASSIN, KILLER, MURDERER** entry.

• MURPHY'S LAW

The law is: If something can go wrong, it will.

• MUSKET

See **WEAPONS.**

• MUSLIMS

See **MOSLEM(S).**

• MUTUAL BROADCASTING SYSTEM, INCORPORATED

Mutual Radio is acceptable in all references. Do not use the abbreviation *M-B-S.*

Headquarters is in Arlington, Virginia.

• MUZAK (MYOO'-ZAK)

A trademark for a type of recorded background music.

• NAIVE

• NAMES

In general, people are entitled to be known however they want to be known, as long as their identities are clear.

When an individual elects to change the name by which he has been known, such as Cassius Clay's transition to Muhammad Ali, provide both names in stories until the new name is known by the public. After that, use only the new name unless there is a specific reason for including the earlier identification.

See the **JUNIOR, SENIOR** entry and the entries under **MIDDLE INITIALS; NICKNAMES;** and **SEX CHANGES.**

• NANO-

A prefix denoting one (b) billionth of a unit. Move the decimal point nine places to the left when converting to the basic unit: two (b) billion nano-seconds equals two seconds.

• NAPHTHA (NAP'-THUH)

See **OIL.**

• NARROW-MINDED

• "NASA"

Acceptable in all references for *National Aeronautics and Space Administration.*

• NATIONAL

See the **CITIZEN, RESIDENT, SUBJECT, NATIONAL, NATIVE** entry.

• NATIONAL AERONAUTICS AND SPACE ADMINISTRATION

"NASA" and *the space agency* are acceptable on all references.

• NATIONAL ASSEMBLY

See **FOREIGN LEGISLATIVE BODIES.**

• NATIONAL ASSOCIATION FOR STOCK CAR AUTO RACING

In general, spell out on first reference.

A phrase such as *"NASCAR" competition* is acceptable on first reference, however, to avoid a cumbersome lead. If this is done, provide the full name later in the story.

• NATIONAL ASSOCIATION FOR THE ADVANCEMENT OF COLORED PEOPLE

N-Double-A-C-P or *N-A-A-C-P* are acceptable on first reference to prevent a cumbersome lead, but make sure to provide the full name of the organization in a subsequent reference.

Headquarters is in New York.

• NATIONAL ASSOCIATION OF LETTER CARRIERS

The shortened form *Letter Carriers union* is acceptable in all references.

Headquarters is in Washington.

• NATIONAL ASSOCIATION OF SECURITIES DEALERS

Do not abbreviate.

The association operates the *National Association of Securities Dealers Automated Quotations* system—*"NASDAQ" (naz'-dak)* on second reference.

Headquarters is in Washington.

• NATIONAL BAPTIST CONVENTION OF AMERICA

See **BAPTIST CHURCHES.**

• NATIONAL BAPTIST CONVENTION, U-S-A, INCORPORATED

See **BAPTIST CHURCHES.**

• NATIONAL BROADCASTING COMPANY

See **N-B-C.**

• NATIONAL COLLEGIATE ATHLETIC ASSOCIATION

N-C-Double-A is acceptable on all references.

• NATIONAL CONFERENCE OF CATHOLIC BISHOPS

See **ROMAN CATHOLIC CHURCH.**

• NATIONAL COUNCIL OF THE CHURCHES OF CHRIST IN THE U-S-A

This interdenominational, cooperative body includes most major Protestant and Eastern Orthodox denominations in the United States.

The shortened form *National Council of Churches* is acceptable in all references.

Headquarters is in New York.

See **WORLD COUNCIL OF CHURCHES.**

• NATIONAL EDUCATION ASSOCIATION

N-E-A is acceptable on second reference.

Headquarters is in Washington.

• NATIONAL GOVERNORS' CONFERENCE

Note the apostrophe. Represents the governors of the 50 states and four territories.

Its office is in Washington.

• NATIONAL GUARDSMAN

Not *guardman.* See **MILITARY TITLES.**

• NATIONAL HURRICANE CENTER

See **WEATHER TERMS.**

• NATIONAL INSTITUTES OF HEALTH

This agency within the Department of Health and Human Services is the principal biomedical research arm of the federal government.

It consists of the National Library of Medicine, eleven separate institutes and various divisions that provide centralized support services for the individual institutes.

The eleven institutes are: National Cancer Institute; National Eye Institute; National Heart, Lung, and Blood Institute; National Institute of Allergy and Infectious Diseases; National Institute of Arthritis, Metabolism, and Digestive Diseases; National Institute of Child Health and Human Development; National Institute of Dental Research; National Institute of Environmental Health Sciences; National Institute of General Medical Sciences; National Institute of Neurological and Communicative Disorders and Stroke; National Institute on Aging.

• NATIONALIST

Generally, this term is descriptive of a person's political philosophy, rather than a specific party affiliation.

• NATIONALITIES AND RACES

See **RACE** for guidelines on when racial identification is pertinent to a story.

Derogatory racial references should be used only when in quoted matter and when essential to the story.

● **NATIONAL LABOR RELATIONS BOARD**

N-L-R-B is acceptable on second reference.

● **NATIONAL LEAGUE OF CITIES**

Its members are the governments of cities and towns and state municipal leagues.

It is separate from the U-S Conference of Mayors, whose membership is limited to mayors of cities with 30-thousand or more residents. The organizations often engage in joint projects, however.

The office is in Washington.

● **NATIONAL ORGANIZATION FOR WOMEN**

Not *of.* *"NOW"* is acceptable on second reference.

Headquarters is in Washington.

● **NATIONAL RIFLE ASSOCIATION**

N-R-A is acceptable in second reference.

Headquarters is in Washington.

● **NATIONAL WEATHER SERVICE**

It is no longer formally called the *U-S Weather Bureau.* But *the weather service* or *the weather bureau* may be used in any reference.

See **WEATHER TERMS.**

● **NATIONWIDE**

● **NATIVE**

See the **CITIZEN, RESIDENT, SUBJECT, NATIONAL, NATIVE** entry.

● **"NATO"** (NAY'-TOH)

Acceptable in all references for the *North Atlantic Treaty Organization,* but use it sparingly. A phrase such as *the alliance* can be used for brevity.

● **NAUTICAL MILE**

Six-thousand, 76-point-12 feet, or one-thousand, 852 meters.

To convert to approximate statute miles—five-thousand, 280 feet—multiply the number of nautical miles by one-point-15.

See **KNOT.**

● **NAVAL, NAVEL**

Naval pertains to a navy.

A *navel* is a bellybutton.

A *navel orange* is a seedless orange, so named because it has a small depression, like a navel, at its apex.

● **NAZI, NAZISM**

After the National Socialist German Workers' Party, the fascist political party founded in 1919 and abolished in 1945. Under Adolf Hitler, it seized control of Germany in 1933.

● **N-B-C**

Acceptable in all references for the *National Broadcasting Company,* a subsidiary of *R-C-A Corporation.*

Divisions are N-B-C News, N-B-C Radio and N-B-C T-V.

Headquarters is in New York.

● **N-C-R CORPORATION**

Formerly National Cash Register Company.

Headquarters is in New York.

● **NEAR EAST**

There is no longer a substantial distinction between this term and *Middle East.*

See the **MIDDLE EAST** entry.

• NEARSIGHTED
When used in a medical sense, it means an individual can see well at close range but has difficulty seeing objects at a distance.

• NEGRO, NEGROES
Use *black* or *Negro,* as appropriate in the context, for both men and women. Do not use *Negress.*
See the **NATIONALITIES AND RACES** entry and **RACE.**

• NEITHER . . . NOR
See the **EITHER . . . OR, NEITHER . . . NOR** entry.

• NETHERLANDS
In datelines and the body of the story, refer to it as it is commonly referred to: *The Netherlands: (AMSTERDAM, THE NETHERLANDS)* --

• NET INCOME, NET PROFIT
See **PROFIT TERMINOLOGY.**

• NEUTRON BOMB
There isn't one. See the next entry.

• NEUTRON WEAPON
A small warhead designed to be mounted on a Lance missile or fired from an eight-inch gun. It produces twice the deadly radiation of older tactical nuclear weapons, but less than one-tenth the explosive power, heat and fallout. This means that the warhead can kill people without causing extensive damage to buildings and other structures.
It is not a *bomb.* It is a *weapon* or *warhead.*
If the term *neutron bomb* is used in a direct quote, explain that it is actually a warhead that would be fired on a missile or from artillery—and not dropped, like a bomb, from a plane.
The formal title for the weapon is *enhanced radiation weapon.*

• NEW BRUNSWICK
One of the three Maritime Provinces of Canada. Do not abbreviate.
See **DATELINES.**

• NEW ENGLAND
Connecticut, Maine, Massachusetts, New Hampshire, Rhode Island and Vermont.

• NEWFOUNDLAND
This Canadian province comprises the island of Newfoundland and the mainland section known as Labrador. Do not abbreviate.
In datelines, use *Newfoundland* after the names of all cities and towns. Specify in the text whether the community is on the island or in Labrador.
See **DATELINES.**

• NEW ORLEANS
The city in Louisiana stands alone in datelines.

• NEW SOUTH
The era that began in the South in the 1960's with a thriving economy and the election of officials who advocated the abolition of racial segregation.
Old South applies to the South before the Civil War.

• NEWSPAPER NAMES
Put all newspaper names in quotes on the first reference: *"The New York Times,"* the *New York "Daily News."*

• NEWSSTAND

• NEW TESTAMENT
See **BIBLE.**

• NEW WORLD
The Western Hemisphere.

• NEW YEAR'S, NEW YEAR'S DAY, NEW YEAR'S EVE
The federal legal holiday is observed on Friday if January First falls on a Saturday, and on Monday if the First falls on a Sunday.

• NEW YORK
Use *New York state* when a distinction must be made between state and city. See **STATE NAMES**.

• NEW YORK CITY
Use *New York* in datelines, not the name of an individual community or borough such as *Flushing* or *Queens*.

Identify the borough in the body of the story if pertinent.

• NEW YORK STOCK EXCHANGE
"NYSE" (ny'-zee) is acceptable on second reference as an adjective. Use *the stock exchange* or *the exchange* for other second references.

The nickname *Big Board* also is acceptable.

• NICKNAMES
A nickname should be used in place of a person's given name in news stories only when it is the way the individual prefers to be known: *Jimmy Carter.*

When a nickname is inserted into the identification of an individual, use quotation marks: *Senator Henry "Scoop" Jackson.* Also: *Jackson is known as "Scoop."*

In sports stories and sports columns, commonly used nicknames may be substituted for a first name without the use of quotation marks: *Woody Hayes, Bear Bryant, Catfish Hunter, Bubba Smith,* etc. But in sports stories where the given name is used, and in all news stories: *Paul "Bear" Bryant.*

• NIGHTCLUB

• NIGHTTIME

• NIT-PICKING

• NITTY-GRITTY

• NOBEL PRIZE, NOBEL PRIZES
The five established under terms of the will of Alfred Nobel are: Nobel Peace Prize, Nobel Prize in chemistry, Nobel Prize in literature, Nobel Prize in physics, Nobel Prize in physiology or medicine.

The Nobel Memorial Prize in Economic Science is not a Nobel Prize in the same sense. The Central Bank of Sweden established it in 1968 as a memorial to Alfred Nobel. References to this prize should include the word *Memorial* to help make this distinction. Explain the status of the prize in the story when appropriate.

• NOBILITY
References to members of the nobility in nations that have a system of rank present special problems because nobles frequently are known by their titles rather than their given or family names. Their titles, in effect, become their names.

The guidelines here relate to Britain's nobility. Adapt them as appropriate to members of the nobility in other nations.

Orders of rank among British nobility begin with the royal family. The term *royalty* is reserved for the families of living and deceased sovereigns.

Next, in descending order, are dukes, marquesses, earls, viscounts and barons. Many hold inherited titles;

others have been raised to the nobility by the soverign for their lifetimes. Occasionally the sovereign raises an individual to the nobility and makes the title inheritable by the person's heirs, but the practice is increasingly rare.

Sovereigns also confer honorary titles, which do not make an individual a member of the nobility. The principal designations, in descending order, are baronet and knight.

Some guidelines and examples:

Royalty: Keep the title as short as possible: *Queen Elizabeth the Second,* rather than *Her Majesty Queen Elizabeth the Second of England.* Also: *the queen, the king, the queen mother.*

Use Prince or *Princess* before the names of a sovereign's children: *Princess Anne, the princess.*

The male heir to the throne normally is designated *Prince of Wales,* and the title becomes, in common usage, an alternate name: *The queen invested her eldest son as Prince of Wales. Prince Charles is now the Prince of Wales. The prince is a bachelor. Charles, Prince of Wales, was married today.*

• NOBODY, NO ONE

• NOLO CONTENDERE

(NOH'-LO KAHN-TEN'-DUH-REE)

The literal meaning is, "I do not wish to contend." Terms such as *no contest* or *no contest plea* are acceptable in all references.

When a defendant in a criminal case enters this plea, it means that he is not admitting guilt but is stating that he will offer no defense. The person is then subject to being judged guilty and punished as if he had pleaded guilty or had been convicted. The principal difference is that the defendant retains the option of denying the same charge in another legal proceeding.

• NO MAN'S LAND

• NON-

Hyphenate all except the following words, which have specific meanings of their own:

NONCHALANCE	NONSENSE
NONCHALANT	NONSENSICAL
NONDESCRIPT	

• NON-ALIGNED NATIONS

A political rather than economic or geographic term. Although non-aligned nations do not belong to Western or Eastern military alliances or blocs, they profess not to be neutral, like Switzerland; but activist alternatives.

Do not confuse *non-aligned* with *Third World,* although many Third World nations belong to the non-aligned group. For example, Yugoslavia is a non-aligned nation because it does not belong to the Warsaw Pact, but it is not a Third World nation.

See the **THIRD WORLD** entry.

• NON-CONTROVERSIAL

All issues are controversial. A *non-controversial issue* is impossible. A *controversial issue* is redundant.

• NONE

It usually means no single one. When used in this sense, it always takes singular verbs and pronouns: *None of the seats was in its right place.*

Use a plural verb only if the sense is no two or no amount: *None of the consultants agree on the same approach. None of the taxes have been paid.*

• NON-RESTRICTIVE CLAUSES

See the **ESSENTIAL CLAUSES, NON-ESSENTIAL CLAUSES** entry.

• NOON

Do not put a *12* in front of it.

• NO ONE

• NORM

See the **AVERAGE, MEAN, MEDIAN, NORM** entry.

• NORTH AMERICA

See **WESTERN HEMISPHERE.**

• NORTH ATLANTIC TREATY ORGANIZATION

"NATO" is acceptable in all references, but use it sparingly.

• NORTH CENTRAL AIRLINES

Headquarters is in Minneapolis.

• NORTH-CENTRAL REGION

As defined by the Census Bureau, the 12-state region is broken into eastern and western divisions.

The five *East North-Central* states are Indiana, Illinois, Michigan, Ohio and Wisconsin.

The seven *West North-Central* states are Iowa, Kansas, Minnesota, Missouri, Nebraska, North Dakota and South Dakota.

See **NORTHEAST REGION; SOUTH;** and **WEST** for the bureau's other regional breakdowns.

• NORTHEAST REGION

As defined by the Census Bureau, the nine-state region is broken into two divisions—the *New England* states and the *Middle Atlantic* states.

Connecticut, Maine, Massachusetts, New Hampshire, Rhode Island and Vermont are the *New England* states.

New Jersey, New York and Pennsylvania are classified as the *Middle Atlantic* states.

See **NORTH-CENTRAL REGION; SOUTH;** and **WEST** for the bureau's other regional breakdowns.

• NORTHERN IRELAND

It is a British province located on the same island as the Republic of Ireland. Use *Northern Ireland* after the names of all communities in datelines.

See **DATELINES** and **UNITED KINGDOM.**

• NORTH SLOPE

The portion of Alaska north of Brooks Range, a string of mountains extending across the northern part of the state.

• NORTHWEST ORIENT AIRLINES

Northwest Airlines is acceptable in all references.

Headquarters is in St. Paul, Minnesota.

• NORTHWEST TERRITORIES

A territorial section of Canada. Do not abbreviate. Use in datelines after the names of all cities and towns in the territory.

If necessary, specify in the text whether the community is in one of the three territorial subdivisions: Franklin, Keewatin and Mackenzie.

See **CANADA.**

• NOUNS

The abbreviation *n.* is used in this book to identify the spelling of the noun forms of words frequently misspelled.

• NOVA SCOTIA

One of the three Maritime Provinces of Canada. Do not abbreviate.

See **DATELINES.**

• NOVOCAIN

A trademark for a drug used as a

local anesthetic. It also may be called *procain.*

• NOWADAYS

Not *nowdays.*

• NUCLEAR REGULATORY COMMISSION

This commission has taken over the regulatory functions previously performed by the Atomic Energy Commission.

N-R-C is acceptable on second reference, but *the agency* or *the commission* is preferred.

• NUCLEAR TERMINOLOGY

In reporting on nuclear energy, include the definitions of appropriate terms, especially those related to radiation.

Core: The part of a nuclear reactor that contains its fissionable fuel. In a reactor core, atoms of fuel, such as uranium, are split. This releases energy in the form of heat which, in turn, is used to boil water for steam. The steam powers a turbine, and the turbine drives a generator to produce electricity.

Fission: The splitting of the nucleus of an atom, releasing energy.

Meltdown: The worst possible nuclear accident, in which the reactor core overheats to such a degree that the fuel melts. If the fuel penetrates its protective housing, radioactive materials will be released into the environment.

Rad: The standard unit of measurement for absorbed radiation. A *millirad* is a thousandth of a rad. There is considerable debate among scientists whether there is any safe level of absorption.

Radiation: Invisible particles or waves given off by radioactive material, such as uranium. Radiation can damage or kill body cells, resulting in latent cancers, genetic damage or death.

Rem: The standard unit of measurement of absorbed radiation in living tissue, adjusted for different kinds of radiation so that one rem of any radiation will produce the same biological effect. A *millirem* is a thousandth of a rem.

A diagnostic chest X-ray involves between 20 millirems and 30 millirems of radiation. Each American, on average, receives 100 millirems to 200 millirems of radiation a year from natural "background" sources, such as cosmic rays, and man-made sources, such as diagnostic X-rays. There is considerable debate among scientists over the safety of repeated low doses of radiation.

Roentgen: The standard measure of X-ray exposure.

Uranium: A metallic, radioactive element used as fuel in nuclear reactors.

• NUMERALS

A numeral is a figure, letter, word or group of words expressing a number.

Roman numerals are not used on the broadcast wires. They should be converted to *Arabic numerals* or words: *World War Two, Native Dancer the Second, King George the Sixth, Pope John the 23rd.*

Arabic numerals use the figures *1, 2, 3, 4, 5, 6, 7, 8, 9 and 0.*

The figures *1, 2, 10, 101,* etc. and the corresponding words—*one, two, ten, one hundred one,* etc.—are called *cardinal numbers.*

The term *ordinal numbers* applies to *1st, 2nd, 10th, 101st* and the corresponding words—*first, second, tenth, one hundred first,* etc.

Usage: Broadcast writing is different. Remember, the goal is to write so that an announcer reading the copy cold can do so easily and correctly.

Imagine trying to read this aloud: *The budget for next year was set at $1,838,763,542.* Now, try this: *Next year's budget was set at roughly one-point-eight (b) billion dollars.*

The following rules have been established to comply with long-standing usage and to ensure that numbers are as easy to read as possible:

Use words alone to express the numbers *one* through *eleven. The number of dead was placed at eleven. Five men were arrested.*

Use figures alone to express the numbers 12 through *999: We've seen 23 movies this year. There were 898 rooms in the hotel.*

Exception: Don't start a sentence with a number. Use words instead: *Eight-hundred-ninety-eight rooms were damaged in the blaze.*

Use words to express *thousands, (m) millions, (b) billions* and *(t) trillions.* Use a hyphen to combine numbers and the word *thousands: It will cost 45-thousand dollars.*

Hyphens are not needed to connect numbers with *(m) millions, (b) billions and (t) trillions.*

To guard against typos, *(m) millions, (b) billions* and *(t) trillions* should be preceded by the word's first letter, in parentheses: *45 (m) million; 118 (b) billion; two (t) trillion.*

Ordinals: Follow the same pattern, with *one* through *eleven* spelled out: *First, fifth, eleventh, etc.*

Use figures to express ordinals 12 through *999: 12th, 14th, 234th, 819th.*

Fractions: Should be spelled out, using the appropriate combination of words: *two-tenths; three-fifths; eight-hundredths.*

Decimals: Always spell them out. Use hyphens, and the word *point: five-point-three, point-two, point-oh-one, 137-point-seven.*

Decimalization should exceed two places only when crucial to the story.

Remember, a number that appears *.0005* in newspaper style needs to be translated for broadcast; it should be treated as a fraction rather than a decimal: *He won by five-thousandths of a second.*

Finally, as noted elsewhere, spell out money amounts: *five dollars, 33 cents, five and a-half dollars,* etc. Never use the $ symbol in copy, except for tabular columns.

- **OASIS, OASES**

- **OBSCENTIES, PROFANTIES, VULGARITIES**

Do not use them in stories unless they are part of direct quotations and there is a compelling reason for them.

When a profanity, obscenity or vulgarity is used, flag the story at the top:

(News directors: portions of the following may be offensive to some listeners.)

In reporting profanity that normally would use the words *damn* or *god,* use the following forms: *damn, damn it, goddamn it.* Do not change the offending words to euphemisms. Do not, for example, change *damn it* to *darn it.*

- **OCCIDENTAL PETROLEUM CORPORATION**

Headquarters is in Los Angeles.

- **OCCUPATIONAL SAFTEY AND HEALTH ADMINISTRATION**

"OSHA" is acceptable on second reference.

- **OCCUR, OCCURRED, OCCURRING**

Also: *occurrence.*

- **OCEAN-GOING**

- **OCEANS**

The five, from the largest to the smallest: Pacific Ocean, Atlantic Ocean, Indian Ocean, Antarctic Ocean, Arctic Ocean.

- **ODD**

Follow with a hyphen:

ODD-LOOKING
ODD-NUMBERED

- **OFF-, -OFF**

Follow Webster's New World Dictionary. Hyphenate if not listed there.

Some commonly used combinations with a hyphen:

OFF-COLOR	OFF-WHITE
OFF-PEAK	SEND-OFF
OFF-SEASON	STOP-OFF

Some combinations without a hyphen:

BLASTOFF	OFFSIDE
CUTOFF	OFFSTAGE
OFFHAND	PLAYOFF
OFFSET	STANDOFF
OFFSHORE	TAKEOFF

- **OFF-BROADWAY, OFF-OFF-BROADWAY**

See the **BROADWAY, OFF-BROADWAY, OFF-OFF-BROADWAY** entry.

- **OFFICEHOLDER**

- **OFF OF**

The *of* is unnecessary: *He fell off the bed.* Not: *He fell off of the bed.*

- **OIL**

In shipping, oil and oil products normally are measured by the ton. For news stories, convert these tonnage figures to gallons.

In international oil transactions, there are 42 gallons to each barrel of oil. The number of barrels per ton varies, depending on the type of oil product.

To convert tonnage to gallons:

—Determine the type of oil.

—Consult the table below to find out how many barrels per ton for that type of oil.

—Multiply the number of tons by the number of barrels per ton. The result is the number of barrels in the shipment.

—Multiply the number of barrels by 42. The result is the number of gallons.

Example: A tanker spills 20-thousand metric tons of foreign crude. The table shows six-point-998 barrels of foreign crude per metric ton. Six-point-998 times 20-thousand equals 139-thousand, 960 barrels, times 42 gallons per barrel equals five (m) million, 878-thousand, 320 gallons.

Table: The table below is based on figures supplied by the American Petroleum Institute.

OIL EQUIVALENCY TABLE

Type of Product	Barrels per Short Ton (2,000 lbs.)	Barrels per Metric Ton (2,204.6 lbs.)	Barrels per Long Ton (2,240 lbs.)
crude oil, foreign	6.349	6.998	7.111
crude oil, domestic	6.770	7.463	7.582
gasoline and naptha	7.721	8.511	8.648
kerosene	7.053	7.775	7.900
distillate fuel oil	6.580	7.253	7.369
residual fuel oil	6.041	6.660	6.766
lubricating oil	6.349	6.998	7.111
lubricating grease	6.665	7.346	7.464
wax	7.134	7.864	7.990
asphalt	5.540	6.106	6.205
coke	4.990	5.500	5.589
road oil	5.900	6.503	6.608
jelly and petrolatum	6.665	7.346	7.464
liquefied pet. gas	10.526	11.603	11.789
Gilsonite	5.515	6.080	6.177

- **OIL, CHEMICAL AND ATOMIC WORKERS INTERNATIONAL UNION**

The shortened forms *Oil Workers union, Chemical Workers union* and *Atomic Workers union* are acceptable in all references.

Headquarters is in Denver.

- **O-K, O-K'D, O-K'ING, O-K'S**

Do not use *okay.*

- **OKLAHOMA CITY**

Stands alone in datelines.

- **OLD CITY OF JERUSALEM**

The walled part of the city.

• OLD SOUTH

The South before the Civil War. See **NEW SOUTH.**

• OLD-TIME, OLD-TIMER, OLD-TIMES

• OLD WEST

The American West as it was being settled in the 19th century.

• OLD WORLD

The Eastern Hemisphere: Asia, Europe, Africa. The term also may be an allusion to European culture and customs.

• OLYMPIC AIRWAYS

Headquarters is in Athens, Greece.

• ON

Do not use *on* before a date or day of the week when its absence would not lead to confusion: *The meeting will be held Monday. He will be inaugurated January 20th.*

Use *on* to avoid an awkward juxtaposition of a date and a proper name: *John met Mary on Monday. He told Carter on Thursday that the bill was doomed.*

Use *on* also to avoid any suggestion that a date is the object of a transitive verb: *The House killed on Tuesday a bid to raise taxes. The Senate postponed on Wednesday its consideration of a bill to reduce import duties.*

• ONE-

Hyphenate when used in writing fractions:

ONE-HALF
ONE-THIRD

Phrases such as *a-half* or *a-third* are also acceptable.

See **FRACTIONS.**

• ONE ANOTHER

See the **EACH OTHER, ONE ANOTHER** entry.

• ONE MAN, ONE VOTE

The adjective form: *one-man, one-vote. He supports the principle of one man, one vote. The one-man, one-vote rule.*

• ONE-SIDED

• ONE TIME, ONE-TIME

He did it one time. He is a one-time winner.

• ONTARIO

This Canadian province is the nation's first in total population and second to Quebec in area. Do not abbreviate.

See **DATELINES.**

• OPINION POLLS

See the **POLLS AND SURVEYS** entry.

• OPOSSUM

The only North American marsupial. No apostrophe is needed to indicate missing letters in a phrase such as *playing possum.*

• OPTION

In a financial sense, the word means an agreement that allows a person or a corporation to buy or sell something, such as shares of stock, within a stipulated time and for a certain price.

A *put option* gives the holder the right to sell blocks of 100 shares of stock within a specified time at an agreed-upon price.

A *call option* gives the holder the right to buy blocks of 100 shares of stock within a specified time at an agreed-upon price.

• ORAL, VERBAL, WRITTEN

Use *oral* to refer to spoken words: *He gave an oral promise.*

Use *written* to refer to words committed to paper: *We had a written agreement.*

Use *verbal* to compare words with some other form of communications: *His tears revealed the sentiments that his poor verbal skills could not express.*

• ORGANIZATION OF AMERICAN STATES

O-A-S is acceptable on second reference.

Headquarters is in Washington.

• ORGANIZATION OF PETROLEUM EXPORTING COUNTRIES

Use the full name for most first references. *"OPEC"* may be used on first reference, but the body of the story should identify it as the shortened form of the name.

The 13 *"OPEC"* members, as of 1981: Algeria, Ecuador, Gabon, Indonesia, Iran, Iraq, Kuwait, Libya, Nigeria, Qatar, Saudi Arabia, United Arab Emirates, Venezuela.

Headquarters is in Vienna, Austria.

• ORGANIZATIONS AND INSTITUTIONS

They are best referred to by their most recognizable names.

For example, the *National Aeronautics and Space Administration* is most commonly called *"NASA"* or *the space agency,* and can be referred to in those ways in all references.

Because broadcast copy is conversational, the names of organizations and institutions should be informalized where appropriate: *"OPEC"—the organization of petroleum exporting countries—can be called the oil cartel.* But do not informalize names when the formal version is better-known: *Massachusetts Institute of Technology* is better than *the technology institute.*

See **ABBREVIATIONS; ACRONYMS;** and **SECOND REFERENCE.**

• ORLON

A trademark for a form of acrylic fiber similar to nylon.

• ORTHODOX CHURCH IN AMERICA

See **EASTERN ORTHODOX CHURCHES.**

• OSCAR, OSCARS

See **ACADEMY AWARDS.**

• OSCILLATING THEORY

See **BIG-BANG THEORY.**

• OTTAWA

The capital of Canada stands alone in datelines.

• OUIJA (WEE'-JUH)

A trademark for a board used in spiritual seances.

• OUNCE (dry)

Units of dry volume are not customarily carried to this level.

See **PINT (DRY).**

• OUNCE (liquid)

See **FLUID OUNCE.**

• OUNCE (weight)

It is defined as 437-point-five grains.

The metric equivalent is about 28 grams.

To convert to grams, multiply by 28: five ounces times 28 equals 140 grams.

See **GRAIN** and **GRAM.**

• OUT-

Follow Webster's New World. Hyphenate if not listed there.

Some frequently used words:

OUTARGUE	OUTPATIENT (n. adj.)
OUTBOX	OUTPOST
OUTDATED	OUTPUT
OUTFIELD	OUTSCORE
OUTFOX	OUTSTRIP

• -OUT

Follow Webster's New World. Hyphenate nouns and adjectives not listed there.

Some frequently used words (all nouns):

COP-OUT	HIDE-OUT
FADE-OUT	PULLOUT
FALLOUT	WALKOUT
FLAMEOUT	WASHOUT

Two words for verbs:

FADE OUT	WALK OUT
HIDE OUT	WASH OUT
PULL OUT	

• OUTER BANKS

The sandy islands along the North Carolina coast.

• OUT OF BOUNDS

But as a modifier: *out-of-bounds. The ball went out of bounds. He took an out-of-bounds pass.*

• OUT OF COURT, OUT-OF-COURT

They settled out of court. He accepted an out-of-court settlement.

• OVAL OFFICE

The White House office of the president.

• OVER

It is not a synonym for *more than.*

Over refers to spatial relationships: *The plane flew over the city. He leaned over the precipice.*

More than is used with figures: *There were more than 40-thousand fans in the stadium. He weighs more than 200 pounds.*

• OVER-

Follow Webster's New World. A hyphen is seldom used. Some frequently used words:

OVERBUY	OVERRATE
OVEREXERT	OVERRIDE

See the **OVERALL** entry.

• -OVER

Follow Webster's New World. Hyphenate if not listed there.

Some frequently used words (all are nouns; some also are used as adjectives):

CARRY-OVER	STOPOVER
HOLDOVER	WALKOVER
TAKEOVER	

Use two words when any of these occurs as a verb.

See **SUFFIXES.**

• OVERALL

A single word in adjectival and adverbial use: *Overall, the Democrats succeeded. Overall policy.*

The word for the garment is *overalls.*

• OVERSEAS NATIONAL AIRWAYS

Headquarters is in New York.

• OZARK AIR LINES

Headquarters is in St. Louis.

• OZARK MOUNTAINS

Or simply: *the Ozarks.*

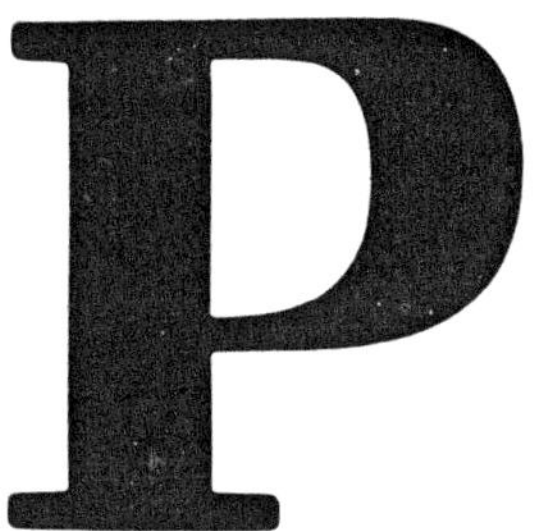

• PACEMAKER

Formerly a trademark, now a generic term for a device that electronically helps a person's heart maintain a steady beat.

• PACIFIC STANDARD TIME (P-S-T), PACIFIC DAYLIGHT TIME (P-D-T)

See **TIME ZONES.**

• PACIFIC TEN CONFERENCE

Arizona, Arizona State, California, Oregon, Oregon State, Southern Cal, Stanford, University of California at Los Angeles (U-C-L-A), Washington, Washington State.

Pac-Ten is acceptable on second reference.

• PADDY WAGON

• PALATE, PALETTE, PALLET

Palate is the roof of the mouth.

A *palette* is an artist's paint board.

A *pallet* is a bed.

• PALESTINE LIBERATION ORGANIZTION

Not *Palestinian. P-L-O* is acceptable on second reference.

• PAN-

No hyphen when combined with a common noun:

PANCHROMATIC
PANTHEISM

Most combinations with *pan-* are proper nouns, however, and they are hyphenated:

PAN-AFRICAN
PAN-AMERICAN
PAN-ASIATIC

• PANAMA CANAL ZONE

In datelines, give the name of a city or town followed by *Canal Zone:*

(BALBOA, CANAL ZONE) --

Do not use the abbreviation *C.Z.*

In text: *the Canal Zone, the canal, the zone.*

• PANAMA CITY

Use *Panama City, Florida,* or *Panama City, Panama,* in datelines to avoid confusion between the two.

• PAN AMERICAN WORLD AIRWAYS

A *Pan Am airliner* is acceptable in any reference.

Headquarters is in New York.

• PANTSUIT

Not *pants suit.*

• PANTYHOSE

• PAPAL NUNCIO

Do not confuse with an *apostolic delegate.* See the **APOSTOLIC DELEGATE, PAPAL NUNCIO** entry.

• PAP TEST, PAP SMEAR

After George Papanicolaou, the anatomist who developed this test for cervical and uterine cancer.

• PARALLEL, PARALLELED, PARALLELING

• PARALLELS

Follow the rules for **NUMERALS**

when referring to the imaginary locater lines that ring the globe from east to west. They are measured in units of zero to 90 degrees north or south of the equator. Note that they are rarely used in routine copy; only when a parallel is used as a specific marker (as in *the 38th parallel* in Korea) should it be referred to in a story.

Examples: *the fourth parallel north, the 89th parallel south.* If, as in the Korean example, the location north or south of the equator is obvious: *the 38th parallel.*

See **LATITUDE AND LONGITUDE.**

• PARDON, PAROLE, PROBATION

The terms often are confused, but each has a specific meaning. Do not use them interchangeably.

A *pardon* forgives and releases a person from further punishment. It is granted by a chief of state or a governor. By itself, it does not expunge a record of conviction, if one exists, and it does not by itself restore civil rights.

A *general pardon,* usually for political offenses, is called *amnesty.*

Parole is the release of a prisoner before the sentence has expired, on condition of good behavior. It is granted by a parole board, part of the executive branch of government, and can be revoked only by the board.

Probation is the suspension of sentence for a person convicted, but not yet imprisoned, on condition of good behavior. It is imposed and revoked only by a judge.

• PARENTHESES

Their major use on the broadcast wires is to set off material which should not be read on the air—datelines, advisories, pronounciations, etc.:

(DENVER) -- Colorado Democrat Patricia Schroeder (shroh'-duhr) reportedly plans to announce her candidacy for the Senate at a (two o'clock) news conference today.

Parentheses should *never* be used instead of a parenthetical clause: *Mrs. Schroeder (who was first elected to Congress in 1972) has never lost a statewide election.*

Parentheses may also be used in rare instances to indicate that an unlikely-looking entry is correct as sent: *An airline spokesman said there were 13 (correct) passengers and 15 crewmembers on board the 747 at the time of the crash.*

• PARENT-TEACHER ASSOCIATION

P-T-A is acceptable in all references.

• PARI-MUTUEL

• PARIS

The city in France stands alone in datelines.

• PARISHIONER

• PARKINSON'S DISEASE

After James Parkinson, the English physician who described this degenerative disease of later life.

• PARKINSON'S LAW

After C. Northcote Parkinson, the British economist who came to the satirical conclusion that work expands to fill the time allotted to it.

• PARLIAMENT

See **FOREIGN LEGISLATIVE BODIES.**

• PAROLE

See the **PARDON, PAROLE, PROBATION** entry.

• PARTIAL QUOTES

See **QUOTATION MARKS.**

• **PARTICLES**
See **FOREIGN PARTICLES.**

• **PART TIME, PART-TIME**
Hyphenate when used as a compound modifier: *She works part time. She has a part-time job.*

• **PARTY**
See the following entry.

• **PARTY AFFILIATION**
Let relevance be the guide in determining whether to include a political figure's party affiliation in a story.

Party affiliation is pointless in some stories, such as an account of a governor accepting a button from a poster child.

It will occur naturally in many political stories.

For stories between these extremes, include party affiliation if listeners need it for understanding or are likely to be curious about what it is.

General Forms: Party affiliations should not be abbreviated in broadcast copy. The following forms are acceptable:

Democratic Senator George McGovern of South Dakota.

Senator George McGovern, the South Dakota Democrat.

Senator George McGovern spoke. The South Dakota Democrat said ...

In stories about party meetings, such as a report on a political convention, no specific reference to party affiliation is needed unless the individual in question is not a member of the party in question.

• **PASS**
See the **ADOPT, APPROVE, ENACT, PASS** entry.

• **PASSENGER LISTS**
When providing a list of victims in a disaster, arrange names alphabetically according to last name, include street address if available, and use a paragraph for each name:

Jones, Joseph, 260 Town Street, Sample, New York.

Williams, Susan, 780 Main Street, Example, New Jersey.

• **PASSENGER-MILE**
One passenger carried one mile, or its equivalent, such as two passengers carried one-half mile.

• **PASSER-BY, PASSERS-BY**

• **PASSOVER**
The week-long Jewish commemoration of the deliverance of the ancient Hebrews from slavery in Egypt. Occurs in March or April.

• **PASTEURIZE**

• **PASTOR**
See **RELIGIOUS TITLES** and the entry for the individual's denomination.

• **PATRIOTS' DAY**
April 19th, a legal holiday in Massachusetts.

• **PATROL, PATROLLED, PATROLLING**

• **PATROLMAN, PATROLWOMAN, POLICEMAN, POLICEWOMAN**
Or *police officer.* But not *cop.*

• **PAYLOAD**

• **PEACEKEEPING**
No hyphen.

• **PEACEMAKER, PEACEMAKING**

• **PEACE OFFERING**

• PEACETIME

• PECK

A unit of dry measure equal to eight dry quarts or one-quarter of a bushel.

The metric equivalent is about eight-point-eight liters.

To convert to liters, multiply the peck measurement by eight-point-eight: five pecks times eight-point-eight equals 44 liters.

See **LITER.**

• PEDAL, PEDDLE

When riding a bicycle or similar vehicle, you *pedal* it.

When selling something, you may *peddle* it. A derogatory usage. Avoid it when possible.

• PEKING

The city China stands alone in datelines.

• PELL-MELL

• PENITENTIARY

See the **PRISON, JAIL** entry.

• PENNSYLVANIA

Legally a commonwealth, not a state.

• PENNSYLVANIA DUTCH

The individuals are of German descent. The word *Dutch* is a corruption of *Deutsch,* the German word for "German."

• PENNY-WISE

See **-WISE.**

Also: *pound-foolish.*

• PENTECOST

The seventh Sunday after Easter.

• PENTECOSTALISM

See **RELIGIOUS MOVEMENTS.**

• PEOPLE, PERSONS

Use them as they are used in conversation.

Person is used when referring to an individual: *One person is waiting for the bus.*

People is used in plural references: *Thousands of people were there. Five people were hurt.*

People also is a collective noun that takes a plural verb when used to refer to a single race or nation: *The American people are united.* In this sense, the plural is *peoples,* as in *freedom-loving peoples everywhere speak the same language.*

• PEOPLE'S

Use this possessive form when the word occurs in the formal name of a nation: *the People's Republic of Albania.*

Use this form also in such phrases as *the people's desire for freedom.*

• PEPSICO, INCORPORATED

Formerly the Pepsi-Cola Company.

Headquarters is in Purchase, New York.

• PERCENT

One word. It takes a singular verb when standing alone or when a singular word follows an *of* construction: *The teacher said 60 percent was a failing grade. He said 50 percent of the membership was there.*

It takes a plural verb when a plural word follows an *of* construction: *He said 50 percent of the members were there.*

• PERCENTAGES

Follow the rules for **NUMERALS; DECIMAL UNITS;** and **FRACTIONS.**

Examples: *one percent, three-tenths of one percent, seven and a-half percent.*

While it is preferable to repeat the

word *percent* with each figure, don't if the construction would be too cumbersome: *The turnout is between ten percent and 30 percent,* but *he says ten to 30 percent of the electorate may not vote.*

• PERIODS

Follow these guidelines:

Abbreviations: Periods generally should not be used—hyphens should. See **ABBREVIATIONS** or individual entries.

End of Declarative Sentence: *The stylebook is finished.*

End of a Mildly Imperative Sentence: *Shut the door.*

Use an exclamation point if greater emphasis is desired: *Be careful!*

End of Some Rhetorical Questions: A period is preferable if a statement is more a suggestion than a question: *Why don't we go.*

End of an Indirect Question: *He asked what the score was.*

Initials: *John F. Kennedy, T.S. Eliot. (No space between T.* and *S.,* to prevent them from being placed on two lines.

Ellipses: See **ELLIPSES.**

Enumerations: After numbers or letters in enumerating elements of a summary: *1. Wash the car. 2. Clean the basement.* Or: *A. Punctuate properly. B. Write simply.*

Placement with Quotation Marks: Periods always go inside quotation marks. See **QUOTATION MARKS.**

• PERK

A shortened form of *perquisite,* often used by legislators to describe fringe benefits. In the state of New York, legislators also use the word *lulu* to describe the benefits they receive in lieu of pay.

When either word is used, define it.

• PERMISSIBLE

• PERSIAN GULF

Use this long-established name unless directly quoting the Iranian government, which calls it the *Gulf of Iran.*

When *Gulf of Iran* is used, explain in the text that this body of water off the southern coast of Iran more commonly is known as the *Persian Gulf.*

• PERSONS

See the **PEOPLE, PERSONS** entry.

• -PERSONS

Do not use coined words such as *chairperson* or *spokesperson* in regular text.

Instead, use *chairman* or *spokesman* if referring to a man or the office in general. Use *chairwoman* or *spokeswoman* if referring to a woman. Or use a neutral word such as *leader* or *representative.*

Use *chairperson* or similar coinage only in direct quotations or when it is the formal description for an office.

• PERSUADE

See the **CONVINCE, PERSUADE** entry.

• PETER PRINCIPLE

It is: Each employee is promoted until he reaches his level of incompetence.

From the book by Laurence Peter.

• PHASE

See the **FAZE, PHASE** entry.

• P-H-D, P-H-D'S

The preferred form is to say a person *holds a doctorate* and name the individual's area of specialty.

See **ACADEMIC DEGREES** and **DOCTOR.**

• PHENOMENA, PHENOMENON

• PHILADELPHIA
The city in Pennsylvania stands alone in datelines.

• PHILIPPINES
Note spelling. In datelines, give the name of the city or town followed by *The Philippines:*
(*MANILA, THE PHILIPPINES*) --
If needed, the name of the individual island can be identified in the text.
The people are *Filipinos* and the institutions are *Philippine: The Philippine government says Filipinos will make more money next year.*

• PHOTOSTAT
A trademark for a type of photocopy.

• PIANO, PIANOS

• PICKET, PICKETS, PICKETED, PICKET LINE
Picket is both the verb and the noun. Do not use *picketer.*

• PICNIC, PICNICKED, PICNICKING, PICNICKER

• PIEDMONT AVIATION
A *Piedmont airliner* is acceptable in any reference.
Headquarters is in Winston-Salem, North Carolina.

• PIGEON

• PIGEONHOLE (n. and v.)

• PIKES PEAK
No apostrophe. After Zebulon Mongomery Pike, an American general and explorer.
The 14-thousand, 110 foot peak is in the Rockies of central Colorado.

• PILE UP (v.)
PILEUP (n. adj.)

• PINT (dry)
Equal to 33-point-six cubic inches, or one-half of a dry quart.
The metric equivalent is about point-55 liters—just over one-half liter.
To convert pints to liters, multiply by point-55: five dry pints times point-55 equals two-point-75—two and three-quarters—liters.
See **LITER** and **QUART (DRY).**

• PINT (liquid)
Equal to 16 fluid ounces, or two cups.
The rough metric equivalents are 470 milliliters or point-47 liters—just under a half-liter.
To convert liquid pints to liters, multiply by point-47: four pints times point-47 equals one-point-88 liters.
See **LITER.**

• PIPELINE

• PISTOL
A pistol can be either an automatic or a revolver, but *automatic* and *revolver* are not synonymous. A revolver has a revolving cylinder that holds the cartridges; an automatic does not.
See **WEAPONS.**

• PLANETS
They are, in order of closeness to the sun: Mercury, Venus, Earth, Mars, Jupiter, Saturn, Uranus, Neptune, Pluto.

• PLANNING
Avoid the redundant *future planning.*

• PITTSBURGH
The city in Pennsylvania stands alone in datelines.
The spelling is *Pittsburg* (no *h*) for communities in California, Illinois, Kansas, New Hampshire, Oklahoma and Texas.

- **PLAY OFF** (v.)
PLAYOFF, PLAYOFFS (n. and adj.)
The noun and adjective forms are exceptions to Webster's New World Dictionary, in keeping with widespread practice in the sports world.

- **PLEAD, PLEADED, PLEADING**
Do not use the colloquial past tense form, *pled.*

- **PLEXIGLAS**
Note the single *s.* A trademark for a synthetic glass, generically called *plexiglass.*

- **PLOW**
Not *plough.*

- **PLURALITY**
See the **MAJORITY, PLURALITY** entry.

- **PLURALS**
Follow these guidelines in forming and using plural words:

Most Words: Add *s: boys, girls, ships, villages.*

Words Ending in *ch, s, sh, ss, x* and *z*: Add *es. Churches, lenses, parishes, glasses, boxes, buzzes.* (*Monarchs* is an exception.)

Words Ending in *is*: Change *is* to *es: oases, parentheses, theses.*

Words Ending in *y*: If *y* is preceded by a consonant or *qu,* change *y* to *i* and add *es: armies, cities, navies, soliloquies.* (See **PROPER NAMES** below for an exception.)

Otherwise add *s: donkeys, monkeys.*

Words Ending in *o*: If *o* is preceded by a consonant, most plurals require *es: buffaloes, dominoes, echoes, heroes, potatoes.* But there are exceptions: *pianos.* See individual entries in this book for many of these exceptions.

Words Ending in *f*: Change *f* to *v* and add *es: leaves, selves.*

Latin Endings: Latin-root words ending in *us* change *us* to *i: alumnus, alumni.*

Most ending in *a* change to *ae: alumna, alumnae* (*formula, formulas* is an exception).

Those ending in *on* change to *a: phenomenon, phenomena.*

Most ending in *um* add *s: memorandums, referendums, stadiums.* Among those that still use the Latin ending: *addenda, curricula, media.*

Use the plural that Webster's New World lists as most common for a particular sense of a word.

Form Change: *Man, men; child, children; foot, feet; mouse, mice; etc.*

Caution: when *s* is used with any of these words it indicates possession and must be preceded by an apostrophe: *men's, children's,* etc.

Words the Same in Singular and Plural: *Corps, chassis, deer, moose, sheep,* etc.

The sense in a particular sentence is conveyed by the use of a singular or plural verb.

Words Plural in Form, Singular in Meaning: Some take singular verbs: *measles, mumps, news.*

Others take plural verbs: *grits, scissors.*

Compound Words: Those written solid add *s* at the end: *cupfuls, handfuls, tablespoonfuls.*

For those that involve separate words or words linked by a hyphen, make the most significant word plural.

When the significant word is first: *adjutants general, aides-de-camp, attorneys general, courts-martial, daughters-in-law, passersby, postmasters general, presidents-elect, secretaries general, sergeants major.*

When the significant word is in the middle: *assistant attorneys general, deputy chiefs of staff.*

When the significant word is last:

assistant attorneys, assistant corporation counsels, deputy sheriffs, lieutenant colonels, major generals.

Words as Words: Do not use *'s: His speech had too many ifs, ands and buts.* (Exception to Webster's New World.)

Proper Names: Most ending in *es* or *z* add *es: Charleses, Joneses, Gonzalezes.*

Most ending in *y* add *s* even if preceded by a consonant: *the Duffys, the Kennedys, the two Germanys, the two Kansas Citys.* Exceptions include *Alleghenies* and *Rockies.*

For others, add *s: the Carters, the McCoys, the Reagans.*

Figures: Add *'s: The custom began in the 1920's. The airline has two 727's. Temperatures will be in the low 20's.*

Single Letters: Use *'s: Mind your p's and q's. He learned the three R's and brought home a report card with four A's and two B's. The Oakland A's won the pennant.*

Multiple Letters: Add *'s: She knows her A-B-C's. I gave him five I-O-U's. Four V-I-P's were there.*

Problems, Doubts: Separate entries in this book give plurals for troublesome words and guidance on whether certain words should be used with singular or plural verbs and pronouns. See also **COLLECTIVE NOUNS** and **POSSESSIVES.**

For questions not covered by this book, use the plural that Webster's New World lists as most common for a particular sense of a word.

Note also the guidelines that the dictionary provides under its "plural" entry.

• P-M, A-M

Hyphens, not periods. Avoid the redundant *ten p-m tonight.*

• POCKET VETO

Occurs only when Congress has adjourned. If Congress is in session, a bill that remains on the president's desk for ten days becomes law without his signature. But if Congress adjourns, a bill that fails to get his signature within ten days is automatically vetoed.

Many states have similar rules.

• POETIC LICENSE

It is valid for poetry—not news or feature stories.

See **COLLOQUIALISMS** and **SPECIAL CONTEXTS.**

• POINSETTIA

Note the *ia.*

• POINT-BLANK

• POLAROID

A trademark for Polaroid Land instant-picture cameras and for transparent material containing embedded crystals capable of polarizing light.

• POLICY-MAKER (n.) POLICY-MAKING (n. and adj.)

• POLIO

The preferred term for *poliomyelitis* and *infantile paralysis.*

• POLITBURO

Acceptable in all references for the *Political Bureau of the Communist Party.* It is the chief policy-making body in the Soviet Union and other Communist nations.

• POLITICKING

• POLITICS

Usually it takes a plural verb: *My politics are my own business.*

As a study or science, it takes a singular verb: *Politics is a demanding profession.*

• POLLS AND SURVEYS

In stories about a canvass of public

opinion, consider the following points, based on questions the National Council on Public Polls has suggested that editors ask before using a poll.

1. Who paid for the poll?

2. When was the poll taken? (Most pollsters concede that rapid, last-minute changes in voter sentiment can take place.)

3. How were the interviews obtained? (Some pollsters think people are less candid on the telephone than in person.)

4. How were the questions worded? (They can be "loaded" to achieve a desired result. Even the sequence of questions should be considered.)

5. Who was interviewed? How were they chosen—from a census list, a voter registration list, a telephone book? How were the selections made from this base—at random or by using some other procedure?

6. How many people were in the group to be contacted? How many responded? What is the margin of error in projecting the results to a larger group? (The larger the number of responses, the smaller the margin for error.)

7. If responses from a group smaller than the total sample are cited, how large was the smaller group and what is the margin of error in projecting the results? (A nationwide poll of 15-hundred people, for example, might show one set of figures on overall attitudes toward abortion, while also reporting on the attitude of Catholics toward abortion. If the attitude of Catholics is cited, how many Catholics were interviewed?)

If a story on the poll is used, provide some indication of the methods the pollster employed.

Remember, polls are not always right, and their findings should not be reported as gospel.

Wrong: *President Carter will be easily re-elected next Tuesday. That's the finding of a nationwide poll made public today.*

Right: *A poll released today estimates that President Carter will win re-election by more than ten (m) million votes next week.*

• POM-POM, POMPON

Pom-pom is sometimes used to describe a rapid-firing automatic weapon. Define the word if it must be used.

A *pompon* is a large ball of crepe paper or fluffed cloth, often waved by cheerleaders or used atop a hat. It is also a flower that appears on some varieties of chrysanthemums.

• POPE JOHN PAUL THE SECOND

See **ROMAN CATHOLIC CHURCH.**

• PORE, POUR

The verb *pore* means to gaze intently or steadily: *She pored over her books.*

The verb *pour* means to flow in a continuous stream: *It poured rain. He poured the coffee.*

• PORTUGUESE NAMES

See the **SPANISH AND PORTUGUESE NAMES** entry.

• POSSESSIVES

Follow these guidelines:

Plural Nouns Not Ending in *s*: Add *'s: the alumni's contributions, women's rights.*

Plural Nouns Ending in *s*: Add only an apostrophe: *the churches' needs, the girls' toys, the horses' food, the ships' wake, states' rights.*

Nouns Plural in Form, Singular in Meaning: Add only an apostrophe: *mathematics' rules, measles' effects.* (But see **INANIMATE OBJECTS**, page 223.)

Apply the same principle when a

plural word occurs in the formal name of a singular entity: *General Motors' profits, the United States' wealth.*

Nouns the Same in Singular and Plural: Treat them the same as plurals, even if the meaning is singular: *one corps' location, the two deer's tracks, the lone moose's antlers.*

Singular Nouns Not Ending in *s*: Add *'s: the church's needs, the girl's toys, the horse's food, the ship's route, the V-I-P's seat.*

Some style guides say that singular nouns ending in *s* sounds such as *ce, x,* and z may take either the apostrophe alone or *'s*. See **SPECIAL EXPRESSIONS** below, but otherwise, for consistency and ease in remembering a rule, always use *'s* if the word does not end in the letter *s: Butz's policies, the fox's den, the justice's verdict, Marx's theories, the prince's life, Xerox's profits.*

Singular Common Nouns Ending in *s*: Add *'s* unless the next word begins with *s: the hostess's invitation, the hostess' seat; the witness's answer, the witness' story.*

Singular Proper Names Ending in *s*: Use only an apostrophe: *Achilles' heel, Agnes' book, Ceres' rites, Descartes' theories, Dickens' novels, Euripides' dramas, Hercules' labors, Jesus' life, Jules' seat, Kansas' schools, Moses' law, Socrates' life, Tennessee Williams' plays, Xerxes' armies.*

Special Expressions: The following exceptions to the general rule for words not ending in *s* apply to words that end in an *s* sound and are followed by a word that begins with *s: for appearance' sake, for conscience' sake, for goodness' sake.* Use *'s* otherwise: *the appearance's cost, my conscience's voice.*

Pronouns: Personal, interrogative and relative pronouns have separate forms for the possessive. None involve an apostrophe: *mine, ours, your, yours, his, hers, its, theirs, whose.*

Caution: If you are using an apostrophe with a pronoun, always doublecheck to be sure that the meaning calls for a contraction: *you're, it's, there's, who's.*

Follow the rules listed above in forming the possessives of other pronouns: *another's idea, others' plans, someone's guess.*

Compound Words: Applying the rules above, add an apostrophe or *'s* to the word closest to the object possessed: *the major general's decision, the major generals' decisions, the attorney general's request, the attorneys general's request.* See the **PLURALS** entry for guidelines on forming the plurals of these words.

Also: *anyone else's attitude, Benjamin Franklin of Pennsylvania's motion.* Whenever practical, however, recast the phrase to avoid ambiguity: *the motion by Benjamin Franklin of Pennsylvania.*

Joint Possession, Individual Possession: Use a possessive form after only the last word if ownership is joint: *Fred and Sylvia's apartment, Fred and Sylvia's stocks.*

Use a possessive form after both words if the objects are individually owned: *Fred's and Sylvia's books.*

Descriptive Phrases: Do not add an apostrophe to a word ending in *s* when it is used primarily in a descriptive sense: *citizens band radio, a Cincinnati Reds infielder, a teachers college, a Teamsters request, a writers guide.*

Memory Aid: The apostrophe usually is not used if *for* or *by* rather than *of* would be appropriate in the longer form: *a radio band for citizens, a college for teachers, a guide for writers, a request by the Teamsters.*

An *'s* is required, however, when a term involves a plural word that does not end in *s: a children's hospital, a people's republic, the Young Men's Christian Association.*

Descriptive Names: Some governmental, corporate and institutional organizations with a descriptive word in their names use an apostrophe; some do not. Follow the user's practice: *Actors Equity, Diners Club, the Ladies' Home Journal, the National Governors' Conference, the Veterans Administration.* See separate entries for these and similar names frequently in the news.

Quasi Possessives: Follow the rules above in composing the possessive form of words that occur in such phrases as *a day's pay, two weeks' vacation, three days' work, your money's worth.*

Frequently, however, a hyphenated form is clearer: *a two-week vacation, a three-day job.*

Double Possessive: Two conditions must apply for a double possessive—a phrase such as *a friend of John's*—to occur: 1. The word after *of* must refer to an animate object, and 2. The word before *of* must involve only a portion of the animate object's possessions.

Otherwise, do not use the possessive form on the word after *of: The friends of John Adams mourned his death.* (All the friends were involved.) *He is a friend of the college.* Not *college's,* because college is inanimate).

Memory Aid: This construction occurs most often, and quite naturally, with the possessive forms of personal pronouns: *He is a friend of mine.*

Inanimate Objects: There is no blanket rule against creating a possessive form for an inanimate object, particularly if the object is treated in a personified sense. See some of the earlier examples, and note these: *death's call, the wind's murmur.*

In general, however, avoid excessive personalization of inanimate objects, and give preference to an *of* construction when it fits the makeup of the sentence. For example, the earlier references to *mathematics' rules* and *measles' effects* would better be phrased: *the rules of mathematics, the effects of measles.*

• POST-

Follow Webster's New World. Hyphenate if not listed there.

Some words without a hyphen:

POSTDATE	POSTNUPTIAL
POSTDOCTORAL	POSTOPERATIVE
POSTELECTION	POSTCRIPT
POSTGRADUATE	POSTWAR

Some words that use a hyphen:

POST-BELLUM
POST-MORTEM

Often, though, it's best to use a different construction: *after the election,* instead of *postelection.*

• POT

Acceptable on second reference for *marijuana.*

• POTATO, POTATOES

• POT-HOLE

• POUND (monetary)

The english pound sign is not used. Spell out the word instead.

Convert the figures to dollars in most cases. Follow the rules for **NUMERALS** and **MONETARY FIGURES.**

• POUND (weight)

Equal to 16 ounces.

The metric equivalent is about 454

grams, or point-45 kilograms—just under half a kilogram.

To convert pounds to kilograms, multiply by point-45: 20 pounds times point-45 equals nine kilograms.

See **GRAM** and **KILOGRAM.**

• POVERTY LEVEL

An income level judged to be the minimum required to provide a family or individual with the essentials of life. The figure for the United States is adjusted regularly to reflect changes in the Consumer Price Index.

• PREFIXES

See separate listings for commonly used prefixes.

Three rules are constant, although they yield some exceptions to first-listed spellings in Webster's New World Dictionary.

—Except for *cooperate* and *coordinate,* use a hyphen if the prefex ends in a vowel and the word that follows begins with the same vowel.

—Use a hyphen if the word that follows is a proper noun.

—Use a hyphen to join doubled prefixes: *sub-subunits.*

• PREMIER, PRIME MINISTER

These two titles often are used interchangeably in translating to English the title of an individual who is the first minister in a national government that has a council of ministers.

Prime minister is the correct title throughout the Commonwealth, formerly the British Commonwealth. See **COMMONWEALTH** for a list of members.

Prime minister is the best or traditional translation from most other languages. For consistency, use it throughout the rest of the world with these exceptions:

—Use *premier* for France and its former colonies.

—Use *premier* for the Communist nations of Eastern Europe and Asia.

—Use *chancellor* in Austria and West Germany.

—Follow the practice of a nation if there is a specific preference that varies from this general practice.

Premier is also the correct title for the individuals who lead the provincial governments in Canada and Australia.

See **TITLES.**

• PREMIERE

A first performance.

• PRE-

The rules in **PREFIXES** apply. The following examples of exceptions to first-listed spellings in Webster's New World are based on the general rule that a hyphen is used if a prefix ends in a vowel and the word that follows begins with the same vowel:

PRE-ELECTION
PRE-EMINENT
PRE-EMPT
PRE-ESTABLISH
PRE-EXIST

Otherwise, follow Webster's New World, hyphenating if not listed there. Some examples:

PREARRANGE
PRECONDITION
PRECOOK
PREDATE
PREDECEASE
PREDISPOSE
PREFLIGHT
PREHEAT
PREHISTORIC
PRE-IGNITION
PREJUDGE
PREMARITAL
PRENATAL
PRE-TAX
PRE-TEST
PRE-WAR

Some hyphenated coinages, not listed in the dictionary:

PRE-CONVENTION
PRE-DAWN

• PREDOMINANT, PREDOMINANTLY

Use these primary spellings listed in Webster's New World for the adjectival and adverbial forms. Do not use the alternates it records, *predominate* and *predominately.*

The verb form, however, is *predominate.*

• PREFERRED STOCK

See the **COMMON STOCK, PREFERRED STOCK** entry.

• PRESBYTERIAN CHURCHES

There are four levels of authority in Presbyterian practice—individual congregations, presbyteries, synods and a general assembly.

Congregations are led by a pastor, who provides guidance in spiritual matters, and by a session, composed of ruling elders chosen by the congregation to represent the members in matters of government and discipline.

A presbytery is composed of all the ministers and an equal number of ruling elders, including at least one from each congregation, in a given district. Although the next two levels are technically higher, the presbytery has the authority to rule on many types of material and spiritual questions.

Presbyteries unite to form a synod, whose members are elected by the presbyteries. A synod generally meets once a year to decide matters such as the creation of new presbyteries and to pass judgment on appeals and complaints that do not affect the doctrine or constitution of the church.

A general assembly, composed of delegations of pastors and ruling elders from each presbytery, meets yearly to decide issues of doctrine and discipline within a Presbyterian body. It also may create new synods, divide old ones and correspond with general assemblies of other Presbyterian bodies.

The assembly also chooses the stated clerk and the moderator for a denomination. The stated clerk, the chief administrative officer, normally serves for an extended period. The moderator, the presiding officer, serves for a year.

The largest Presbyterian body in the United States is the United Presbyterian Church in the United States of America. It has some two (m) million, 700-thousand members throughout the nation, although membership is concentrated in the north.

The Presbyterian Church in the United States, with just under one (m) million members, is the principal Southern body.

Beliefs: The characteristic teachings rely heavily on the writings of John Calvin, a 16th-century French lawyer turned theologian who emphasized the "sovereignty of God." He taught that church government is a purely human organization, quasi-democratic in nature. Christ, rather than any human individual, is the only real head of the church.

Presbyterians believe in the Trinity and the humanity and divinity of Christ. Baptism, which may be administered to children, and the Lord's Supper are the only sacraments.

The basic doctrinal standard is the Westminster Confession of Faith, a document drawn up by an assembly of leaders who met from 1643 to 1648 in England.

Clergy: All Presbyterian clergymen may be described as *ministers. Pastor* applies if a minister leads a congregation.

On first reference, use *the Reverend* before the name of a man or woman.

Do not carry the title through to subsequent references.

Other officials: The preferred form for elected officials such as *elders* or *deacons* is to put the title after the name, set off with commas.

• PRESENTLY

Use it to mean *in a little while* or *shortly,* but not to mean *now.*

• PRESIDENT

The formal title of the chief executive of the United States.

Also the formal title of national leaders in some other nations. In some cases, the president is a ceremonial official, with the true power residing with the *prime minister* or *premier.*

In most cases, the first name of a current or former president is not necessary on the first reference. But use it if confusion might otherwise result: *President Andrew Johnson, President Lyndon Johnson.*

For presidents of other nations and of organizations and institutions, use the full name on first reference. Do not carry the title through on subsequent references.

• PRESIDENTIAL MEDAL OF FREEDOM

This is the nation's highest civilian honor. It is given by the president, on the recommendation of the Distinguished Civilian Service Board, for "exceptionally meritorious contribution to the security of the United States or other significant public or private endeavors." Until 1963 it was known as the Medal of Freedom.

• PRESS CONFERENCE

News conference is preferred.

• PRESS SECRETARY

News secretary or *presidential spokesman* is preferred for the White House official.

The formal title is *assistant to the president for press relations.*

In other cases, *spokesman* is preferred: *a spokesman for Chrysler Corporation, the Chrysler spokesman.*

• PRETENSE, PRETEXT

A *pretext* is something that is put forward to conceal a truth: *He was discharged for tardiness, but the reason given was only a pretext for general incompetence.*

A *pretense* is a false show, a more overt act intended to conceal a truth: *My profuse compliments were all pretense.*

• PRICE-EARNINGS RATIO

The price of a share of stock divided by earnings per share for a 12-month period.

In Associated Press stock tables, the ratios reflect earnings for the most recent 12 months.

For example, a stock selling for 60 dollars per share and earning six dollars per share would be selling at a price-earnings ratio of ten-to-one.

See **PROFIT TERMINOLOGY.**

• PRIME MINISTER

See the **PREMIER, PRIME MINISTER** entry.

• PRIME RATE

The interest rate that commercial banks charge on loans to their borrowers with the best credit ratings.

Fluctuations in the prime rate seldom have an immediate impact on consumer loan rates. Over the long term, however, consistent increases (or decreases) in the prime rate can lead to increases (or decreases) in the interest rates for mortgages and all types of personal loans.

PRINCE EDWARD ISLAND

One of the three Maritime Provinces of Canada. Do not abbreviate.

See **DATELINES.**

PRINCIPAL, PRINCIPLE

Principal is a noun and adjective meaning someone or something first in rank, authority, importance or degree: *She is the school principal. He was the principal player in the trade. Money is the principal problem.*

Principle is a noun that means a fundamental truth, law, doctrine or motivating force: *They fought for the principle of self-determination.*

PRIOR TO

Before is less stilted for most uses. *Prior to* is appropriate, however, when a notion of requirement is involved: *The fee must be paid prior to the examination.*

PRISON, JAIL

Do not use the two words interchangeably.

Prison is a generic term that may be applied to the maximum security institutions often known as *penitentiaries* and to the medium security facilities often called *correctional institutions* or *reformatories.* All such facilities confine persons serving sentences for felonies.

Do not construct a substitute when the formal name is commonly accepted: It is *the Colorado State Penitentiary,* for example, not *Colorado State Prison.*

On second reference, any of the following may be used: *the state prison, the prison, the state penitentiary, the penitentiary.*

A *jail* is a facility normally used to confine persons serving sentences for misdemeanors, persons awaiting trial or sentencing on either felony or misdemeanor charges, and persons confined for civil matters such as failure to pay alimony and other types of contempt of court.

See the **FELONY, MISDEMEANOR** entry.

Federal Institutions: Maximum security institutions are known as *penitentiaries: the U-S Penitentiary at Lewisburg* or *Lewisburg Penitentiary* on first reference; *the federal penitentiary* or *the penitentiary* on second reference.

Medium security institutions include the word *federal* as part of their formal names: *the Federal Correctional Institution in Danbury, Connecticut.* On second reference: *the correctional institution, the federal prison, the prison.*

Most federal facilities used to house persons awaiting trial or serving sentences of a year or less have the proper name *Federal Detention Center.* The term *Metropolitan Correctional Center* is being adopted for some new installations. On second reference: *the detention center, the correctional center.*

PRISONER OF WAR

P-O-W is acceptable on second reference.

As a compound modifier: *a prisoner-of-war trial* or *a P-O-W trial.*

PRIVILEGE, PRIVILEGED

PRO-

Use a hyphen when coining words that denote support for something. Some examples:

PRO-BUSINESS	PRO-LIFE
PRO-LABOR	PRO-WAR

No hyphen when *pro* is used in other senses: *produce, profile, pronoun,* etc.

• PROBATION

See the **PARDON, PAROLE, PROBATION** entry.

• PROCTER AND GAMBLE COMPANY

Do not use the abbreviation *P-and-G.*

Headquarters is in Cincinnati.

• PROFANITY

See the **OBSCENITIES, PROFANITIES, VULGARITIES** entry.

• PROFESSIONAL GOLFERS' ASSOCIATION

Note the apostrophe. In general, spell out on first reference.

A phrase such as *P-G-A tournament* may be used on first reference, however, to avoid a cumbersome lead. If this is done, provide the full name later in the story.

• PROFIT-SHARING (n. and adj.)

The hyphen for the noun is an exception to Webster's New World.

• PROFIT-TAKING (n. and adj.)

• PROFIT TERMINOLOGY

Note the meanings of the following terms in reporting a company's financial status. Always be careful to specify whether the figures given apply to quarterly or annual results.

The terms, listed in the order in which they might occur in analyzing a company's financial condition:

Revenue: The amount of money a company took in, including interest earned and receipts from sales, services provided, rents and royalties.

The figure also may include excise taxes and sales taxes collected for the government. If it does, the fact should be noted in any report on revenue.

The terms *gross earnings* and *gross income* are seldom-used synonyms for *revenue.*

Sales: The money a company received for the goods and services it sold.

In some cases the figure includes receipts from rents and royalties. In others, particularly when rentals and royalties make up a large portion of a company's income, figures for these activities are listed separately.

Gross Profit: The difference between the sales price of an item or service and the expenses directly attributed to it, such as the cost of raw materials, labor and overhead linked to the production effort.

Income before Taxes: Gross profits minus company-wide expenses not directly attributed to specific products or services. These expenses typically include interest costs, advertising and sales costs, and general administrative overhead.

Net Income, Profit, Earnings: The amount left after taxes have been paid.

A portion may be committed to pay preferred dividends. Some of what remains may be paid in dividends to holders of common stocks. The rest may be invested to obtain interest revenue or spent to acquire new buildings or equipment to increase the company's ability to make future profits.

To avoid confusion, do not use the word *income* alone—always specify whether the figure is *income before taxes* or *net income.*

The terms *profit* and *earnings* commonly are interpreted as meaning the amount left after taxes. The terms *net profit* and *net earnings* are acceptable synonyms.

Earnings per Share: The figure obtained by dividing the number of outstanding shares of common stock into the amount left after dividends have been paid on any preferred stock.

Dividend: The amount paid per share per year to holders of common stock. Payments generally are made in quarterly installments.

The dividend usually is a portion of the earnings per share. However, if a company shows no profit during a given period, it may be able to use earnings retained from profitable periods to pay its dividend on schedule.

Return on Investment: A percentage figure obtained by dividing the company's assets into its net income.

Extraordinary Loss, Extraordinary Income: An expense or source of income that does not occur on a regular basis, such as a loss due to a major fire or the revenue from the sale of a subsidiary. Extraordinary items should be identified in any report on the company's financial status to avoid creating the false impression that its overall profit trend has suddenly plunged or soared.

• PROHIBITION

The period that began when the 18th amendment to the Constitution was put into law, prohibiting the manufacture, sale or transportation of alcoholic liquors.

The amendment was declared ratified on January 29th, 1919, and took effect on January 16th, 1920. It was repealed by the 21st Amendment, which took effect on December fifth, 1933, the day it was declared ratified.

• PRONOUNCERS

Always try to provide a pronunciation guide for words that are unusual and which the broadcaster is unlikely to recognize.

The pronouncer should be in parentheses and immediately follow the word in question: *Police in Tucson are trying to regain control of the Pima (pee'-muh) County Jail. A spokesman for Ayatollah Khomeini (hoh-may'-nee) says the religious leader is ill.*

In general, the AP tries to provide pronouncers for proper nouns, technical terms and obscure words which are not in general usage. It is not, however, the AP's responsibility to interpret words that the average journalist should already know.

Try to err on the side of caution. If you know the pronunciation of a potentially puzzling word, by all means use it—but first ask yourself if you should be using the word at all. If it's so unusual that no one will know how to pronounce it, it is highly likely that no one will know what it means either.

When handling foreign copy, try to eliminate as many non-essential names as possible. If you are using a technical term, try to find a simpler, generic term which will work just as well. *The fire victim spoke monotonically to reporters* might be better rendered as: *The fire victim seemed dazed. He spoke in a dull, wooden voice.*

Be careful about providing pronouncers for private citizens' names unless you have spoken to the person in question. Stations often want pronouncers for the names of accident victims, criminal defendants, etc. But if you have obtained the name from a police officer, the prosecutor or some other third party, remember that the third party may not know how the person pronounces his name either.

In other words, don't guess. If you don't know, don't use it.

The most serious obstacle to providing proper pronunciation guides is that the teleprinters used by AP and other services do not have nearly enough characters to reproduce the standard phonetic alphabet used by dictionaries and other linguistic guides.

All we can do is provide a very rough approximation of what the word sounds like.

Here are the basic sounds represented by the wire-service phonetic symbols:

Vowel Sounds:
a — bat, apple
ah — father, arm
aw — raw, board
ay — fate, ace
e, eh — bed
ee — feel, tea
i, ih — pin, middle
y, eye — ice, time, guide
oh — go, oval
oo — food, two
ow — scout, crowd
oy — boy, join
u — curl, foot
uh — puff
yoo — fume, few

Consonants:
g — got, beg
j — job, gem
k — keep, cap
ch — chair, butcher
sh — shut, fashion
zh — vision, mirage
th — thin, path
kh — guttural "k"

• PROPELLER

• PROPHECY (n.)
PROPHESY (v.)

• PROSTATE GLAND
Not *prostrate.*

• PROTESTANT, PROTESTANTISM
They refer either to denominations formed as a result of the break from the Roman Catholic Church in the 16th century or to the members of these denominations.

Church groups covered by the term include Anglican, Baptist, Congregational, Methodist, Lutheran, Presbyterian and Quaker denominations. See separate entries for each.

Protestant is not generally applied to Christian Scientists, Jehovah's Witnesses or Mormons.

Do not use *Protestant* to describe a member of an Eastern Orthodox church. Use a phrase such as *Orthodox Christian* instead.

See **RELIGIOUS MOVEMENTS.**

• PROTESTANT EPISCOPAL CHURCH
See **EPISCOPAL CHURCH.**

• PROTESTER
Not *protestor.*

• PROVE, PROVED, PROVING
Use *proven* only as an adjective: *a proven remedy.*

• PROVINCES
Names of provinces are set off from community names—just as state names are set off from community names. thus: *Halifax, Nova Scotia.*

See **DATELINES.**

• P-T-A
See **PARENT-TEACHER ASSOCIATION.**

• P-T BOAT
It stands for *patrol torpedo boat.*

• PUBLIC BROADCASTING SERVICE
It is not a network, but an association of public television stations organized to buy and distribute programs selected by a vote of the members.

P-B-S is acceptable on first reference only within contexts such as a television column. Otherwise, do not use *P-B-S* until second reference.

• **PULITZER PRIZES**

These yearly awards for outstanding work in journalism and the arts were endowed by the late Joseph Pulitzer, publisher of the New York World, and first given in 1917. They are awarded by the trustees of Columbia University on recommendation of an advisory board.

Awards in the journalism category are for: public service, national reporting, international reporting, general local reporting, special local reporting, editorial writing, editorial cartooning, spot news photography, feature photography, commentary, criticism.

Awards in the arts category are for: biography, drama, fiction, general nonfiction, history, music, poetry.

• **PULL BACK** (v.)
PULLBACK (n.)

• **PULL OUT** (v.)
PULLOUT (n.)

• **PULPIT**

See the **LECTERN, PODIUM, PULPIT, ROSTRUM** entry.

• **PUNCTUATION**

Think of it as a service to the newscaster, designed to help him understand a story.

Inevitably, a mandate of this scope involves gray areas. For this reason, punctuation entries in the handbook refer to guidelines rather than rules.

See separate entries under: **COLON; COMMA; DASH; DOUBLE DASH; ELLIPSIS; EXCLAMATION MARK; HYPHEN; PARENTHESES; PERIOD; QUESTION MARK; QUOTATION MARKS;** and **SEMICOLON.**

• **PUPIL, STUDENT**

Use *pupil* for children in kindergarten through eighth grade.

Student or *pupil* is acceptable for grades nine through 12.

Use *student* for college and beyond.

• **PUSH-BUTTON** (n., adj.)

• **PUSH UP** (v.)
PUSH-UP (n., adj.)

• **PUT OUT** (v.)
PUTOUT (n.)

• **PYGMY**

• **QANTAS** (KWAHN'-TUHS) **AIRWAYS**

Headquarters is in Sydney, Australia.

• **"Q-E-TWO"**

Acceptable on second reference to the ocean liner *"Queen Elizabeth Two."*

• **Q-TIPS**

A trademark for a brand of cotton swabs.

• **QUAKERS**

This informal name may be used in all references to members of the *Religious Society of Friends,* but always include the full name in a story dealing primarily with Quaker activities.

The denomination originated with George Fox, an Englishman who objected to Anglican emphasis on ceremony. In the 1640s, he said he heard a voice that opened the way for him to develop a personal relationship with Christ, described as the Inner Light, a term based on the Gospel description of Christ as the "true light."

Brought to court for opposing the established church, Fox tangled with a judge who derided him as a "Quaker" in a reference to his agitation over religious matters.

The basic unit of Quaker organization is the weekly meeting, which corresponds to the congregation in other churches. A monthly meeting receives and records members, extends spiritual care and, if necessary, material aid for members of one or more weekly meetings.

A quarterly meeting consists of representatives from several monthly meetings. Quarterly meetings unite into larger groups called yearly meetings, which are the rough equivalent of conventions, conferences, synods or dioceses in other faiths.

Various yearly meetings form larger associations that assemble at intervals of a year or more. The largest is the Friends United Meeting. Its 15 yearly meeting members represent about half the Friends in the world.

Others include the Evangelical Friends Alliance and the Friends General Conference. Members of the conference include some yearly meetings that also are affiliated with the Friends United Meeting.

Overall, Friends count about 120-thousand members in the United States and Canada, and a total of 200-thousand world-wide.

Beliefs: Fox taught that the Inner Light emancipates a person from adherence to any creed, ecclesiastical authority or ritual forms. Many weekly meetings of worship involve silent meditation, in which any participant may speak when spiritually moved to do so. In others, there is a service of prayer and preaching.

Clergy: There is no recognized ranking of clergy over lay people. However, meeting officers, called *elders* or *ministers,* are chosen by acclamation for their ability in leadership. But they do not go through an ordination ceremony. Many Quaker ministers, particularly in the Midwest and West, use *the Reverend* before their names and describe themselves as *pastors.*

Use *the Reverend* before a name on the first reference. Do not carry the title through to subsequent references.

- **QUART** (dry)

Equal in volume to 67-point-two cubic inches. The metric equivalent is about one-point-one liters.

To convert to liters, multiply by one-point-one: five dry quarts times one-point-one equals five and a-half liters.

See **LITER.**

- **QUART** (liquid)

Equal in volume to 57-point-75—57 and three-quarters—cubic inches. It also equals 32 fluid ounces.

The approximate metric equivalents are 950 militers or point-95 liters.

To convert to liters, multiply by point-95: four quarts times point-95 equals three-point-eight liters.

See **LITER.**

- **QUASAR** (KWAY'-ZAHR)

Acceptable in all references for a *quasi-stellar astronomical object,* often a radio source. Most astronomers consider quasars the most distant objects observable in the heavens.

- **QUEBEC**

The city in Canada stands alone in datelines.

Use *Quebec City* in the body of a story if the city must be distinguished from the province.

Do not abbreviate any reference to the province of Quebec, Canada's largest in area and second-largest in population.

See **DATELINES.**

- **QUEEN MOTHER**

The mother of a reigning monarch. See **NOBILITY.**

- **QUESTION MARK**

Follow these guidelines:

End of a Direct Question: *Who started the riot?*

Did he ask who started the riot? (The sentence as a whole is a direct question despite the indirect question at the end.)

You started the riot? (A question in the form of a declarative statement.)

Interpolated Question: *You told me—Did I hear you correctly?—that you started the riot.*

Multiple Questions: Use a single question mark at the end of the full sentence:

Did you hear him say, "What right have you to ask about the riot?"

Did he plan the riot, employ assistants, and give the signal to begin?

Or, to cause full stops and throw emphasis on each element, break into separate sentences: *Did he plan the riot? Employ assistants? Give the signal to begin?*

Caution: Do not use question marks to indicate the end of indirect questions:

He asked who started the riot. To ask why the riot started is unnecessary. I want to know what the cause of the riot was. How foolish it is to ask what caused the riot.

Placement with Quotation Marks: Inside or outside, depending on the meaning:

Who wrote "Gone With the Wind"?

He asked, "How long will it take?"

Miscellaneous: The question mark supersedes the comma that normally is used when supplying attribution for a quotation: *"Who is there?" she asked.*

- **QUESTIONNAIRE**

- **QUICK-WITTED**

• QUOTATION MARKS

They serve as visual cues to the broadcaster that the quoted words deserve special treatment: They are direct quotes, proper names or unusual terms.

But remember: Only the newscaster sees them. They are invisible to the listeners and viewers. They must therefore be used with great care.

Direct Quotations: This is the most common and the most dangerous usage of quotation marks. Direct quotes are very hard for broadcasters to handle and it is usually better to paraphrase. It is especially important to avoid the first-person pronoun whenever possible.

The sheriff told reporters: *"I am outraged by the order and I will not obey it. This is the first time I have seen it."*

Better: *The sheriff said he is "outraged" by the order and will not obey it. He said he had not seen it before today's meeting.*

It is always dangerous to use any direct quotation of more than one sentence, since the listener can lose the sense of who is speaking. He may end up blaming the newscaster for injecting his own opinions into the story.

The sheriff said he "would not believe anything the attorney general said. The attorney general is a damned liar."

This is what can happen when a harried writer tries to eliminate the "I" without paraphrasing the entire passage. It could sound, to some, as if the newscaster called the attorney general a liar. It's better to rewrite it:

The sheriff called the attorney general -- in his words -- "a damned liar," and said he would not believe anything the attorney general said.

There are many phrases which can be used to emphasize that the next few words are those of the person being quoted, not those of the newscaster. Even though these phrases may be stilted, they should still be used whenever there is any danger of misinterpretation.

The attorney general said that the sheriff -- as he put it -- "has never had a reputation for excessive honesty."

The sheriff denounced the attorney general again today as he called him -- quote -- "a damned liar."

The attorney general put it bluntly today. He used two words to describe the sheriff. Those two words were: "damned fool."

The sheriff accused the attorney general of dishonesty. He called him -- and we use his exact words -- "a crook."

The attorney general responded quickly. Speaking of the sheriff, he made this statement: "I hate him."

These are examples of unusual—but certainly not rare—utterances. To omit them entirely is to lose much of the flavor of the story, but to use them improperly is to invite trouble.

There are many other quotes that can be very easily omitted in broadcast writing.

The senator says the proposal is "too inflationary" and should not be considered "until next year."

These quotes add nothing at all. They can be omitted with no damage.

The senator says the proposal is too inflationary and should be put off until next year.

Other uses of quotation marks:

Acronyms: Use quotation marks around all acronyms: *"NATO," "NASA," "SALT," "CORE."*

Abbreviations: Do not use them around abbreviations.

Composition Titles: Use them

around the names of books, newspapers, magazines, plays, television and radio programs and movies: *"20-20," "60 Minutes," "The New York Times," "History of Rock and Roll."*

See **COMPOSITION TITLES.**

Proper Names: Use quotation marks around the proper names of ships, airplanes and other craft: *U-S-S "Enterprise," "Air Force One," "Apollo-Eleven."*

Also, use quotation marks around the names of performing groups: *"Pink Floyd," "Alice Cooper," "Earth, Wind and Fire."* Do not use them for orchestras: *The Chicago Symphony, The Academy of St. Martin In The Fields.*

Irony: Put quotation marks around any statement or description that is intended to be ironical: *The "Great Debate" turned into a shouting match.*

This is not intended, however, to encourage irony or innuendo. Their use should be very limited.

Unfamiliar Terms: Words or phrases which are likely to be new to the broadcaster and hence to the listener should be in quotation marks so they are read with special emphasis: *Broadcast frequencies are now being measured in something called "kilohertz."*

Special Emphasis: Any words needing special emphasis in a sentence can be put in quotation marks: *The word "silly" has a negative connotation to many people. The word "crook" was used for the first time today in the sheriff's trial.*

Quotes within Quotes: Avoid them. They don't work in broadcast copy.

Placement with Other Punctuation: There are well-established rules governing such matters:

—The period and the comma always go within the quotation marks.

—The dash, the semicolon, the question mark and the exclamation point go within the quotation marks when they apply to the quoted matter only. Otherwise, they go outside.

See **COMMA.**

Slang, Dialect: It is common practice to correct the errors in grammar and word usage which often occur in informal speech.

It would be unusual to quote such matter verbatim:

The mayor said: "Hey look, it's the first -- I didn't see it until he gave it to me and I just, uh, kinda don't know, you know?"

Similarly, do not use abnormal spellings such as *gonna* in an attempt to convey regional dialects.

Obviously, there are rare occasions when such usages may be appropriate in a feature item.

• RABBI

See **JEWISH CONGREGATIONS.**

• RACOON

• RACE

Identification by race is pertinent:

—In biographical and announcement stories, particularly when they involve a feat or appointment that has not routinely been associated with members of a particular race.

—When it provides the listener with a substantial insight into conflicting emotions known or likely to be involved in a demonstration or similar event.

—When describing a person sought in a manhunt.

In some stories that involve a conflict, it is equally important to specify that an issue cuts across racial lines. If, for example, a substantial number of whites are involved in a demonstration by supporters of busing to achieve racial balance in schools, that fact should be noted.

Do not use racially derogatory terms unless they are part of a quotation that is essential to the story.

See the **OBSCENITIES, PROFANITIES, VULGARITIES** entry and the **NATIONALITIES AND RACES** entry.

• RACK, WRACK

The noun *rack* applies to various types of framework; the verb *rack* means to arrange on a rack, to torture, trouble or torment: *He was placed in the rack. She racked her brain.*

The noun *wrack* means ruin or destruction, and generally is confined to the phrase *wrack and ruin.*

The verb *wrack* has substantially the same meaning as the verb *rack,* which is preferred.

• RACKET

Not *racquet,* for the light bat used in tennis and badminton.

• RADICAL

In general, avoid this description in favor of a more precise definition of an individual's political views.

When used, it suggests that an individual believes change must be made by tearing up the roots or foundation of the present order.

Although *radical* often is applied to individuals who hold strong socialist or communist views, it also is applied at times to individuals who believe an existing form of government must be replaced by a more authoritarian or militaristic one.

See the **LEFTIST, ULTRA-LEFTIST** and **RIGHTIST, ULTRA-RIGHTIST** entries.

• RADIO

When the term is used before the name of a city, as in *Radio Moscow,* the reference is to the official voice of the government.

When the term is used after the city name, as in *Havana radio,* it refers merely to broadcasts in that city.

• RAINSTORM

See **WEATHER TERMS.**

• RAISED, REARED

Only humans may be *reared.*

Any living thing, including humans, may be *raised.*

• RANGES

Strive for informality, but be careful to avoid confusion when dealing with ranges of numbers.

For example, the phrase *12 to 14 (m) million dollars* is preferable to *12 (m) million to 14 (m) million dollars*—unless the context makes it confusing.

You need not state the units on the first reference in a range unless failure to do so would leave the broadcaster and listeners confused.

• RANK AND FILE (n.)

The adjective form: *rank-and-file.*

• RARELY

It means seldom. *Rarely ever* is redundant, but *rarely if ever* is often the appropriate phrase.

• RATIOS

Use hyphens and the word *to* and follow the rules for **NUMERALS** when describing a ratio: *It was a 75-to-one shot; He beat the president two-to-one.* Or, better still: *He beat the president by a two-to-one margin.*

Use the term *ratio* or *margin* if there might be confusion between the ratio and the actual figures.

• RAVAGE, RAVISH

To ravage is to wreak great destruction or devastation: *Union troops ravaged Atlanta.*

To ravish is to abduct, rape or carry away with emotion: *Soldiers ravished the women.*

Although both words connote an element of violence, they are not interchangeable. Buildings and towns cannot be *ravished.*

• R-C-A CORPORATION

Formerly *Radio Corporation of America.* The abbreviation *R-C-A* is acceptable on all references.

Headquarters is in New York.

• RE-

The rules in **PREFIXES** apply. The following examples of exceptions to first-listed spellings in Webster's New World are based on the general rule that a hyphen is used if a prefix ends in a vowel and the word that follows begins with the same vowel:

RE-ELECT	RE-ENLIST
RE-ELECTION	RE-ENTER
RE-EMERGE	RE-ENTRY
RE-EMPLOY	RE-EQUIP
RE-ENACT	RE-ESTABLISH
RE-ENGAGE	RE-EXAMINE

For many other words, the sense is the governing factor:

RECOVER (REGAIN)	RE-COVER (COVER AGAIN)
REFORM (IMPROVE)	RE-FORM (FORM AGAIN)
RESIGN (QUIT)	RE-SIGN (SIGN AGAIN)

Otherwise, follow Webster's New World. Use a hyphen for words not listed there unless the hyphen would distort the sense.

• REALTOR

The term *real estate agent* is preferred. Use *realtor* only if there is a reason to indicate that the individual is a member of the National Association of Real Estate Boards.

See **SERVICE MARK.**

• REARED

See the **RAISED, REARED** entry.

• REBUT, REFUTE

Rebut means to argue to the contrary: *He rebutted his opponent's statement.*

Refute connotes success in argument and almost always implies an editorial judgment. Instead, use *deny, dispute, rebut* or *respond to.*

- **RECONNAISSANCE**

- **RECONSTRUCTION**
The process of reorganizing the Southern states after the Civil War.

- **RECORD**
Avoid the redundant *new record.*

- **RECORD HOLDER**

- **RECTOR**
See **RELIGIOUS TITLES.**

- **RECUR, RECURRED, RECURRING**
Not *reoccur.*

- **RED CHINA**
See **CHINA.**

- **RED-HAIRED, REDHEAD, REDHEADED**
All are acceptable for a person with red hair.
Redhead also is used colloquially to describe a type of North American diving duck.

- **RED-HANDED** (adj. and adv.)

- **RED-HOT**

- **REDNECK**
From the characteristic sunburned neck acquired in the fields by farm laborers. It refers to poor, white rural residents of the South and often is a derogatory term.

- **RE-ELECT, RE-ELECTION**

- **REFER**
See the **ALLUDE, REFER** entry.

- **REFERABLE**

- **REFERENDUM, REFERENDUMS**

- **REFORMATORY**
See the **PRISON, JAIL** entry.

- **REFORM JUDAISM**
See **JEWISH CONGREGATIONS.**

- **REFUTE**
See the **REBUT, REFUTE** entry.

- **REGIME**
See the **GOVERNMENT, JUNTA, REGIME** entry.

- **REIGN, REIN**
The leather strap for a horse is a *rein,* hence figuratively: *seize the reins, give free rein to, put a check rein on.*
Reign is the period a ruler is on the throne: *The king began his reign.*

- **RELEASE TIMES**
Material is sometimes provided by a source on the condition that it not be broadcast or published until a specific time.
This arrangement is beneficial to all members, since it permits the AP to transmit the material in full so that members have it ready to use at the specific release time.
Government agencies often provide complex reports, studies or speeches with the understanding that they will not be broadcast or published until after the news conference at which they are explained.
Without such agreements, members would receive the material much later than is now the case. Members should note that their membership contracts specifically require them to observe release times.
If the source does not specify a particular time but says the material is

for release in morning papers, the automatic release time for broadcast and print is 6:30 p-m Eastern time.

If the source says only that material is for release in afternoon papers, the automatic release time for broadcast and print is 6:30 a-m Eastern time.

Such stories should carry slugs indicating the release times:

(Following advance for use at 6:30 p-m E-S-T)

Followed by a line at the end of the text:

(Above advance for use at 6:30 p-m E-S-T)

If the material is to be held until the beginning of a news conference or until the beginning of a speech, it should be slugged:

(Hold for release, expected at 10:30 a-m)

Followed by

(Note: The above is to be held for release until about 10:30 a-m, when the president expects to begin his remarks).

When the material is released, an advisory should be sent to that effect:

A D V I S O R Y

INAUGURAL SPEECH RELEASED. THE PRESIDENT HAS BEGUN SPEAKING. HIS PREPARED TEXT MAY NOW BE RELEASED.

• RELIGIOUS MOVEMENTS

The terms that follow have been grouped under a single entry because they are interrelated and frequently cross denominational lines.

Evangelical: Historically, *evangelical* was used as an adjective describing dedication to conveying the message of Christ. Today it also is used as a noun, referring to a category of doctrinally conservative Christians. They emphasize the need for a definite, adult commitment or conversion to faith in Christ and the duty of all believers to persuade others to a decision accepting Christ.

Evangelicals make up some conservative denominations and are numerous in broader denominations. Evangelicals stress both doctrinal absolutes and vigorous efforts to win others to belief.

The National Association of Evangelicals is an interdenominational, cooperative body of relatively small, conservative Protestant denominations. It has a total of about two (m) million, 500-thousand members, and has headquarters in Wheaton, Illinois.

Evangelism: The word refers to activity directed outside the church fold to influence others to commit themselves to faith in Christ, to his work of serving others and to infuse his principles into society's conduct.

Styles of evangelism vary from direct preaching appeals at large public meetings to practical deeds of caring in the name of Christ, indirectly conveying the same call to allegiance to him.

The word *evangelism* is derived from the Greek *evangelion,* which means the gospel or good news of Christ's saving action in behalf of humanity.

Fundamentalist: The word gained usage in an early 20th century fundamentalist-modernist controversy within Protestantism. In recent years, however, *fundamentalist* has to a large extent taken on pejorative connotations except when applied to groups that stress strict, literal interpretations of Scripture and separation from other Christians.

In general, do not use *fundamentalist* unless a group applies the word to itself.

Liberal: In general, avoid this word as a descriptive classification in religion. It has objectionable implications to many believers.

Acceptable alternate descriptions include *activist, more flexible* and *broadview.*

Moderate is appropriate when used by the contending parties, as is the case in the conflict between the moderate or more flexible wing of the Lutheran Church-Missouri Synod and conservatives, who argue for literal interpretations of biblical passages others consider symbolic.

Do not use the term *Bible-believing* to distinguish one faction from another, because all Christians believe the Bible. The differences are over interpretations.

Neo-Pentecostal, Charismatic: These terms apply to a movement that has developed within mainline Protestant and Roman Catholic denominations since the mid-20th century. It is distinguished by its emotional expressiveness, spontaneity in worship, speaking or praying in "unknown tongues" and healing. Participants often characterize themselves as "spirit-filled" Christians.

Unlike the earlier Pentecostal movement, which led to separate denominations, this movement has swelled within major churches.

Pentecostalism: A movement that arose in the early 20th century and separated from historic Protestant denominations. It is distinguished by belief in tangible manifestations of the Holy Spirit, often in demonstrative, emotional ways such as speaking in "unknown tongues" and healing.

Pentecostal denominations include the Assemblies of God, the Pentecostal Holiness Church, the United Pentecostal Church and the International Church of the Foursquare Gospel founded by Aimee Semple McPherson.

• RELIGIOUS SOCIETY OF FRIENDS

See **QUAKERS.**

• RELIGIOUS TITLES

The first reference to a clergyman, clergywoman or nun should include the formal title before the individual's name.

In many cases, *the Reverend* is the designation that applies. Use *the Reverend Doctor* only if the individual has earned a doctoral degree—Doctor of Divinity degrees frequently are honorary—and the reference to the degree is relevant. *The Reverend Martin Luther King Junior* is preferable to *the Reverend Doctor Martin Luther King Junior* except in special contexts.

On second references, do not carry the title through unless the individual is best known with it: *the Reverend Billy Graham,* but *Graham* on the second reference.

Detailed guidance on specific titles and descriptive words are provided in the entries for the major denominations.

• RELUCTANT, RETICENT

Reluctant means unwilling to act: *He is reluctant to enter the primary.*

Reticent means unwilling to speak: *The candidate's husband is reticent.*

• REORGANIZED CHURCH OF JESUS CHRIST OF LATTER DAY SAINTS

Not properly described as a *Mormon church.* See the explanation under **CHURCH OF JESUS CHRIST OF LATTER-DAY SAINTS.**

• REPUBLICAN, REPUBLICAN PARTY

G-O-P may be used on second reference.

• REPUBLICAN GOVERNORS' ASSOCIATION

Note the apostrophe.

REPUBLICAN NATIONAL COMMITTEE

On second reference: *the national committee, the committee.*

Similarly: *Republican State Committee, Republican County Committee, Republican City Committee, the state committee, the county committee, the city committee, the committee.*

REPUTATION

See the **CHARACTER, REPUTATION** entry.

RESERVE OFFICERS' TRAINING CORPS

The *s'* is military practice. *R-O-T-C* is acceptable in all references.

When the service is specified, use it before the *R-O-T-C* reference: *Army R-O-T-C, Navy R-O-T-C.* But not *A-R-O-T-C* or *N-R-O-T-C.*

RESIDENT

See the **CITIZEN, RESIDENT, SUBJECT, NATIONAL, NATIVE** entry.

RESISTIBLE

RESTAURATEUR

Not *restauranteur.*

RESTRICTIVE CLAUSES

See the **ESSENTIAL CLAUSES, NON-ESSENTIAL CLAUSES** entry.

RESTRICTIVE PHRASES

See the **ESSENTIAL CLAUSES, NON-ESSENTIAL CLAUSES** entry.

RETAIL CLERKS INTERNATIONAL ASSOCIATION

The shortened form *Retail Clerks union* is acceptable in all references.

Headquarters is in Washington.

RETAIL SALES

The sales of retail stores, including merchandise sold and receipts for repairs and similar services.

A business is considered a *retail store* if it is engaged primarily in selling merchandise for personal, household or farm consumption.

RETURN ON INVESTMENT

See **PROFIT TERMINOLOGY.**

REUTERS (ROY'-TUHRS)

A private British news agency, named for Baron Paul Julius von Reuter, the founder.

The official name is *Reuters Limited.* It is referred to as *Reuters.* When it is used as an adjective, the *s* is dropped: *a Reuter correspondent, a Reuter story.*

REVENUE

See **PROFIT TERMINOLOGY.**

REVENUE BOND

See **PROFIT TERMINOLOGY.**

REVOLUTIONS PER MINUTE

The abbreviation *R-P-M* is acceptable on first reference in specialized contexts such as an auto column. Otherwise, do not use it until second reference.

REVOLVER

See **PISTOL** and **WEAPONS.**

R-H FACTOR

Also: *R-H negative, R-H positive.*

RHODE ISLAND

It is the smallest of the 50 states in terms of total land area: one-thousand, 49 square miles.

RICHTER SCALE

See **EARTHQUAKE.**

RIFLE

See **WEAPONS.**

- **RIFLE, RIFFLE**

To rifle is to plunder or steal.

To riffle is to leaf rapidly through a book or pile of papers.

- **RIGHT HAND** (n.)
RIGHT-HANDED (adj.)
RIGHT-HANDER (n.)

- **RIGHTIST, ULTRA-RIGHTIST**

In general, avoid these terms in favor of more precise descriptions of an individual's political philosophy.

As popularly used today, particularly abroad, *rightist* often applies to someone who is conservative or opposed to socialism. It also often indicates an individual who supports an authoritarian government that is militantly anti-communist or anti-socialist.

Ultra-rightist suggests an individual who subscribes to rigid interpretations of a conservative doctrine or to forms of fascism that stress authoritarian, often militaristic views.

See **RADICAL** and the **LEFTIST, ULTRA-LEFTIST** entry.

- **RIGHT OF WAY, RIGHTS OF WAY**

- **RIGHT-TO-WORK** (adj.)

A right-to-work law prohibits a company and a union from signing a contract that would require the affected workers to be union members.

Federal labor laws generally permit such contracts. There is no federal right-to-work law, but Section 14B of the Taft-Hartley Act allows states to pass such laws if they wish. Many states have done so.

The repeal of Section 14B would have the effect of voiding all right-to-work laws. By itself, the repeal would not require workers to be union members, but in states that now have right-to-work laws, the repeal would open the way to contracts requiring union membership.

See **CLOSED SHOP** for definitions of various agreements that require union membership.

- **RIGHT WING** (n.)

But: *right-wing* (adj.), *right-winger* (n.).

- **RINGLING BROTHERS AND BARNUM AND BAILEY CIRCUS**

Headquarters is in Washington.

- **RIO GRANDE**

Not *Rio Grande River.* (*Rio* means river.)

- **RIP OFF** (v.)
RIP-OFF (n., adj.)

Use this term sparingly.

- **ROAD**

Do not abbreviate. See **ADDRESSES.**

- **ROARING 20'S**

See **DECADES.**

- **ROBBERY**

See the **BURGLARY, LARCENY, ROBBERY, THEFT** entry.

- **ROCK'N'ROLL**

Rock-and-roll is better.

- **ROCKY MOUNTAINS**

Or simply: *the Rockies.*

- **ROLL CALL** (n.)
ROLL-CALL (adj.)

- **ROLLS-ROYCE**

Note the hyphen in this trademark for a make of automobile.

- **ROLY-POLY**

- **ROMAN CATHOLIC CHURCH**

The church traces its origin to

Christ's choice of the apostle Peter to lead his church on earth and his promise that "whatever you bind on earth shall be bound in heaven and whatever you loose on earth shall be loosed in heaven."

The church teaches that its bishops have been established as the legitimate successors of the apostles through generations of ceremonies in which authority was passed down by a laying-on of hands.

Responsibility for teaching the faithful and administering the church rests with the bishops. However, the church holds that the pope has final authority over their actions because he is the bishop of Rome, the office that it teaches was held by Peter at his death.

The shared teaching power—often called *collegiality*—of the bishops is particularly manifest when a pope summons an ecumenical council, a meeting of all bishops to regulate church worship and define new expressions of its teachings. Council actions must be approved by the pope, however, before they can take effect.

Although the pope is empowered to speak infallibly on faith and morals, he does so only in formal pronouncements that specifically state he is speaking from the chair (*ex cathedra*) of St. Peter. This rarely used prerogative was most recently invoked in 1950, when Pope Pius the 12th declared that Mary was assumed bodily into heaven.

The *Curia* serves as a form of governmental cabinet. Its members, appointed by the pope, handle both administrative and judicial functions.

The pope also chooses members of the *College of Cardinals,* who serve as his principal counselors. When a new pope must be chosen, they meet in a conclave to select a new pope by majority vote. In practice, cardinals are bishops, but there is no requirement that a cardinal be a bishop.

In the Latin Rite used by Catholics in the Western world, there are no national "churches" in the sense that applies in other denominations. Bishops in various nations do, however, organize conferences that develop programs to further the needs of the church in their nations. The National Conference of Catholic Bishops is the national organization of Roman Catholic bishops in the United States. Its administrative arm is the United States Catholic Conference, with offices in Washington.

In the Eastern Rite, followed by many Roman Catholics who live in the Middle East or trace their origins to it, there are national churches. They and the archbishops (often called *patriarchs*) who head them have considerable autonomy in ritual and discipline, but they acknowledge the authority of the pope. See the **EASTERN RITE** entry.

In the United States, the church's principal organizational units are archdioceses and dioceses. They are headed, respectively, by archbishops and bishops, who have final responsibility for many activities within their jurisdictions and report directly to Rome. Although the seat of an archdiocese once served as a meeting place for the bishops of other dioceses within a region, there is little practical difference between the two in the Latin Rite. An archbishop, however, is required to report to Rome if he believes that abuses have occurred in a diocese within his region.

Membership: The church counts more than 600 (m) million members worldwide. In the United States it has more than 48 (m) million members, making it the largest single body of Christians in the nation.

Beliefs: Roman Catholics believe in the Trinity—that there is one God who exists as three divine persons, the Father, the Son and the Holy Spirit. They believe that the Son became man as Jesus Christ.

Other beliefs include salvation through Christ, and everlasting heaven and hell.

The essential elements of belief are contained in the Bible and in "tradition," the body of teachings passed on both orally and in writing by the apostles and their successors.

The Mass is the central act of worship. Christ is believed to be present in the Holy Eucharist, which is consecrated during Mass.

In addition to the Holy Eucharist, there are six other sacraments—baptism, confirmation, penance (often called the sacrament of reconciliation), matrimony, holy orders, and the sacrament of the sick (formerly extreme unction).

Clergy: Ranks below the pope are, in descending order, cardinal, archbishop, bishop, monsignor, priest and deacon. In religious orders, some men who are not priests have the title brother.

The first-reference forms for titles follow. Use only last names on second reference.

Cardinals: *Cardinal Timothy Manning.* The usage *Timothy Cardinal Manning,* a practice traceable to the nobility's custom of identifications such as *William, Duke of Norfolk,* is still used in formal documents but otherwise is considered archaic.

Archbishops: *Archbishop Joseph Bernardin,* or *the Most Reverend Joseph Bernardin, archbishop of Cincinnati.*

Bishops: *Bishop Bernard Flanagan,* or *the Most Reverend Bernard Flanagan, bishop of Worcester.*

Monsignors: *Monsignor Joseph Vogt.* Do not use the abbreviation *Msgr.* or *the Right Reverend* or *the Very Reverend*—this distinction between types of monsignors no longer is made.

Priests: *the Reverend John Paret.* When necessary in quotations on second reference: *Father Paret.*

Deacons: *Deacon Mark Smith.*

Brothers: *Brother Thomas Garvey.*

Nuns: See the **SISTER** entry.

See **RELIGIOUS TITLES.**

- **ROMANIA**

Not *Rumania.*

- **ROMANIAN ORTHODOX CHURCH**

The Romanian Orthodox Church in America is an autonomous archdiocese of the Romanian Orthodox Church. The Romanian Orthodox Episcopate of America is an autonomous archdiocese within the Orthodox Church in America.

See **EASTERN ORTHODOX CHURCHES.**

- **ROMAN NUMERALS**

See **NUMERALS.**

- **ROME**

The city in Italy stands alone in datelines.

- **ROQUEFORT CHEESE, ROQUEFORT DRESSING**

A trademark for a blue cheese.

- **ROSARY**

It is *recited* or *said,* never *read.*

- **ROSH HASHANA** (ROHSH HA-SHAH'-NAH)

The Jewish new year. Occurs in September or October.

- **ROSTRUM**

See the **LECTERN, PODIUM, PULPIT, ROSTRUM** entry.

• R-O-T-C

Acceptable in all references for *Reserved Officers' Training Corps.* See that entry.

• ROUND UP (v.)
ROUND-UP (n.)

• ROYAL DUTCH-SHELL GROUP OF COMPANIES

This holding company, based in London and The Hague, owns substantial portions of the stock in numerous corporations that specialize in petroleum and related products. Most have *Shell* in their names.

Among them is Shell Oil Company, an American corporation, with headquarters in Houston.

• RUBBER STAMP (n.)
RUBBER-STAMP (v. and adj.)

• RUBELLA (ROO-BEL'-UH)

Also known as *German measles.*

• RUNNER-UP, RUNNERS-UP

• RUNNING MATE

• RUSH HOUR (n.)
RUSH-HOUR (adj.)

• RUSSIA, SOVIET UNION

Soviet people and *the Soviets* are acceptable umbrella terms in referring to all the people who live within the 15 republics that make up the *Union of Soviet Socialist Republics,* popularly known as the *Soviet Union.*

The Russian Soviet Federated Socialist Republic is the dominant state, and its leaders effectively control the other 14 republics. For this reason, *Russia, Russian* and *Russians* are acceptable synonyms for *Soviets* and *Soviet Union* when referring to the governmental apparatus. For example: *Russia is considering the U-S proposal. The United States is negotiating with the Russians.*

Do not, however, use *Russia, Russian* or *Russians* in references to all the people of the Soviet Union. Make it *Soviet hockey team,* for example, not *Russian hockey team,* in a story about a group that includes Soviet citizens of many nationalities.

When relevant, identify the nationalities of the individuals involved. While a first reference might say *Soviet gymnast,* for example, indicate later in the story where the individual comes from in the Soviet Union.

In addition to the *Russians,* national groups within the Soviet Union include *Armenians, Georgians, Latvians, Lithuanians* and *Ukrainians.*

Datelines: *Moscow* stands alone. Follow all other community names with *Soviet Union.*

Identify a republic in the text if relevant.

Republics: The Russian republic includes Moscow and pre-revolutionary Russia. It is the largest in area and population.

The other 14, from the most populous to the least populous, are: the Ukrainian, Byelorussian, Uzbeck, Kazakh, Georgian, Azerbaidzhan, Lithuanian, Moldavian, Latvian, Kirgiz, Tadzhik, Armenian, Estonian and Turkmen Soviet Socialist Republics.

The Ukrainian and Byelorussian republics have their own memberships in the United Nations.

• RUSSIAN NAMES

When a first name in Russian has a close phonetic equivalent in English, use the equivalent in translating the name: *Alexander Solzhenitsyn* rather than *Aleksandr,* the spelling that would result from a transliteration of the Russian letters into the English alphabet.

When a first name has no close phonetic equivalent in English, express it with an English spelling that approximates the sound in Russian: *Nikita,* for example.

For last names, use the English spelling that most closely approximates the pronunciation in Russian.

If an individual has a preference for an English spelling that is different from the one that would result by applying these guidelines, follow the individual's preference.

Women's last names have feminine endings. But use them only if the woman is not married or if she is known under that name (*the ballerina Maya Plissetskaya*). Otherwise, use the masculine form: *Victoria Brezhnev,* not *Brezhneva.*

Russian names never end in *off,* except for common mistransliterations such as *Rachmaninoff.* Instead, the transliterations should end in *ov: Romanov.*

Always use pronouncers.

- **RUSSIAN ORTHODOX CHURCH**

See EASTERN ORTHODOX CHURCHES.

- **RUSSIAN REVOLUTION**

Also: *The Bolshevik Revolution.*

SABENA (SUH-BEE′-NUH) **BELGIAN WORLD AIRLINES**
A *Sabena airliner* is acceptable in any reference.
Headquarters is in Brussels, Belgium.

SABOTEUR

SACRILEGIOUS

SAINT
Abbreviate as *St.* in the names of saints, cities and other places: *St. Jude, St. Paul, Minnesota,* and the *St. Lawrence Seaway.*
But see the entries for **SAINT JOHN** and **SAULT STE. MARIE.**

SAINT JOHN
The spelling for the city in New Brunswick.
To distinguish it from *St. John's, Newfoundland.*

SALABLE

SALES
See **PROFIT TERMINOLOGY.**

"SALT"
See **STRATEGIC ARMS LIMITATION TALKS.**

SALT LAKE CITY
Stands alone in datelines.

"SALT-TWO"

SALVO, SALVOS

"SAM," "SAMS"
Acceptable on second reference for *surface-to-air missile(s).*

SANDBAG (n.)
The verbs: *sandbagged, sandbagging.* And: *sandbagger.*

SAN DIEGO
The city in California stands alone in datelines.

SANDSTORM
See **WEATHER TERMS.**

SAN FRANCISCO
The city in California stands alone in datelines.

SANITARIUM, SANITARIUMS

SARDINIA
Use instead of *Italy* in datelines on stories from communities on this island.

SASKATCHEWAN
A province of Canada north of Montana and North Dakota. Do not abbreviate.
See **DATELINES.**

SATELLITES
See **SPACECRAFT DESIGNATIONS.**

"SATURDAY NIGHT SPECIAL"
See **WEAPONS.**

SAULTE STE. MARIE (SOO SAYNT MUH-REE′), **MICHIGAN; SAULTE STE. MARIE, ONTARIO**
The abbreviation is *Ste.* instead of

St. because the full name is *Saulte Sainte Marie.*

• SAVINGS AND LOAN ASSOCIATIONS

They are not banks. Use *the association* on second reference.

• SAVIOR

Use this spelling for all senses, rather than the alternate form, *saviour.*

• SCANDINAVIAN AIRLINES SYSTEM

S-A-S is acceptable on second reference.

Headquarters is in Stockholm, Sweden.

• SCISSORS

Takes plural verbs and pronouns: *The scissors are on the table. Leave them there.*

• SCORES

Use hyphens and the word *to,* and, in exception to the rules in **NUMERALS,** use figures only: *The Mets beat the Giants 6-to-5. It was a 12-to-3 victory.*

However, when reporting one team's score in the text of the story, follow the rules for **NUMERALS:** *The six-run effort; the Yankees scored a total of seven runs; the Packers rolled up 24 points.* But: *it was Boston 6, Baltimore 5.*

• SCOT, SCOTS, SCOTTISH

A native of Scotland is a *Scot.* The people are *the Scots,* not *the Scotch.*

Somebody or something is *Scottish.*

• SCOTCH WHISKY

A type of whiskey distilled in Scotland from malted barley. The malt is dried over a peat fire.

Use the spelling *whisky* only when the two words are used together.

Use the spelling *whiskey* for generic references to the beverage, which may be distilled from any of several grains.

The verb *to scotch* means to stamp out, put an end to.

• SCOTLAND

Use *Scotland* after the names of Scottish communities in datelines.

See **DATELINES** and **UNITED KINGDOM.**

• SCULPTOR

Use for both men and women.

• SCURRILOUS

• SEABOARD WORLD AIRLINES

Headquarters is in New York.

• SEA ISLANDS

A chain of islands off the coasts of South Carolina, Georgia and Florida.

Islands within the boundaries of South Carolina include Parris Island, Port Royal Island, and St. Helena Island.

Those within Georgia include Cumberland Island (largest in the chain), St. Simons Island and St. Catherines Island (no apostrophes), and Sea Island.

Amelia Island is within the boundaries of Florida.

Several communities have names taken from the island name—Port Royal is a town on Port Royal Island, Sea Island is a resort on Sea Island, and St. Simons Island is a village on St. Simons Island.

In datelines:

(PORT ROYAL, SOUTH CAROLINA) - -

(ST. SIMONS ISLAND, GEORGIA) - -

• SEARS, ROEBUCK AND COMPANY

Headquarters is in Chicago.

• SEATTLE

The city in the state of Washington stands alone in datelines.

• SECOND GUESS (n.)

The verb from: *second-guess.* Also *second-guesser.*

• SECOND HAND (n.)
SECONDHAND (adj. and adv.)

Secondhand Rose had a watch with a second hand that she bought secondhand.

• SECOND-RATE (adj.)

All uses: *A second-rate play. The play is second-rate.*

• SECOND REFERENCE

When used in this handbook, the term applies to all references other than the primary reference to an organization or individual within a story.

Generally speaking, *the first reference* to a subject comes in the lead of the story, and the *second reference* covers all subsequent mentions. But, in broadcast writing, where the full reference to a subject can make a lead impossibly cumbersome, the writer may choose to lead with the second-reference form of the name or term, and treat the subsequent mention as the primary reference. For example:

The U-A-W is on strike. Members of the United Auto Workers Union walked off car assembly lines across the country at midnight.

In cases where the second-reference term is used in the lead, be sure to use full reference in the following sentence.

Acceptable abbreviations and acronyms for organizations frequently in the news are listed under the organization's full name. A few prominent acronyms acceptable on first reference also are listed alphabetically according to the letters of the acronym.

The listing of an acceptable term for second reference does not mean that it always must be used after the first reference. Often a generic word such as *the agency, the commission* or *the company* is more appropriate and less jarring to the listener. At other times, the full name may need to be repeated for clarity.

For additional guidelines that apply to organizations, see **ABBREVIATIONS** and **ACRONYMS.**

For additional guidelines that apply to individuals, see **COURTESY TITLES** and **TITLES.**

• SECRETARY-GENERAL

Note hyphen.

• SECRETARY-TREASURER

Note hyphen.

• SECRET SERVICE

A federal agency administered by the Treasury Department.

• SECURITIES AND EXCHANGE COMMISSION

S-E-C is acceptable on second reference only in business copy—not in general news stories. Instead, use *the commission.*

The related legislation is the *Securities Exchange Act.* Note: no *and.*

• SECURITY COUNCIL

Precede it with *U-N* or *United Nations* on the first reference. On second reference: *the council.*

• SEEING EYE DOG

A trademark for a guide dog.

• SEE-SAW

SELF-

Always hyphenate:

SELF-ASSURED
SELF-DEFENSE
SELF-GOVERNMENT

SELL OUT (v.)
SELLOUT (n.)

SEMI-

The rules in **PREFIXES** apply, but in general, no hyphen. Some examples:

SEMIFINAL
SEMI-INVALID
SEMIOFFICAL
SEMITROPICAL

SEMIANNUAL

It means twice a year—and is best said that way.

Biannual Means the same thing—and ought to be similarly avoided.

Biennial means once every two years. Avoid it, too.

SEMICOLON

Not often used in broadcast writing, it indicates a greater separation of thought and information than a comma can convey but less than a period provides.

The basic guidelines:

To Clarify a Series: Semicolons can separate elements of a series when individual segments contain material that must also be set off by commas:

He leaves a son, John Smith of Kansas City, Missouri; a daughter, Jane Smith of Kansas City, Kansas; and a brother, Joe Smith of East St. Louis, Illinois.

Note that the semicolon is used before the final *and* in such a series.

To Link Independent Clauses: A semicolon can be used when a coordinating conjunction such as *and, but* or *for* is not present: *The package was due last week; it arrived today.*

See the **COMMA; DOUBLE DASH** and **ELLIPSIS** entries for alternate forms of punctuation.

SEND OFF (v.)
SEND-OFF (n.)

SENIOR

See the **JUNIOR, SENIOR** entry.

SENIOR CITIZEN

Use the term sparingly. See **ELDERLY.**

SERIAL NUMBERS

Use them in stories only when they are essential.

Use figures and hyphens. If there is a space between a string of letters or numbers, use a comma: *A013467* should be expressed as *serial number A-0-1-3-4-6-7,* while *a09 87b* should be expressed as *a-0-9, 8-7-b.* The comma is the visual cue to pause.

SERVICEABLE

SERVICEMAN, SERVICEWOMAN

SERVICE MARK

A brand, symbol or word, used by a supplier of services and protected by law to prevent a competitor from using it: *Realtor,* for a member of the National Association of Real Estate Boards, for example.

The preferred form, however, is to use a generic term unless the service mark is essential to the story.

See **BRAND NAMES** and **TRADEMARK.**

SESQUICENTENNIAL

Every 150 years. Say it that way.

● **SET UP** (v.)
SETUP (n. and adj.)

● **SEVEN SEAS**

Arabian Sea, Atlantic Ocean, Bay of Bengal, Mediterranean Sea, Persian Gulf, Red Sea, South China Sea.

● **SEVEN SISTERS**

The colleges are: Bryn Mawr, Connectitcut College for Women, Mount Holyoke, Radcliffe, Smith, Vassar and Wellesley.

Also a nickname for the world's largest privately-operated oil companies: British Petroleum, Exxon, Gulf, Mobil, Royal Dutch-Shell, Standard Oil Company of California and Texaco.

● **SEVENTH-DAY ADVENTIST CHURCH**

The denomination is traceable to the preaching of William Miller of New Hampton, New York, a Baptist layman who said his study of the Book of Daniel showed that the end of the world would come in the mid 1840s.

When the prediction did not come true, the Millerites split into smaller groups. One, influenced by visions described by Ellen Harmon, later Mrs. James White, is the precursor of Seventh-day Adventist practice today.

The General Conference, which meets every four years, has authority to make decisions that affect the denomination worldwide. In descending order of authority come divisions for various sections of the world, union conferences for major areas within a division, and, in the United States, state conferences. Members at each level participate in electing representatives to higher levels.

The office of General Conference, located in Washington, lists American membership at 500-thousand, and worldwide membership at two (m) million, 500-thousand.

Beliefs: The description *adventist* is based on the belief that a second coming of Christ is near. Believers hold that events leading to the coming began in the mid-1840s and will continue until the completion of a process that will identify those worthy of joining in the resurrection at the second coming of Christ.

Seventh-day derives from the contention that the Bible permits no deviation from observing the seventh day of the week as the Sabbath.

Baptism, by immersion, is reserved for those old enough to understand its meaning. Baptism and the Lord's Supper are the only sacraments.

Clergy: The head of the General Conference holds the formal title of *president.* The formal titles for ministers are *pastor* or *elder.*

The designation *the Reverend* is not used.

See **RELIGIOUS TITLES.**

● **SEVEN WONDERS OF THE WORLD**

The Egyptian pyramids, the hanging gardens of Babylon, the Mausoleum at Halicarnassus, the temple of Artemis at Ephesus, the Colossus of Rhodes, the statue of Zeus by Phidias at Olympia and the Pharos or lighthouse at Alexandria.

● **SEWAGE, SEWERAGE**

Sewage is waste matter.

Sewerage is the drainage system.

● **SEX CHANGES**

Follow these guidelines in using proper names or personal pronouns when referring to an indivdual who has had a sex-change operation:

—If the reference is to an action before the operation, use the proper name and gender of the individual at that time.

—If the reference is to an action after the operation, use the new proper name and gender.

For example:

Dr. Richard Raskind was a first-rate amateur tennis player. He won several tournaments. Ten years later, when Dr. Renee Richards applied to play in tournaments, many women players objected on the ground that she was the former Richard Raskind, who had undergone a sex-change operation. Miss Richards said she was entitled to compete as a woman.

• **SEXISM**
See **WOMEN.**

• **SHAKE UP** (v.)
SHAKE-UP (n. and adj.)

• **SHALL, WILL**
Use *shall* to express determinations: *We shall overcome. You and he shall stay.*

Either *shall* or *will* may be used in first-person constructions that do not emphasize determinations: *We shall hold a meeting. We will hold a meeting.*

For second- and third-person constructions, use *will* unless determination is stressed: *You will like it. She will not be pleased.*

See the **SHOULD, WOULD** entry and **SUBJUNCTIVE MOOD.**

• **SHAPE UP** (v.)
SHAPE-UP (n. and adj.)

• **SHARIAH** (SHUH-REE'-UH)
The legal code of Islam. It is roughly comparable to the Talmudic tradition in Judaism.

• **SHAVUOT** (SHUH-VOO'-OHT)
The Jewish Feast of Weeks, commemorating the receiving of the Ten Commandments. Occurs in May or June.

• **SHE**
Do not use this pronoun in references to ships or nations.

Use *it* instead.

• **SHEET METAL WORKERS INTERNATIONAL ASSOCIATION**
The shortened form *Sheet Metal Workers union* is acceptable in all references.

Headquarters is in Washington.

• **SHEETROCK**
A trademark for a brand of gypsum wallboard.

• **SHELL**
See **WEAPONS.**

• **SHELL OIL COMPANY**
This American company, with headquarters in Houston, is part of the Royal Dutch-Shell Group of Companies. The group owns more than half of the stock in Shell Oil.

• **SHERIFF**

• **SHIPS**
See the **BOATS, SHIPS** entry.

• **SHIRT SLEEVE, SHIRT SLEEVES** (n.)
SHIRT-SLEEVE (adj.)

• **SHOESHINE, SHOESTRING**

• **SHOPWORN**

• **SHORTCHANGE**

• **SHORT-LIVED** (adj.)
A short-lived plan. The plan was short-lived.

• **SHORT TON**
Equal to two-thousand pounds. See **TON.**

• **SHOT**
See **WEAPONS.**

• **SHOTGUN**
See **WEAPONS.**

• **SHOULD, WOULD**
Use *should* to express an obligation. *We should help the needy.*
Use *would* to express a customary action: *In the summer we would spend hours by the seashore.*
Use *would* also in constructing a conditional past tense, but be careful:
Wrong: *If Soderholm would not have had an injured foot, Thompson would not have been in the lineup.*
Right: *If Soderholm had not had an injured foot, Thompson would not have been in the lineup.*
See **SUBJUNCTIVE MOOD.**

• **SHOWCASE, SHOWROOM**

• **SHOW OFF** (v.)
SHOW-OFF (n.)

• **SHUT DOWN** (v.)
SHUT-DOWN (n.)

• **SHUT-IN**

• **SHUT OFF** (v.)
SHUT-OFF (n.)

• **SHUT OUT** (v.)
SHUTOUT (n.)

• **SICILY**
Use instead of *Italy* in datelines on stories from communities on this island.

• **SIDE BY SIDE, SIDE-BY-SIDE**
They walked side by side. The stories received side-by-side display.

• **SIERRA NEVADA, THE**
Not *Sierra Nevada Mountains. Sierra* means mountains.
Not *Sierras* or *Sierra Nevadas. Sierra* is plural.

• **SIGHTSEEING, SIGHTSEER**

• **SIMONIZ** (SY'-MUH-NYZ)
A trademark for a brand of auto wax.

• **SINAI**
Not *the Sinai.* But: *The Sinai Desert, the Sinai Peninsula.*

• **SINGAPORE**
Stands alone in datelines.

• **SINGLE-HANDED, SINGLE-HANDEDLY**

• **SISTER**
If no surname is given, the name is the same in all references: *Sister Agnes Rita.*
If a surname is used in first reference, drop the given name on second reference: *Sister Clair Regina Torpy* on first reference, *Sister Torpy* in subsequent references.
Use *mother* the same way when referring to a woman who heads a group of nuns.
See **RELIGIOUS TITLES.**

• **SISTER-IN-LAW, SISTERS-IN-LAW**

• **SIT DOWN** (v.)
SIT-DOWN (n. and adj)

• **SIT IN** (v.)
SIT-IN (n. and adj.)

• **SITUATION**
A tired and overworked word that usually can be eliminated—or replaced with something better.

Generally, when the word *situation* is preceded by an adjective (as in *hostage situation* or *economic situation*), the word isn't needed at all. In both of the examples, it is non-descriptive—and wasted.

Better would be *hostage standoff* or *the holdout;* and *the recession* or, simply, *the economy.*

• **SIZABLE**

• **SKEPTIC**
See the **CYNIC, SKEPTIC** entry.

• **SKI, SKIS, SKIER, SKIED, SKIING**
Also: *ski jump, ski jumping.*

• **SKID ROAD, SKID ROW**
The term originated as *Skid Road* in the Seattle area, where dirt roads were used to skid logs to the mill. Over the year, *Skid Road* became a synonym for the area where loggers gathered, usually down among the rooming houses and saloons.

In time, the term spread to other cities as a description for sections, such as the Bowery in New York, that are havens for derelicts. In the process, *row* replaced *road* in many references.

Use *Skid Road* for this section in Seattle; either *Skid Road* or *Skid Row* for other areas.

• **SKILLFUL**

• **SLANG**
In general, avoid slang, the highly informal language that is outside of conventional or standard usage.

See **COLLOQUIALISMS; DIALECT;** and **WORD SELECTION.**

• **SLAYING**
See the **HOMICIDE, MURDER, MANSLAUGHTER** entry.

• **SLEDGEHAMMER**

• **SLEET**
See **WEATHER TERMS.**

• **SLEIGHT OF HAND**

• **SLOWDOWN**

• **SLUMLORD**

• **SLUSH FUND**

• **SMALL-ARMS FIRE**

• **SMALL-BUSINESS MAN**

• **SMASH UP** (v.)
SMASHUP (n. and adj.)

• **SMITHSONIAN INSTITUTION**
Not *Smithsonian Institute.*

• **SMOKE BOMB, SMOKE SCREEN**

• **SMOKEY**
Or *Smokey Bear.* Not *Smokey the Bear.*

But: *A smoky room,* the *Smoky Mountains.*

• **SNOWDRIFT, SNOWFALL, SNOWFLAKE, SNOWMAN, SNOWPLOW, SNOWSHOE, SNOWSTORM, SNOWSUIT**

• **SO CALLED** (adv.)
SO-CALLED (adj.)

• SOCIETY FOR THE PREVENTION OF CRUELTY TO ANIMALS
S-P-C-A is acceptable on second reference.

The *American Society for the Prevention of Cruelty to Animals* is limited to the five boroughs of New York City.

The autonomous chapters in other cities ordinarily precede the organization by the name of the city: On first reference, the *Philadelphia Society for the Prevention of Cruelty to Animals;* on second, the *Philadelphia S-P-C-A* or *S-P-C-A,* as appropriate in the context.

• SOCIETY OF FRIENDS
See **QUAKERS.**

• SOFT-SPOKEN

• SOLICITOR
See **LAWYER.**

• SOLID SOUTH
Those Southern states traditionally regarded as supporters of the Democratic Party.

• SOLILOQUY, SOLILOQUIES

• SON-IN-LAW, SONS-IN LAW

• S-O-S
The distress signal.

• SOUND BARRIER
The speed of sound, no longer a true barrier because aircraft have exceeded it. See **MACH NUMBER.**

• SOUTH
As defined by the Census Bureau, the 16-state region is broken into three divisions.

The four *East South-Central* states are Alabama, Kentucky, Mississippi and Tennessee.

The eight *South Atlantic* states are Delaware, Florida, Georgia, Maryland, North Carolina, South Carolina, Virginia and West Virginia.

The four *West South-Central* states are Arkansas, Louisiana, Oklahoma and Texas.

See **NORTH-CENTRAL REGION; NORTHEAST REGION;** and **WEST** for the bureau's other regional breakdowns.

• SOUTH AMERICA
See **WESTERN HEMISPHERE.**

• SOUTHEAST ASIA
The nations of the Indochinese Peninsula and the islands southeast of it: Burma, Cambodia, Indonesia, Laos, Malaysia, New Guinea, the Philippines, Singapore, Thailand and Vietnam.

See **ASIAN SUBCONTINENT** and **FAR EAST.**

• SOUTHEAST ASIA TREATY ORGANIZATION
"SEATO" is acceptable on second reference. But use *the alliance* in some references to reduce the frequency of alphabet soup.

• SOUTHEASTERN CONFERENCE
Alabama, Auburn, Florida, Georgia, Kentucky, Louisiana State, Mississippi, Mississippi State, Tennessee, Vanderbilt.

• SOUTHWEST CONFERENCE
Arkansas, Baylor, Houston, Rice, Southern Methodist, Texas, Texas A-and-M, Texas Christian, Texas Tech.

• SOVIET UNION
Acceptable in all references to *Union of Soviet Socialist Republics.*

See the **RUSSIA, SOVIET UNION** entry for guidance in using *Soviet* and for a list of the 15 republics that make up the nation.

• SPACE AGE

It began on October fourth, 1957, with the launching of the Soviets' *"Sputnik-One."*

• SPACE AGENCY

See **NATIONAL AERONAUTICS AND SPACE ADMINISTRATION.**

• SPACE CENTERS

See **JOHN F. KENNEDY SPACE CENTER** and **LYNDON B. JOHNSON SPACE CENTER.**

• SPACECRAFT

The plural also is *spacecraft.*

• SPACECRAFT DESIGNATIONS

Follow the rules for **NUMERALS.** Place all formal names in quotes and hyphenate between the name and number: *"Gemini-Seven," "Apollo-Eleven,"* but no hyphen after a pronouncer: *"Soyuz (Soy'-uz) 35."*

• SPACESHIP

• SPACE SHUTTLE

The first American shuttle is a reusable winged aircraft capable of carrying scientists and cargo into Earth orbit. It is designed to take off vertically with the aid of booster rockets. After an orbital mission, re-entry begins with the firing of engines that send the craft back into Earth's atmosphere. The final leg of the return trip is a powerless glide to a landing strip.

• SPANISH-AMERICAN WAR

• SPANISH AND PORTUGUESE NAMES

The family names of both the father and mother usually are considered part of a person's full name. In everyday use, customs vary widely with individuals and countries.

The normal sequence is given name, father's family name, mother's family name: *Jose Lopez Portillo.*

On second reference, use only the father's family name (*Lopez*), unless the individual prefers or is widely known by a multiple last name (*Lopez Portillo*).

Some individuals use a *y* (for *and*) between the two surnames: *Jose Lopez y Portillo.* Include the *y* on second reference only if both names are used: *Lopez y Portillo.*

In the Portuguese practice common in Portugal and Brazil, some individuals use only the mother's family name on second reference. If the individual's preference is not known, use both family names on second reference: *Humberto Castello Branco* on first reference, *Castello Branco* on second.

A married woman frequently uses her father's family name followed by the particle *De* (for *of*) and her husband's name. A woman named *Irma Perez* who married a man named *Anibal Gutierrez* would be known as *Irma Perez de Gutierrez.* Use *Mrs. Gutierrez* on second reference.

• SPECIAL CONTEXTS

When this term is used in this book, it means that the material described may be used in a regular column devoted to a specialized subject or when a particular literary effect is suitable.

Special literary effects generally are suitable only in feature copy, but even there they should be used with care. Most feature material should follow the same style norms that apply to regular news copy.

• SPECIES

Same in singular and plural. Use singular or plural verbs and pronouns depending on the sense: *The species has been unable to maintain itself. Both species are extinct.*

• SPEECHMAKER, SPEECHMAKING

• SPEED OF SOUND
See **MACH NUMBER.**

• SPEED UP (v.)
SPEEDUP (n. and adj.)

• SPELLING
The basic rule when in doubt is to consult this handbook followed by, if necessary, a dictionary under conditions described in the **DICTIONARIES** entry.

Memory Aid: Noah Webster developed the following rule of thumb for the frequently vexing question of whether to double a final consonant in forming the present participle and past tense of a verb:

—If the stress in pronunciation is on the first syllable, do not double the consonant: *combat, combating, combated; cancel, canceling, canceled.*

—If the stress in pronunciation is on the second syllable, double the consonant: *control, controlling, controlled; refer, referring, referred.*

—If the word is only one syllable, double a consonant unless confusion would result: *jut, jutted, jutting.* An exception to avoid confusion with *buss*, is *bus, bused, busing.*

• SPILL, SPILLED, SPILLING
Not *spilt* in the past tense.

• SPLIT INFINITIVE
See **VERBS.**

• SPOKESMAN, SPOKESWOMAN
But not *spokesperson.* Use *a representative* if you do not know the sex of the individual.

• SPOUSE
Use when some of the persons involved may be men. For example: *physicians and their spouses,* not *physicians and their wives.*

• SPRINGTIME

• SQUALL
See **WEATHER TERMS.**

• SQUINTING MODIFIER
A misplaced adverb that can be interpreted as modifying either of two words: *Those who lie often are found out.*

Place the adverb where there can be no confusion, even if a compound verb must be split: *Those who often lie are found out.* Or if that was not the sense: *Those who lie are often found out.*

• SRI LANKA (SHREE LAHN'-KUH)
Formerly Ceylon. Use *Sri Lanka* in datelines and other references to the nation.

The people may be called either *Sri Lankans* or *Ceylonese.*

Before the nation was called Ceylon, it was Serendip, whence comes the word *serendipity.*

• S.S. KRESGE COMPANY
Headquarters is in Troy, Michigan.

• S-S-T
Acceptable in all references for a *supersonic transport.*

• STADIUM, STADIUMS

• STALIN, JOSEF
Not *Joseph.*

• STANCH, STAUNCH
Stanch is a verb: *He stanched the flow of blood.*

Staunch is an adjective: *She is a staunch supporter of equality.*

• "STANDARD AND POOR'S REGISTER OF CORPORATIONS"
The source for determining the formal name of a business. See **COMPANY NAMES.**

The register is published by Standard and Poor's Corporation of New York.

• STANDARD-BEARER

• STANDARD OIL COMPANY (INDIANA)
Indiana Standard or *Standard of Indiana* is acceptable on second reference.

On first reference: *Standard Oil of Indiana,* or simply *Standard Oil Company of Indiana.*

Amoco is a company trademark. Headquarters is in Chicago.

• STANDARD OIL COMPANY (NEW JERSEY)
The former name of *Exxon Corporation.*

• STANDARD OIL COMPANY OF CALIFORNIA
Socal (soh'-cal) is acceptable on second reference.

Headquarters is in San Francisco.

• STANDARD OIL COMPANY (OHIO)
Sohio (soh-hy'-oh) is acceptable on the second reference.

Headquarters is in Cleveland.

• STAND IN (v.)
STAND-IN (n. and adj.)

• STAND OFF (v.)
STANDOFF (n. and adj.)

• STAND OUT (v.)
STANDOUT (n. and adj.)

• "THE STAR-SPANGLED BANNER"

• STATE
Four American states—Kentucky, Massachusetts, Pennsylvania and Virginia—legally are commonwealths rather than states. But the distinction is necessary only in formal uses: *The Commonwealth of Kentucky filed a suit.*

For usual geographic references, these states may be handled as all the others are.

• STATEHOUSE

• STATE NAMES
Some guidelines:

Abbreviations: Don't use them in the body of the story or the dateline.

Punctuation: Place one comma between the city and the state name, and another comma after the state name, unless ending a sentence: *He was traveling from Nashville, Tennessee, to Austin, Texas, to Show Low, Arizona. She said Cook County, Illinois, was Mayor Daley's stronghold.*

Miscellaneous: Use *New York city* or *New York State* when the distinction is necessary.

Use *the state of Washington* or *Washington state* when confusion with Washington D-C would otherwise result.

• STATES' RIGHTS

• STATEWIDE

• STATIONARY, STATIONERY
To stand still is to be *stationary.* Writing paper is *stationery.*

• STATION WAGON

• STATUTE MILE
It equals five-thousand, 280 feet, or roughly one-point-six kilometers.

To convert to approximate nautical miles, multiply the number of statute miles by point-869.

See **KILOMETERS**; **KNOT**; **MILE**; and **NAUTICAL MILE**.

- **STAUNCH**

See the **STANCH, STAUNCH** entry.

- **STEADY-STATE THEORY**

See **BIG-BANG THEORY**.

- **STEPBROTHER, STEPFATHER**

Also: *stepsister, stepmother.*

- **STEPPINGSTONE**

- **STIFLING**

- **ST. JOHN'S**

The city in the Canadian province of Newfoundland.

Not to be confused with *Saint John, New Brunswick.*

- **ST. LOUIS**

The city in Missouri stands alone in datelines.

- **STOCK**

See the **COMMON STOCK, PREFERRED STOCK** entry.

- **STOCKBROKER**

- **STOCK MARKET PRICES**

Spell out any fractions or decimals—fractions are preferred.

Follow the rules for **NUMERALS**; **FRACTIONS**; and **DECIMALS**.

Some examples: *The stock went up three-quarters of a point. It has risen one and a-half points over the past week. A-T-T was up six and five-eighths.*

- **STOCKMEN'S ADVISORY**

See **WEATHER TERMS**.

- **STOPGAP**

- **STORM**

See **WEATHER TERMS**.

- **STRAIGHT-LACED, STRAIT-LACED**

Use *straight-laced* for someone strict or severe in behavior or moral views.

Reserve *strait-laced* for the notion of confinement, as in a corset.

- **STRAITJACKET**

Not *straightjacket.*

- **STRATEGIC AIR COMMAND**

"SAC" is acceptable on second reference.

- **STRATEGIC ARMS LIMITATION TALKS**

"SALT" or *"SALT-Two"* are acceptable on the second reference.

To avoid alphabet soup, also use such references as *the talks, the arms talks* or *the negotiations.*

Similarly, with regard to completed pacts, use *the treaty* or similar references.

- **STRIKEBREAKER**

- **STRONG-ARM** (v. and adj.)

- **STRONG-WILLED**

- **STUDENT**

See the **PUPIL, STUDENT** entry.

- **SUB-**

The rules in **PREFIXES** apply, but in general, no hyphen. Some examples:

SUB-BASEMENT	SUBMACHINE GUN
SUBCOMMITTEE	SUB-ORBITAL
SUBCULTURE	SUBTOTAL
SUBDIVISION	SUB-ZERO

• SUBCOMMITTEE

Spelling out the full name and affiliation of a congressional subcommittee can spell the death of an otherwise lively sentence. Therefore, informalize where possible: *The Health and Research Subcommittee of the Senate Health and Labor Committee* is best referred to as either *a senate health subcommittee* or *the health and research subcommittee.*

Generally, subcommittee action is required before a full congressional committee will report a bill to the floor. Be sure to make the distinction between subcommittee action and full committee action.

• SUBJECT

See the **CITIZEN, RESIDENT, SUBJECT, NATIONAL, NATIVE** entry.

• SUBJUNCTIVE MOOD

Use the subjunctive mood of a verb for contrary-to-fact conditions, and expressions of doubts, wishes or regrets:

If I were a rich man, I wouldn't have to work hard.

I doubt that more money would be the answer.

I wish it were possible to take back my words.

Sentences that express a contingency or hypothesis may use either the subjunctive or the indicative mood depending on the context. In general, use the subjunctive if there is little likelihood that a contingency might come true:

If I were to marry a millionaire, I wouldn't have to worry about money.

If the bill should overcome the opposition against it, it would provide extensive tax relief.

But:

If I marry my millionaire beau, I won't have to worry about money.

If the bill passes as expected, it will provide an immediate tax cut.

See the **SHOULD, WOULD** entry.

• SUBMACHINE GUN

See **WEAPONS.**

• SUBPOENA, SUBPOENAED, SUBPOENAING

• SUBS

A wire substitution is sent when a story contains an error in a vital respect and must therefore be replaced. It differs from an updated story—generally a *tops*—in that the replacement is necessary because of an error, not new material.

Wire subs must be so slugged and contain an advisory as to what has been fixed in the story:

SUBS AND CORRECTS

PLEASE SUBSTITUTE THE FOLLOWING FOR THE FIRST ITEM IN THE FIFTH SUMMARY TO MAKE CLEAR THAT THE ALBATROSS IS NOT IN NEW YORK CITY.

Subs should be sent with urgent priority codes.

• SUCARYL (SOO'-KUH-RIL)

A trademark for a brand of non-caloric sweetener.

• SUCCESSOR

• SUFFIXES

See separate listings for commonly used suffixes.

Follow Webster's New World Dictionary for words not in this book.

If a word combination is not listed in Webster's New World, use two words for the verb form; hyphenate any noun or adjective forms.

• SUIT (SOOT), **SUITE** (SWEET)

You may have a *suit* of clothes a *suit* of cards, or be faced with a *lawsuit.*

There are *suites* of music, rooms and furniture.

- **SUKKOT** (SOO'-KOHT)

The Jewish Feast of Tabernacles, celebrating the fall harvest and commemorating the desert wandering of the Jews during the Exodus. Occurs in September or October.

- **SUMMERTIME**

- **SUNBATHE**

The verb forms: *sunbathed, sunbathing.* Also: *sunbather.*

- **SUN BELT**

Generally those states in the South and West, ranging from Florida and Georgia through the Gulf states into California.

- **SUPER**

Avoid the slang tendency to use it in place of *excellent* or *wonderful.*

- **SUPER-**

The rules in **PREFIXES** apply, but in general, no hyphen. Some frequently used words:

SUPERAGENCY	SUPERHIGHWAY
SUPERCARRIER	SUPERPOWER
SUPERCHARGE	SUPERTANKER

As with all prefixes, however, use a hyphen if the word that follows is a proper noun: *super-Republican.*

- **SUPERINTENDENT**

- **SUPERIOR COURT**

See **COURT NAMES.**

- **SUPERSEDE**

- **SUPERSONIC**

See **MACH NUMBER.**

- **SUPERSONIC TRANSPORT**

S-S-T is acceptable in all references.

- **SUPRA-**

The rules in **PREFIXES** apply, but in general, no hyphen. Some examples:

SUPRAGOVERNMENTAL
SUPRANATIONAL

- **SUPREME COURT OF THE UNITED STATES**

The chief justice is properly the *chief justice of the United States,* not *of the Supreme Court: Chief Justice Warren Burger.*

The proper title for the eight other members of the court is *associate justice.* When used as a formal title before a name, it should be shortened to *justice* unless there are special circumstances: *Justice William Rehnquist, Associate Justice William Rehnquist.*

See **JUDGE.**

- **SUPREME COURTS OF THE STATES**

If a court with this name is not a state's highest tribunal, the fact should be noted. In New York, for example, the Supreme Court is a trial court. Appeals are directed to the Appelate Division of the Supreme Court. The state's highest court is the Court of Appeals.

- **SUPREME SOVIET**

The principal legislative body of the Soviet Union.

- **SURFACE-TO-AIR MISSILE(S)**

"SAM" and *"SAMS"* may be used on second reference.

But avoid the redundant *"SAM" missiles.*

- **SWASTIKA**

- **SWEAT PANTS, SWEAT SHIRT, SWEAT SUIT**

- **SWIMMING**

Scoring is in minutes, if appropriate, seconds and tenths of a second. Extend to hundredths if available.

Events in the United States normally are measured in yards. Olympic contests and other international events are measured in metric units.

Identify events as *100-yard freestyle, women's 100-meter backstroke,* etc., on first reference. Condense to *men's 100 freestyle, women's 100 backstroke* on second reference.

- **SWISSAIR**

Headquarters is in Zurich, Switzerland.

- **SYLLABUS, SYLLABUSES**

- **SYNAGOGUE**

- **SYNAGOGUE COUNCIL OF AMERICA**

See **JEWISH CONGREGATIONS.**

- **SYNOD**

A council of churches or church officials. See the entry for the denomination in question.

- **SYRIAN CATHOLIC CHURCH**

See **EASTERN RITE CHURCHES.**

- **TABLESPOON, TABLESPOONFULS**

Equal to three teaspoons or one-half a fluid ounce.

The metric equivalent is approximately 15 milliliters.

See **LITER.**

- **TABULAR MATTER**

Exceptions may be made to the normal rules for abbreviations, as necessary to make material fit. But make any abbreviations as clear as possible.

- **TAILSPIN**

- **TAIL WIND**

- **TAIWAN**

Use *Taiwan,* not *Formosa,* in references to the Nationalist government on Taiwan and to the island itself.

See **CHINA.**

- **TAKES**

To make the copy as easy to handle as possible, long stories are broken into pages, called *takes.* The number of takes in a script should be kept to the minimum to reduce the chance of any single take getting lost or delayed in transmission.

Generally, a take should run no more than 40 lines, and the first take of a multi-take script should indicate the total number of takes in the slug:

THE SUNRISER (THREE TAKES)

Subsequent takes should also be numbered in the slug:

THE SUNRISER-TAKE 2

- **TAKE-HOME PAY**

- **TAKE OFF** (v.)
TAKEOFF (n. and adj.)

- **TAKE OUT** (v.)
TAKEOUT (n. and adj.)

- **TAKE OVER** (v.)
TAKEOVER (n. and adj.)

- **TAKE UP** (v.)
TAKE-UP (n. and adj.)

- **TALMUD** (TAHL'-MUD)

The collection of writings that constitute the Jewish civil and religious law.

- **TANKS**

Follow the rules for **HYPHEN** and **NUMERALS.** Do not put generic names in quotation marks: *M-60, M-60's.*

- **TAPE RECORDING**

The noun. But hyphenate the verb form: *tape-record.*

- **TASS**

The Soviet government's news agency.

- **TEACHERS COLLEGE**

No apostrophe.

- **TEAM**

See **COLLECTIVE NOUNS.**

- **TEAMMATE**

- **TEAMSTERS UNION**

Acceptable in all references to the

International Brotherhood of Teamsters, Chauffeurs, Warehousemen and Helpers of America.

See the entry under that name.

• TEAR GAS

Two words. See **CHEMICAL MACE.**

• TEASPOON

Equal to one-sixth of a fluid ounce, or one-third of a tablespoon.

The metric equivalent is approximately five milliliters.

See **LITER.**

• TEASPOONFUL, TEASPOONFULS

Not *teaspoonsful.*

• TEEN, TEEN-AGER (n.) **TEEN-AGE** (adj.)

• TELECAST (n.) **TELEVISE** (v.)

• TELEPHONE NUMBERS

Use them only when vital to the story, or, in feature material, when they will provide the listener with extra information that he might find useful.

Wire features should generally move such numbers in an advisory sent with the story, so members have the option of not using them.

When using telephone numbers, use figures and hyphens. Between the exchange and the second set of numbers, use a space, a hyphen and a space: *2-6-2 - 4-0-0-0.* If an area code is used, indicate so in the text: *area code 2-1-2, 2-6-2 - 4-0-0-0* or *the area code is 2-1-2 and the number is 2-6-2 - 4-0-0-0.*

• TELEPROMPTER

A trademark for a type of cuing device.

It is no relation to *Teleprompter corporation,* a cable television company with headquarters in New York.

• TELETYPE

A trademark for a brand of teleprinters and teletypewriters.

• TELEVISION PROGRAM TITLES

Follow the guidelines in **COMPOSITION TITLES.**

Put quotation marks around *show* only if it is part of the formal name. The word *show* may be dropped when it would be cumbersome, such as in a set of listings.

Treat programs named for the star in any of the following ways as appropriate in text or listing: *"The Mary Tyler Moore Show," "Mary Tyler Moore,"* or *the Mary Tyler Moore show.* But be consistent in a story or set of listings.

Use quotation marks also for the title of an episode: *"Chuckles Bites the Dust," an episode* of *"The Mary Tyler Moore Show."*

• TELEVISION STATIONS

See **CALL LETTERS.**

• TELLTALE

• TEMBLOR

See **EARTHQUAKES.**

• TEMPERATURE-HUMIDITY INDEX

See **WEATHER TERMS.**

• TEMPERATURES

Follow the rules for **NUMERALS.** Use a word, not a minus sign, for temperatures below zero.

Some examples:

The day's low was minus ten.

It hit ten below zero at noon.

It's 65 degrees all across the country.

It wil be in the 70's in the southwest.

Temperatures get *higher* or *lower*—not *warmer* or *cooler*.

Wrong: *Cool temperatures dominated the Northwest.*

Right: *Low temperatures dominated the Northwest,* or *cool weather dominated the Northwest.*

See **FAHRENHEIT**; **CELSIUS**; and **WEATHER TERMS.**

• TENDERHEARTED

• TENFOLD

• TENNESSEE VALLEY AUTHORITY

T-V-A is acceptable on second reference.

Headquarters is in Knoxville, Tennessee.

• TENNIS

The scoring units are points, games, sets and matches.

A player wins a point if his opponent fails to return the ball, hits it into the net or hits it out of bounds. A player also wins a point if his opponent is serving and fails to put the ball into play after two attempts (*double faults,* in tennis terms).

A player must win four points to win a game. In tennis scoring, both players begin at love, or zero, and advance to 15, 30, 40 and game. (The numbers 15, 30 and 40 have no point value as such—they are simply tennis terminology for one point, two points and three points.)

The server's score is always called out first.

If a game is tied at 40-all, or *deuce,* play continues until one player has a two-point margin.

A set is won if a player wins six games before his opponent has won five. If a set becomes tied at five games apiece, it goes to the first player to win seven games. If two players who were tied at five games apiece also tie at six games apiece, they normally play a tie-breaker—a game that goes to the first player to win seven points. In some cases, however, the rules call for a player to win by two games.

A match may be either a best-of-three contest that goes to the first player or team to win two sets, or a best-of-five contest that goes to the first player or team to win three sets.

In reporting on a match, some typical sentences might read:

—*Chris Evert won the first set from Sue Barker 6-0, lost the second 3-6 and won the third 7-6.*

—*Chris Evert won her match, defeating Sue Barker 6-0, 3-6, 7-6.*

Note that this format is an exception to usual score style.

• TERA-

A prefix denoting one (t) trillion units of a measure. Move a decimal point 12 places to the right, adding zeros if necessary, to convert to the basic unit: Five-point-five teratons equals five (t) trillion, 500 (m) million tons.

• TEXACO INCORPORATED

Headquarters is in Harrison, New York.

• TEXAS

The state with the second-most land in terms of total area: 262-thousand, 134 square miles.

• THAI

A native or the language of Thailand.

Siam and *Siamese* are historical only.

• THANKSGIVING, THANKSGIVING DAY

The fourth Thursday in November.

• THAT (conjunction)

Use the conjunction *that* to introduce a dependent clause if the sentence sounds or looks awkward without it. There are no hard-and-fast rules, but in general:

—*That* usually may be omitted when a dependent clause immediately follows a form of the verb *to say: The president said he had signed the bill.*

—*That* should be used when a time element intervenes between the verb and the dependent clause: *The president said Monday that he had signed the bill.*

—*That* usually is necessary after some verbs. They include: *advocate, assert, contend, declare, estimate, make clear, point out, propose,* and *state.*

—*That* is required before subordinate clauses beginning with conjunctions such as *after, although, because, before, in addition to, until* and *while: Haldeman said that after he learned of Nixon's intention to resign, he sought pardons for all connected with Watergate.*

When in doubt, include *that.* Omission can hurt.

• THAT, WHICH, WHO, WHOM (pronouns)

Use *who* and *whom* in referring to persons and to animals with a name: *John Jones is the man who helped me.* See the **WHO, WHOM** entry.

Use *that* and *which* in referring to inanimate objects and to animals without a name.

See the **ESSENTIAL CLAUSES, NONESSENTIAL CLAUSES** entry for guidelines on using *that* and *which* to introduce phrases and clauses.

• THEATER

Use this spelling also in all names: *Shubert Theater.*

• THEFT

See the **BURGLARY, LARCENY, ROBBERY, THEFT** entry.

• THEIR, THERE, THEY'RE

Their is a possessive pronoun: *They went to their house.*

There is an adverb indicating direction: *We went there for dinner.*

There also is used with the force of a pronoun for impersonal constructions in which the real subject follows the verb: *There is no food on the table.*

They're is a contraction for *they are.*

• THERETOFORE

Use *until then.*

• THIRD WORLD

The economically developing nations of Africa, Asia and Latin America.

Do not confuse with *non-aligned,* which is a political term. See **NON-ALIGNED.**

• THREE-D

• THREE R'S

They are: *reading, 'riting* and *'rithmetic.*

• THREESOME

• THROWAWAY (n. and adj.)

• THUNDERSTORM

See **WEATHER TERMS.**

• TIDBIT

• TIE, TIED, TYING

• TIE IN (v.)
TIE-IN (n. and adj.)

• TIE UP (v.)
TIE-UP (n. and adj.)

• TIME ELEMENT

Use *today, this morning, this after-*

noon, tonight, and similar terms as appropriate. Do not use the day of the week for references to *yesterday* or *tomorrow.* See **TODAY.**

In references to days within the past seven or within the upcoming seven (a total span of 14 days), use the day of the week. The tense—past or future—will serve to indicate which day of the week you mean: *He made the statement Tuesday. He will make the next announcement Tuesday.* This will enable you to avoid the confusing *last Tuesday, or next Tuesday.*

Avoid awkward placements of the time element, particularly those that suggest the day of the week is the object of a transitive verb: *The police jailed Tuesday.* Potential remedies include the use of the word *on* (see the **ON** entry), rephrasing the sentence, or placing the time element in a different sentence.

• TIME OF DAY

The exact time of day that an event has happened or will happen is not necessary in most stories. Follow these guidelines to determine when it should be included and in what form:

When To Be Specific: There are circumstances under which a specific clock reference is called for.

—Whenever it gives the reader a better picture of the scene: Did the earthquake occur when people were likely to be home asleep or at work? A clock reading for the time in the datelined community is acceptable, although *predawn hours* or *rush hour* often is more graphic.

—Whenever the time is critical to the story: When will the rocket be launched? When will a major political address be broadcast? What is the deadline for meeting a demand?

Deciding on Clock Time: When giving a clock reading, use the time in the community where the story occurred—usually the datelined community—and say so in the body of the story: *It was 3 a-m in London when the first blast occurred.*

Any story or table that involves television or radio programs should use Eastern time, and indicate so. If the program will not be broadcast simultaneously all across the nation, indicate the differing local transmission times.

Zone Abbreviations: See **A-M, P-M.** When adding a zone abbreviation to a time, use a comma: *8 a-m, P-S-T. 9:30 p-m, E-D-T.* But when an A-M or P-M designation is not made, do not use a comma: *tomorrow morning at 9 E-D-T.* The same guidelines apply when spelling out such terms as *Eastern Time, Pacific Daylight Time.*

Such zonal references should be used only if:

—The story involves travel or other activities, such as the closing hour for polling places or the time of an event likely to affect people or developments in more than one time zone.

—The item involves radio or television programs (see above).

—The item is an advisory.

Converting to Eastern Time: Do not convert clock times from other time zones in the continental United States to Eastern time.

If the time is critical in a story from outside the continental United States, provide a conversion to Eastern time using this form:

The kidnappers set a deadline of 9 a-m—that's 3 a-m, Eastern time.

See **TIME ZONES.**

• TIMES

Use figures, except for *noon* and *midnight.* Use a colon to separate hours from minutes, and hyphenate a-m or p-m: *11 a-m, 12:30 p-m.*

Avoid such redundancies as *10 a-m*

this morning or *10 p-m tomorrow night.*

The construction *4 o'clock* is acceptable, but listings with a-m or p-m are preferred.

See **MIDNIGHT** and **TIME ZONES.**

• TIME SEQUENCES

Spell them out in all contexts: *2:30:21.65* should be expressed as *two hours, 30 minutes, and 21-point-65 seconds,* or *two and a half hours, 21-point-65 seconds.*

Tenths and hundredths of a second may be expressed that way—instead of as decimals.

See **NUMERALS; DECIMALS;** and **FRACTIONS.**

• TIME ZONES

See **TIME OF DAY** for guidelines on when to use the clock time and when to use the zonal reference.

Time zones should be spelled out when not accompanied by a clock reading: *Chicago is in the Central time zone.*

When the time zone is abbreviated, use hyphens. If the clock reading includes A-M or P-M, set off the zone with a comma: *9 E-D-T* but *9 a-m, E-D-T.*

Any references to time zones outside of the continental United States are best informalized: *it's 6 a-m in Anchorage* as opposed to *6 a-m, Alaska Standard Time.* Do not abbreviate such time zones.

One exception: *Greenwich Mean Time* may be abbreviated *G-M-T* on the second reference.

• TIPTOP

• TITLEHOLDER

• TITLES

They are getting longer and longer. There are only two ways to handle them in broadcast—make them shorter or arrange the story so the newscaster doesn't turn blue before he gets through the sentence.

Charles Robertson, Undersecretary of State for Economic Affairs, spoke.

Too long.

Try this: *The speaker was Charles Robinson. He's the Undersecretary of State for Economic Affairs.*

Or: *The State Department's top economist, Charles Robinson, spoke.*

When informally shortening a title, however, try to use the complete title somewhere in the story, even if it's the last line. It should be there for members who want to expand on the story themselves.

Abbreviated Titles: The only titles which should be abbreviated are *Mr., Mrs., Ms., and Dr.* Spell out all others.

Past and Future Titles: Use *former,* not *ex-,* for one who no longer holds the title. One who is about to take on a job is the *designate: Secretary of State-designate Haig,* or *President-elect Reagan.*

Unique Titles: If a title applies to only one person in an organization, it should be preceded by *the: George Bush is the vice president.*

See **COURTESY TITLES; MILITARY TITLES; COMPOSITION TITLES.**

• T-N-T

Acceptable in all references for *trinitrotoluene.*

• TOBACCO, TOBACCOS

• TODAY

Use it. Also use *yesterday, last night, tomorrow* and *tonight.* But don't get much more specific than that, especially when writing for the national wires.

When it's *tonight* in New York, it's still *this afternoon* in Hawaii.

Remember, too, that the copy may not be used right away at member stations.

Example: *He will be appearing in court in a few hours.* By the time this is read, the defendant may already have appeared.

Instead, use: *He appears in court today.* Or: *The case of John Smith is on the docket today.*

• TOKYO

Stands alone in datelines.

• TOMORROW

See **TODAY.**

• TOMMY GUN

Alternate trademark for *Thompson submachine gun.*

See **WEAPONS.**

• TON

There are three types:

A *short ton* is equal to two-thousand pounds.

A *long ton,* also known as a *British ton,* is equal to two-thousand, 240 pounds.

A *metric ton* is equal to one-thousand kilograms—roughly two-thousand, 204-point-62 pounds.

Conversion Equations:

Short to long: Multiply by .89 (5 short tons x .89 = 4.45 long tons).

Short to metric: Multiply by .9 (5 short tons x .9 = 4.5 metric tons).

Long to short: Multiply by 1.12 (5 long tons x 1.12 = 5.6 short tons).

Long to metric: Multiply by 1.02 (5 long tons x 1.02 = 5.1 metric tons).

Metric to short: Multiply by 1.1 (5 metric tons x 1.1 = 5.5 short tons).

Metric to long: Multiply by .98 (5 metric tons x 98 = 4.9 long tons).

See **METRIC SYSTEM.**

See **KILOTON** for units used to measure the power of nuclear explosions.

See **OIL** for formulas to convert the tonnage of oil shipments to gallons.

• TONIGHT

All that's necessary is *8 tonight,* or *8 p-m.* Avoid the redundant *8 p-m tonight.*

See **TODAY.**

• TOPS

A tops is a separate that provides significant new material to a story already covered in the day's report. After a story breaks, it may be topped out several times. If a story's first use is in a summary, and it is updated then with a separate, that can be slugged tops:

HOSTAGES (TOPS)

If the updating material is of an urgent nature, the story can also be slugged:

U R G E N T

HOSTAGES (TOPS)

But do not use the urgent slug if the story is a detailed analysis or if it is an advance item.

• TORNADO

See **WEATHER TERMS.**

• TORONTO

The city in Canada stands alone in datelines.

• TORY, TORIES

An exception to the normal practice when forming the plural of a proper name ending in y.

The words are acceptable on second reference to the *Conservative Party* in Britain and its members.

• **TOTAL, TOTALED, TOTALING**
The phrase *a total of* often is redundant.
It may be used, however, to avoid a figure at the start of a sentence: *A total of 650 people were killed in holiday traffic accidents.*

• **TOWARD**
Not *towards.*

• **TRACK AND FIELD**
Scoring is in distance or time, depending on the event.
Distance events in the United States are normally in feet and yards. Olympic contests and other international events are measured in metric units.
Spell out all times in the body of the story. Extend times to hundredths if available: *six seconds; seven and 45-hundredths; four hours, 35 minutes; 24 and three-tenths seconds.*
Follow the rules for **NUMERALS; DECIMALS; FRACTIONS.**

• **TRADE IN** (v.)
TRADE-IN (n. and adj.)

• **TRADEMARK**
A trademark is a brand, symbol or word used by a manufacturer or dealer and protected by law to prevent a competitor from using it: *Astroturf,* for a type of artificial grass, for example.
In general, use a generic equivalent unless the trademark name is essential to the story.
Many trademarks are listed separately in this book, together with generic equivalents.
The U-S Trademark Association, located in New York, is a helpful source of information about trademarks.
See **BRAND NAMES** and **SERVICE MARKS.**

• **TRADE OFF** (v.)
TRADE-OFF (n. and adj.)

• **TRAFFIC, TRAFFICKED, TRAFFICKING**

• **TRANS-**
The rules in **PREFIXES** apply, but in general no hyphen. Some examples:

TRANSCONTINENTAL	TRANSSEXUAL
TRANSMIGRATE	TRANSSHIP
TRANSOCEANIC	TRANS-SIBERIAN

Also: TRANS-ATLANTIC and TRANS-PACIFIC. These are exceptions to Webster's New World in keeping with the general rule that a hyphen is needed when a prefix precedes a capitalized word.

• **TRANSFER, TRANSFERRED, TRANSFERRING**

• **TRANSSEXUALS**
See **SEX CHANGES.**

• **TRANS WORLD AIRLINES**
A *T-W-A airliner* is acceptable in any reference.
Headquarters is in New York.

• **TRAVEL, TRAVELED, TRAVELING, TRAVELER**

• **TRAVELOGUE**
Not *travelog.*

• **TREASURER**
Caution: The secretary of the U-S Department of the Treasury is not the same person as the U-S treasurer.

• **TREASURY BILLS, TREASURY BONDS, TREASURY NOTES**
See **LOAN TERMINOLOGY.**

• **TRIBES**
See the **NATIONALITIES AND RACES** entry.

• TRIGGER-HAPPY
Use the term with caution.

• TRINIDAD AND TOBAGO
In datelines on stories from this island nation, use a community name followed by either *Trinidad* or *Tobago* —but not both—depending on where the community is located.

• TRISTAR
The proper name that Lockheed Aircraft Corporation uses for its L-Ten-Eleven jetliner.

• TROOP, TROOPS, TROUPE
A *troop* is a group of persons or animals. *Troops* mean several such groups, particularly groups of soldiers.

Use *troupe* only for ensembles of actors, dancers, singers, and the like.

• TROPICAL DEPRESSION
See **WEATHER TERMS.**

• TRUMAN, HARRY S.
With a period after the initial. Truman once said there was no need for the period because the *S* did not stand for a name. Asked in the early 1960's about his preference, he replied, "It makes no difference to me."

AP style has called for the period since that time.

• TRUSTEE (TRUHS-TEE')
A person to whom another's property or the management of another's property is entrusted.

• TRUSTY (TRUHS'-TEE)
A prison inmate granted special privileges as a trustworthy person.

• TRY OUT (v.)
TRYOUT (n.)

• TSAR
Use *czar.*

• T-SHIRT

• TUBERCULOSIS
T-B is acceptable on second reference.

• TUNE UP (v.)
TUNEUP (n. and adj.)

• TURBOPROP
See **AIRCRAFT TERMS.**

• T-V
Acceptable as an adjective or in such constructions as *cable TV.* But do not normally use as a noun unless part of a quotation.

• 20TH CENTURY-FOX, TWENTIETH CENTURY FUND, TWENTIETH CENTURY LIMITED
Follow an organization's practice. See **COMPANY NAMES.**

• TYPHOONS
Use *it* or *its*—not *he* or *she* or *her* or *his*—when referring to typhoons.

Put the proper name of the storm in quotation marks: *typhoon "Alexis."*

And do not let the presence of women's name, when it is used, provide an excuse for the use of sexist images in describing the behavior of the storm.

See **WEATHER TERMS.**

• U-BOAT

• U-F-O, U-F-O'S

Acceptable in all references to *Unidentified Flying Object(s).*

• U-H-F

Acceptable in all references for *ultrahigh frequency.*

• UKRAINIAN CATHOLIC CHURCH

See **EASTERN RITE CHURCHES**

• UKRAINIAN SOVIET SOCIALIST REPUBLIC

See the **RUSSIA, SOVIET UNION** entry.

• UKULELE

• ULSTER

A colloquial synonym for *Northern Ireland.* See **UNITED KINGDOM.**

• ULTRA-

The rules in **PREFIXES** apply, but in general, no hyphen. Some examples:

ULTRAMODERN	ULTRASONIC
ULTRANATIONALISM	ULTRAVIOLET

• ULTRAHIGH FREQUENCY

U-H-F is acceptable in all references.

• UN-

The rules in **PREFIXES** apply, but in general, no hyphen. Some examples:

UN-AMERICAN	UNNECESSARY
UNARMED	UNSHAVEN

• U-N

Used as an adjective, but not as a noun, for *United Nations.*

See **UNITED NATIONS.**

• UNCLE TOM

A term of contempt applied to a black person, taken from the main character in Harriet Beecher Stowe's novel *"Uncle Tom's Cabin."* It describes the practice of kowtowing to whites to curry favor.

Do not apply it to an individual. It carries potentially libelous connotations of having sold one's convictions for money, prestige or political influence.

• UNDER-

The rules in **PREFIXES** apply, but in general, no hyphen. Some examples:

UNDERDOG	UNDERSHERIFF
UNDERGROUND	UNDERSOLD

• UNDERSECRETARY

One word.

• UNDER WAY

Two words in virtually all uses: *The project is under way. The naval maneuvers are under way.*

One word only when used as an adjective before a noun in a nautical sense: *an underway flotilla.*

• UNEMPLOYMENT RATE

In the United States, this estimate of the number of unemployed residents seeking work is compiled monthly by the Bureau of Labor Statistics, an agency of the Labor Department.

Each month the bureau selects a nationwide cross section of the population and conducts interviews to determine the size of the work force.

The *work force* is defined as the number of persons with jobs and the number looking for jobs.

The *unemployment rate* is expressed as a percentage figure. The essential calculation involves dividing the total work force into the number of persons looking for jobs, followed by adjustments to reflect variable factors such as seasonal trends.

• "UNESCO"

Acceptable on first reference for the *United Nations Educational, Scientific and Cultural Organization,* but a subsequent reference should give the full name.

• "UNICEF"

Acceptable in all references for the *United Nations Children's Fund.* The words *International* and *Emergency,* originally part of the name, have been dropped.

• UNIFORM CODE OF MILITARY JUSTICE

The laws covering members of the armed forces.

• UNINTERESTED

See the **DISINTERESTED, UNINTERESTED** entry.

• UNION NAMES

The formal names of unions may be condensed to conventionally accepted short forms.

Follow union practice in the use of the word *worker* in shortened forms. Among major unions, all except the *United Steelworkers* use two words: *United Auto Workers, United Mine Workers.*

When *worker* is used generically, make *autoworkers* one word in keeping with widespread practice; use two words for other job descriptions: *bakery workers, mine workers, steel workers.*

See the individual entries for more information on many of these unions frequently in the news:

AMALGAMATED CLOTHING AND TEXTILE WORKERS UNION OF AMERICA
AMALGAMATED TRANSIT UNION
AMERICAN FEDERATION OF GOVERNMENT EMPLOYEES
AMERICAN FEDERATION OF LABOR AND CONGRESS OF INDUSTRIAL ORGANIZATIONS
AMERICAN FEDERATION OF MUSICIANS
AMERICAN FEDERATION OF STATE, COUNTY AND MUNICIPAL EMPLOYEES
AMERICAN FEDERATION OF TEACHERS
AMERICAN FEDERATION OF TELEVISION AND RADIO ARTISTS
AMERICAN POSTAL WORKERS UNION
BAKERY AND CONFECTIONARY WORKERS' INTERNATIONAL UNION OF AMERICA
BRICKLAYERS, MASONS AND PLASTERERS' INTERNATIONAL UNION OF AMERICA
BROTHERHOOD OF RAILWAY, AIRLINE AND STEAMSHIP CLERKS, FREIGHT HANDLERS, EXPRESS AND STATION EMPLOYEES
COMMUNICATIONS WORKERS OF AMERICA
HOTEL AND RESTAURANT EMPLOYEES AND BARTENDERS INTERNATIONAL UNION
INTERNATIONAL ASSOCIATION OF MACHINISTS AND AEROSPACE WORKERS
INTERNATIONAL BROTHERHOOD OF ELECTRICAL WORKERS
INTERNATIONAL BROTHERHOOD OF PAINTERS AND ALLIED TRADES OF THE UNITED STATES AND CANADA
INTERNATIONAL BROTHERHOOD OF TEAMSTERS, CHAUFFEURS, WAREHOUSEMEN AND HELPERS OF AMERICA
INTERNATIONAL LADIES' GARMENT WORKERS UNION

INTERNATIONAL LONGSHOREMEN'S ASSOCIATION
LABORERS' INTERNATIONAL UNION OF NORTH AMERICA
NATIONAL ASSOCIATION OF LETTER CARRIERS
NEWSPAPER GUILD, THE
OIL, CHEMICAL AND ATOMIC WORKERS INTERNATIONAL UNION
RETAIL CLERKS INTERNATIONAL ASSOCIATION
SHEET METAL WORKERS INTERNATIONAL ASSOCIATION
UNITED AUTOMOBILE, AEROSPACE AND AGRICULTURAL IMPLEMENT WORKERS OF AMERICA
UNITED BROTHERHOOD OF CARPENTERS AND JOINERS OF AMERICA
UNITED ELECTRICAL, RADIO AND MACHINE WORKERS OF AMERICA
UNITED MINE WORKERS OF AMERICA
UNITED RUBBER, CORK, LINOLEUM AND PLASTIC WORKERS OF AMERICA
UNITED STEELWORKERS OF AMERICA

• UNION OF AMERICAN HEBREW CONGREGATIONS

See **JEWISH CONGREGATIONS.**

• UNION OF ORTHODOX JEWISH CONGREGATIONS OF AMERICA

See **JEWISH CONGREGATIONS.**

• UNION OF SOVIET SOCIALIST REPUBLICS

Do not use the abbreviation U-S-S-R in any context.

Use *Soviet Union* in datelines and as the first reference in the body of a story.

Neither term is synonymous with *Russia;* see **RUSSIA, SOVIET UNION** for details and a list of the republics.

• UNION SHOP

See **CLOSED SHOP.**

• UNIQUE

It means one of a kind. Do not describe something as *rather unique* or *most unique.*

• UNITED AIRLINES

A subsidiary of *U-A-L Incorporated.* Headquarters is in Chicago.

• UNITED ARAB EMIRATES

Do not abbreviate in any context. Generally, on second reference, *the Emirates.*

• UNITED AUTOMOBILE, AEROSPACE AND AGRICULTURAL IMPLEMENT WORKERS OF AMERICA

The shortened forms *United Auto Workers* and *United Auto Workers union* are acceptable in all references.

U-A-W and *the Auto Workers* are acceptable on second reference.

Use *autoworker* or *autoworkers* in generic references to workers in the auto industry.

Headquarters is in Detroit.

• UNITED BROTHERHOOD OF CARPENTERS AND JOINERS OF AMERICA

The shortened form *Carpenters union* is acceptable in all references.

Headquarters is in Washington.

• UNITED CHURCH OF CHRIST

See **CONGREGATIONALIST CHURCHES.**

• UNITED ELECTRICAL, RADIO AND MACHINE WORKERS OF AMERICA

The shortened form *Electrical Workers union* is acceptable in all references.

Headquarters is in New York.

• UNITED KINGDOM

It consists of Great Britain and Northern Ireland.

Great Britain (or *Britain*) consists of England, Scotland and Wales.

Ireland is independent of the United Kingdom.

See **DATELINES** and **IRELAND.**

• UNITED KLANS OF AMERICA

See **KU KLUX KLAN.**

• UNITED METHODIST CHURCH

See **METHODIST CHURCHES.**

• UNITED MINE WORKERS OF AMERICA

The shortened forms *United Mine Workers* and *United Mine Workers union* are acceptable in all references.

U-M-W and *the Mine Workers* are acceptable on second reference.

Use *mine workers* or *miners* in generic references to workers in the industry.

Headquarters is in Washington.

• UNITED NATIONS

Spell it out. The abbreviation *U-N* may be used only as an adjective.

In datelines:

(UNITED NATIONS) - -

Use *U-N General Assembly, U-N Secretariat* and *U-N Security Council* on the first reference. The *U-N* can be dropped in subsequent references.

Only the Security Council has the power of enforcement in the United Nations. But it also is subject to the veto power of the five permanent members.

• UNITED PRESBYTERIAN CHURCH IN THE UNITED STATES OF AMERICA

See **PRESBYTERIAN CHURCHES.**

• UNITED PRESS INTERNATIONAL

A privately-owned news agency formed in 1958 in a merger of the United Press and the International News Service.

Use the full name on the first reference. *U-P-I* is acceptable on second reference.

• UNITED RUBBER, CORK, LINOLEUM AND PLASTIC WORKERS OF AMERICA

The shortened forms *United Rubber Workers* and *United Rubber Workers union* are acceptable in all references.

Use *rubber workers* in generic references to workers in the rubber industry.

Headquarters is in Akron, Ohio.

• UNITED SERVICE ORGANIZATIONS

U-S-O is acceptable on second reference.

• UNITED STATES

U-S is acceptable in all references.

For organizations with names beginning with the words United States, see entries alphabetized under U-S.

• UNITED STEELWORKERS OF AMERICA

The shortened forms *United Steelworkers* and *United Steelworkers union* are acceptable in all references.

Use *steel workers* (two words) in generic references to workers in the steel industry. (Many Steelworkers are employed in other industries and thus are not steel workers.)

Headquarters is in Pittsburgh.

• UNITED SYNAGOGUE OF AMERICA

Not *synagogues.* See **JEWISH CONGREGATIONS.**

• UP-

The rules in **PREFIXES** apply, but in general, no hyphen. Some examples:

UP-END	UPSTATE
UPGRADE	UPTOWN

• -UP

Follow Webster's New World Dictionary. Hyphenate if not listed there.

Some frequently used words (all are nouns, some also are used as adjectives):

BREAKUP	MAKEUP
BUILDUP	MIX-UP
CALL-UP	MOCK-UP
CHANGE-UP	PILEUP
CHECKUP	PUSH-UP
CLEANUP	ROUNDUP
CLOSE-UP	RUNNERS-UP
COVER-UP	SETUP
CRACKUP	SHAKE-UP
FOLLOW-UP	SHAPE-UP
FRAME-UP	SMASHUP
GROWN-UP	SPEEDUP
HOLDUP	TIE-UP
LETUP	WALK-UP
LINEUP	WINDUP

Use two words when any of these occurs as a verb.

See **SUFFIXES.**

• UPDATES

These are story-related advisories for AP members. They are not air-ready, and are designed solely to inform newsrooms of new developments on an urgent basis—before a story can be written. In addition, they often provide information on the way the updated story will be handled.

UPDATE
PRESIDENT REAGAN HAS LEFT FOR CAMP DAVID, AND IS EXPECTED TO ARRIVE IN ABOUT 20 MINUTES. DETAILS IN THE UPCOMING FIFTH SUMMARY.
THE AP

• U-P-I

Acceptable on second reference for *United Press International.*

• UPSIDE DOWN (adv.)
UPSIDE-DOWN (adj.)

The cat turned upside down. She made an upside-down cake. The book is upside-down.

• UPWARD

Not *upwards.*

• URGENTS

An urgent is a short, separate story providing an update on a story of importance and urgency.

Generally, urgents are sent on newswires when expected developments occur in major stories, or when new stories of moderate—but not overwhelming—importance break. They take three bells.

Extremely important stories take *bulletin* treatment. Transcendant stories are treated as *flash* material. These are quite rare.

The form for urgents:

U R G E N T
(WASHINGTON) - - PRESIDENT KENNEDY HAS SIGNED THE NUCLEAR TEST BAN TREATY. IN A WHITE HOUSE CEREMONY . . .

See **BULLETIN** and **FLASH.**

• U-S

Acceptable in all references to *United States.*

• U-S-AIR

Formerly Allegheny Airlines. Headquarters is in Washington.

• U-S AIR FORCE

See **AIR FORCE; MILITARY ACADEMIES;** and **MILITARY TITLES.**

• U-S ARMY

See **MILITARY ACADEMIES** and **MILITARY TITLES.**

• U-S COAST GUARD

See **COAST GUARD; MILITARY ACADEMIES;** and **MILITARY TITLES.**

• U-S CONFERENCE OF MAYORS

The members are mayors of cities with 30-thousand or more residents. See **NATIONAL LEAGUE OF CITIES.**

Use *the conference* or *the mayors conference* on the second reference.

There is no organization with the name *National Mayors' Conference.*

• U-S COURT OF APPEALS

The court is divided into eleven circuits:

District of Columbia Circuit.

First Circuit: Maine, Massachusetts, New Hampshire, Rhode Island, Puerto Rico. Based in Boston.

Second Circuit: Connecticut, New York, Vermont. Based in New York.

Third Circuit: Delaware, New Jersey, Pennsylvania, Virgin Islands. Based in Philadelphia.

Fourth Circuit: Maryland, North Carolina, South Carolina, Virginia, West Virginia. Based in Richmond, Virginia.

Fifth Circuit: Alabama, Florida, Georgia, Louisiana, Mississippi, Texas, Canal Zone. Based in New Orleans.

Sixth Circuit: Kentucky, Michigan, Ohio, Tennessee. Based in Cincinnati.

Seventh Circuit: Illinois, Indiana, Wisconsin. Based in Chicago.

Eighth Circuit: Arkansas, Iowa, Minnesota, Missouri, Nebraska, North Dakota, South Dakota. Based in St. Louis.

Ninth Circuit: Alaska, California, Hawaii, Idaho, Montana, Nevada, Oregon, Washington, Guam. Based in San Francisco.

Tenth Circuit: Colorado, Kansas, New Mexico, Oklahoma, Utah, Wyoming. Based in Denver.

The courts do not always sit in cities where they are based. Sessions may be held in other major cities within each region.

Reference Forms: A phrase such as *a federal appeals court* is acceptable on first reference.

On first reference to the full name, use *U-S Court of Appeals* or a circuit name: *Eighth U-S Circuit Court of Appeals* or *the U-S Court of Appeals for the Eighth Circuit.*

U-S Circuit Court of Appeals without a circuit number is a misnomer and should not be used.

In shortened and subsequent references: *the Court of Appeals, the Second Circuit, the appeals court, the appellate court(s), the circuit court(s), the court.*

Do not create non-existent entities such as *San Francisco Court of Appeals.* Make it *the U-S Court of Appeals in San Francisco.*

Jurists: The formal title for the jurists on the court is *judge: U-S Circuit Judge Homer Thornberry* is preferred to *U-S Appeals Judge Homer Thornberry,* but either is acceptable.

See **JUDGE.**

• U-S COURT OF CLAIMS

This court handles suits against the federal government. It is based in Washington.

• U-S COURT OF CUSTOMS AND PATENT APPEALS

This court handles appeals involving customs, patents and copyrights. It is based in Washington.

• USHER

Use for both men and women.

U-S INFORMATION AGENCY
The abbreviation *U-S-I-A* is acceptable on second reference.

U-S MILITARY ACADEMY
See **MILITARY ACADEMIES.**

U-S NAVY
See **MILITARY ACADEMIES** and **MILITARY TITLES.**

U-S POSTAL SERVICE
The Postal Service is acceptable on any reference.

U-S POSTAL SERVICE DIRECTORY OF POST OFFICES
The reference for U-S place names not covered in this book.

U-S-S
Stands for *United States Ship, Steamer* or *Steamship.* It is used before the name of a vessel, and is preceded by *the: The U-S-S "Enterprise."* Note that U-S-S does not go inside the quotation marks.

In datelines:

(ABOARD THE U-S-S "IOWA") - -

U-S SUPREME COURT
See **SUPREME COURT OF THE UNITED STATES.**

U-S TAX COURT
This is an administrative body within the U-S Treasury Department rather than part of the judicial branch. It handles appeals in tax cases.

U-TURN (n. and adj.)

V
See **VERBS.**

VACUUM

VALIUM
A trademark for a brand of tranquilizer and muscle relaxant. It also may be called *diazepam.*

VARIG BRAZILIAN AIRLINES
Headquarters is in Rio de Janeiro.

VATICAN CITY
Stands alone in datelines.

V-E DAY
May Eighth, 1945, the day the surrender of Germany was announced, officially ending the European fighting in World War Two.

V-EIGHT
An engine configuration.

VENDOR

VENEREAL DISEASE
V-D is acceptable on second reference.

VERBAL
See the **ORAL, VERBAL, WRITTEN** entry.

VERBS
The abbreviation *v.* is used in this book to identify the spelling of the verb forms of words frequently misspelled.

Split Forms: In general, avoid awkward constructions that split infinitive forms of a verb (*to leave, to help*) or compound forms (*had left, are found out*).

Awkward: *She was ordered to immediately leave on an assignment.*

Preferred: *She was ordered to leave immediately on an assignment.*

Awkward: *There stood the wagon that we had early last autumn left by the barn.*

Preferred: *There stood the wagon that we had left by the barn early last autumn.*

Occasionally, however, a split is not awkward and is necessary to convey the meaning:

He wanted to really help his mother. Those who lie are often found out. How has your health been? The budget was tentatively approved.

VERNACULAR
The native language of a country or place. A vernacular term that has achieved widespread recognition may be used without explanation if appropriate in the context.

Terms not widely known should be explained when used. In general, they are appropriate only when illustrating vernacular speech.

See **COLLOQUIALISMS** and **DIALECT.**

VERSUS
Do not abbreviate.

VERY HIGH FREQUENCY
V-H-F is acceptable in all references.

• VETERANS ADMINISTRATION
No apostrophe. *V-A* may be used on second reference.

• VETERANS DAY
Formerly Armistice Day, November Eleventh, the anniversary of the armistice that ended World War One in 1918.

• VETERANS OF FOREIGN WARS
V-F-W is acceptable on the second reference.
Headquarters is in Kansas City.

• VETO, VETOES (n.)
The verb forms: *vetoed, vetoing.*

• V-H-F
Acceptable in all references for *very high frequency.*

• VICE-
Use two words: *vice admiral, vice chairman, vice chancellor, vice consul, vice president, vice principal, vice regent, vice secretary.*
Several are exceptions to Webster's New World. The two-word rule has been adopted for consistency in handling the similar terms.

• VICE PRESIDENT
See **PRESIDENT.** The first name of the vice president of the United States may be dropped on the first reference.

• VICE-VERSA

• VIDEOTAPE (n. and v.)

• VIE, VIED, VYING

• VIET CONG

• V-I-P, V-I-P'S
Acceptable in all references to *very important people.*

• VIRGINIA
Legally a commonwealth, not a state.

• VIRGIN ISLANDS
Use with a community name in datelines on stories from the U-S Virgin Islands. Do not abbreviate.
Identify an individual island in the text if relevant.
See **DATELINES** and **BRITISH VIRGIN ISLANDS.**

• VITAMINS
Hyphenate their names, following the rules for **NUMERALS:** *vitamin b-12, vitamin a.*

• V-J DAY
The day of victory for the Allied Forces over Japan in World War Two.
It can be marked on two days: August 15th, 1945, the day fighting ended, or September second, 1945, the day Japan officially surrendered.

• V-NECK (n. and adj.)

• VOLKSWAGEN OF AMERICA, INCORPORATED
The name of the American subsidiary of the German carmaker known as *Volkswagen A-G.*
American headquarters is in Englewood Cliffs, New Jersey.

• VOLLEY, VOLLEYS

• VOLUNTEERS IN SERVICE TO AMERICA
"VISTA" is acceptable on second reference.

• VOODOO

• VOTE-GETTER

• VOTE TABULATIONS

For treatment of voter returns in the body of a story, see **ELECTION RETURNS.**

When tabulating returns, always use figures, since this is source material, not air-ready copy:

CARTER	*40,825,839*
FORD	*39,147,770*

• VULGARITIES

See the **OBSCENITIES, PROFANITIES, VULGARITIES** entry.

• "WAC"

"WAC" is no longer used by the military, but is an acceptable term in a reference to a woman who served in what used to be the *Women's Army Corps.*

"WAC" is acceptable on second reference to the corps.

• **WAITER** (male)
WAITRESS (female)

• **WALES**

Use *Wales* after the names of Welsh communities in datelines.

See **DATELINES** and **UNITED KINGDOM.**

• **WALK UP** (v.)
WALK-UP (n. and adj.)

• **WALL STREET**

• **WARHEAD**

• **WAR HORSE, WARHORSE**

Two words for a horse used in battle.

One word for a veteran of many battles: *He is a political warhorse.*

• **WARLIKE**

• **WARLORD**

• **WARNER COMMUNICATIONS INCORPORATED**

Headquarters is in New York.

The motion picture division is Warner Brothers.

• **WARRANT OFFICER**

See **MILITARY TITLES.**

• **WARTIME**

• **WASHED-UP**

• **WASHINGTON**

Use *Washington state* or *state of Washington* if necessary to distinguish between the state and Washington D-C.

See **STATE** and **STATE NAMES.**

• **WASHINGTON'S BIRTHDAY**

It is calculated as February 22nd.

The federal legal holiday is the third Monday in February.

• **WASTEBASKET**

• **WATERSPOUT**

See **WEATHER TERMS.**

• **WAVE, "WAVES"**

Wave is no longer used by the military, but is acceptable in a reference to a woman who served in the Navy.

"WAVES" is acceptable on second reference to the *Women's Auxiliary Volunteer Emergency Service,* an organizational distinction made for women in the Navy during World War Two but subsequently discontinued.

• **WEAK-KNEED**

• **WEAPONS**

Gun is an acceptable term for any firearm. Note the following definitions and forms in dealing with weapons and ammunition:

Anti-aircraft: A heavy-caliber cannon that fires explosive shells. It is designed for defense against air attack. The form: *a 105-millimeter anti-aircraft gun.*

Artillery: A carriage-mounted cannon.

Automatic: A kind of pistol designed for automatic or semiautomatic firing.

Its cartridges are held in a magazine. The form: *a 22-caliber automatic.*

Buckshot: See *shot,* page 284.

Bullet: The projectile fired by a rifle, pistol or machine gun. Together with metal casing, primer and propellant, it forms a *cartridge.*

Caliber: A measurement of the diameter of the inside of a gun barrel except for most shotguns. Measurement is in either millimeters or decimal fractions of an inch. The word *caliber* is not used when giving the metric measurement.

The forms: *a nine-millimeter pistol, a 22-caliber rifle.*

Cannon: A large-caliber weapon, usually supported on some type of carriage, that fires explosive projectiles. The form: *a 105-millimeter cannon.*

Carbine: A short-barreled rifle. The form: *an m-three carbine.*

Cartridge: See *bullet* above.

Colt: Named for Samuel Colt, it designates a make of weapon or ammunition developed for Colt handguns. The forms: *a "Colt" 45-caliber revolver, a "Colt-45,"* and *45 "long Colt"* ammunition.

Gauge: This word describes the size of a shotgun. Gauge is expressed in terms of the number per pound of round lead balls with a diameter equal to the size of the barrel. The bigger the number, the smaller the shotgun.

Some common shotgun gauges:

Gauge	Interior Diameter
10	.775 inches
12	.729 inches
16	.662 inches
20	.615 inches
28	.550 inches
.410	.410 inches

The 410 actually is a caliber, but commonly is called a gauge. The forms: *a 12-gauge shotgun, a 410-gauge shotgun.*

Howitzer: A cannon shorter than a gun of the same caliber employed to fire projectiles at relatively high angles at a target, such as opposing forces behind a ridge. The form: *a 105-millimeter howitzer.*

Machine Gun: An automatic gun, usually mounted on a support, that fires as long as the trigger is depressed. The forms: *a 50-caliber "browning" machine gun.*

Magnum: A trademark for a type of high-powered cartridge with a larger case and a larger powder charge than other cartridges of approximately the same caliber. The form: *a 357-caliber "magnum" a 44-caliber "magnum."*

M-one, M-14: These and similar combinations of a letter and figure(s) designate rifles used by the military. The forms: *an M-one rifle, an M-14 carbine.*

Musket: A heavy, smooth-bore, large-caliber shoulder firearm fired by means of a matchlock, a wheel lock, a flintlock or a percussion lock. Its ammunition is a musket ball.

Pistol: A hand weapon. It may be a *revolver* or an *automatic.* Its measurements are in calibers. The form: *a 38-caliber pistol.*

Revolver: A kind of pistol. Its cartridges are held in chambers in a cylinder that revolves. The form: *a 45-caliber revolver.*

Rifle: A firearm with a rifled bore. It uses bullets or cartridges for ammunition. Its size is measured in calibers. The form: *a 22-caliber rifle.*

Saturday Night Special: The popular name for the type of cheap pistol used for impulsive crimes, often committed Saturday nights.

Shell: The word applies to military or naval ammunition and to shotgun ammunition.

Shot: Small lead or steel pellets fired by shotguns. A shotgun shell usually contains one to two ounces of shot. Do not use *shot* interchangeably with *buckshot,* which refers only to the largest shot sizes.

Shotgun: A small-arms gun with a smooth bore, sometimes double-barreled. Its ammunition is shot. Its size is measured in gauges. The form: *a 12-gauge shotgun.*

Submachine Gun: A lightweight automatic or semiautomatic gun firing small-arms ammunition.

• WEATHER-BEATEN

• WEATHER BUREAU

See NATIONAL WEATHER SERVICE.

• WEATHERMAN

The preferred term is *forecaster.*

• WEATHER TERMS

The following are based on definitions used by the National Weather Service. All temperatures are Fahrenheit.

Blizzard: Wind speeds of 35 miles-an-hour and considerable falling and-or blowing of snow with visibility near zero.

Coastal Waters: The waters within about 20 miles of the coast, including bays, harbors and sounds.

Cyclone: A storm with strong winds rotating about a moving center of low atmospheric pressure.

The word sometimes is used in the United States to mean *tornado* and in the Indian Ocean area to mean *hurricane.* Because of the confusion that can result, use the more precise words *tornado* or *hurricane.*

Degree-Day: A degree-day is a computation that gauges the amount of heating or cooling needed for a building. An uninsulated building will maintain an inside temperature of 70 degrees if the outside temperature is 65 degrees. A degree-day is a one-degree difference in this equilibrium for one day (a temperature of 64 degrees for 24 hours), or its equivalent such as a two-degree difference for half a day (a temperature of 63 for 12 hours).

A temperature of ten below zero for 24 hours yields 75 degree-days. A temperature of 85 degrees for six hours yields five degree-days.

Dust Storm: Visibility of one-half mile or less due to dust and wind speeds of 30 miles-an-hour or more.

Flash Flood: A sudden, violent flood. It typically occurs after a heavy rain or the melting of a heavy snow.

Flash Flood Warning: Warns that flash flooding is imminent or in progress. People in the affected area should take necessary precautions immediately.

Flash Flood Watch: Alerts the public that flash flooding is possible. Those in the affected area are urged to be ready to take additional precautions if a flash flood warning is issued or if flooding is observed.

Flood: Stories about floods usually tell how high the water is and where it is expected to crest. Such a story should also, for comparison, list flood stage and how high the water is above, or below, flood stage.

Wrong: *The river is expected to crest at 39 feet.*

Right: *The river is expected to crest at 39 feet, 12 feet above flood stage.*

Freeze: Describes conditions when the temperature at or near the surface is expected to be below 32 degrees during the growing season. Adjectives such as *severe* or *hard* are used if a cold spell exceeding two days is expected.

A freeze may or may not be accompanied by the formation of frost. However, use of the term *freeze* usually is restricted for occasions when wind or other conditions prevent frost.

Freezing Drizzle, Freezing Rain: Synonyms for *ice storm.*

Frost: Describes the formation of thin ice crystals, which might develop under conditions similar to dew except for the minimum temperatures involved. Phrases such as *frost in low places* or *scattered light frost* are used when appropriate. The term *frost* seldom appears in state forecasts unless rather heavy frost is expected over an extensive area.

Funnel Cloud: A violent, rotating column of air that does not touch the ground, usually a pendant from a cumulonimbus (kyoo-myoo-loh-nim'-buhs) cloud.

Gale: Sustained winds within the range of 39 to 54 miles-an-hour—34 to 47 knots.

Heavy Snow: It generally means:

—A fall accumulating to four inches or more in six hours, or

—One accumulating to six inches or more in 24 hours.

High Wind: Normally indicates that sustained winds of 39 miles-per-hour or greater are expected to persist for one hour or longer.

Hurricane or Typhoon: A warm-core tropical cyclone in which the minimum sustained surface wind is 74 miles-an-hour or more.

Hurricanes are spawned east of the international date line. Typhoons develop west of that line.

When a hurricane or typhoon loses strength—as measured by its wind speed—it is reduced to *tropical storm* status. This usually happens after the storm hits land.

Hurricane Eye: The relatively calm area in the center of the storm. In this area, winds are light and the sky is often covered only partly by clouds.

Hurricane Season: The portion of the year that has a relatively high incidence of hurricanes. In the Atlantic, Caribbean and Gulf of Mexico, it is from June through November. In the eastern Pacific, it is June through November 15th. In the central Pacific, it is June through October.

Hurricane Tide: Same as *storm tide.*

Hurricane Warning: Warns that one or both of these dangerous effects of a hurricane are expected in a specified coastal area in 24 hours or less:

—Sustained winds of 74 miles-an-hour—64 knots—or higher.

—Dangerously high water or a combination of dangerously high water and exceptionally high waves, even though winds expected may be less than hurricane force.

Hurricane Watch: An announcement for specific areas that a hurricane or incipient hurricane conditions may pose a threat to coastal and inland communities.

Ice Storm, Freezing Drizzle, Freezing Rain: Describes the freezing of drizzle or rain on objects as it strikes them. *Freezing drizzle* and *freezing rain* are synonyms for *ice storm.*

Ice Storm Warning: Reserved for occasions when significant, and possibly damaging, accumulations of ice are expected.

National Hurricane Center: The National Weather Service's National Hurricane Center in Miami has overall responsibility for tracking and providing information about tropical depressions, tropical storms and hurricanes in the Atlantic Ocean, Gulf of Mexico and Caribbean Sea.

The service's Eastern Pacific Hurricane Center in San Francisco is responsible for hurricane information in the Pacific Ocean area north of the equator and east of 140 degrees west longitude.

The service's Central Pacific Hurricane Center in Honolulu is responsible for hurricane information in the Pacific Ocean area north of the equator from 140 degrees west longitude to 180 degrees.

Nearshore Waters: The waters extending to five miles from shore.

Offshore Waters: The waters extending to about 250 miles from shore.

Sandstorm: Visibility of one-half mile or less due to sand blown by winds of 30 miles-an-hour or more.

Severe Blizzard: Wind speeds of 45 miles-an-hour or more, great density of falling and-or blowing snow with visibility frequently near zero and a temperature of ten degrees or lower.

Severe Thunderstorm: Describes either of the following:

Thunderstorm-related surface winds sustained or gusts 50 knots or greater.

Surface hail three-quarters of an inch in diameter or larger. The word *hail* in a watch implies hail at the surface and aloft unless qualifying phrases such as *hail aloft* are used.

Sleet (one form of ice pellet): Describes generally solid grains of ice formed by the freezing of raindrops or the refreezing of largely melted snowflakes. Sleet, like small hail, usually bounces when hitting a hard surface.

Sleet (heavy): Heavy sleet is a fairly rare event in which the ground is covered to a depth of significance to motorists and others.

Snow Avalanche Bulletin: Snow avalanche bulletins are issued by the U-S Forest Service for avalanche-prone areas in the western United States.

Squall: A sudden increase of wind speed by at least 16 knots and rising to 25 knots or more and lasting for at least one minute.

Stockmen's Advisory: Alerts the public that livestock may require protection because of certain combinations of cold, wet and windy weather, specifically cold rain and-or snow with temperatures 45 degrees or lower and winds of 25 miles-per-hour or higher. If the temperature is in the mid-30s or lower, the wind speed criterion is lowered to about 15 miles-per-hour.

Tornado: A violent rotating column of air forming a pendant, usually from a cumulonimbus cloud, and touching the ground. It usually starts as a funnel cloud and is accompanied by a loud roaring noise. On a locale scale, it is the most destructive of all atmospheric phenomena.

Tornado Warning: Warns the public of an existing tornado or one suspected to be in existence.

Tornado Watch: Alerts the public to the possibility of a tornado.

Traveler's Advisory: Alerts the public that difficult traveling or hazardous road conditions are expected to be widespread.

Tropical Depression: A tropical cyclone in which the maximum sustained surface wind is 38 miles-per-hour (33 knots) or less.

Tropical Storm: A warm-core tropical cyclone in which the maximum sustained surface wind ranges from 39 to 73 miles-per-hour (34 to 63 knots) inclusive.

Typhoon: See *hurricane or typhoon* in this listing.

Waterspout: A tornado over water.

Wind Chill Index: No hyphen. The wind chill index is a calculation that describes the combined effect of the wind and cold temperatures on outdoor activities. The wind chill index would be minus 22, for example, if the temperature was 15 degrees and the wind was blowing at 25 miles per hour —in other words, the combined effect would be the same as a temperature of 22 below zero with no wind.

The higher the wind at a given temperature, the lower the wind chill reading, although wind speeds above 40 miles-per-hour have little additional chilling effect.

Winter Storm Warning: Notifies the public that severe winter weather conditions are almost certain to occur.

Winter Storm Watch: Alerts the public to the possibility of severe winter weather conditions.

• WEATHER VANE

• WEEKEND

• WEEK-LONG

• WEIRD, WEIRDO

• WELL

Hyphenate as part of a compound modifier: *She is a well-dressed woman. She is well-dressed.*

See the **HYPHEN** entry for guidelines on compound modifiers.

• WELL BEING

• WELL-TO-DO

• WELL-WISHERS

• WEST

As defined by the U-S Census Bureau, the 13-state region is broken into two divisions.

The eight *Mountain division* states are Arizona, Colorado, Idaho, Montana, Nevada, New Mexico, Utah and Wyoming.

The five *Pacific division* states are Alaska, California, Hawaii, Oregon and Washington.

See **NORTH-CENTRAL REGION; NORTHEAST REGION;** and **SOUTH** for the bureau's other three regional breakdowns.

• WESTERN AIRLINES

Use this spelling of *airlines,* which Western has adopted for its public identity. Only its incorporation papers still read *air lines.*

Headquarters is in Los Angeles.

• WESTERN ATHLETIC CONFERENCE

Arizona, Arizona State, Brigham Young, Colorado State, New Mexico, Texas El Paso, Utah, Wyoming.

• WESTERN HEMISPHERE

The continents of North and South America, and the islands near them.

It frequently is subdivided as follows:

Caribbean: The islands from the tip of Florida to the continent of South America, plus, particularly in a political sense, French Guiana, Guyana and Surinam on the northeastern coast of South America.

Major island elements are the Bahamas, Cuba, Hispaniola (the island shared by the Dominican Republic and Haiti), Jamaica, Puerto Rico, and the West Indies islands.

Central America: The narrow strip of land between Mexico and Colombia. Located there are Belize, Costa Rica, El Salvador, Guatemala, Honduras, Nicaragua and Panama.

Latin America: The area of the Americas south of the United States where Romance languages (those derived from Latin) are dominant. It applies to most of the region south of the United States except areas with a British heritage: the Bahamas, Barbados, Belize, Grenada, Guyana, Jamaica, Trinidad and Tobago, and various islands in the West Indies. Surinam, the former Dutch Guiana, is an additional exception.

North America: Canada, Mexico, the United States and the Danish territory of Greenland. When the term is used in more than its continental sense, it also may include the islands of the Caribbean.

South America: Argentina, Bolivia, Brazil, Chile, Colombia, Ecuador, Paraguay, Peru, Uruguay, Venezuela, and in a purely continental sense, French Guiana, Guyana and Surinam. Politically and psychologically, however, the latter three regard themselves as part of the Caribbean.

West Indies: The term no longer is used extensively, but it applies to the Caribbean islands east of Puerto Rico southward to South America.

Major island elements are the nations of Barbados, Grenada, and Trinidad and Tobago, plus smaller islands dependent in various degrees on:

—Britain: British Virgin Islands, Anguilla, and the West Indies Associated States, including Antigua, Dominica, St. Lucia, St. Vincent and St. Christopher-Nevis.

—France: Guadeloupe (composed of islands known as Basse-Terre and Grande-Terre, plus five other islands) and Martinique.

—Netherlands: Netherlands Antilles, composed of Aruba, Bonaire, Curacao, Saba, St. Eustatius and the southern portion of St. Martin Island (the northern half is held by France).

—United States: U-S Virgin Islands, principally St. Croix, St. John and St. Thomas.

• WEST GERMANY

Use in datelines instead of the *Federal Republic of Germany.*

See **BERLIN** and **EAST GERMANY.**

• WEST INDIES

See **WESTERN HEMISPHERE.**

• WEST POINT

Acceptable on second reference to the *U-S Military Academy.*

See **MILITARY ACADEMIES.**

In datelines:

(WEST POINT, NEW YORK) - -

• WHEAT

It is measured in bushels domestically, in metric tons for international trade.

There are 36-point-seven bushels of wheat in a metric ton.

• WHEELCHAIR

• WHEELER-DEALER

• WHEREABOUTS

Takes a singular verb: *His whereabouts is a mystery.*

• WHEREVER

• WHICH

See the **ESSENTIAL CLAUSES, NON-ESSENTIAL CLAUSES** entry; the **THAT, WHICH** entry; and the **WHO, WHOM** entry.

• WHISKEY, WHISKEYS

Use the spelling *whisky* only in conjunction with *Scotch.* See the **SCOTCH WHISKY** entry.

• WHITE-COLLAR (adj.)

• WHITEWASH (n., v. and adj.)

• WHO, WHOM

Use *who* and *whom* for references to human begins and to animals with a name. Use *that* and *which* for inanimate objects and animals without a name.

Who is the word when someone is the subject of a sentence, clause or phrase: *The woman who rented the room left the window open. Who is there?*

Whom is the word when someone is the object of a verb or preposition: *The woman to whom the room was rented left the window open. Whom do you wish to see?*

See the **ESSENTIAL CLAUSES, NON-ESSENTIAL CLAUSES** entry for guidelines on how to punctuate clauses introduced by *who, whom, that* and *which.*

• WHOLE-HEARTED

• WHOLESALE PRICE INDEX

A measurement of the changes in the average prices that businesses pay for a selected group of industrial commodities, farm products, processed foods and feed for animals.

Recent adjustments in the factors comprising the index have led to formulation of a *Producer Price Index,* which more accurately reflects the price movements for finished goods.

The U-S index is issued monthly by the Bureau of Labor Statistics, an agency of the Labor Department.

• WHOLE-WHEAT

• WHO'S, WHOSE

Who's is a contraction for *who is,* not a possessive: *Who's there?*

Whose is the possessive: *I do not know whose coat it is.*

• WIDE-

Usually hyphenated. Some examples:

WIDE-ANGLE	WIDE-EYED
WIDE-AWAKE	WIDE-OPEN
WIDE-BRIMMED	

Exception: WIDESPREAD.

• -WIDE

No hyphen. Some examples:

CITYWIDE	NATIONWIDE
CONTINENTWIDE	STATEWIDE
COUNTRYWIDE	WORLDWIDE
INDUSTRYWIDE	

• WIDOW, WIDOWER

In obituaries: A man *is survived by his wife,* or *leaves his wife.* A woman *is survived by her husband,* or *leaves her husband.*

Guard against the redundant *widow of the late.* Use *wife of the late* or *widow of.*

• WIDTHS

See **DIMENSIONS.**

• WILDLIFE

• WILKES-BARRE (WILKS-BAYR), **PENNSYLVANIA**

• WILL

See the **SHALL, WILL** entry and **SUBJUNCTIVE MOOD.**

• WILSON'S DISEASE

After Samuel Wilson, an English neurologist. A disease characterized by abnormal accumulation of copper in the brain, liver and other organs.

• WIND CHILL INDEX

See **WEATHER TERMS.**

- **WINDOW DRESSING**

The noun. But as a verb: *window-dress.*

- **WIND-SWEPT**

- **WIND UP** (v.)
WINDUP (n. and adj.)

- **WINGSPAN**

- **WINTERTIME**

- **WIRETAP, WIRETAPPER**

The verb forms: *wiretap, wiretapped, wiretapping.*

- **-WISE**

No hyphen when it means *in the direction of* or *with regard to.* Some examples:

CLOCKWISE	OTHERWISE
LENGTHWISE	SLANTWISE

Avoid contrived combinations such as *moneywise, religionwise.*

The word *penny-wise* is spelled with a hyphen because it is a compound adjective in which *wise* means *smart,* not an application of the suffix *-wise.* The same for *street-wise* in *street-wise youth.*

- **WOMAN'S CHRISTIAN TEMPERANCE UNION**

Not *Women's.*

- **WOMEN**

Women should receive the same treatment as men in all areas of coverage. Physical descriptions, sexist references, demeaning stereotypes and condescending phrases should not be used.

To cite some examples, this means that:

—Copy should not assume maleness when both sexes are involved, as in *Jackson told newsmen* or in *the taxpayer ... he* when it easily can be said *Jackson told reporters* or *taxpayers ... they.*

—Copy should not express surprise that an attractive woman can be professionally accomplished, as in: *Mary Smith doesn't look the part but she's an authority on ...*

—Copy should not gratuitously mention family relationships when there is no relevance to the subject, as in: *Golda Meir, a doughty grandmother, told the Egyptians today ...*

—Use the same standards for men and women in deciding whether to include specific mention of personal appearance or marital and family situation.

In other words, treatment of the sexes should be even-handed and free of assumptions and stereotypes. This does not mean that valid and acceptable words such as *mankind* or *humanity* cannot be used. They are proper.

See **COURTESY TITLES; DIVORCEES;** the **MAN, MANKIND** entry; and the **-PERSONS entry.**

- **WOMEN'S ARMY CORPS**

See the "**WAC**" entry.

- **WOOLWORTH'S**

Acceptable in all references for *F.W. Woolworth Company.*

- **WORD-OF-MOUTH** (n. and adj.)

- **WORDS AS WORDS**

The meaning of this phrase, which appears occasionally in this book and similar manuals that deal with words, is best illustrated by an example: In this sentence, *woman* appears solely as a word rather than as the means of representing the concept normally associated with the word.

When italics are available, a word used as a word should be italicized. Entries in this book use italics when a word or phrase is discussed in this sense. Note, for example, the italics used on *woman* in this sentence and in the example sentence.

Italics are not available to highlight this type of word use on the news wires. When a news story must use a word as a word, place quotation marks around it instead.

See **ITALICS** and **PLURALS.**

• WORD SELECTION

In general, any word with a meaning that is universally understood is acceptable unless it is offensive or below the normal standards for literate writing.

In broadcast, you are writing for the ear. Choose words and constructions that are in common conversational use and evoke clear images.

This handbook lists many words with cautionary notes about how they should be used. The entries in Webster's New World provide cautionary notes, comparisons and usage guidelines to help a writer choose the correct word for a particular context.

Any word listed in Webster's New World may be used for the definitions given unless this handbook restricts its use to only some of the definitions recorded by the dictionary or specifies that the word be confined to certain contexts.

If the dictionary cautions that a particular usage is objected to by some linguists or is not accepted widely, be wary of the usage unless there is a reason in the context.

The dictionary uses the description *substandard* to identify words below the norms for literate writing.

The dictionary provides guidance on many idiomatic expressions under the principal word in the expression. The definition and spelling of *under way*, for example, are found in the "way" entry.

If it is necessary to use an archaic word or an archaic sense of a word, explain the meaning.

Additional guidance on the acceptability of words is provided in this book under: **AMERICANISMS; COLLOQUIALISMS; DIALECT; FOREIGN WORDS; JARGON; SPECIAL CONTEXTS;** and **VERNACULAR.**

See also the **OBSCENITIES, PROFANITIES AND VULGARITIES** entry.

• WORKDAY

• WORKING CLASS (n.) WORKING-CLASS (adj.)

• WORKOUT

• WORKWEEK

• WORLD BANK

Acceptable in all references for *International Bank for Reconstruction and Development.*

• WORLD COUNCIL OF CHURCHES

This is the main international, interdenominational cooperative body of Anglican, Eastern Orthodox, Protestant and old or national Catholic churches.

Roman Catholicism is not a member but cooperates with the council in various programs.

Headquarters is in Geneva, Switzerland.

• WORLD COURT

This was an alternate name for the *Permanent Court of International Justice* set up by the League of Nations.

See the entry for the **INTERNA-**

TIONAL COURT OF JUSTICE, which has replaced it.

• WORLD HEALTH ORGANIZATION

W-H-O is acceptable on second reference.

Headquarters is in Geneva, Switzerland.

• WORLD WAR ONE, WORLD WAR TWO

• WORLDWIDE

• WORN-OUT

• WORSHIP, WORSHIPED, WORSHIPING, WORSHIPER

• WORTHWHILE

• WOULD

See the **SHOULD, WOULD** entry.

• WRACK

See the **RACK, WRACK** entry.

• WRESTLING

Identify events by weight divisions.

The key words to indicate winners are *pinned* and *outpointed.*

• WRITE IN (v.) WRITE-IN (n. and adj.)

• WRONGDOING

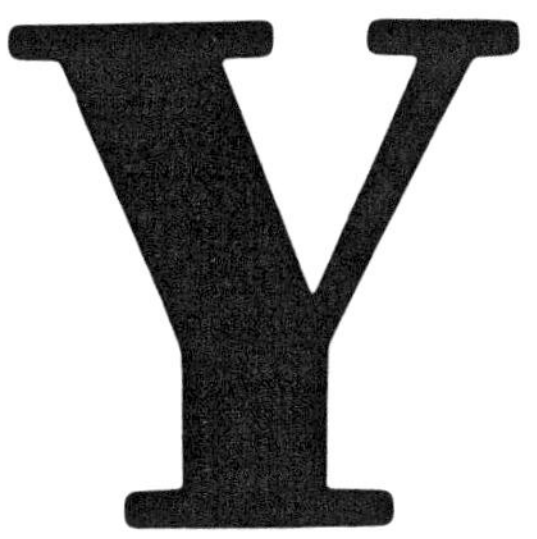

• X

The motion picture rating that denotes *individuals under 17 are not admitted.* See **MOVIE RATINGS.**

• XEROX

A trademark for a brand of photocopy machine. Never a verb.

• X-RAY (n., v. and adj.)

Use for both the photographic process and the radiation particles themselves.

• YAM

Botanically, yams and sweet potatoes are not related, although several varieties of moist-fleshed sweet potatoes are popularly called *yams* in some parts of the United States.

• YANKEE CONFERENCE

Boston University, Connecticut, Maine, Massachusetts, New Hampshire, Rhode Island, Vermont.

• YARD

Three feet.

The metric equivalent is about point-91 meters—just over nine-tenths of a meter.

To convert to meters, multiply the number of yards by point-91: five yards times point-91 equals four-point-55 meters.

See **FOOT; METER;** and **DISTANCES.**

• YARD LINES

Follow the rules for **NUMERALS** when indicating the dividing lines on football fields and the distance traveled: *The five-yard line, the 40-yard line, he plunged in from the two, it was a six-yard run, he gained seven yards.*

• YEAR-END (adj.)

• YEARLING

An animal one year old or in its second year. The birthdays of all thoroughbred horses arbitrarily are set at January first. On that date, any foal born in the preceding year is reckoned one year old—a *yearling.*

• YEAR-LONG

• YEARS

Use figures, without commas: *1975.* Use an *s* with an apostrophe to indicate spans of decades or centuries: *the 1890's, the 1800's.*

Years are the lone exception to the general rule in **NUMERALS** that a figure is not used to start a sentence: *1976 was a very good year.*

See **B-C**; **DECADES**; and **MONTHS**.

• YELLOW JOURNALISM

The use of cheaply sensational methods to attract or influence readers. The term comes from the "Yellow Kid," a comic strip in the New York World in 1895.

• YEOMAN (YOH'-MUHN)

See **MILITARY TITLES.**

• YESTERYEAR

• YIELD

In a financial sense, the annual rate of return on an investment, as paid in dividends or interest. It is expressed as a percentage obtained by dividing the market price for a stock or bond into the dividend or interest paid in the preceding 12 months.

See **PROFIT TERMINOLOGY.**

• YOM KIPPER

The Jewish Day of Atonement. Occurs in September or October.

• YOUNG MEN'S CHRISTIAN ASSOCIATION

Y-M-C-A is acceptable in all references.

Headquarters is in New York.

• YOUNG WOMEN'S CHRISTIAN ASSOCIATION

Y-W-C-A is acceptable in all references.

Headquarters is in New York.

• YOUTH

Applicable to boys and girls from age 13 to their 18th birthday. Use *man* or *woman* for individuals 18 and older.

• YO-YO

Formerly a trademark, now a generic term.

• YUKON

A territorial section of Canada. Do not abbreviate. Use in datelines after the names of communities in the territory.

See **CANADA.**

• YULE, YULETIDE

• **ZERO, ZEROES**

• **ZIGZAG**

• **ZIONISM**

The effort of the Jews to regain and retain their biblical homeland. It is based on the promise of God in the Book of Genesis that Israel would forever belong to Abraham and his descendants as a nation.

The term is named for Mount Zion, the site of the ancient temple in Jerusalem. The Bible also frequently uses *Zion* in a general sense to denote the place where God is especially present with his people.

• **ZIP CODES**

It stands for *Zone Improvement Program,* and the lack of quotation marks is an exception to the rule.

Hyphenate the five-digit codes, setting them off with the word *ZIP* or *the ZIP code is*: *ZIP 1-0-0-2-0, the ZIP code is 1-0-0-2-0.*

INDEX